OUTSTANDING DISSERTATIONS IN

MUSIC FROM BRITISH UNIVERSITIES

edited by
JOHN CALDWELL
OXFORD UNIVERSITY

A GARLAND SERIES

MUSIC AT THE ROYAL COURT AND CHAPEL IN POLAND, c. 1543–1600

TOMASZ M.M. CZEPIEL

GARLAND PUBLISHING, INC.
NEW YORK & LONDON / 1996

Copyright © 1996 Tomasz M.M. Czepiel
All rights reserved

Library of Congress Cataloging-in-Publication Data

Czepiel, Tomasz M. M.
    Music at the royal court and chapel in Poland, c. 1543–1600 / Tomasz M.M. Czepiel.
        p.   cm. — (Outstanding dissertations in music from British universities)
    Includes bibliographical references and index.
    ISBN 0-8153-2237-2 (alk. paper)
    1. Music—Poland—16th century—History and criticism. I. Title. II. Series.
ML297.2.C9   1996
780'.9438'09031—dc20   95-51816
                                                            MN

Printed on acid-free, 250-year-life paper
Manufactured in the United States of America

CONTENTS

	Page	
Contents		v
List of tables		ix
Preface		xi
Acknowledgments		xv
Notes		xvii
Abbreviations		xix

Introduction. Poland: A Brief Summary of Its History, and the State of the Country and Its Monarchy in the Sixteenth Century ... 3

The history of Poland up to the sixteenth century ... 3
Poland in the sixteenth century ... 4
Zygmunt I Stary (1467-1548) ... 5
Zygmunt II August (1520-1572) ... 8
The monarchy during the last quarter of the sixteenth century ... 10
The implications of Polish history for music in the sixteenth century ... 11
Notes ... 12

PART I. THE RORANTISTS' COLLEGE AND ITS REPERTORY, 1543-1600 ... 13

I The Rorantists' College: Its Foundation and History, 1543-1600 ... 15

The cathedral on Wawel Hill: an outline ... 15
The cathedral staff, the endowment of chantries and colleges of priests ... 16
Zygmunt's chapel: the building ... 20
The creation of the Rorantists' College ... 21
Aspects of the Rorantists' College as an institution ... 23
The Rorantists' College, 1543-1548 ... 27
The Rorantists during the reign of Zygmunt II August and the second foundation of 1552 ... 28
The interregna and the instability of the Rorantists' College ... 31

    Anna Jagiellonka's patronage of the Rorantists and the third
        foundation of 1584   32
    The Rorantists' College: conclusions   36
    Notes   37

II The Rorantists' Liturgy and Plainchant Repertory   45

    The contemporary inventories and extant liturgical books   45
    The Rorantists' Missal and its calendar   48
    The Rorantists' Gradual   50
    The college liturgy: conclusions   57
    Notes   58

III The Rorantists' Polyphonic Repertory as found in their Manuscript   61
    Partbooks and Prints

    The Rorantists' repertory recorded in contemporary inventories   61
    The music manuscripts   66
    Kk I.3: The earliest extant manuscript belonging to the Rorantists   66
    Kk I.1: Music for the high altar of the cathedral   76
    Kk I.4: Additional music for use in chapel and at the high altar of the   100
        cathedral
    Kk I.5: A composite manuscript containing music for use in chapel   112
        and at the high altar of the cathedral
    The Rorantists' printed repertory   115
    The Rorantists' polyphonic repertory: conclusions   116
    Notes   118

PART II. THE MUSICAL ESTABLISHMENT AT THE
COURT OF ZYGMUNT II AUGUST (1543-1572)
AND THE MUSIC OF THE ROYAL CHAPEL

IV The Musical Establishment at the Court of Zygmunt II August   129

    The Royal Chapel   129
    The groups of instrumentalists   141
    Soloists   147
    The musical establishment: conclusions   150
    Notes   152

V	The Music of Zygmunt II August's Chapel	161
	Jurek Jasivcicz and the inventory of music manuscripts and prints of 1572	161
	Wacław of Szamotuły	173
	Notes	176

CONCLUSIONS 181

APPENDICES

I	Map of the Jagiellonian Realm (c. 1569)	185
II	The Rorantists' acts	186
III	Membership of the Rorantists' College (1543-1599)	230
IV	Documents concerning the prefects of the Rorantists' College	241
V	Rorantists' inventories containing lists of books (selections)	243
VI	The calendar of the Rorantists' Missal, Kk 4	259
VII	Extract from Bishop Jerzy Radziwiłł's decree of 1597 mandating the use of the Roman Missal	268
VIII	Catalogue of the Rorantists' Gradual	269
IX	Catalogues of the Rorantists' partbooks	279
X	Register of courtiers and servants employed at the court of Zygmunt II August (RK 110) (selection)	308
XI	Pensions (Privilegia) granted to musicians at Zygmunt II August's court	332
XII	Membership of Zygmunt II Augusts' musical establishment	336
XIII	The inventory of Jurek Jasivcicz (1572)	352
XIV	Music from the Rorantists' repertory: transcriptions	371

BIBLIOGRAPHY 393

Index 403

LIST OF TABLES

II.1	Rorantists' liturgical books recorded in contemporary inventories	47
II.2	The layout and contents of the Rorantists' Gradual (Kk 46)	52
II.3	The Alleluia and verses and Tracts of the Rorantists' Gradual and the seasonal designated use of the texts as found in the *Missale Cracoviensis*, 1532	53
III.1	Kk Inv. 67: List of musical items found in the Rorantists' library in 1599	62
III.2	Le Roy and Ballard prints listed in Surzyński, *Monumenta musices sacrae* (1885) and Chybiński, 'Zbiory muzyczne' (1910)	63
III.3	Orlando di Lasso prints listed in Chybiński, *Materjały* (1910)	65
III.4	Scribal analysis of the Second Mass of the Annunciation (Kk I.3, item 6)	67
III.5	General layout of Kk I.3	68
III.6	Layers and contents of Kk I.1	78
III.7	Copies of masses from *Missae cum quatuor vocibus paribus...* (Scotto, Venice, 1542) found in Kk I.1	81
III.8	Layout of Mass Propers in Kk I.1 and their liturgical use	82
III.9	Additional Marian Propers of Kk I.1 and their use in the TridentineGradual	98
III.10	Overview of Kk I.4	101
III.11a	Propers for Easter in Kk I.4	103
III.11b	Propers for Pentecost in Kk I.4	103
III.12	The Pre-Tridentine and the Tridentine cycle of the Annunciation and the Votive Mass during Advent	104
III.13	Sections of the Mass for the feast of the Annunciation and the daily Votive Mass in Kk I.4	105
III.14	Layers of Kk I.5, with their watermarks, scribes, and principal contents	112

PREFACE

In the sixteenth century, Poland was a powerful kingdom, and its monarchs ruled over large territories, which extended far beyond its present limits. It was, militarily and politically, a force to be reckoned with. Internal trade thrived with the help of the river Wisła, and foreign trade, via Gdańsk and the Baltic sea, linked Poland with the whole of the known world. Culturally, the sixteenth century is regarded as Poland's 'Złoty wiek' (Golden Age). The achievements here may not have matched those which took place in Italy during the same period, though given the peripheral location of Poland far from Italy and the Netherlands, they were of crucial significance for the development of that country. In the capital, Kraków, the university flourished and learned societies were established. Wealthy magnates sent their sons abroad for an education, especially to Italian universities. Printing had been introduced in the last quarter of the fifteenth century and had now become the main vehicle for new ideas. The historian Marcin Kromer (c. 1512-89) compiled a history of Poland, *De origine et rebus gestis Polonorum* (Kraków, 1555), which proved to be an essential textbook for foreigners interested in the affairs of the country. The Polish language ceased to be a *lingua vulgaris*: it was now codified, the orthography was standardized through prints, and it was used by most writers and poets, most notably Jan Kochanowski. Mikołaj Kopernik (Nicolaus Copernicus) (1473-1543) published his *De revolutionibus orbium coelestium* (Nuremberg, 1543), in which he established the earth's movement around the sun, thus providing the foundations of modern astronomy. It was, however, the royal court which became the main focal point of cultural life in Poland. In particular, Zygmunt I 'Stary' (1467-1548) and his son Zygmunt II August (1520-72) surrounded themselves with educated men and artists, and with music and musicians.

This study presents two different facets of musical patronage of the Polish monarchy during the second half of the sixteenth century. The first part discusses the so-called Rorantists' College, a body of chaplains established by Zygmunt I in the chapel which he had built onto the cathedral on Wawel Hill. The survey covers the period from the college's foundation in 1543 to the end of the century, that is, until the death of Queen Anna Jagiellonka (1596), the last Jagiellonian patron of the chapel. It deals with the foundation itself and the subsequent changes made by Zygmunt I's successors (Chapter I), the liturgy and plainchant tradition of the chapel (Chapter II) and its polyphonic repertory (Chapter III). The second part of the study presents the musical establishment created by Zygmunt II August: the royal household chapel (different from the Rorantists' College) and the various groups of instrumentalists. It describes their formation and activities during the three decades of the court's existence (Chapter IV). There is also a discussion of the repertory of the royal chapel (Chapter V). As this work is addressed primarily to non-Polish readers, the study is introduced by some relevant background information on Poland's history (Introduction). With the main text, the book also contains copious appendices. These include diplomatic transcriptions of source material, most of which is unavailable in microfilm or other photographic form, graphs mapping out the membership of the respective institutions, and catalogues of the Rorantists' manuscripts containing plainchant and polyphony. Finally, there are some transcriptions of the Rorantists' music.

To a large extent, the scope and content of this study have been determined by the available source material. Poland's cultural and musical heritage has suffered immense losses over the centuries, particularly during the Swedish invasions of the seventeenth century and during the Second World War, making it practically impossible to produce a comprehensive study of music in Poland in the sixteenth century. Thus it was deemed more sensible to focus on the two areas of study outlined above for which sufficient sources are available. For the Rorantists, there are the original founding acts, illuminated with royal crests and containing the signatures and seals of the monarchs; these are preserved in the cathedral archive on Wawel Hill. Here too is the college account-book and contemporary inventories which include lists of liturgical and music books. We have most of the Rorantists' music manuscripts produced in the sixteenth century, which, after being taken from the cathedral archive at the end of the nineteenth century and dispersed throughout Poland and beyond, have only recently returned to their original home (1982-3).[1]

The main source of information on the musical establishment of Zygmunt II August are the royal account-books: manuscript volumes of payments made by the royal treasury to the court singers and musicians. More than a hundred such volumes are preserved in the Main Archive of Old Acts in Warsaw, and amongst these is a register of courtiers and servants employed at the court between 1543 and 1572. Individual volumes of royal payment books are also preserved in other libraries in Poland (Wrocław, Ossoliński Library, and Kraków, Czartoryski Library). Further supporting archival information can be found in the archives on Wawel Hill and that of the bishop's palace, Kraków.[2] As for the music of the royal chapel, although all of the prints and manuscripts have been lost, these were recorded in an inventory of 1572, which is extant. Finally, a few compositions by the chapel's principal composer, Wacław of Szamotuły, have survived in foreign printed anthologies.

The scholarly literature on the subject is surprisingly limited, predominantly in Polish, and mostly out of date. The Rorantists' College as an institution has been examined only once in detail, by Adolf Chybiński in his *Materyały do dziejów król. kapeli Rorantystów na Wawelu. Część pierwsza: 1540-1624* (Kraków, 1910). This study presented a transcription of a copy of the Rorantists' founding act of 1543 and an alphabetic list of the college members which he derived from the first college account-book. It also gave a list of the manuscripts and prints which Chybiński found in the cathedral archive on Wawel Hill and which he assumed belonged to the Rorantists. This work was pioneering for its time, though it included some serious mistakes and omissions. To be fair, subsequent articles by Chybiński in part correct his earlier work. Since then, all of the literature has basically repeated Chybiński's conclusions. More recently, Zygmunt M. Szweykowski initiated a series of thematic catalogues of Polish music manuscripts. So far, six fascicli devoted to the Rorantist repertory have been published, covering seven sets of partbooks and including the four extant sets produced in the sixteenth century. Each fascicle has an introduction to the respective manuscript, containing a summary of the literature, some basic palaeographical information, and dating.[3] However, some of the dating in the catalogues is incorrect, and the liturgical purpose of the individual compositions is unfortunately based on the Tridentine missal, as opposed to the local pre-Tridentine missal. As yet, the principal archival documents of the Rorantists' foundation, which determined the structure of the college, as well as their liturgical and thus musical duties, have not yet been examined. Likewise, the Rorantists' repertory has never been examined as a whole, though it has to be said that the whole corpus of manuscripts has only relatively recently been made available for study. Yet even those individual compositions which have been analysed have never been placed in their appropriate context.

As for the literature on Zygmunt II August's musical establishment, several general accounts are available, the most recent of which is Elżbieta Głuszcz-Zwolińska's *Muzyka nadworna ostatnich Jagiellonów* (Kraków, 1988), which deals with music at the court of both Zygmunt I Stary and Zygmunt II August. Despite discussing certain important aspects, such as the basic organization of musical establishments and the social and economic position of the members, as well as providing extensive (although not exhaustive) indexes of members with source references, Głuszcz-Zwolińska does not present the precise make-up of the establishment, nor does she discuss the changes that took place within it over the period covered. Her tables mapping out the membership at the royal court on three A3 pages are not easy to read and distort the true orientation of some of the individuals within it. Other works, including Mirosław Perz's *Mikołaj Gomółka* (Kraków, 1981) or the article on Wacław of Szamotuły by Zygmunt and Anna Szweykowski (*Muzyka*, 1964, no. 1) are devoted to individuals and only superficially mention the whole of the musical establishment, and this has led to some misleading generalizations. In all fairness, the source material is not complete and contains some inconsistencies and mistakes. Inevitably, this has resulted in misinterpretations in the literature, especially when the information was taken at face value. As for the repertory of the royal chapel, no substantive account has yet been produced. It was mentioned, albeit briefly, in Aleksander Poliński's pioneering book on Polish music of 1907.[4] An annotated transcription of the 1572 inventory was published by Chybiński in 1912,[5] providing the possible identifications of several printed items based on Eitner's *Quellen-Lexikon*. Since then, all books and articles which refer to the inventory duplicate Chybiński's work. Even the most recent account in Głuszcz-Zwolińska's *Muzyka nadworna* provides little new information on the inventory, and on some counts falls short of Chybiński's work.[6]

NOTES

[1] Z. Szweykowski, Editor's note to *Musicalia Vetera: Thematic Catalogue of Early Musical Manuscripts in Poland*, Vol. I, fasc. 1 (Kraków, 1969), Editor's Note, p. 7.

[2] Kk and Kku respectively.

[3] Exceptionally, Kk I.5 (*olim* Ch. 58) is included with Kk I.4 (*olim* Ch. 191) in one fascicle.

[4] A. Poliński, *Dzieje muzyki polskiej w zarysie* (Lwów, 1907), p. 58.

[5] A. Chybiński, 'Krakowskie inwentarze muzyczne z XVI wieku', *Kwartalnik Muzyczny* (1912), no. 3, pp. 253-8.

[6] E. Głuszcz-Zwolińska (in *Muzyka nadworna*) provides a reduced facsimile of the inventory (ill. 27-32, between p. 80-1) and a selective list of composers and items, with some information on genre and scoring. She omits several prints and two composers (Ghibelli and Londariti) identified by Chybiński. A more serious omission is the exclusion of all the anthologies, which represent a significant portion of the collection.

ACKNOWLEDGMENTS

My first and greatest debt is to Professor John Harper, for his great help and warm encouragement while I was writing the original doctoral thesis. He was exceptionally generous with his time, and always offered positive advice on my work. My sincere thanks also to Dr Bojan Bujić for his help during the early stages of my work in Oxford, and to Professor Zygmunt M. Szweykowski, with whom I consulted during my years in Poland. Many others deserve mention for their help given over the years, in particular, Professor B. Przybyszewski, for his advice on the archival sources, Professor J. Pikulik, who helped me with liturgical matters, as well as Dr Tim Carter, Stefan Czepiel, Dr Simon Heighes, Dr Piotr Poźniak, and Dr Sally Roper. My thanks also go to Bonie Blackburn for proof-reading this text.

Mention must also be made of several libraries and their staff. I wish to thank the Cathedral Archive on Wawel Hill, Kraków, and in particular the archivist there, Sister Klara Antosiewicz, the Archive of the Bishop's Palace in Kraków, the Main Archive of Old Acts in Warsaw, the Czartoryski Library in Kraków, the Ossoliński Library in Wrocław, the Music Department Library of the Jagiellonian University and the Jagiellonian Library in Kraków, the Bodleian Library and the Music Faculty Library, Oxford, and the British Library. I should also like to extend my gratitude to those who facilitated my search for and work on source materials as well as secondary sources: Dr Zofia Dobrzańska, Stanisław Hrabia, Dorota Maciejewicz, Hania Murłowska, Darek Sokołowski, Barbara Strzałkowska, and Wojtek Strojny.

I am also indebted to the Principal and Fellows of Hertford College for electing me to the Starun Senior Scholarship, and to the British Council and Polish Government for awarding me a scholarship for two years to carry out my research in Poland. My sincere thanks to my parents, for their generous moral and financial support, not to mention their faith in me and my work. Last, but by no means least, I would like to thank my wife, Małgosia, for her constant support and encouragement.

NOTES ON NAMES, PLACES, QUOTATIONS, MUSICAL EXAMPLES, APPENDICES, AND CURRENCY

All the sources discussed in this study are of Polish origin, unless otherwise stated. The standard *Répertoire International des Sources Musicales (RISM)* system of library identification has been adopted throughout for both music manuscripts and prints, and this system has also been adapted for the non-musical source material. A list of the important manuscripts, together with a key to the manuscript abbreviations, appears on pp. xix-xxii Manuscripts and printed sources preserved in the cathedral archive on Wawel Hill have been given their current shelf-mark in their various forms: this includes Igancy Polkowski's published catalogue numbers for manuscript liturgical books (1884), a nineteenth-century card catalogue of legal documents and acts (possibly also by Polkowski), a typescript list of Bishops' Visitations (in German), a temporary numbering of other archival manuscripts (Inventories), Sister Klara Antosiewicz's typescript catalogue of printed liturgical books, and Tadeusz Maciejewski's music manuscript numbering system (under review). Former shelf-marks of the music manuscripts (which appear in the literature) are also provided. Work is currently under way to organize the whole of this archive, under the direction of Sister Klara Antosiewicz, and this should result in a more comprehensive classification system of all manuscripts and prints preserved therein, though some of the shelf-marks may well be changed.

All the quotations in the main text as well as in the appendices have been taken from the original sources, unless otherwise stated. These are diplomatic transcriptions and retain the original Latin or Polish orthography, including errors and inconsistencies. Likewise all the abbreviations and contractions of the original texts are also reproduced. Exceptionally, the symbol for the suffix 'que', which cannot be reproduced satisfactorily, has been expanded without square brackets. Titles of compositions and plainchant, as well as other notes, are also unchanged; text incipits, however, have been standardized.

Musical examples, both those within the main text and in Appendix XIV, are accurate transcriptions of the original sources, unless otherwise stated, though note-values have been halved. On those occasions where a set is incomplete, the missing part has been shown by an open stave. Within the text, pitch is indicated in accordance with the Helmholtz system: C below the bass stave to low B in the bass stave are referred to as *C-B*; notes in the next octave *c - b*; middle C to B in the soprano clef *c' -b'*.

For ease of reference, the catalogues of the Gradual, music manuscripts, and book inventories presented in the appendices, include item-numbering systems (editorial or occasionally original). These numberings will also be used in the main text.

For the purpose of this study, an approach to names has been taken which is a compromise, but perhaps most accessible to the English reader. All Polish names and surnames are presented in the vernacular form, with a standardized spelling. For all those identified by a birth-place, their Polish forename is followed by 'of' and the name of the town of origin, e.g. Mikołaj of Poznań. This approach avoids the need to present a declined version of the place of birth which occurs in Polish. Names of foreigners are given in the form that appears within the sources. All Polish cities and towns are also presented in their modern version.

The principal currencies used in sixteenth-century Poland included the mark, floren (later złoty), and grosz (pl. groszy). In spite of the general devaluation, the relative value of these coins was maintained: 1 mark = 48 groszy; 1 floren = 1 złoty = 30 groszy.

ABBREVIATIONS

1. Source Abbreviations

Kc MS 1033	Kraków, Biblioteka Narodowa im. Czartoryskich, MS 1033, *Regestrum racionis generalis S.M.R. 1544*
Kc MS 1059	Kraków, Biblioteka Narodowa im. Czartoryskich, MS 1059, *Summariusz Przywileiów w Archiwum Katedry Krakowskiej*
Kc MS 3084	Kraków, Biblioteka Narodowa im. Czartoryskich, MS 3084, *Inwentarz funduszów XX Mansionarze w Krakowie*
Kj 1267	Kraków, Biblioteka Jagiellońska, MS 1267
Kk 4	Kraków, Archiwum Kapituły Metropolitalnej Krakowskiej, MS 4, ('Rorantists' Missal')
Kk 42	Kraków, Archiwum Kapituły Metropolitalnej Krakowskiej, MS 42, ('Olbracht Gradual, vol. III: Marian')
Kk 43	Kraków, Archiwum Kapituły Metropolitalnej Krakowskiej, MS 43, ('Olbracht Gradual, vol. II: Sanctorale')
Kk 44	Kraków, Archiwum Kapituły Metropolitalnej Krakowskiej, MS 44, ('Olbracht Gradual, vol. I: Temporale')
Kk 45	Kraków, Archiwum Kapituły Metropolitalnej Krakowskiej, MS 45
Kk 46	Kraków, Archiwum Kapituły Metropolitalnej Krakowskiej, MS 46, ('Rorantists' Gradual')
Kk 58	Kraków, Archiwum Kapituły Metropolitalnej Krakowskiej, MS 58, ('Gosławski Cancionale')
Kk 239	Kraków, Archiwum Kapituły Metropolitalnej Krakowskiej, MS 239, *Kalendarium et Statuta Dominorum Vicariorum Ecclesie Cathedralis*
Kk Capit. Crac. 3	Kraków, Archiwum Kapituły Metropolitalnej Krakowskiej, *Acta Capitularia Ecclesiae Cracoviensis*, vol. 3 (1524-1543)

Kk Capit. Crac. 5	Kraków, Archiwum Kapituły Metropolitalnej Krakowskiej, *Acta Capitularia Ecclesiae Cracoviensis*, vol. 5 (1555-1564)
Kk Capit. Crac. 7	Kraków, Archiwum Kapituły Metropolitalnej Krakowskiej, *Acta Capitularia Ecclesiae Cracoviensis*, vol. 7 (1577-1587)
Kk Capit. Crac. 9	Kraków, Archiwum Kapituły Metropolitalnej Krakowskiej, *Acta Capitularia Ecclesiae Cracoviensis*, vol. 9 (1600-1614)
Kk dyp. 110	Kraków, Archiwum Kapituły Metropolitalnej Krakowskiej, dyplom 110
Kk dyp. 1123	Kraków, Archiwum Kapituły Metropolitalnej Krakowskiej, dyplom 1123
Kk dyp. 1172	Kraków, Archiwum Kapituły Metropolitalnej Krakowskiej, dyplom 1172
Kk dyp. 1184	Kraków, Archiwum Kapituły Metropolitalnej Krakowskiej, dyplom 1184
Kk dyp. 1190	Kraków, Archiwum Kapituły Metropolitalnej Krakowskiej, dyplom 1190
Kk Inv. 22	Kraków, Archiwum Kapituły Metropolitalnej Krakowskiej, Inventarz 22, ('Liber retaxatiarum, 1529')
Kk Inv. 29	Kraków, Archiwum Kapituły Metropolitalnej Krakowskiej, Inwentarz 29, *Anno Domini 1563 mense septembri Inventarium rerum, facultatum et suppellectillis sacrae ecclesiae cathedralis Cracoviensis*
Kk Inv. 64	Kraków, Archiwum Kapituły Metropolitalnej Krakowskiej, Inwentarz 64, *Regestrum Generale omnium Perceptorum et Expensarum Collegij RR Rorantistarum 1624-1698*.
Kk Inv. 65	Kraków, Archiwum Kapituły Metropolitalnej Krakowskiej, Inwentarz 65, *Elenchus omnium perceptorum et expositarum ex proventibus Sacelli Regii Rorantistarum Ab anno 1543 ad Annum 1631*
Kk Inv. 66	Kraków, Archiwum Kapituły Metropolitalnej Krakowskiej, Inwentarz 66, ('Decreta Trzebickiego, 1680')
Kk Inv. 67	Kraków, Archiwum Kapituły Metropolitalnej Krakowskiej, Inwentarz 67, *Apparatus Ecclesiasticus Capellæ Sacre Regie M̄tis Rorā dictæ ... M.D.XC. nono conscriptus per Job*

Abbreviations

Kk Inv. 68	Kraków, Archiwum Kapituły Metropolitalnej Krakowskiej, Inwentarz 68, *Opisanie Kaplicy Królewskiej Zygmuntowskiej Rorantystów zwany* (1834)
Kk Inv. 69	Kraków, Archiwum Kapituły Metropolitalnej Krakowskiej, Inwentarz 69, *Visitatio Capellæ SRM Rorantia dictae 1602*
Kk Visit. 51-53	Kraków, Archiwum Kapituły Metropolitalnej Krakowskiej, Wizytacje 51-53, *Acta Visitationis ... Andreae Trzebicki ... 1670*
Kk Visit. 64	Kraków, Archiwum Kapituły Metropolitalnej Krakowskiej, Wizytacje 64 (1584)
Kku Episc. Crac. 18	Kraków, Archiwum Kurii Metropolitalnej, Acta Episcopalia Cracoviensis, vol. 18 (1538-40)
Kku Episc. Crac. 20	Kraków, Archiwum Kurii Metropolitalnej, Acta Episcopalia Cracoviensis, vol. 20 (1543-44)
Kku Episc. Crac. 30	Kraków, Archiwum Kurii Metropolitalnej, Acta Episcopalia Cracoviensis, vol. 30 (1572-77)
Kku Episc. Crac. 32	Kraków, Archiwum Kurii Metropolitalnej, Acta Episcopalia Cracoviensis, vol. 32 (1592-96)
Kku Offic. Crac. 47	Kraków, Archiwum Kurii Metropolitalnej, Acta Officialia, vol. 47
Kku Offic. Crac. 100	Kraków, Archiwum Kurii Metropolitalnej, Acta Officialia, vol. 100
Kku Offic. Crac. 107	Kraków, Archiwum Kurii Metropolitalnej, Acta Officialia, vol. 107
Kpa Advoc. Crac. 142	Kraków, Wojewódzkie Archiwum Państwowe w Krakowie, Acta Advocatialia Cracoviensis, vol. 142 (1547)
Kpa Advoc. Crac. 200	Kraków, Wojewódzkie Archiwum Państwowe w Krakowie, Acta Advocatialia Cracoviensis, vol. 200 (1580-1583)
Kpa Advoc. Crac. 226	Kraków, Wojewódzkie Archiwum Państwowe w Krakowie, Acta Advocatialia Cracoviensis, vol. 226 (1602-1603)
Kpa K 466	Kraków, Wojewódzkie Archiwum Państwowe w Krakowie, MS K 446, *Liber officiosum Inventariorum ...* (1571-1573)
Wagad RK 110	Warszawa, Archiwum Główne Akt Dawnych, Archiwum Skarbu Koronnego, Rachunki Królewskie, MS 110

WRo 180 II	Wrocław, Biblioteka Zakładu im. Ossolińskich, MS 180 II
WRo 9789 II	Wrocław, Biblioteka Zakładu im. Ossolińskich, MS 9789 II

2. Bibliographical Abbreviations

Briq	Briquet, C.M., *Les Filigranes: Dictionnaire historique des marques du papier de leur apparition vers 1282 jusqu'en 1600* (facsimile edition of the Paris 1907 print, ed. A. Stevenson, Amsterdam, 1968).
Czap	Siniarska-Czaplicka, J., *Filigrany papierni położonych na obszarze Rzeczypospolitej Polskiej od początku XVI do połowy XVIII wieku*, ed. A. Gryczowa, W. Korotaj and H. Kapełuś (Książka w dawnej kulturze polskiej, 15; Wrocław, 1969).
LU	Liber Usualis, (Solesmes, Tournai, 1963)
MCh XI	Simmons, J.S.G. (ed.), *Tromonin's Watermark Album*, ed. E. J. Labarre (Monumenta Chartae Papyriceae Historiam Illustrata, 11; Hilversum, 1965).
WDMP	Wydawnictwo Dawnej Muzyki Polskiej (Editions of Early Polish Music), books 1-74+.

3. Liturgical Abbreviations

All.	Alleluia
BVM	Blessed Virgin Mary
Com.	Communion
Grad.	Gradual
Intr.	Introit
Offer.	Offertory
Sequ.	Sequence
Tr.	Tract

4. General Abbreviations

adol.	adolescent
ap.	apprentice
b.	boy
cl.	clerk
d.	died
vol.	volume

Music at the Royal Court and Chapel in Poland, c. 1543–1600

INTRODUCTION

Poland: A Brief Summary of Its History, and the State of the Country and Its Monarchy in the Sixteenth Century

THE HISTORY OF POLAND UP TO THE SIXTEENTH CENTURY

It was the Piasts who rose in the tenth century to be the first real leaders of Poland, a territory extending from the Baltic sea in the north to the Tatra mountains in the south, and from the Odra river in the west to beyond the Wisła river in the east.[1] The first important event in Poland's early history was the conversion of Mieszko I to Christianity in 966: this act brought the country into the realm of Western Christianity, together with its politics and culture. Mieszko's descendants ruled in direct succession for over a century, beginning with his son, Bolesław Chrobry, the first crowned king, in 1025, and ending with Bolesław III Krzywousty (d. 1138). On the latter's death, the Polish lands were divided between his four sons, and for the next two hundred years the various branches of the Piast family fought for supremacy, bringing internal fragmentation and exposing the country to foreign attacks. Only at the beginning of the fourteenth century did the situation improve. Władysław I Łokietek (c. 1260-1333) outmanoeuvred and outlived all of his rival relatives and emerged as the unchallenged ruler of the kingdom. He made his base in Kraków and it was here, in the cathedral on Wawel Hill, that he was crowned king on 20 January 1320. Władysław I was also the first Polish king to be acknowledged by the pope.[2] His son, Kazimierz III Wielki ('the Great') (1310-70) consolidated the monarch's position, particularly over the Polish magnates, and made further territorial gains for his kingdom. He organized the country's defence by building numerous castles and other fortifications, and by enforcing military service. During his reign, the laws of the kingdom were codified and became the basis of the legal system for centuries to come. Internal trade flourished, and many new towns were established, including Kazimierz (named after him), situated just outside Kraków. King Kazimierz also founded the University of Kraków in 1364.

Only in one respect did Kazimierz fail: he did not produce a male heir to the throne. In view of this he made arrangements for his nephew, Louis of Anjou (1326-82), the King of Hungary, to succeed him. However, Louis was little concerned with Poland: following his coronation in 1370, the country was managed by regents in his absence, and the nobility succeeded in gaining many long-term concessions from him in return for their immediate loyalty.

After Louis's death, the fate of the monarchy lay very much in the hands of the nobility. In 1384 they elected Louis's daughter Jadwiga (Hedviga of Anjou) Queen of Poland, and in the following year they offered her together with the Polish crown to Jogaila (c. 1351-1434), the pagan Grand Duke of Lithuania. In February 1386 Jogaila was baptized, he married Jadwiga, and in March their joint coronation took place. So began the union between Poland and Lithuania under the Jagiellonian monarchy. During the reign of Jogaila, now Władysław II Jagiełło, both countries prospered. Their security was not seriously threatened by neighbouring countries, and the various confrontations with the Teutonic Order, most notably the battle of Grunwald in 1410, served only to strengthen their position and diminish the Order's power. As for the union itself, the Polish and Lithuanian nobility continued to make further clarifications and changes, and by 1413 they had agreed that decisions concerning both countries were to be made by common consent. They also strove to diminish the power of the monarch and to do away with the strict hereditary principle of royal succession, so much so that towards the end of his life, Władysław was obliged to bargain with the nobility to secure the crown for his son. On his death, he was indeed succeeded by his nine-year-old son Władysław (1425-44). During his short reign, he was also elected to the Hungarian crown and subsequently led a crusade against the Turks. This ill-fated expedition ended with his death at Varna in 1444.

By contrast, the reign of Władysław II Jagiełło's second son, Kazimierz IV Jagiellończyk (1427-92) was both long and successful. He managed to maintain his authority at home and made further accretions to the kingdom, most notably that of Royal Prussia in 1466. By the last decade of the fifteenth century, he had established a firm position for the Jagiellonian dynasty in the international politics of central Europe.[3] His first son, Władysław (1456-1516), was elected King of Bohemia in 1471 and King of Hungary in 1490. On Kazimierz's death in 1492, the Polish throne was given to his third son Jan Olbracht (1459-1501), and the Duchy of Grand Lithuania to his fourth son Aleksander (1461-1506).

POLAND IN THE SIXTEENTH CENTURY

By the sixteenth century, Poland's political framework, with its rigid social structure, had been put into place. The monarchy was now only nominally hereditary, and successive kings were chosen by the nobility. A two-chamber Parliament had been created in 1493.[4] The upper chamber (Senate), which had previously been the king's council, included the monarch himself, the archbishops and bishops, the palatines and castellans. Their deliberations were concerned primarily with international matters. The lower chamber consisted of representatives or envoys from every province in the kingdom. Sessions of Parliament (Sejm) met at least once every two years to discuss all matters of state, including taxation. In 1505, the principle of *Nihil Novi* was established, which prevented any law or important decision from being passed without the consent of the whole nobility. In effect, this placed ultimate power in their hands.

Church affairs were dominated by internal matters as well as conflict with the papacy. From 1417 the country had its own primate, and from 1513 all bishops were to be elected by the monarch. Membership of the higher clergy (bishops and canons) was restricted to the nobility. The Reformation, imported from Poland's western neighbour, spread across the kingdom with great speed. However, it did not have the same response here as it did in the German speaking lands. Even so, efforts were made by both the established Church and the monarchy to suppress such new religions, but the nobility protested in principle against any such action, and religious tolerance was generally observed.

The relative stability of the country encouraged both internal and external trade. Following the incorporation of Royal Prussia in 1466, the Wisła river became the main trade route for the whole of the kingdom, and the grain trade flourished in particular. The seaport of Gdańsk (Danzig) became Poland's main port, handling the majority of the country's foreign trade. Printing and the sale of books also became a thriving industry, especially following the influx of several enterprising Germans and Silesians to Kraków in the last decades of the fifteenth century.[5] Many of these people maintained links with their former counterparts, especially in Germany, often commissioning them to produce books for the Polish market. The more prestigious printers gained royal or ecclesiastical privileges, giving them monopolies to publish and sell certain books for limited periods of time.

ZYGMUNT I STARY (1467-1548)

Zygmunt I, later referred to as 'Stary' ('the Elder'), was born on 1 January 1467, the fifth son of King Kazimierz IV Jagiellończyk and Elizabeth of Austria. He was educated, together with his elder brothers, by Jan Długosz (1415-80), a canon of Kraków, now regarded as the first Polish historian.[6] With central Europe divided between his three elder brothers, Zygmunt had no real prospects of gaining a kingdom of his own; however, due to the unexpected deaths in the family, he rose to power almost effortlessly. Following his father's death in 1492, he was invited by his brother Władysław to the Hungarian court in Buda. In 1498 Władysław entrusted Zygmunt with the small kingdom of Głogów, and three years later the kingdom of Opawa. In 1501, King Jan Olbracht died, and although

Władysław nominated Zygmunt for election to the Polish crown, the Polish nobility elected his brother Aleksander, currently the Grand Duke of Lithuania. Undeterred, Władysław placed Zygmunt in charge of Silesia in 1504, which he administered competently in the name of his elder brother.[7] In 1506 King Aleksander's health deteriorated rapidly, so much so that the summer session of Parliament turned its attention to the question of succession. It was here that Zygmunt's supporters promoted his cause. In August 1506 King Aleksander died without issue. Zygmunt was chosen by the nobles of Lithuania as their Grand Duke, and soon afterwards a special session of Parliament elected him to the Polish crown.[8] Zygmunt's coronation took place in the cathedral on Wawel Hill on 7 January 1507.

Zygmunt married twice. His first wife, Barbara Zapolya (d. 1507), was the daughter of a Hungarian magnate, whom Zygmunt met during his time at the court of his elder brother in Buda. The wedding took place in February 1512, on Wawel Hill in Kraków. Barbara died just three years later, in December 1515, following the birth of their second daughter. Barbara's death had a profound effect on Zygmunt, and it was at this time that he made initial enquiries about building a chapel at the cathedral on Wawel Hill.[9] Since Barbara had not produced a male heir, Zygmunt was obliged to remarry. Of the several suitable candidates, he chose Bona Sforza, daughter of Gian Galeazzo, Duke of Milan. The wedding of Zygmunt and Bona took place in Kraków amid great festivity on 18 April 1518. Bona did produce a male heir, Zygmunt August, born on 1 August 1520; she also gave birth to four daughters. Polish historians have presented conflicting opinions of Bona as a person, wife, and mother. However, few disagree that she was a determined woman with strong political and economic convictions. She promoted anti-Habsburg policies in Parliament and constantly strove to strengthen the monarch's position in the country. She mistrusted the nobility and despised them for hampering her plans.

During Zygmunt's reign, the Polish crown saw the incorporation of Prussia and Mazowsze.[10] Prussia had been a fief of the Polish kingdom since 1466. Albrecht von Hohenzollern, the Grand Master of the Teutonic Order (and Zygmunt's nephew), had begun to ignore his commitments with regard to the Treaty of Toruń (1466) and, in particular, was amassing a significant army. In 1519 war broke out: though Zygmunt defeated the Grand Master and drove him back to Königsberg, he agreed to a cease-fire and a truce in 1521. Fortunately for Zygmunt, the truce coincided with the advent of the Reformation. Within just four years many of the knights of the Teutonic Order were converted and even Albrecht von Hohenzollern himself became a Calvinist; consequently the Order disintegrated. This seriously de-stabilized the state and made it vulnerable to external attack. Albrecht turned to Zygmunt for protection, and in 1525 Prussia was incorporated into the Polish kingdom as a secular state, with the Grand Master becoming the hereditary Duke.

The situation with Mazowsze was a different matter. Mazowsze, with its capital Warsaw, had been controlled by the descendants of the Piast dynasty right up until 1526, the year in which the last prince, Janusz III, died. It was reported that Janusz did not die a natural death but was poisoned, and the chief suspect was Queen Bona. In spite of the protestations and claims of succession on the part of Piast relatives, the lands were confiscated by the crown, and placed under Bona's direct management.

On his accession, Zygmunt had also inherited a number of Poland's international problems, the most disturbing being the threat posed by the Muscovites, who periodically attacked Lithuania's eastern borders. Particularly destructive were the invasion of 1507-8, the ten-year war (1512-22), and the campaign of 1537; each of these conflicts ended with a truce, with neither side gaining any territory.[11] Another threat came in the form of the expansionism of the Austrian Habsburgs. In their eagerness to crush the Jagiellonian Empire, the Habsburgs sought an alliance with the Muscovites and the Teutonic Order in Prussia to achieve their end. However, after a decisive victory over the Muscovites at Orsza in 1514, Zygmunt exposed the Habsburgs' plot, and they, in order to maintain their international reputation, were obliged to seek a more cordial relationship with the Jagiellonians. Thus the Congress of Vienna of 1515, which brought together the Jagiellonian kings Władysław of Hungary and Zygmunt of Poland, and the Emperor Maximilian Habsburg, resulted in a double marriage uniting the two families. Władysław's son, Louis Jagiellończyk, married Maria of Castile (the Emperor's granddaughter), and Ferdinand Habsburg (Emperor, 1556-1564) married Anna, Władysław's daughter. This linked the future of the two empires and, perhaps more importantly, established peace in the area. Unfortunately for the Jagiellonians, Louis died in 1526 childless, and Bohemia and Hungary passed without question to the Habsburgs.

One of Zygmunt's most significant achievements was the election and coronation of his son, Zygmunt August, to the Grand Duchy of Lithuania in 1529, and to the Polish crown in 1530. This was unique in that he was the only monarch who managed to have his son crowned during his own lifetime, even if it was accomplished by deceit and by-passing the usual procedure. The Polish nobility guarded strongly their right to elect the king, and this was to take place at a specially convened session of Parliament. On this occasion, Zygmunt won over the magnates individually, and then surprised the session of Parliament of early 1530 with the decision as a *fait accompli*. Few of the nobility opposed the decision, and on 20 February 1530 the nine-year-old prince was elected.

In spite of the conflicting interests of the monarch, magnates, and nobility, the delicate internal *status quo* prevailed for the majority of Zygmunt's reign. This is even more remarkable, given the political advantage gained by the nobility during the short and unstable reigns of both Jan Olbracht and Aleksander. However, several events strained this fragile relationship, most notably the Mazowsze affair and the election of Zygmunt August to the crown, not to mention the constant interference of Queen Bona (especially in the last years of Zygmunt's life, by which time he had become senile). Of particular gravity was the armed rebellion of the nobility against the monarch in 1537. The king had clearly been violating the rule of law, and the nobility took it upon themselves to bring him into line. Zygmunt was forced into submission and at the next sessions of Parliament (1538 and 1539), he promised to uphold all of the laws.[12]

Zygmunt was an ardent defender of the Catholic Faith. He spoke out against the 'new religions' of the Reformation and sought their suppression in Poland. In a whole series of edicts from 1520 to 1534, he banned the teachings of Luther, prohibited scholars from attending Protestant academies, and gave the Church the right to censor printed books. In spite of these edicts, the nobility, part of which had converted to different denominations, prevented any extreme action on the part of the monarch.

By all accounts, Zygmunt was a keen patron of the arts, especially architecture. As a prince at the court of his brother Władysław in Buda, he had come into contact with many Italian artists, and throughout his reign encouraged them to come to Poland. The whole of the palace on Wawel Hill was rebuilt in the Italian style between 1507 and 1535 under the direction of Franciscus Italus of Florence. His successor, Bartolomeo Berrecci, was in charge of much of the interior decoration of the palace; he was also responsible for the new royal chapel built onto the adjoining cathedral. It was here, on Wawel Hill, that King Zygmunt resided with his court for long periods of time surrounded by educated courtiers, poets, and artists.

ZYGMUNT II AUGUST (1520-1572)

Zygmunt II August - the last of the Jagiellonian kings - was born on 1 August 1520, only son of king Zygmunt I Stary and his second wife, Bona Sforza. Zygmunt August's early development and education were fostered by his mother. In 1529 she entrusted a Sicilian, Andreas Silvius, with the young prince's education. Judging by contemporary reports, Silvius was an unsuitable tutor for the prince,[13] and in 1535 he was dismissed. Following a brief period during which a royal scribe called Scipionus acted as tutor, in 1537 Piotr Opaliński, the Castellan of Gniezno, was appointed the next royal tutor. It is said that Zygmunt August had a 'soft' character, no doubt as a result of being close to his mother during his formative years and, according to Piotr Zborowski, the castellan of Małogoszcz, he was able in feminine activities such as dancing and singing,[14] something which undoubtedly influenced his attitude to music in later life.

Zygmunt August's political future had been secured by his father while he was still a boy, being chosen the next Grand Duke of Lithuania and king of Poland in 1529 and 1530 respectively. Of course, these elections did not take effect immediately: Zygmunt transferred control of Lithuania to his son in

October 1544, and Zygmunt August became king of Poland on his father's death in 1548.

Zygmunt August was a conscientious monarch. He endorsed the rule of law, which had previously been abused by his father,[15] and attended every session of Parliament (seventeen between the years 1548 and 1572). Amongst his most important achievements were the organization of a permanent army which defended the borders of the country, and the creation of a fleet, which guarded the Baltic coastline. In foreign matters, the king's main concern was Poland's northeast neighbour, Livonia. The Reformation movement had greatly de-stabilized the country, and this made it vulnerable to the expanding power of the Swedes to the north and the Muscovites to the east. When in 1558-9 a Muscovite army did invade, the Grand Master of the Knights of the Sword, Gottard von Kettler, turned to Zygmunt August for help. He agreed to protect Livonia on condition that it be incorporated into the Polish kingdom.[16] Kettler and the Livonian nobility accepted, and following their act of homage to Zygmunt August in 1561, Livonia became a fief of the Polish kingdom. On the negative side, his most serious mistake was the granting of hereditary succession for the Dukes of Prussia. This may not have been such a drastic concession at the time, although this act had far-reaching consequences in the next two centuries, as it was in part responsible for the ultimate break-up of the kingdom in the latter part of the eighteenth century.

The last decade of Zygmunt August's life was also marked by his efforts to consolidate the Polish-Lithuanian union. The original union, which served the Jagiellonian monarchy for the best part of two centuries, was now out of date. Internal organization needed general overhauling, as did public financing. Of particular importance was the funding of the army, even more so in view of the constant attacks by the Muscovites. One other important consideration was also apparent. Zygmunt had not produced an heir, and without the appropriate mechanism for electing the monarchy, potential differences between the Poles and the Lithuanians could have lead to the break-up of the union. After lengthy and at times heated discussions at several sessions of Parliament, and many compromises and reassurances to the nobility on the part of the monarch, a new constitution was drawn up, and on 1 July 1569 the Union of Lublin was signed and sealed by the senate. Poland and Lithuania were to be joined into one so-called Republic, with one elected king, one Parliament, consisting of both Polish and Lithuanian representatives, and one currency.

Zygmunt August was interested in the new religions of the Reformation, although he himself remained a Catholic throughout his life. In this way, he was one of the first kings to approve the recommendations of the Council of Trent, whilst at the same time paving the way for religious tolerance in Poland, which was made law 28 January 1573, less than a year after his death.

Zygmunt August married three times. His first marriage, to Elizabeth Habsburg, was arranged in the 1530s by Zygmunt I and Elizabeth's father, Ferdinand. The wedding took place in 1543, and after a short and unhappy two years Elizabeth died. By the time of her death, Zygmunt August had already met Barbara, daughter of Mikołaj Radziwiłł, the Lithuanian Hetman. After a secret affair, the two were married in 1547 without the knowledge of his parents or the senate; consequently the union was not recognized, nor was Barbara accepted as queen. Zygmunt August fought for her recognition, and this was granted only in 1550. Barbara was crowned Queen of Poland in December of that year. However, their happiness was short-lived; Barbara died just five months later. Zygmunt's third wife was Catherine Habsburg, Elizabeth's younger sister. This was a political marriage and, like the first, was disastrous. Soon after the wedding and coronation, which took place on Wawel Hill amongst great festivities on 29 and 30 July 1553, Catherine's interference in the country's politics gained her the king's displeasure. This rift grew with time; by 1562 the royal couple had separated, and in 1566 Catherine left Poland.

Unlike his father, King Zygmunt August spent very little time in Kraków, the capital of Poland. After his wedding to Catherine Habsburg in 1553, he made only two short visits there in 1558 and 1559. He was clearly more attached to his residence in Vilnius (Wilno in Polish), which he extended quite substantially in the 1550s, and where he established and maintained his extensive personal library. It was here that he retreated between sessions of Parliament. Towards the end of his life, Zygmunt August spent most of his time in Warsaw, and here too, he rebuilt the royal palace. He had one further favourite residence in Knyszyn, half-way between Warsaw and Vilnius, where he often travelled in later years, and it was here, on 7 July 1572, that he died.

THE MONARCHY DURING THE LAST QUARTER OF THE SIXTEENTH CENTURY

The death of Zygmunt August put the new electoral system of the 1569 constitution to its first test. The electoral session of Parliament was convened in the Spring of 1573 just outside Warsaw. The choice was not easy, since there was no obvious candidate, and there was the added problem of the middle-aged daughter of Zygmunt I, Anna Jagiellonka, who had never married and had remained in Poland. Of the several frontrunners, all foreign monarchs and dukes, the nobility chose Prince Henry Valois of France. The details of the election, including marriage to Anna, were accepted by Henry in September 1573, and on 21 February 1574 he was crowned. Henry concerned himself little with Polish affairs and did not fulfil his marriage obligation to Anna. More importantly, on 30 May 1574, his elder brother, King Charles IX of France, died without issue, and on hearing the news, Henry fled Poland to take his place on the French throne. He never returned to Poland, and in May 1575 the Polish nobility declared the throne vacant.

In the ensuing interregnum, Poland's infrastructure began to crumble, and the country lay defenceless against the attacks of Muscovites in Livonia and the Tartars in the south-east. The nobility themselves were divided over the choice of the next monarch. Only after long deliberations did they elect Stefan Batory, the Transilvanian. On 1 May 1576 he married Anna Jagiellonka and was crowned king. During his ten-year reign, Batory managed to restore order in Poland: he controlled the magnates, replenished the royal coffers, and reformed the army. He was also successful in defeating the Muscovites, thus regaining the Livonian lands.

Following the death of Stefan Batory on 12 December 1586, the country was thrown into yet another interregnum and an electoral session of Parliament. On this occasion, the nobility chose Prince Zygmunt Vasa, the son of King John III Vasa of Sweden and Katarzyna Jagiellonka, and he was crowned in December 1588. Although Zygmunt III Vasa lost the Swedish throne to his brother Charles, he was the father of the next dynasty of Polish kings.

THE IMPLICATIONS OF POLISH HISTORY FOR MUSIC IN THE SIXTEENTH CENTURY

Several important factors emerge from this historical outline. The first is geographical (in its political dimension). The Jagiellonian monarchy 'ruled' over a relatively large portion of central and eastern Europe, comprising Poland and Lithuania, later on also Prussia, Mazowsze, and Livonia. (See Map of the Jagiellonian Realm, Appendix I.) This had a positive effect in that the royal chest acquired additional sources of income, allowing a larger court to be financed. The introduction of the elected monarchy, following the death of the last Jagiellonian king, resulted in very different personalities being elected to the Polish crown. This too had a serious implications on royal patronage.

Though this study emphasizes Kraków and Wawel Hill in particular as the centre of the royal household, it was not the only centre. It was favoured by Zygmunt as his principal residence, but not by his son Zygmunt August, who preferred Vilnius. As ruler of such a large kingdom, the monarch was obliged to spend a significant portion of his time travelling to the various parts of the kingdom, be it for sessions of Parliament, or for military reasons. Such patterns affected patronage and the movement of musicians and singers of the chapel.

Finally, the cultural and commercial contacts with Italy and with the German-speaking states emphasize Poland's position as an international state, and one whose facets (including those of musical practice and patronage) reflect the broad pattern observed in the rest of Europe. Nevertheless, the country's individual political history and cultural traits were responsible for certain unique features which are not found elsewhere.

NOTES

[1] The best account of Polish history of the period is N. Davies, *God's Playground: A History of Poland*, i: *The Origins to 1795* (Oxford, 1981). This book presents the main events of Poland's history in an objective light and, unlike some of the recent histories by Poles, is not inspired by any particular ideology.

[2] Ibid., pp. 72, 93-5.

[3] Ibid., p. 138.

[4] M. Biskup (ed.), *Historia dyplomacji polskiej*, i: *Połowa X wieku - 1572*, (Warsaw, 1982), pp. 729-30.

[5] J. Ptaśnik (ed.), *Cracovia impressorum XV et XVI ss.* (Monumenta Poloniae Typographica, 1; Warsaw, 1979; reprint of Lwów, 1922 edition).

[6] His twelve-volume *Historia Polonica* records all of the major events in the country's history. See Davies, *God's Playground*, pp. 5-6.

[7] J. Gierowski, *Historia Polski*. ii: *1505-1764* (Warsaw, 1986), p. 93. All further references are to this volume.

[8] Zygmunt nevertheless was obliged to return control of Silesia back to Władysław.

[9] S. Komornicki, 'Kaplica Zygmuntowska w katedrze na Wawelu', *Rocznik Krakowski* (1932), no. 23, p. 53.

[10] See Appendix I: Map of the Jagiellonian Realm

[11] Davies, *God's Playground*, pp. 142-3.

[12] Gierowski, *Historia Polski*, p. 97.

[13] L. Kolankowski, *Zygmunt August, Wielki Książę Litwy do roku 1548* (Lwów, 1913), p. 78.

[14] Ibid., p. 79: 'in mulierum coetu et puellarum grege craciviæ choreis et cantibus potissimam ætatis partem conterit'.

[15] J. Prus, 'Król Zygmunt August i jego zasługi dla polskiej kultury', *Studia Historyczne*, 17 (1974), no. 4, p. 540.

[16] See Appendix I.

Part I

The Rorantists' College
and its Repertory, 1543-1600

I

The Rorantists' College: Its Foundation and History, 1543-1600

In 1543 Zygmunt I Stary established a college of chaplains in his newly built chapel at the cathedral on Wawel Hill in Kraków. The college soon became known as the 'Rorantists', the name originating from the first word of the introit 'Rorate caeli desuper', which the college sang daily to polyphony. The Rorantists were active for more than three centuries; only after the partition of Poland and the confiscation of funds by the Austrian authorities in 1872 was the college forced to disband. During this time it cultivated the art of *a cappella* singing and its membership included a number of notable Polish composers. This chapter will describe the foundation of the Rorantists' college, its membership and its duties. It will also discuss the development of the college until the close of the sixteenth century, that is until the death of Queen Anna Jagiellonka in 1596, the last of the Jagiellonian patrons. In particular, it will include a discussion of the additional requirements made of the college by Zygmunt II August (in 1550-1552) and Anna Jagiellonka (in 1584). The main sources of information for this subject are the legal documents issued by the monarchs as well as the bishops which survive in the cathedral archive on Wawel Hill. These are presented, in dyplomatic transcriptions, in Appendix II.

THE CATHEDRAL ON WAWEL HILL: AN OUTLINE

In order fully to appreciate the nature of the Rorantists' college and its place within the cathedral complex, it is necessary to provide some basic information on the cathedral, and its other foundations.[1] The original cathedral was built in the eleventh century following the decision at the Congress of Gniezno in 1020 to create a diocese in Kraków. This building was damaged by fire in the 1080s, and work began on a second cathedral in the 1090s. Initially consecrated in 1118, the building was re-consecrated in 1142 after further improvements. It was in this second cathedral that Władysław I Łokietek was crowned king of Poland on 20

January 1320. Later that year, and on his initiative, work began on the third and present cathedral. The main part of the building took over forty years to complete, and was finally consecrated on 28 March 1364.[2] The cathedral assumed a central role in the events of Poland, being the place of coronation for the Polish monarchy, as well as their final place of rest.

Over the centuries, numerous side-altars were erected in the cathedral by monarchs, bishops, and magnates. These were located throughout the building: in the nave of the building against the pillars, and in the side-aisles. Each altar was dedicated to a saint or saints, or to the Blessed Virgin Mary. Some of the monarchs and bishops built side-chapels onto the cathedral, which also served as their mausoleums, and these also included an altar. One such chapel was that of the Assumption of the Blessed Virgin Mary, founded by Kazimierz III Wielki in 1340. Although these chapels had their usual dedication, they were often referred to in the sources by their founder's name. By the time of the 1563 cathedral inventory and description, there were over fifty altars located throughout the building, including those in the seventeen side-chapels.

THE CATHEDRAL STAFF, THE ENDOWMENT OF CHANTRIES AND COLLEGES OF PRIESTS

The cathedral on Wawel Hill was, of course, the seat of the bishop of Kraków. It was staffed by a chapter of canons, which numbered thirty-six in the sixteenth century, and amongst these were six senior canons or prelates: the Dean, Archdeacon, Prefect, Scholastic, Cantor, and Custodian. Each of the canons had a substitute (known as a vicar), and from the latter the prelates chose their deputies. It was the duties of the canons, or their deputies in their absence, to provide the liturgy at the main altar as well as to recite the breviary in the canons' stalls.

The cathedral also accommodated a large number of priests who held chantries at a given altar, or prebends in a given chapel. Initially, each new altar was accompanied by the establishment of a chantry. The establishment of such chantries was reserved for members of the royal family, the high nobility, and bishops, though some were created by influential canons of the cathedral chapter. With time, space in the building became scarce and secondary chantries were established at pre-existing altars. These chantries were intended to be perpetual: the benefactor secured funds which provided the salary of the chaplain;[3] he also donated the necessary items for the celebration of the liturgy (the liturgical apparatus and vestments). The liturgy observed by the chantry priest comprised the recitation of a number of masses every week, invariably including prayers for the well-being of the benefactor and, following his death, for his soul. The benefactor held jurisdiction over the chantry, giving him or her the right to choose the chantry priest. Finally, provisions were always made for the continuation of patronage after the benefactor's death.[4] A more substantial form of endowment at the cathedral was the establishment of a college of priests. By the beginning of the sixteenth century there were four such institutions: the so-called 'Mansionarii', the 'Psalterists', and two 'royal' colleges based in the chapels of the Holy Trinity and the Holy Cross. In principle, all four were similar: each was essentially a body of chaplains responsible for the liturgy at an altar or chapel. As with the single chantries, the pattern of liturgical observance of each college was set out by the benefactor, though their liturgical duties were more extended, including both communal and individual duties. In detail, however, the four colleges were quite different. They varied in size and form, and each one had its own specific liturgy to celebrate. Their role in the liturgical and musical life of the cathedral should not be underestimated, and all four deserve description here.

The first institution, the 'Mansionarii', was established in 1381 by Bishop Zawisza of Kurozwęka (d. 1382).[5] From 1374 he served as chancellor to Louis of Anjou, King of Hungary and Poland, and from 1381 as Louis's regent in Poland. In the final two years of his life he was also the Bishop of Kraków.[6] Zawisza of Kurozwęka established a college of eight chaplains: one Precentor and seven Mansionarii, including one clerk. The Mansionarii were sited in the chapel built by the Zawisza family (Rosarum Sacellum), located in the south-west corner of the cathedral. Their communal duties included the reciting of the canonic hours, and a sung mass every day in honour of the Assumption of the Blessed Virgin Mary. Each Thursday they were required to say Matins of nine lessons, and on Friday to celebrate a Requiem mass for the soul of the benefactor. Every Mansionarius was also obliged to celebrate three masses per week in the chapel. The college was given a house within the walls of the castle on Wawel Hill, where its members lived and shared a communal table.[7] The location of the Mansionarii and their chapel seems not to have been an ideal one since their duties overlapped with those of the college in the adjacent chapel of the Holy Cross and the singing of the two chapels clashed.[8] In view of this, Jan Radlica, the Bishop of Kraków and the next patron of the chapel, moved the college in 1390 to the chapel of the Nativity of the Blessed Virgin Mary, at the opposite end of the cathedral behind the main altar. Over the years, several additional benefices, albeit smaller, were given to the Mansionarii. One such addition of King Zygmunt I dates from 1518, which gave them a sum of 20 marks per year from the royal salt-mines in return for several masses, including a Sunday mass in honour of the Assumption of the Blessed Virgin Mary.[9]

The second college comprised the 'Psalterists' (Communitatis Psalteristarum), so named from their main duty of singing the psalter. The Psalterists were founded in 1393 by Queen Jadwiga, with the consent and financial support of her husband, King Władysław II Jagiełło.[10] The institution received papal approval from Pope Boniface IX in 1397.[11] Jadwiga established a body of sixteen Psalterists, including the prefect, and one clerk. Unlike the other choral institutions, the Psalterists were not based in a side-chapel, but at the altar of St. Christopher, located in the nave of the cathedral in front of the chapel of Sts Peter and Paul (now the Vasa chapel).[12] The Psalterists' main responsibility was the continual recitation of the psalter, and not just the canonic hours. They were not all required to attend at any one time, but in groups of four during the day and two at night: 'ad decantationem Psalterii dies et noctes alternis vicibus, quorum in die quattuor presbiteri, nocte vero per duos presbiteros'.[13] Presumably their number allowed for a reasonable rota system. The Psalterists were also required to celebrate four masses every day, and sing Matins of nine lessons once a week. Their principal income was the sum of 300 marks from the royal salt-mines - each psalterist received 18 marks per year and the clerk was given 8 marks.[14] Like the Mansionarii, they had the use of a house on Wawel Hill.[15]

The third college of chaplains served in the chapel of the Holy Trinity. The chapel itself was built in 1431-3 in the north-west corner of the cathedral on the left of the west door. The various acts and documents pertaining to this college indicate that its establishment was a long and drawn-out affair. Most sources name Queen Zofia (1405-61), the fourth wife of King Władysław II Jagiełło, as the founder of the college in 1458,[16] although Władysław himself had already allocated certain funds for the chapel in 1431 and 1433.[17] Furthermore, it was their son, King Kazimierz IV Jagiellończyk, who provided the main source of the college's income - 100 marks from the royal salt-mines in 1464 - three years after Zofia's death.[18] They were also given a house in the castle, next to the Mansionarii.[19] The college consisted of nine members: the prefect, who held one of the cathedral canonries from 1474,[20] seven prebendaries ('praebendarii'), and the clerk. The main duty of this college was to sing a daily mass in honour of the Holy Trinity, which all members - including the clerk - had to attend. Each prebendary was also required to celebrate three masses per week, the first for Corpus Christi, the second in honour of the Assumption of the Blessed Virgin Mary, and the third a Requiem mass for the benefactors. The college was to remain under royal jurisdiction, giving successive monarchs the right to grant new funds and request further duties, as well as nominate all new members.

The fourth college was established in the chapel of the Holy Cross. The present chapel was built in 1470 in the south-west corner of the cathedral, on the right of the west door, very much in the same style as, and no doubt as a complement to, the chapel of the Holy Trinity on the other side of the west door. There is little doubt that an earlier chapel of the same name stood here and which was staffed by a college of chaplains by 1390 at the latest; as mentioned above, it was on their count that the Mansionarii in the adjacent chapel were moved due to overlapping duties. However, it has not been possible to find source information on the former chapel or its original institution; very few documents pertaining to this chapel have survived and information on the chapel is available only in secondary accounts which post-date its rebuilding in 1470. It was in this new chapel that King Kazimierz IV Jagiellończyk and his wife, Queen Elizabeth of Austria, established a college in 1477.[21] It comprised nine members: eight prebendaries (including the prefect) and a clerk. The prefect's post also included one of the cathedral's canonries. The main income of 100 marks came from the royal salt-mines. The communal duties included a daily mass and the hours of the Holy Cross as well as a Requiem for the benefactors. To avoid any confusion, the sources stipulate that this was to commence just after the end of the daily mass in the Holy Trinity chapel.[22] The prebendaries were also required to sing a mass and Matins of nine lessons on the respective anniversaries of the founders' deaths (Kazimierz on 7 June 1492 and Elizabeth on 30 August 1505). Each prebendary was to recite two masses per week - the first 'pro peccatis', the second for the dead.[23] As with the college of the Holy Trinity, this college was also under royal jurisdiction. Likewise it was granted a communal house on Wawel Hill.

These four colleges continued to be active throughout the sixteenth century and beyond. However, by the time of the Rorantists' establishment in the 1540s a hierarchy of the colleges seems to have emerged. This can be deduced from the movement, presumably promotion, of chaplains from one college to another. At the forefront were the Psalterists, followed by the Holy Trinity college, the Mansionarii, and finally the Holy Cross college. It is possible that this hierarchy arose from the endowment of the respective groups, and more specifically, the salaries offered to their members. Nevertheless, the chapel of the Holy Trinity maintained its 'royal' status right up to the establishment of the Rorantists: it was the only institution to be clearly described as such in contemporary cathedral records.[24] Furthermore, it was arguably the most musically orientated chapel: its membership included two of the more notable figures involved in music at the royal court: Alexander Pesenti (de Pesentis) and Jan Wierzbkowski. Alexander Pesenti, nephew of the Italian composer Michael Pesenti, was previously organist to Cardinal Ippolito d'Este. It is believed that Pesenti travelled with the cardinal to Kraków in 1518 for the wedding of Bona Sforza and Zygmunt I. After the cardinal's death in 1520, Pesenti returned to Poland and entered Queen Bona's service as a musician. It is not known when he was elected to a prebend in the Holy Trinity chapel, nor for how long he served there. However, a record of his resignation from the college, dated 4 August 1537, is preserved in the chapter records, and thus his membership cannot be disputed.[25] Jan Wierzbkowski, canon of the cathedral, and earlier holder of a prebend in the chapel of the Holy Cross, was elected to Holy Trinity chapel on 28 November 1537, and held a prebend here for six years. Wierzbkowski resigned on 27 July 1543,[26] less than a month before departing with Zygmunt August to Vilnius, where he subsequently became the prefect of the latter's new chapel.

All these institutions were initially complete, with most aspects of the duties and running of the college established; it was neither foreseen nor intended that later alterations should be made. With time, however, each of the four institutions changed and developed to some degree. New funds were provided, and further liturgical obligations in view of those funds were included in the chapel's duties. Some of these took the form of additional chantries, incorporated into the foundation and allocated either to individuals or given to the college as a whole. These additions were introduced by the patron of the institution (the king or queen in the case of the Psalterists and the chapels of the Holy Trinity and Holy Cross, and the Bishop of Kraków in the case of the Mansionarii); occasionally others sponsored the institutions, but only with the patron's permission. One of the more interesting changes was the inclusion of the cathedral organist in the ranks of the Psalterists at some stage before 1526.[27] This was a practical measure, made to ensure the organist's salary without having to find a new source of income. It is not clear, however, whether or not the organist was required to take part in the Psalterists' duties at the altar of St Christopher.

ZYGMUNT'S CHAPEL: THE BUILDING

Whilst on a visit to Vilnius in 1517, King Zygmunt I wrote to his banker in Kraków stating that he had seen a model of a chapel by an Italian architect (who is not named in the letter),[28] and had commissioned the latter to build the chapel onto the cathedral on Wawel Hill in Kraków.[29] The architect in question was undoubtedly Bartolomeo Berrecci, who was not only responsible for the building itself, but also the six statues it housed.[30] Very little is known about Berrecci's early life. He was born near Florence,[31] and had spent some time in Hungary prior to his arrival in Kraków in about 1516.[32] No earlier examples of his works are known to exist either in Italy or Hungary, and this chapel is the earliest known building by him in Poland. The new building was modelled on the centrally planned Italian buildings of the early Renaissance. Its base took the form of a cube, with each side measuring just over 8 metres on the exterior and 6 metres inside. Over this cube there was an octagonal drum, with its diameter also just over 8 metres. Each of the eight sides contained circular windows,[33] which provided the principal source of natural light for the chapel. Over the drum there was a dome 4 metres high and above that a lantern, 2.5 metres in diameter and 9 metres in height. In all, the chapel was 25 metres high. The choice of site for the new building is interesting, if difficult to explain. It was to be located at the mid-point of the cathedral on the south side, on the site of the early fourteenth-century chapel of the Assumption of the Blessed Virgin Mary, built by Kazimierz III. Whilst there was room available on the north side of the cathedral, this side may have been regarded as unsuitable due to the lack of light. It is also possible that the original chapel of the Assumption was in a poor state and was not worth maintaining.

Demolition work on the old chapel probably began immediately in 1517 and, by the beginning of 1518, work on the new chapel had commenced.[34] The foundations were laid just over a year later, and in 1520 the corner-stone was laid, probably by Zygmunt himself.[35] By 1524 the sandstone walls which constitute the base of the chapel were erected, and within the next two years the octagonal drum and windows, the dome, and the lantern were completed. In 1526 work began on the interior of the chapel and in 1529 Berrecci was commissioned to sculpt the six statues, which took two years to complete. By 1531 the building of the chapel was finished; it had taken over a decade to build and had cost 20, 000 złoty. In 1532 the chapel furnishings were installed and a bronze screen which separated the chapel from the nave of the cathedral was erected. The final item of the chapel was the altar. An initial plan was drawn up around 1531: its reredos was to take the form of a triptych, with a painted wooden exterior, and an interior of pure silver. The exterior panels were painted by Georgio Pinczestein, for which he received 290 florens in 1533; the interior was carried out by a silversmith in Nuremberg, one Melchior Bayer, at a cost of 5, 801 florens and 8 groszy, paid to him in 1535. The whole altar was completed in 1538.[36] Meanwhile, on 9 May 1533, Bishop Piotr Tomicki and the cathedral chapter formally gave their permission for sung masses to take place in the chapel.[37] A month later, on 8 June, the chapel was consecrated and dedicated to the Assumption of the Blessed Virgin Mary, St Sigismund, and St Barbara. Thus the original dedication was maintained, with the addition of the king's name saint and that of his first wife. Zygmunt's new chapel was a magnificent building, and it undoubtedly stood out and above the Gothic cathedral and surrounding chapels.

THE CREATION OF THE RORANTISTS' COLLEGE

There is evidence to support the claim that Zygmunt I intended his chapel to be staffed by a college of chaplains from the outset. A letter from Bishop Tomicki to Seweryn Boner, the royal banker and keeper of the royal salt-mines, dated 21 August 1533, reveals that the king had asked Tomicki to prepare a founding act or document pertaining to the college. Tomicki therefore needed to know from Boner what funds were to be made available for it. Thus by the time of the chapel's completion, the whole process of establishing a new college had been put into motion:

> *Praeterae a Dominatione Vestra rogo, quamadmodum et prius rogavi, ut me certiorem facere velit, quam summam census annui ex salinis habituri sunt sacerdotes in sacello regia maiestatis divinis procurandis instituendi: ut scire possim, quo pacto litterae erectionis sint conficiendae, quas confectas et scriptas maiestas regia ad se Vilnam mitti mandavit.*[38]

Within two months, the bishop had drawn up the document and sent it to the king as requested. Zygmunt, however, seems not to have been satisfied with the document, and made his views known in a letter to the bishop of 14 October 1533:

> Super ordinatione facienda de mansionariis capellae nostrae non censemus, quod hic bene constituere possimus, et proinde suspendemus deliberationem nostram ad reditum illuc nostrum felicem, ubi commodius Paternitati Vestrae Reverendissimae verbis quam per litteras animi nostri intentionem explicare et per mutuam conferentiam pervestigatis bene rerum circumstantiis, non tam praesentibus quam futuris, prospicere melius poterimus.[39]

Clearly, the king felt that a comprehensive document could not be drawn up adequately by correspondence, and suggested that the whole matter be suspended until his return to Kraków, when it could be discussed with the bishop in person. However, it is uncertain whether such a discussion took place, or indeed whether another document was produced. Zygmunt returned to Kraków on 8 August 1535, but remained there for less than two months: he left for Vilnius on 4 October. After this initial activity in 1533, several years elapsed before the actual founding documents were produced. Several facts may explain this. Between 1533 and 1538, Zygmunt I spent most of his time away from Kraków, including three years in Vilnius.[40] He was much preoccupied with matters of state, not to mention the military campaign against Moldavia.[41] The death of Bishop Tomicki in 1535 may also have been a set-back for the king.

Then, at the beginning of 1540, two acts were issued, one each by Zygmunt I (9 January) and Bishop Sebastian Branicki of Poznań (14 January). It may be no coincidence that they were produced during the king's first extended residence in Kraków for several years (20 March 1538 - 24 April 1540). Both documents deal with new funds for the chapel: certain tithes which came from royal land in the diocese of Poznań, formerly allocated to the local parish church of Wiszkitki, were 'released' and now transferred to the new royal chapel. The decision to take funds from land so far away from the capital cannot be easily explained, although given that the king had appointed Branicki as Bishop of Poznań just a few months earlier,[42] it is possible that the latter's actions were in gratitude to the king.

It was another three years before the next acts were produced. This delay, like the previous one, may be attributed to the absence of the king from Kraków between April 1540 and May 1542.[43] The four documents, which appeared in March and August 1543, mark an important stage in the creation of the college. The first, dated 27 March 1543,[44] takes the form of a decree or public notice and announces the forthcoming establishment of the royal college. It was issued by Piotr Gamrat, Bishop of Kraków, and affixed to the doors of the cathedral three weeks later by Andrzej Radomski, the Vicar-General of the cathedral. The second, again by Piotr Gamrat, dated 23 July, is a confirmation of the election of Mikołaj of Poznań as the first prefect of the chapel.[45] The third, Zygmunt's act of 28 August, seems to be retrospective,[46] and confirms the donation of the house and the granting of funds from the royal salt-mines, which already appear in earlier documents. The fourth and final document, also dated 28 August 1543, was issued by Piotr Gamrat.[47] It contains a substantial section covering the many details of the chapel's liturgical duties, funding, salaries, internal structure, and management. It affirms royal jurisdiction over the chapel, even naming Zygmunt August as the next patron.[48] It also contains a copy of all of the earlier acts and decrees with an introduction by Gamrat to each one. This document can be regarded as the definitive founding act of the Rorantists' college. It gave the college the right to exist, and was essentially its guarantee of funding. (See Appendix II.2, Kk dyp. 1184.)

Before focusing on the Rorantists' college itself, it should be understood that the above-mentioned founding act of 1543 encompasses the whole of the liturgical staff who served in the new chapel. It therefore includes two other separate chantries, those of St Mary of Egypt and Sts Felix and Adauct.[49] The first of these was originally located in the twelfth-century 'rotunda' of the Blessed Virgin Mary, and the second in the fourteenth-century chapel built by Kazimierz III Wielki. Both these chapels were demolished in the first decade of the century when the royal palace was rebuilt by Zygmunt. He was therefore obliged to preserve the chantries established by his predecessors and relocated them in his own newly-built chapel in the cathedral. For the moment, they remained independent chantries under the jurisdiction of the monarchy.

ASPECTS OF THE RORANTISTS' COLLEGE AS AN INSTITUTION

Size and organization

The Rorantists' college was to have a prefect ('præfectus'), nine prebendaries (the acts refer to them as 'præbendarii', 'mansionarii', or 'sacellani'), and one clerk ('clericus').[50] The actual number of chaplains was stipulated in Gamrat's decree of 27 March 1543 and his document of 28 August 1543; all other documents, including those issued by the king refer only to 'a certain number of chaplains' ('certum sacerdotum numerum').[51] It is possible that only at the very end, when the various funds were secured, was it possible to determine the precise size of the college.

The prefect was to hold the original chantry of the Assumption of the Blessed Virgin Mary which had been transferred from the former chapel to the new one, and he was to draw the income from it. The others were to be given benefices of the newly formed college. This distinction between the prefect and the prebendaries is not insignificant. The prefect was chosen by the king, he had tenure for life ('perpetuum'),[52] and could be dismissed only by the king himself. The prefect was nevertheless free to resign if and when he so wished. By contrast, the prebendaries and the clerk were stipendiary members of the college.[53] They were not appointed by the king, but employed by the prefect, who also had the power to dismiss them without reference to the king. Furthermore, and unlike the prefect, the prebendaries were forbidden from holding any other church benefice or stipend: 'nulla alia beneficia ecclesiastica . . . habent'.[54]

It was the prefect's duty to choose suitable priests for the college, who were well versed in the art of singing and chanting, possessing good, sonorous voices: 'Ad huiusmodi autem præbendas et clericaturam non nisi personas abiles et idonei actu præsbiteri, qui ex arte cantare et psallere sciant cum bona et sonorosa uoce.'[55] Each candidate was to pass a formal examination before he could be accepted. Likewise the prefect was charged with employing a suitable clerk to serve in chapel. The clerk did not have to be an ordained priest, but could be just in minor orders. If the clerk had a good voice, he was to be promoted by the prefect to a prebend at the next opportunity,[56] presumably assuming that he had by that time been ordained. The prefect was also responsible for monitoring the behaviour of the college members. He was to punish those who were disobedient or committed an offence, and in extreme cases, with the college's consent, he was to remove a chaplain who was unsuitable: 'Qui tandem non nisi ex legitima causa et intolerabili excessu removeri.'[57]

The college's finances

Of all the aspects covered in the founding act, the sections dealing with the college's finances are perhaps the most comprehensive. They stipulate precisely what funds were secured for the foundation and give unambiguous directives concerning the college's expenditure, so as to prevent any financial manipulation or abuse.

There were several sources of income for the college. First, there was the income from the pre-existing chantry of the Assumption of the Blessed Virgin Mary.[58] This was itself made up of smaller constituent parts. 12 marks per annum came from the royal salt-mines, a further 10 marks and 32 groszy from the royal treasury, and church tithes from four villages: Słomniki, Szczepanowice, Poznachowice (or Górna Wieś), and Winiary. The total income of the chantry, according to the founding act, was 43 marks.[59] This sum now became the prefect's income. Next, the college was granted tithes from several royal villages: Kąski, Czerwona Niwa, and Kozłowicze, formerly ceded to the Wiszkitki parish. As these tithes were set by location, their monetary value was not fixed, but varied according to the crop and its value. In the first year, 1543, these tithes brought the college a total of 155 marks and 26 groszy.[60] The college had one further source of income, namely the sum of 100 marks per annum from the royal salt-mines of Bochnia, just outside Kraków. This was to be paid by the keeper of the mines in quarterly instalments. The acts do not stipulate how the funds were to reach the college, but it is evident from the sources that the Rorantists themselves travelled to the respective locations and collected the sums in person.[61]

In addition to these funds, the Rorantists were provided with a communal house on Wawel Hill which stood adjacent to the north gate of the castle. The house was formerly part of a building used as a warehouse for storing grain. Two-thirds of this warehouse was rebuilt at the king's expense and given to the Rorantists, while the third part remained a store for the king's grain.[62] The house became the property of the college, and the members lived there free of charge. It was also exempt from church tax: 'domum pro eiusdem sacerdotibus donatam libertati et immunitati Ecclesiasticæ ascribimus'.[63] The members of the college were not only required to live in the house, they were also obliged to eat their meals there: 'in prænominata domo . . . simul habitare et communem mensam tenere debeant et teneantur'.[64] Provisions were also made for the employment of two house-servants. The first was to be an 'honest and mature woman', who washed and maintained the chapel vestments and linen, as well as preparing the meals for the college.[65] The other was a house-servant who was at the chaplains' disposal.[66]

The college expenditure can be divided into salaries, chapel costs, and household costs. As already mentioned, the prefect was given the total income from the chantry of the Assumption of the Blessed Virgin Mary, namely 43 marks per year. Each of the prebendaries received 20 marks per year, and the clerk 16 marks. The cook/cleaner and the servant received 5 and 3 marks respectively.[67] The act made provisions for the smooth running of the chapel liturgy, thus 10 marks per annum was allocated for wax candles, whilst the bread and wine used during mass was to be supplied by the cathedral. 35 marks was given to the communal household: 25 for food, and 10 for firewood. Finally, an additional sum of 10 marks was set aside for the maintenance of the chapel and house. The remaining sum of money was to be kept in a chest located in the chapel itself, made safe with two locks, to which the prefect and a senior prebendary each had a key.

The prefect was ultimately responsible for the college's finances. He was required to keep an account-book in which he was to record the income from the salt-mines and tithes, as well as the expenditure (the salaries and the other costs incurred): 'librum authenticum in quo proventus omnes conscribere, et de expositis rationem reddere possit'.[68] Fortunately, the first account-book of the college, containing detailed accounts for the years 1543 to 1624, has survived: the *Elenchus omnium perceptorum et expositorum ex proventibus Sacelli Regii*, Kk Inv 65 (henceforth *Elenchus*). The prefect was also obliged to present the accounts to the college every year for its approval.

Chapel duties

The chapel duties, both communal and individual, are also clearly laid out in the founding act. First and foremost, the college was to celebrate a daily mass in honour of the Annunciation of the Blessed Virgin Mary, the so-called 'Rorate' mass. The whole college was expected to attend this mass and to adorn the liturgy with polyphony. For most of the liturgical year, this mass was to be celebrated between the Mass and Prime sung by the Mansionarii; in Advent, it was to follow the morning mass sung by the vicars of the cathedral.[69] It is clear that there was not always sufficient time for the Rorantists to celebrate their mass during Advent, since the act stipulates certain days on which they were instructed to omit their mass and give priority to the chapel of the Holy Cross and the Mansionarii. These days include all Sundays, the feasts of St Andrew, St Nicholas, St Thomas the Apostle, the Conception of the Blessed Virgin Mary, and Christmas.

> Statuimus et ordinamus, ut Præpositus et Præbendarii dictæ Capellæ pro tempore existentes Missam Rorate de Anunctiatione Beatissime Virginis Mariæ in eadem Capella cantu figurato als na Szorth singulis diebus et perpetuis temporibus in continenti post missam: et ante primam: Mansionariorum omnibus temporibus Anni præterquam in Adventu: quæ max post missam Rorate, in choro a vicariis decantari solitam, in dicta Capella siue oraculo concinna et sonorosa uoce simul omnes ... Et quia tempus aliquando non fert, ut officium iuxta fundationes suas proprias expleantur, quamobrem obmittere oportebit missam hanc nouæ fundationis, iuxta missas aliarum fundationum, puta missas Sanctæ Crucis, et Beate Virginis Mariæ Mansionariorú, potissimum hiis diebus in Adventu videlicet Dominicis diebus, die sancti Andreæ, Sancti Nicolai, Conceptionis Beatissimæ virginis, Thomæ Apostoli, Natiuitatis domini, ... '[70]

The whole college was also required to sing matins every month, which was to include prayers for the benefactor, and after his death for his soul. This was to take place on the first ferial day of the month.[71]

The prefect and the prebendaries also had their own specific duties. As the holder of the chantry of the Assumption of the Blessed Virgin Mary, the prefect was obliged to celebrate four masses every week. None of the extant sources specifies what sort of masses these were to be, although one might expect one of these to be in honour of the Virgin Mary, and another a requiem mass for the founder, Kazimierz III. The prefect was also required to celebrate a 'Rorate' mass, in honour of the Blessed Virgin Mary, on the feasts of Easter, Pentecost, and Christmas, and on the major feasts of the Virgin Mary. This last duty was probably linked with the prefecture of the college and not the chantry of the Assumption. Each prebendary was required to celebrate two masses every week. The first was a dedication mass, in honour of the Assumption of the Blessed Virgin Mary, with a collect for the benefactors of the chapel, both living and dead. The second was also for the founders, the community, and the faithful departed: 'pro fundatoribus, famula, et fidelium'.[72]

Finally, one should mention the chapel duties of the clerk. He was required to serve the prefect and prebendaries during masses and other services in the chapel, though may well have joined in with the actual singing. He was also responsible for the maintenance of the chapel apparatus and vestments.

The Rorantists and the other cathedral colleges

A comparison of the Rorantists with the other cathedral institutions, particularly the chapels of the Holy Trinity and the Holy Cross, reveals similarities of concept and form. They had a prefect, a number of prebends, and a clerk. In funding, Zygmunt followed his predecessors' example by granting the Rorantists a significant sum from the royal salt-mines, tithes from royal land, and similarly, he gave the college a communal house. Like the other colleges, the Rorantists' duties included a principal mass and other services at which the whole college had to be present, as well as masses which each member had to celebrate individually. Common to all were the prayers and petitions for the respective founders. Finally, jurisdiction over the Rorantists was reserved for the monarch. The Rorantists, however, differed in several important aspects. The most significant departure from the pattern of the other institutions was Rorantists' obligation to adorn the daily mass with polyphony. The others presumably relied on chant.[73] In connection with this, it is also important to remember that only in the Rorantists college were candidates required to be competent singers and subject to a vocal test on entry. Excluding the Psalterists, who worked according to a rota system, the Rorantists were also the largest foundation.[74]

THE RORANTISTS' COLLEGE, 1543-1548

Notification of the king's intent to establish a college was made public in April 1543. By this time, the funds were secured and the college house was being prepared. The following month, on 31 May, the king appointed Mikołaj of Poznań as the first college prefect.[75] This decision was implemented by Bishop Gamrat a month later, on 25 June.[76] Very little is biographical information is available on Mikołaj of Poznań, although we know that he was a canon of the cathedral, serving as its vice-dean.[77]

On his election, Mikołaj of Poznań set about enlisting prebendaries. However, there were immediate problems with recruiting chaplains, with only three employed in June or July and a fourth in August.[78] The *Elenchus* refers to an outbreak of the plague at the time, and it is possible that this may have hindered the prefect's task.[79] It was therefore with these four prebendaries and the clerk that the college first began its duties in the chapel on Sunday, 19 August 1543. (A table mapping out the college membership is given in Appendix III.) The king himself was not present at this occasion; he had left the capital at the beginning of August probably on account of the plague.[80] One should add here that Mikołaj of Poznań made use of two substitutes for four and five weeks respectively, at some stage between August and December 1543 (the lack of dates in the *Elenchus* makes it impossible to say exactly when they were employed, or whether they were employed together or consecutively).[81] Such use of substitutes was not mentioned in the founding act; it is nevertheless clear that they were used to enlarge the body of singers during the daily mass only and were not obliged to celebrate the weekly masses required of the prebendaries.[82] In subsequent years the use of such chapel substitutes became commonplace due to a constant lack of prebendaries.

By the time of the king's return in October of 1544, the college included eight prebendaries and the clerk. The college maintained this size for the next three years until the death of Zygmunt in April 1548, one prebendary short of the ideal size envisaged in the founding act.

THE RORANTISTS DURING THE REIGN OF ZYGMUNT II AUGUST AND THE SECOND FOUNDATION OF 1552

Zygmunt II August, the last of the Jagiellonian kings, was also the first not to have built his own chapel onto the cathedral in Kraków and thus did not establish his own college of chaplains there. Several possible explanations may be offered for this. First, he seems not to have been particularly attached to the royal residence on Wawel Hill, especially after the death of his second wife, Barbara Radziwiłł, in 1551. Secondly, he spent very little time in Kraków, preferring the residence in Vilnius, which he did rebuild quite substantially in the 1550s. Thirdly, Zygmunt August had already created a musical establishment at his court which included a chapel choir. This chapel was initially located in Vilnius, where he resided as the Grand Duke of Lithuania, and following his accession to the Polish throne it moved with the whole court to Kraków. Although Kraków served as the chapel's base, it acquired a mobile character, accompanying the king and his court on many of his journeys.[83] Zygmunt August nevertheless showed interest in the Rorantists' college. In the year following his accession to the throne, he provided some financial assistance to the college in the form of two measures of salt ('duas metretas . . . salis') quarterly from the royal mines. The document concerning this donation, Kk dyp. 1123, states that this gift would have been given by Zygmunt I Stary, had it not been for his death.[84] One should note that following his accession to the Polish throne, Zygmunt August granted many such 'gifts' to individuals at his court and the cathedral.[85]

The first two years of Zygmunt August's reign were problematic for the Rorantists' college. Even before the old king's death, there was a large turnover of prebendaries, and the college had great difficulty maintaining its numbers. In the first seven years, no fewer than sixteen were employed; only two are known to have died, whilst the rest resigned or left, possibly dismissed. Piotr of Samborz (Rorantist August 1543 - April 1545), for instance, left for the service of Queen Bona, and Franciszek of Poznań (Rorantist 25 February 1544 - 8 August 1545) was lured by Zygmunt August for his own newly established chapel. Other candidates were not employed because, according to the prefect, they were deemed unsuitable to sing in the college.[86] Consequently, between 1548 and 1549 the number of prebendaries fell from eight to just four. Furthermore, from the spring of 1548 no new prebendaries were recruited until 1552. In order to maintain a reasonable size choir, Mikołaj of Poznań had to rely on an increasing number of substitutes. Clearly the prerequisites of the founding act were impractical and suitable singers who were also priests could not be found. One might also presume that the substitutes, some of whom where employed for two or more years at a stretch, were not ordained priests.

Zygmunt August's efforts to rectify the shortage of prebendaries were taken as part of a larger programme of funding and change which took place between 1550 and 1552. During these three years a number of individual documents were produced: two by the king himself (2 January 1550 and 21 May 1551), one by Mikołaj Dzierzgowski, Archbishop of Gniezno and Primate of Poland (13 June 1550), and one final document by Andrzej Zebrzydowski, the Bishop of Kraków (10 December 1552). This last document, Kk dyp. 1172, includes a copy of all the others (see Appendix II.3).

The most significant change was the establishment of permanent ('perpetuum') prebendaries by Zygmunt August on 21 May 1551. This was taken, as the king's act states, 'in order to make the prebendaries more attractive' and 'that appropriate and accomplished singing in the chapel should be maintained in accordance with the wishes of the founder'.[87] The candidates still had a formal examination on entry and presumably were chosen by the prefect; however, the successful ones were now to be appointed to their prebend by the bishop of Kraków and not just employed by the prefect, as had hitherto been the practice. In effect, this gave them tenure for life, or as long as they wished to remain in the college; they could be dismissed only by the bishop in extreme cases of disobedience or negligence, at the college's request. The clerk was not included in this change of status, and remained an expendable employee of the college.

Further funds were also secured for the Rorantists, so that their salaries could be increased, thus encouraging appropriate candidates. Zygmunt August allocated tithes from the royal villages of Rzgów, Gatka, Chocianowice, and Lasłowice in the vicinity of Pabianice, a town not far from Piotrków. As with the other tithes granted to the college, the monetary value of these was not set, although in 1554 - the first year in which the full amount was paid - the tithes brought the college a sum of 135 marks. These new funds enabled the salaries to be improved quite substantially. In addition to the old chantry worth 43 marks, the prefect was now given a further 20 marks; the salaries of the prebendaries rose from 20 to 30 marks, and the clerk's from 16 to 20 marks. The two servants were also given one additional mark each.

In return for the new funds, the college was required to fulfil further duties over and above those set out in the original act. The college was now responsible for providing polyphony for High Mass at the main altar of the cathedral on all the major Marian feasts: Purification (2 February), Annunciation (25 March), Visitation (2 July), Assumption (15 August), Nativity (8 September), and Conception (8 December):

> *Id circo nos ex commisione et voluntate Sacræ Regiæ M^{tis} Statuimus et ordinamus ut ipse Prepositus cum omnibus Prebendariis dicte Capelle summam missam in festiuitatibus solennibus. Purificacionis Anunciacionis. Visitacionis. Assumpcionis. Natiuitatis. et Concepcionis gloriosæ virginis sanctæ Marie dominæ nostre, in ecclesia nŕa Cathedrali cantu figurato canant, et canere annis singulis tempore sempiterno teneantur.*[88]

This is the first instance at the cathedral where a college was required to participate in the liturgy of the main altar, though there do seem to be good reasons for such a move. The cathedral itself did not have its own choir capable of singing polyphony and thus relied on the resources of the king's private chapel. With the king absent from Kraków for long periods of time, a permanent arrangement for polyphonic music seems to have been sought. It is therefore possible that the king and the bishop of Kraków took advantage of the college's potential, and ensured polyphony at the main altar of the cathedral, if only on the Marian feasts.

Two further aspects affecting the chapel are included in Bishop Zebrzydowski's document of 10 December 1552. The first addresses the use of substitutes. The large number of such additional singers employed by Mikołaj of Poznań in the preceding years undoubtedly gave cause for concern, and this procedure needed to be formalized. The bishop made it clear that such singers could only be used as substitutes for prebendaries who, for a good reason, were not able to attend chapel. These singers were themselves to have the same singing abilities as required of the prebendaries on entry.[89] The implication here is that the prefect was obliged to maintain a full complement of prebendaries and not to use substitutes when their number was low. The second aspect addressed the role of the clerk, who was now allowed to sing with the prebendaries in chapel, as long as he had a suitable voice.[90]

Zygmunt August's foundation was initially successful in encouraging new prebendaries and in increasing the size of the college. Within a year of the foundation, the number of prebendaries rose from four to eight. In the summer of 1554, a ninth was appointed and for the first time in its history the chapel had a full complement of prebendaries. However, the following years (1555-6), saw significant changes in the college. In 1555 the college lost three prebendaries (two of whom died and the third resigned) and at the end of that year the prefect Mikołaj of Poznań died. The actual date of his death was probably 28 December: the cathedral calendar *Kalendarium et statuta Dominorum Vicariorum* (Kk 239) records a mass to be said in his intention.[91] This date seems all the more plausible in view of the fact that Mikołaj received a full salary for the year,[92] usually paid at the end of the year, and that a note in the cathedral records dated 3 January 1556 refers to 'the late' Mikołaj of Poznań.[93]

The election of the next prefect, Krzysztof Borek, seems to have been more the result of circumstance than a planned decision on the part of the king. Borek had been employed as a chaplain at the court of Bona Sforza since the 1540s, and from 1547 he was placed in charge of the boys at her court, presumably choristers.[94] Following the death of her husband in 1548, Bona moved with her court to Mazowsze and resided there until 1556. At the beginning of this year, she dissolved her court and on 1 February left Poland to return to her native Italy.[95] The dissolution of Bona's court, therefore, coincided with the vacancy in the Rorantists' chapel: Borek was an obvious candidate, and on 17 March 1556 (or just prior to that date) Zygmunt August appointed him the new prefect.[96] For this first year in office, Borek allowed himself a full year's salary, although he had not held the post for the full length of time.

Judging from the *Elenchus*, the fifteen years of Borek's prefecture appear to have been stable years for the college. The changes in the status of the prebendaries introduced a few years earlier by Zygmunt August seem to have had a positive effect on the college membership. During the late 1550s and early 1560s, the size of the college remained relatively stable, with rarely less than seven prebendaries at any one time. Between 1556 and 1574 only six prebendaries died or left (as opposed to twelve between 1543 and 1550). This small turnover of members also eased the previous strain of recruiting appropriate chaplains.

THE INTERREGNA AND THE INSTABILITY OF THE RORANTISTS' COLLEGE

After this period of stability, the 1570s saw a downturn in the fortunes of the Rorantists' chapel, reflecting the state of the monarchy and the country in general.

On 20 February 1572 the prefect Krzysztof Borek died.[97] A few months later (7 July 1572), King Zygmunt August also died, without having appointed a new prefect.[98] Thus for the next two years, the Rorantists found themselves without a patron and a prefect. Their membership fell from eight to seven, and no new prebendary was appointed. The accounts for these years were entered into the *Elenchus* by one of the prebendaries, Stanisław Zając, probably at a later date.[99]

On 21 February 1574 Henry Valois of France was crowned King of Poland and seven weeks later the new patron appointed Benedykt of Stryków as the next prefect of the college (9 April 1574).[100] Benedykt was an experienced chaplain who had served in Zygmunt August's household chapel for over twenty years, from 1551 until the eventual dissolution of the court in 1574. Nothing is known of Benedykt's time in the Rorantists' college, save the fact that he resigned from his post less than a year later.[101] One can only speculate as to the reason for his departure so soon after being made prefect; though it is tempting to suggest that after the musical splendour and variety of the royal chapel maintained by Zygmunt August, the specific and unchanging 'musical' duties of the Rorantists' chapel did not suit him. As for King Henry Valois, he left Poland in June 1574 to take his place on the French throne.

Until the Polish nobility declared the Polish throne vacant in May 1575, Henry was still officially the king and also the patron of the Rorantists' chapel. Indeed, the document of 23 March 1575, recording the election of the next prefect, Stanisław Zając of Pabianice, states that the latter was appointed by Henry: 'Stanislaum Zaiancz vicarium Cathedralę ecclesie Cracouien, ad prítationem Serenissimi dni Henrici Dei grá Regis Polonie'.[102] However, Henry's role in this appointment is questionable. He had, after all, left Poland several months earlier. It is therefore more likely that Zając was actually chosen by somebody else, most probably Anna Jagiellonka, and the appointment was only formally approved by Henry. As for the new prefect, the appointment of Zając was neither extraordinary nor surprising; the latter had held a prebend since 1553 and, by the time of his promotion, was one of the most senior members of the college.

ANNA JAGIELLONKA'S PATRONAGE OF THE RORANTISTS AND THE THIRD FOUNDATION OF 1584

Anna Jagiellonka was the only daughter of Zygmunt Stary and Bona not to have been given away in marriage, and she remained in Poland for the whole of her life. Following Zygmunt August's death in 1572, Anna took it upon herself to take care of the college. In a letter of 4 June 1573 to the members of the college, still without a prefect at that time, Anna committed herself to 'dealing with all major arrangements concerning the chapel on her return to the capital'.[103] This interest in her father's chapel persisted not only during the difficult interregna of the 1570s, but for the rest of her life: throughout the ten-year reign of her husband King Stefan Batory (1576-86), and for the first nine years of the reign of her nephew, Zygmunt III Vasa, right up till her death in 1596. On several occasions, she interceded on the college's behalf when tithes from the royal lands were not paid. She herself gave sums of money to the college, and donated vestments and liturgical apparatus. Anna even provided the college with two chaplains in 1577 and 1584 to improve the singing in chapel.[104]

Almost from the start of Zając's time as prefect, there seems to have been trouble with the chapel duties due to the negligence of the prebendaries. Some of the priests, contrary to the rules, were concurrently holding other benefices and stipends to supplement their income, and as a result they were not attending chapel services. In a letter of 26 February 1577, Anna ordered Zając to stop such malpractice among the priests, and stated that she would rather see such offenders dismissed.[105] In the same letter, she made it clear that she intended to make the prebends more attractive.[106] She kept her word, and the foundation of 1584 (the college's third), included a number of organizational changes as well as financial improvements.

As with the earlier foundations, several documents were issued in 1584, three by Anna herself (9 January, 27 February, and 28 June 1584), two by her husband, King Stefan Batory (11 and 21 February 1584), and a final document issued by Bishop Piotr Myszkowski on 11 July 1584, containing a copy of all the others. This last 'presentation' document was printed, although it does contain the bishop's written signature at the very end.[107] (See Kk 1190, Appendix II.4.)

Undoubtedly the most significant change regarded the election of the college prefect. Until now, it had been the privilege and duty of the monarch to appoint the prefect. However, the difficulties during the two interregna of the 1570s had revealed the inadequacies of this procedure. Anna was also aware of the fact that the Jagiellonian dynasty was at its end, and with the advent of the elected monarch in Poland, interest in the Jagiellonian chapel on the part of future monarchs could not be guaranteed. Under the new procedure, the prebendaries were to nominate a candidate from their own ranks. This was to be done by secret ballot and in the presence of a notary. They were instructed to choose the most appropriate person for the post, and not to be motivated by personal interest or favours. The candidate with the most votes would then be considered for election by the monarch. This procedure moved the burden of prefectural election from the monarch to the college itself, although the monarch's patronal rights were affirmed in the acts, and he could, if he so wished, elect his own candidate:

Antequam Præbendarii Capellæ præfatæ ad electionem novi Præpositi accedant, quilibet et eorum singulatim & seorsim expressis verbis in manibus Notarii, tactis sacri Evangelii scripturis, iuret, & iuramentum corporale præstare debebit. Quod videlicet ad electionem novi Præpositi accedet, illumque ex gremio confratrum suorum, qui sibi idoneus, & in psallendo ac musica magis peritior videbitur, non amore, favore, factione, prece, vel pretio, aut alia ipse recompensæ ... talem qui pluralitate vocum suffultus fuerit, pro electo Præposito nominabit & declarabit ... Mtas autem Regia neminem alium præter huiusmodi electum & declaratum Lociordinario ad institutendum, iuxta Privilegium super hoc per suam concessum, præsentabit.[108]

The 1584 foundation also changed the status of the two independent chantries of Sts Felix and Adauct, and St Mary of Egypt, which had coexisted in the royal chapel since 1543. Two documents issued by Stefan Batory and Anna (11 February and 28 June respectively) now incorporated these two chantries into the Rorantists' foundation. Henceforth, the chantry of Sts Felix and Adauct was to be given automatically to the prefect, and that of St Mary of Egypt to the senior prebendary. They were to receive the income from their respective chantry and were therefore also bound by its liturgical duties.[109] The actual income of the chantries as well as the appropriate duties are not discussed in the act itself, but this information can be found in another source, namely the manuscript recording Bishop Bernard Maciejowski's visitation of the cathedral in 1599.[110] The chantry of Sts Felix and Adauct brought the prefect the income from the tithes of three villages: Nigra, Łobzów, and Biskupice. The monetary value of the chantry is not mentioned in the sources. The prefect was obliged to celebrate three masses every week, one 'pro peccatis', the second for the dead, and the third for the Blessed Virgin Mary. The chantry of St Mary of Egypt brought the senior prebendary an additional 20 marks from the royal salt-mines. For this, he was instructed to say just two masses each week, the first for the founder of the chantry (Queen Elizabeth, third wife of King Władysław Jagiełło), and the second for the kings of Poland, both living and dead.

The 1584 foundation included one other organizational change. The college clerk, previously an expendable employee of the college, now was to be appointed in the same manner as the prebendaries. He was therefore given the same rights as the prebendaries, that is, tenure for life or for as long as he pleased.[111]

As for improving the financial state of the college, Anna provided the Rorantists with a substantial new source of income. She purchased some land for the college from Hieronim Konarski at a cost of 6,000 Polish florens. The land in question, the village of Szwosowice with an estate including the villages of Mękarzowice and Korytko in the Wiślica district of Sandomierz, was to bring the college an annual income of 500 florens in rent. The documents stipulate how this sum was to be spent: 50 florens was to be put into the communal chest, $7\frac{1}{2}$ florens was to be spent for wax candles, the clerk was given 10 florens, each prebendary received one-ninth of the remaining money, and the amount left over (when the college did not have its full complement of nine prebendaries) was to be deposited in the chest.

The 1584 foundation also introduced further liturgical duties both at the main altar of the cathedral and in the chapel. The college's activities at the main altar were now extended to include High Mass on Christmas, Easter, and Pentecost. As with the duties on the Marian feasts introduced by Zygmunt August three decades earlier, the Rorantists were charged with adorning these masses with polyphony. As for the chapel duties, Anna requested a daily mass to be recited for her health and 'sins' and, following her death, for her soul. This mass was to be recited by a single prebendary, presumably on a rota system. This broke away from the existing pattern of binding every prebendary to one mass per week, but ensured a daily mass including regular prayers for the queen regardless of the actual number of prebendaries.

> *Idem Prębendarii ratione & respectu eiusmodi prouentuum auctionis, pręter priora onera & ordinationes, perpetuo quolibet die in eadem Capellam alternatim unam lectam sacrificii Missæ pro salute & peccatis Serenissimæ Reginæ Annæ quoad vixerit, post mortem vero illius pro anima, obire debebunt & tenebunt.*

There is little doubt that one of the main aims of the foundation of 1584 was to make the prebends more attractive, and to remove the need for prebendaries to seek additional benefices. Anna herself makes this clear in a letter to Zając dated 21 June 1585: 'And it was for this reason that we provided the funds, so that there should be no other chaplains, except those who are content with the benefice alone.'[112] However, in this respect, Anna's foundation was not entirely successful, as some of the prebendaries continued to hold additional benefices. On several occasions, the queen asked the prefect to deal with this problem, and to ensure that the liturgy in the chapel was maintained in accordance with the foundation. From the constant reminders, it is clear that this was a recurring problem; Zając may not have had sufficient authority over the prebendaries, or else he was unwilling to deal with the offenders.

Following the death of Stefan Batory, the next king of Poland, Zygmunt Vasa of Sweden, affirmed his right of patronage and jurisdiction over the college on 19 September 1588.[113] But it was his aunt, Anna Jagiellonka, who continued to take the initiative in college matters. When in 1590 the cathedral was being re-roofed, Anna decided that the chapel should also be given a new roof.[114] She also wrote to the cathedral chapter and requested that their building be covered as soon as possible to avoid any damage to the royal chapel.[115] When, in the mid 1590s, there seem to have been some problems with the ageing prefect,[116] Anna took matters into her own hands. Towards the end of his life (from about 1594),[117] Zając had problems with his eyesight and may even have gone blind. He no longer recorded the accounts in the *Elenchus*, and his continuing management of the college was now in serious doubt. In a letter of 27 September 1595, Anna reproached the college for not having chosen a successor to Zając, given the latter's condition. She also informed the membership that she had appointed one Wojciech Chotelski to a college prebend and intended him to succeed Zając as prefect.[118] On the same day, Anna also wrote to Chotelski, informing him of her plans. It is evident from this letter that Chotelski was uneasy about the arrangements being made, and that he was looking for a position elsewhere. In the event, Anna's plan was not carried out and she died in Warsaw on 9 September 1596. It is doubtful whether Chotelski ever became a member of the college,[119] but even if he did, he would have held a prebend for less than a year, since on 8 July 1596 he was appointed a canon in Wiślica.[120] Stanisław Zając, in spite of not being able to fulfil his duties as prefect, retained his post for a further six years until his death on 18 January 1601.[121]

THE RORANTISTS' COLLEGE: CONCLUSIONS

By the end of the sixteenth century, the first chapter of the Rorantists' history had come to a close. With the death of Anna Jagiellonka in 1596, direct patronage of the royal family which founded the chapel came to an end,[122] and successive monarchs did not show as much interest in the Jagiellonian chapel and its staff. With the advent of the Vasa dynasty, the main royal residence was established in Warsaw,[123] and this further distanced the monarchy from the Rorantists. Another factor which took the college into a new era came with the death of the prefect, Stanisław Zając in 1601. From the beginning of the seventeenth century, the new procedure of presenting a candidate for appointment was to be set into motion, in effect, creating a self-perpetuating institution.

The first fifty or so years of the Rorantists' activity were characterized by changes made on the part of the patron and fluctuating fortunes of the college membership. To begin with, the original founding act of 1543 proved to be less than perfect in several organizational respects when put into practice. The most notable of these included the inadequate status of the prebendaries and the election of the prefects during the interregnum of 1572-4. The appropriate amendments were introduced, though not immediately. Judging by the account-book and the letters of Anna Jagiellonka, there was also the problem of finding suitable candidates for the college. Again, the initial prerequisites of Zygmunt, that the college should only accept ordained priests with good voices, may have proved too strict in practice. As it was, the average membership for the period was about seven prebendaries, which, in addition to the clerk, gave a choir of eight men. We know nothing on the background of the vast majority of the men who served in the chapel during the sixteenth century, the exceptions being Krzysztof Borek, Benedykt of Stryków, Tomasz Szadek, and Szymon Buczkowski, all of whom also served at the royal court.

NOTES

[1] A history of the cathedral is available in English: M. Rożek, *The Royal Cathedral on Wawel Hill* (Warsaw, 1981).

[2] Ibid., p. 44.

[3] In the case of a monarch, funds came from the royal salt-mines or taxes from land belonging to the Crown; funds for those founded by a bishop or canon were raised from tithes on church land.

[4] Royal and bishops' chantries remained under the jurisdiction of successive kings and bishops; those established by the canons were subsequently administered by the cathedral chapter.

[5] A college record book (Kc MS 3084 II), dating from the sixteenth century, contains much information about the college's foundation and duties. This manuscript includes a reference to the founding act which was dated 11 May 1381.

[6] A. Bochnak, *Inwentarz katedry wawelskiej z roku 1563* (Źródła do dziejów Wawelu, 10; Kraków, 1979), p. 294.

[7] Kc MS 3084 II, fol. 8rv: 'Domus murata in Castro Cracovien. ad Mansionariorum Cracovien. pertinens iuxta murum Castren. versi occidentem, inter domum Joannis Głowacz de Oliessnicza Palatini Sandomirien., et domum Praebendariorum de Capello Zophiae Regia sita. In qua Mansionarii habent perpetuu. domicilium et cameras et mensam comunem.'

[8] Kk Visit. 51, p. 298.

[9] Kc 3084 II, fol. 35v: 'eiusque Praebendariorum et respective Mansionariorum diversa officia eodem tempore decantantium notabilis dissonantia, confusio et impedimentum hinc et inde mutuo resultaret . . .'.

[10] Kk Visit. 52 (1670), p. 118.

[11] Kk dyp. 233 (15 July 1397).

[12] On the death of King Władysław in 1434, his tomb was not placed in a side-chapel, but here, next to St Christopher's altar.

[13] Kk Inv. 29 (1563), fol. 106r. See Bochnak, *Inwentarz*, p. 145.

[14] Kk Inv. 22, Liber retaxationum Beneficiorum . . . 1529, transcribed in Z. Leszczyńska-Skrętowa, *Księga dochodów beneficjów diecezji krakowskiej z roku 1529 (tzw. Liber Retaxationum)* (Materiały Komisji Nauk Historycznych, 13; Wrocław, 1968), p. 315.

[15] Kk Visit. 52, p. 121.

[16] Kk Visit. 52, p. 206; Kk Inv. 29 (1563), fol. 83. See Bochnak, *Inwentarz*, p. 113 (name only).

[17] Kk dyp. 320 (25 March 1431) and Kk dyp. 329 (21 March 1433).

[18] Kk dyp. 452, (15 June 1464).

[19] This can be deduced from Czart 3084 II, fol. 8rv, see n. 7.

[20] Kc MS 1059, p. 18: '1474 Transumptum Bullae Eugenii IV incorporationis Canonicatus Praepositurae SS. Trinitatis'; and Kk Visit. 52 (1670), p. 213: '8mum. Executio literarum Eugenii quarti et Nicolai quinti Pontificium super incorporatione Canonicatus et Praebendae Rzemenczyce [Rzemieńczyce, a village near Kielce] ad praeposituram eiusdem capellae. 9mum. Transumptum Bullae Eugenii super eadem incorporatione continens'.

[21] Kk dyp. 52 (1670), p. 186: 'Et primo est erectio primaeva eiusdem Cappellae est Praebendariorum per Serenissimum olim Andream Casimirum Regem Fundatorem procurata ... de anno 1477 die septima Mensis Octobris.'

[22] Kk Inv. 29, for. 89r: 'Item praefati praebendarii ad missam de Sancta Cruce singulis diebus cantandam, idque mox post finita missa in capella Sanctissimae Trinitatis inchoandam, que tandem missa sua finita, mox missam defunctorum pro famulo et famula voce submissa etiam diebus singulis decantare tenentur.' In Bochnak, *Inwentarz*, p. 122.

[23] Ibid.

[24] This can be seen in the acts and decrees of the Bishop (Kku Episc. Crac.) and the decrees and proclamations of the cathedral chapter (Kk Capit. Crac.).

[25] Kk Capit. Crac. 3, fol. 176v.

[26] Kku Episc. Crac. 20, fol. 253v.

[27] The first reference to the organist as a member of the Psalterists is dated 10 February 1526. Kk Capit. Crac. 3, fol. 15v.

[28] The fact that Zygmunt chose an Italian architect for his chapel is not surprising. As a prince, he had come into contact with Italian architects in Buda, at the court of his elder brother, King Władysław of Hungary, and throughout his life he encouraged architecture in the Italian style in Poland. Following the death of King Jan Olbracht in 1501, Zygmunt commissioned the Italian architect and sculptor Franciscus of Florence to build a sarcophagus for his elder brother. Franciscus came to Kraków in 1502, and completed the commission in the same year. At this time too, he was commissioned by Queen Elizabeth, to rebuild the east wing of the palace on Wawel Hill which had been damaged in a fire in 1499. Following Zygmunt I Stary's accession to the Polish throne, the king commissioned Franciscus to rebuild the rest of the palace in the Italian style. Work began the following year and was completed in 1517, a year after the architect's death.

[29] S. Wiliński, 'O renesansie wawelskim', in T. Jaroszewski (ed.), *Renesans* (Warsaw, 1976), p. 215.

[30] Following the completion of the chapel, Berrecci was placed in charge of other work on the chambers in the royal palace on Wawel Hill.

[31] J. Bierzanówna and J. Małecki, *Kraków w wiekach XVI-XVIII*, ed. J. Bierzanówna, J. Małecki, and J. Mitkowski, (Dzieje Krakowa, 2; Kraków, 1984), p. 115.

[32] This can be deduced from the reference in the same letter to 'Hungarian' marble, which the architect recommended as being ideal for the commission in question.

[33] Five of the windows were 'external', permitting natural light to enter. Of the other three, the centre window looked onto the south aisle of the cathedral and the other two were incorporated into the abutment with the cathedral.

[34] This can be inferred from a letter of Pope Leo X (10 February 1518) giving his permission for the building of the new chapel 'which was in progress'. Komornicki, 'Kaplica Zygmuntowska', p. 56.

[35] One of the inscriptions on the exterior of the chapel reads: 'Sigismundi I . . . sacellum hoc . . . conduit anno salutis MDXX.'

[36] A. Bochnak, 'Mecenat Zygmunta Starego w zakresie rzemiosła artystycznego', in J. Szablowski (ed.), *Studia do dziejów Wawelu* ii (Kraków, 1961), pp. 179-180.

[37] Kk Capit. Crac. 3, fol. 99rv. See B. Przybyszewski, (ed.), *Wypisy źródłowe do dziejów Wawelu 1530-1533* (Źródła do dziejów Wawelu, 11/1-4; Kraków, 1984-7), pp. 232-3. This mass was to start after the masses of the chapel of the Holy Cross and the Mansionarii of the Lady Chapel behind the main altar, and finish prior to Prime, said by the vicars of the cathedral: '. . . finitis missis capellarum S. Crucis et post maius altare Beata Virginis incipiendam et ante vicarialis Prime incepcionem finiendam, sic ut a nullo cuiuscumque officii cantu pro tunc impediretur . . .'.

[38] L. Kalinowski, 'Treści artystyczne i ideowe kaplicy Zygmuntowskiej', in J. Szablowski (ed.), *Studia do dziejów Wawelu* ii (Kraków, 1961), p. 76.

[39] Ibid.

[40] A. Gąsiorowski, 'Itineraria dwu ostanich Jagiellonów', *Studia Historyczne*, 16, (1973), no. 2, pp. 265-6.

[41] In the summer of 1537, he accompanied his armies on a campaign against Moldavia; close to Lwów, a portion of Polish nobility revolted against the Crown, criticizing the policies of the Senate and demanding their rights. The following sessions of parliament at the beginning of 1538 dealt with this matter and ended, as did so many other sessions, in a delicate compromise which pleased no one.

[42] K. Mazurkiewicz and W. Pociecha 'Sebastjan Branicki', *Polski Słownik Biograficzny*, ii (1936), pp. 409-411.

[43] Gąsiorowski, 'Itineraria', pp. 266-7.

[44] The original has not survived, but a copy is preserved in the founding act (Kk dyp. 1184, fol. 15-16), which is dated 28 August 1543.

[45] The original is to be found in Kku Episc. Crac. 20, fol. 221r, and this was also copied into Kk dyp. 1184.

[46] Kk dyp. 764.

[47] Kk dyp. 1184. Chybiński found a copy of this act in the Jagiellonian University Library, Kraków, MS 5541, and presented a transcription in his *Materyały do dziejów królewskiej kapeli rorantystów na Wawelu*, i: *1540-1624* (Kraków, 1910), pp. 43-60. He discussed the contents of the act, although not in any detail, and not all his conclusions are correct.

[48] Kk dyp. 1184, p. 13.
[49] Ibid., p. 14.
[50] Ibid., p. 5.
[51] Ibid., p. 9.
[52] Ibid., p. 12.
[53] Ibid.
[54] Ibid.
[55] Ibid.
[56] Ibid.
[57] Ibid.
[58] A transcript of the legal document pertaining to this chantry, Kk dyp. 110 (dating from 1430), can be found in Appendix II.
[59] Kk dyp. 1184, p. 5. Chybiński, *Materyały*, p. 12, mistakenly claimed that the income from the tithes alone amounted to 43 marks.
[60] Kk Inv. 56, fol. Vr.
[61] Kk Inv. 56.
[62] Kk dyp. 1184, p. 10.
[63] Ibid., p. 11.
[64] Ibid., pp. 12-3.
[65] Ibid., p. 13: 'Præpositus et Præbendarii tenebunt in eadem domo communi aliquam mulierem maturam et honestam, quæ vestes Sacras et mensæ domus mundet, ac abluat, et curam omnem ciborum pro communi mensa domus habeat.'
[66] Ibid: 'servitorem . . . præpositi et præbendarii in eadem domo ad illis serviendum habeant'.
[67] Ibid.
[68] Ibid.
[69] The morning mass sung by the vicars of the cathedral during Advent was also called a 'Rorate Mass', and previous musicologists have often confused this mass with the Rorantists' mass.
[70] Kk dyp. 1184, p. 11.
[71] Ibid.
[72] Since the act does not include the prefect here, one might assume that the latter was not obliged to recite these two masses every week.
[73] This can be concluded from the lack of reference to polyphonic music in all of the sources pertaining to the other colleges, as well as the liturgical books

which were to be found in the possession of the respective colleges in an inventory of 1563. See Bochnak, *Inwentarz*.

[74] Although the Psalterists numbered seventeen, they operated on a rota system, with a maximum of four chaplains fulfilling the foundation's duties at any one time.

[75] Kk Inv. 65, fol. IIrv: 'Sigismúdus Rex Polonie . . . sue Prepositum et rectoré p̄mú sacelli illius Venrabilé Doiṁ Nicolaú de Poznania viccariú et Vicedecanú arcie Cracovień Anno 1543 Die 31 May institutus. (See Appendix IV.1)

[76] Ibid, fol. IIIv: Institucio Prepositi Venerabilis Dóinus Nicolaus de Poznania Viccarius et Vicedecanus Ecclesie Cathedrali Craé Prep̄tus Capelle nove Fúdacionis Regie Maiét ac rector p̄mus Institutus est. Per Rṅdissīm in Chró prém et dóim Dóim Petrú de Gamrat Archip̄sulé et Ep̄m Cracouień legatú natú primatem Regni Anno dōi 1543 25 Junij.

[77] Ibid.

[78] This is evident from the payments made at the end of the year.

[79] Kk Inv. 65, fol 1r: 'Maxime hys [praebendariorum] qui tempore suspecto pestilencie suscepti sunt...'

[80] Gąsiorowski, 'Itineraria', p. 267. The king left Kraków in early August for Niepołomice, later travelling to Wielowieś, Piotrków, and Warsaw. He returned to Kraków more than a year later.

[81] Kk Inv. 56, fol. 1v.

[82] The *Elenchus* (Kk Inv. 56) often refers to these substitutes as 'singing with the choir', e.g., fol. 6v: 'Item d. Stanislao Bawol de posnania laboranti in choro nobiscum . . .'.

[83] Zygmunt II August's chapel is discussed in Chapter IV.

[84] Kk dyp.1123: 'Sal tamen in usum illorum, morte impeditus, non concessit [i.e. Zygmunt I], Volentes autem nos, quod a Maiestate illius omissum est supplere, communitate sacerdotum prædictorum, domuique illorum, duas metretas quas vulgo Czwierthnie uocant, salis minuti, ex zuppis nostris singulis anni quartalibus dandas et conferendas duximus, damusque et conferimus præsentibus litteris perpetuo et in euum.'

[85] A number of such donations are recorded in WRo 180 II.

[86] Kk Inv. 65, fol. 17r. Daniel of Górka and Maciej of Kosmirek were two such priests.

[87] Kk dyp. 1172, fol. 4r: '. . . ut cantus in eo ipso sacello ex animi sentencia sanctæ memoriæ parentis nr̄i institutus, recte et concinne perficiatur.'.

[88] Kk dyp. 1172, fol. 4v.

[89] Kk dyp. 1172, fol. 5r: '. . . sic ut per se ipsum cantare officiumque suum facere non ualeret in eo casu licebit illi, seu illis de consensu prepositi pro

tempore existentis. substitutos idoneos, et in cantu figurato doctos, et ex arte voce bona canentes. habere. et loco sui substituere.'

[90] Kk dyp. 1172, fol. 5r: '... Qui nichilominus debet esse idoneus, et sufficienter in cantu figurato peritus. sic ut cum prebendariis capellæ missas cantare ualeat.'

[91] Kk ms 239, p. 77: 'XXVIII [Decembris] Innocentum. Votive due fundatæ per h. d. Nicolaum a Posnania Vicedecanum una de S. Trinitatis cum tricesima Altera Humiliavit etiam cum tricesima, a quibus penduntur març quinque et super memoria eiusdem marca una grossi xii a cóitate nostra.'

[92] Kk Inv. 56, fol. 47rv.

[93] Kk Capit. Crac. 5, fol. 209v: '[3 January 1556]: morte et obitum Venerabilis d. Nicolai a poznania Vicedecani eiusdem ecclesia crac...'.

[94] Wagad RK 141, fol. 101v.

[95] D. Wójcik-Góralska, *Niedoceniona królowa* (Warszawa, 1987), p. 239.

[96] Kku, Offic. Crac, 100 (1556) fol. 1154v: '[17 March 1556] V. do. chrofeus Borek Sacelli Regii Novi in arci Cracc Preptus et ad eccliam Palem in Sandissow pntates apud acta pncia...'. This entry is not clear as to whether Borek was elected to both the prefect's post and the benefice in the parish of Sandiszów at this time, or whether he was already the prefect, and now given the other post. The whole record can be found in Appendix IV.2.

[97] The *Elenchus* has a note '... post mortem preposito 20 Februari...' (Kk Inv. 65, fol. 79r), which, although it does not name Borek, can refer only to him.

[98] This is evident in the document concerning the next prefect's election, which states that the previous prefect had indeed been Borek.

[99] The confirmation of the accounts by the college membership for these years dates from 1578. Kk Inv. 56, fol. 79r.

[100] Kku, Episc. Crac. 30, fol. 207r. This record is presented in Appendix IV.3.

[101] The document relating to the election of the next prefect (Kku Offic. Crac. vol. 107, p. 252) stipulates that Benedykt resigned his post: '... per liberam resignationem honorabilis Benedicti de Strikow... dicte prepositure ultimi ac immediati possessoris...'.

[102] Kku Offic. Crac. 107, p. 252. The whole document can be found in Appendix IV.4.

[103] '... aż do szczęsliwego dali Bóg przyjazdu naszego, gdzie o wszytkim postanowienie gruntowniejsze uczyniemy.' The whole letter can be found in A. Przeździecki, *Jagiellonki polskie w XVI wieku*, 5 vols. (Kraków, 1868-78), pp. 277-8.

[104] In a letter of 26 February 1577, she mentioned a singer with a beautiful voice for the discantus whom she found and was to send to the chapel: 'jakoż i

teraz zjednaliśmy jednego do dyszkantu z pięknym głosem, który W.T. potem poślemy z prezentacja'. A second letter of 14 September 1584 mentioned another singer who had been sent to the chapel, whom Anna wished to become a priest and remain a prebendary: 'Temubyś też radzi, aby tamten dobry człowiek któregoście do kaplicy przyjęli, kapłanem został i tam się z W.W. zadzierżał na co pilnie namawiajcie.' Both these letters were published by Przeździecki, *Jagiellonki polskie*, iv, pp. 288-9 and 299 respectively.

[105] Letter of 26 February 1577. See Przeździecki, *Jagiellonki polskie*, iv, p. 288.

[106] Ibid.

[107] Kk dyp. 1190.

[108] Ibid., fol. 8r.

[109] Kk dyp. 1190, fols. 5v-6r: 'quæ Prepositus & Prębendarius eiusdem Capellæ senior, nunc & pro tempore existenteń, cum suis fundis, censibus, decimis, iuxta illorum erectiones teneant, . . . & tales qui illic perpetuo resideń munia sua debita & officia ex fundatione competentia obeant'.

[110] Kk Inv. 69, pp. 7-8.

[111] Kk dyp. 1190, fol. 7v.

[112] Przeździecki, *Jagiellonki polskie*, iv, p. 300: 'A iż dla tegośmy prowentu przyczynili, żeby nie inakszy kaplani byli, jedno beneficium przestawali.'

[113] The affirmation was recorded in the act Kk dyp. 863.

[114] A. Grabowski, *Kraków i jego okolice* (Warszawa, 1981; repr. of 5th edn., Kraków, 1866), p. 367.

[115] A. Grabowski, *Starożytności historyczne; czyli, Pisma i pamiętniki do dziejów dawnej Polski* (Kraków, 1840), pp. 236-7: 'odkrywszy kościoł na zamku krakowskim, dachu nie kończycie: dlaczego się kaplica nasza królewska zamkowa od dżdżu psuje od strony kościelniej odkrytej. A tak niejedno napominamy, ali prosimy W.M. raczcie się do tego a pilnością mieć, jakoby dla odkrytego kościoła kaplica się nasza niepsowała.' ('. . . having uncovered the church in the castle in Kraków [the cathedral], you do not finish the roof. Why should the royal chapel in the castle be damaged from the rain entering from the church which is uncovered. And so we request and ask that you see to this matter urgently, so that our chapel is not damaged from the side of the uncovered church.')

[116] According to the inscription on the memorial stone on the wall just west of the entrance to Zygmunt's chapel, Zając died at the age of 80.

[117] This can be assumed from the fact that his last entry in the *Elenchus* dates from this year.

[118] Grabowski, *Starożytności historyczne*, p. 38.

[119] The *Elenchus* does not contain the accounts for the years 1595-7, so it is possible that Chotelski was actually admitted to the college in 1595 or even 1596.

[120] Kku Episc. Crac. 32, fol. 47v.

[121] Kk Inv. 67, p 44: 'Prædictus vero Rdus D. Stanislaus Zaiąc Præptus Sacelli Regii Roran, plenus dierum obdormivit in Dno die 18 January in Anno Dni 1601 hora noctis 4 cuius anima requiescat in pace.'

[122] Appropriately, Anna's sarcophagus was located, presumably on her request, in the chapel together with those of her father and brother, and not in the Lady chapel next to the monument she had erected for her late husband, Stefan Batory.

[123] Although the year 1596 is often given as the date of the transfer of the royal court to Warsaw, no such transfer took place. Warsaw had long since become an important political centre of the Polish-Lithuanian commonwealth, and it was here that the vast majority of the sessions of parliament were held after 1569. For King Zygmunt III, too, it was much more geographically suitable, being closer to his native Sweden.

II

The Rorantists' Liturgy and Plainchant Repertory

The Rorantists' college was essentially a liturgical staff responsible for the liturgy in Zygmunt I's chapel. As an extension of the cathedral, the Rorantists might be expected to have some connection with the local liturgy, as well as draw upon the pre-existing plainchant tradition. However, as a new foundation with very specific duties, it had its own unique liturgical practice. In this chapter some basic liturgical issues, hitherto neglected by musicologists will be explored. An examination of contemporary inventories can establish what liturgical books the college possessed during the sixteenth century and the extant books will be surveyed in some detail. In particular, the Rorantists' plainchant repertory will be discussed and compared with that of the cathedral.

THE CONTEMPORARY INVENTORIES AND EXTANT LITURGICAL BOOKS

There are three manuscript inventories of 1563, 1584 and 1599 which record the Rorantists' liturgical books. (A transcription of the respective parts of the inventories, together with translation and identification of the surviving books, is provided in Appendix V.) The first of these, Kk Inv. 29, is a substantial document (170 folios of text) dealing with the whole of the cathedral on Wawel Hill in 1563.[1] It encompasses a systematic description of the building, the high altar, its artefacts, vestments, and ornaments, all of the altars and side-chapels together with their respective chantries or colleges of priests, and finally their vestments and ornaments. The Rorantists' chapel is described on fols. 112r - 116v,[2] and amongst the altar apparatus are listed six liturgical books.[3] The second manuscript, Kk Visit. 64, contains an inventory of the chapel (pp. 12-15), which was made at the request of Anna Jagiellonka in 1584. The inventory is dated 26 April and is signed by the queen at the end. This is a useful inventory since it provides an ordered and detailed list of the items preserved in the chapel, including four Missals. It also includes a separate list of items which were presented to the chapel by Anna herself. These donations are entered chronologically, dating from Easter Saturday of 1546 to Christmas Eve of 1583. It is here that a fifth Missal is recorded. The date of the inventory and its layout suggests that it was a copy of an earlier manuscript which has not survived. The third manuscript, Kk Inv. 67, is devoted exclusively to the Rorantists and contains two complete inventories of 1599 and 1647. The first of these (dated 11 June 1599) was prepared by Job of Wiślica (prebendary 1577-1601), at the request of Jerzy Radziwiłł, Bishop of Kraków. The inventory, written in Polish, covers both the Rorantists' chapel and their communal house. It is a more comprehensive and detailed inventory than the previous ones: the items are more fully described and are often accompanied by a note of their donor. Judging by the order of the manuscript, as well as certain mistakes and corrections it contains,[4] this inventory may well have been a copy, at least in part, of the inventory of 1584. By this time, the college possessed seven liturgical books, which were kept in the chapel. These are entered on page 23 under the heading 'Mszały' ('Missals').

The three inventories (henceforth *1563, 1584,* and *1599*) are not only a record of the liturgical books which belonged to the Rorantists' college at these points in time (See Table II.1); they also provide some useful information on the chronology of their acquisition. It would appear that the Rorantists possessed at least three Missals during the early years of their activity, if not from the college's inception in the summer of 1543. The first two were copies of the printed Kraków Missal of Bishop Piotr Tomicki,[5] *Missale Secundum Ritum Insignis Ecclesie Cathedralis Cracoviensis Noviter Emendatum* (P. Lichtenstein, Venice, 1532).[6] One of these may have been donated to the chapel on its consecration in 1533 and used by the chaplain who held the original chantry of the Assumption in the decade prior to the foundation of the Rorantists' college.[7] The third was a manuscript Missal, which, according to *1599,* was donated by Zygmunt,[8] and so was in the college's possession by 1548 at the latest. Apart from these Missals, the college possessed a manuscript Gradual, described in *1563* as being a very distinct manuscript. Although absent in both *1584* and *1599,* this manuscript is recorded in an inventory of 1647.[9] As will be discussed later in the chapter, this Gradual was produced by the Rorantists themselves in the initial years of the college's activity.

Over the next half century, the college acquired further liturgical books. The first of these was a printed Missal, recorded in *1563* as a newly printed Missal ('novum impressum') (item 2). Its use seems to have been short-lived since it was not recorded in *1599.* The next book was a manuscript Missal donated to the college by Anna Jagiellonka just prior to Easter 1576. Judging by its description in both *1584* and *1599,* it was clearly an expensive manuscript, lavishly ornamented with miniatures within, and gilded studs without. Two further Missals are recorded only in *1599.* The first was a Roman Missal printed

Table II.1: Rorantists' liturgical books recorded in contemporary inventories.
(The item numbers, which are editorial, are given in square brackets).

1563 Inventory	1584 Inventory	1599 Inventory
A good Missal, printed in Kraków, of the late [Bishop] Tomicki . . . in the middle of which [there is] a shield of an Eagle and the Pogoń[10] . . . [1]	Tomicki's printed Missal with studs with silver studs and clamps [1]	A Tomicki Missal with ten silver studs [and] silver clamps (Zygmunt) [1]
Another Missal, newly printed [2]	Another Tomicki printed Missal [2]	A second old [Bishop] Tomicki Missal (Zygmunt) [2]
A third Missal, written on parchment [3]	A Missal written on parchment [4]	A manuscript Missal [written on] parchment (Zygmunt) [4]
Two other daily Missals [4 and 5]	A daily Missal [3]	A Kraków Missal [of Bishop] Fryderyk (Zygmunt) [3]
A good Gradual noted on parchment written with care, covered with leather, ornamented with bulging studs [6]		
	A parchment Missal beautifully decorated with miniatures and ten silver studs and two [silver] clamps [5]	An expensive parchment Missal written with miniatures, in brown velvet, with nine gilded silver studs, [and] clamps likewise gilded (Anna) [5]
		Roman Missal of 1595 printed in Venice [6]
		A second Roman Missal [7]

in Venice in 1595, and the second is described as being similar to the first. The appearance of these books at the end of the sixteenth century, almost three decades after the initial production of the Roman Missal, is easily explained. Although the Catholic Church produced the revised Roman Breviary (1568) and the Roman Missal (1570) and endorsed their use throughout the Church, it did allow places which had observed their own liturgy for more than 200 years to preserve their particular Use. This was the case in Kraków up until 1597. On 20 January of this year, Jerzy Radziwiłł, the bishop of Kraków (1591-1600), issued an edict in which he mandated the use of the Roman Breviary and the Roman Missal by the vicars of the cathedral, and presumably all of its chantry priests and colleges, including the Rorantists.[11] We can therefore confine the date of acquisition of these Roman Missals to a two-year period between 1597 and 1599.

There remain a small number of other Missals recorded in the three inventories. *1563* lists two daily Missals (items 4 and 5); *1584* refers to a daily Missal (item 3), and *1599* records a 'Fridericii' Missal (item 3). Whilst there is no conclusive evidence, these items may well be linked. The two items referred to in *1563* are the last of the Missals and are, unlike the others, grouped together. It is possible that these two Missals did not originally belong to the Rorantists' college, but to the two chantries of Sts Felix and Adauct, and St Mary of Egypt which were located in the chapel. Indeed, *1563* mentions that these two chantries were moved together with their 'duties and apparatus',[12] and so the chantry chaplains would have had their own Missals. This proposition is further substantiated by the reference in the 1599 inventory to a 'Fridericii' Missal, namely the *Missale secundum rubricam Cracoviensem* of Bishop Fryderyk Jagiellończyk,[13] which dates from 1494,[14] and thus long before the establishment of the Rorantists' college. Although it would appear that the other Missal was lost or discarded at some stage before the 1584 inventory, the Fryderyk Missal became college property after the incorporation of the two chantries into the Rorantists' foundation in the same year.

Of the liturgical books which belonged to the Rorantists' college during the sixteenth century, just two manuscripts are still extant, both preserved in the cathedral archive on Wawel Hill. The first, Kk 4, is the manuscript Missal donated by Zygmunt. The second, Kk 46, is the Rorantists' Gradual. Both of these provide an insight into the college's liturgical practice and plainchant repertory, and will presently be examined. With these manuscripts, one print should be included in the discussion of the Rorantists' liturgy, namely the *Missale Secundum Ritum Insignis Ecclesie Cathedralis Cracoviensis Noviter Emendatum* (P. Lichtenstein, Venice, 1532). We know the Rorantists had a copy of this print, referred to as the 'Tomicki' Missal in all three inventories, although neither of the two copies preserved in the cathedral archive (Kk M. 157 and Kk M. 135) appears to have belonged to the college. This Missal represents an important bridge between the Rorantists' liturgical practice and the local use of the cathedral, and will be referred to in this chapter and the next.

THE RORANTISTS' MISSAL AND ITS CALENDAR

The Rorantists' Missal, Kk 4, is a parchment manuscript covered in blue velvet material. Although all three inventories refer just to a manuscript Missal and *1599* names the donor, there is little doubt that Kk 4 is the manuscript given to the Rorantists by Zygmunt. The crucial link between the original references and the extant manuscript can be found in a college inventory of 1843 (Kk Inv. 68). Here there is an entry which describes a parchment manuscript, bound in blue

The Rorantists' Liturgy and Plainchant Repertory

velvet without any protective metal corners or studs, which was given by Zygmunt: 'Mszał pargaminowy pisany Goczkim haracterem z figurami maluwanemi przez K. Zygmunta I dany w Axamicie Niebieskim bez okucia' (see Appendix V.4, item 149). One might finally add that if the covers are original, such a plain description in the earlier inventories would have been in order.

The principal value of this Missal for this study is the liturgical calendar located at the front of the manuscript (fols. 1r-6v). (A transcription of this calendar can be found in Appendix VI.) It presents all of the fixed feasts, saints' days, vigils and octaves of more important feasts, and finally, the classification of feasts. Judging by the similarities between this calendar and the one printed in *Missale Cracoviensis*, of 1532, it appears to have been based on the local model. The vast majority of the feast-days and saints' days are reproduced exactly. There are only a relatively small number of differences, and most of these concern minor saints. The Rorantists' calendar, however, does not include some feasts of local importance: the slaying of St Stanisław (11 April), Władysław, King and Confessor (27 June), or the Virgin Mary of the Snows (5 August). One can only suggest that these changes reflect the specific nature of the liturgy observed in the chapel.

More important is the classification of feasts. The Rorantists' calendar has four classes. The first were the solemn feasts, reserved for the most important days in the liturgical year: Christmas (25 December), the Circumcision of Christ (1 January), All Saints (1 November), and all six Marian feasts: Purification (2 February), Annunciation (25 March), Visitation (2 August), Assumption (15 August), Nativity (8 September), and Conception (8 December). There were of course other solemn feasts, including Easter, Ascension, Pentecost, and Corpus Christi. However, as movable feasts, they were not included in the calendar. Next were the double feasts: Apostles, Evangelists, and the more important martyrs and saints, particularly some local saints. The largest group was that of the single feasts, which encompassed the majority of the remaining saints and martyrs. The last group were the commemoration feasts, which included minor saints, martyrs, confessors, and bishops. This classification had important implications for the celebration of the daily liturgy in the Rorantists' chapel. Firstly, it determined the content of the Mass Ordinary. On solemn feasts and Sundays, the Mass Ordinary comprised all five sections: Kyrie, Gloria, Credo, Sanctus, and Agnus Dei. On double feasts the Credo was omitted. On single feasts, commemorations, and ferial days, the Mass Ordinary was reduced to the Kyrie, Sanctus, and Agnus Dei only.[15] Secondly, it usually determined the Mass Ordinary setting used on a given day; as will be discussed presently, many of the ordinary sections are labelled by class.

THE RORANTISTS' GRADUAL

The manuscript, its notation and dating

The Rorantists' Gradual, Kk 46, comprises 120 parchment folios, with modern foliation. The initial single folio contains a title-page. The main part of the manuscript, which contains plainchant, is made up of fourteen gatherings of four bi-folios each (fols. 2-111; two folios are missing). This is followed by a printed insert of two gatherings of two bi-folios each (fols. 112-119). There is finally a single folio which is joined to the previous two gatherings. The manuscript block presently measures 41 x 30 cms; however, it is clear that the manuscript was renovated at some stage and the pages trimmed. The manuscript has wooden boards covered with two layers of leather: an older, presumably original, frontispiece mounted onto a newer layer which covers the wooden boards and spine of the Gradual.[16]

The title-page on the initial folio (1v) names Mikołaj of Poznań (prefect 1543-56) as the collector/editor of the Gradual and Walentyn of Jastrząb (prebendary 1543-7) as its scribe. It also names the foundation to which it belonged:

> *Liber iste. opera et industria Venerabilis uiri Nicolai a Posnania. Primi huius sacelli prepositi: est collectus: ac per honorabilem Valentinum Iastrzębsky eiusdem sacelli prebédarium notatus: In quo sacello: officia diuina. iuxta erectionem fundatoris Serenissimi Principis Sigismundi primi regis Polonię die dominico infra octavam Assumcionis uirginis Marie decima nona mensis Augusti Anno salutis . M . D . XL . III . inicium sumserunt . . .*

The title-page does not record the date of the Gradual's production; instead, it provides the day on which the college began its activities, 19 August 1543. In his article on this manuscript, Jerzy Pikulik understood this to be the *terminus ante quem* of the Gradual's completion and suggested that work on the manuscript was carried out between 1540 and 1543, when he believed other preparations for the chapel were being made.[17] In the light of the information presented in the founding acts, Pikulik's dating is questionable. The king made public his intention to establish a college in his chapel only in April 1543; Mikołaj of Poznań was appointed the first prefect on 31 May 1543 and only took up his post on 25 June.[18] Since it was the prefect's function to employ prebendaries, Walentyn presumably was recruited after this date and before the inception of the chapel on 19 August. The salary he received at the end of the year corresponds approximately to such a period of service. As such, it is more probable that work on selection and copying began in the summer of 1543, and that only a portion was ready for the college's first Mass in August. As for the time of the Gradual's completion, it would seem that the manuscript was ready by the summer of the following year. On 22 July 1544 Mikołaj of Poznań received a payment from the royal treasury for the sum of 17 florens for a Gradual, almost certainly the manuscript in question: 'Item d. 22 Julii Solvi Préto capellae Regiae quos exposuit in libr. graduali eiusdem capellae mo fl. 17 gr. 0'.[19]

The scribe, Walentyn of Jastrząb, was responsible for the vast majority of the manuscript. He used Gothic notation for the chant, with the neumes written on a five-line stave, with seven staves per page.[20] This format and style is characteristic of the extant pre-Tridentine manuscript Graduals of the cathedral on Wawel Hill. The actual production of the Gradual appears to have been carried out in two phases. The first constituted the initial production, possibly up till the summer of 1544, and this seems to have been followed by a period of about three years, that is, up till Walentyn's death in 1547, during which certain additions were made. In this state, the manuscript remained unchanged until the end of the century, at which time a small number of further items were introduced, no doubt in response to the Tridentine Gradual. Two scribes in particular can be identified here, Job of Wiślica (prebendary 1577-1601) and Jan Mirmicus (prebendary 1595/7-1623). Finally, a small number of entries date from the middle of the seventeenth century and even later, though these fall outside the limits of this survey.

Layout and content

The Gradual is a functional manuscript, its layout being determined by its use and content. The editor, or possibly the scribe, divided it into three sections and apportioned a suitable number of gatherings for the respective parts. The first five gatherings (fols. 2-41) were allocated to the settings of Mass Ordinary sections (Kyrie, Gloria, Sanctus, and Agnus Dei), the next seven gatherings (fols. 42-96) were used for the Mass Propers as well as settings of the Credo, and the last two gatherings (fols. 97-111) were set aside for the chants for Matins. Following the initial phase of copying, each of these three sections had some free space, particularly the second, and this space was subsequently used for additions. (A summary of the Gradual's contents is provided in Table II.2 below. A full catalogue, with editorial numbers for each item, can be found in Appendix VIII. This numbering will be adopted here.)

The Gradual contains a selection of chants for the Ordinary of the Mass: thirteen settings of the Kyrie (items 1-10, 32, 33, 35), ten settings of the Gloria (items 2-6, 9-11, 88, 91) and twenty settings of the Sanctus and Agnus Dei chants (items 12-31). Many of the Kyrie and Gloria sections are paired together, as are all of the Sanctus and Agnus Dei. With these are six settings of the Credo (items 75-7, 80, 90, 92), which were entered after the Mass Proper cycle. This reflects the layout of the other near contemporary Graduals preserved in the cathedral archive on Wawel Hill. The titles of these sections indicate their use, be it for the appropriate class of feasts (solemn, double, during octaves), individual feast-days (Easter, Pentecost) and even certain days of the week (Saturday in particular).

Table II.2: The layout and contents of the Rorantists' Gradual (Kk 46)

Folio	Initial production (WJ)	First additions (WJ)	Additions c. 1600	Later additions
1r	title-page			
2r-18v	Ordinary: Kyrie. Gloria			
19r-40r	Ordinary: Sanctus. Agnus Dei			
40r-41r		Additional Kyrie		
41rv				Gloria (c.1658)
42r-43r	Propers: Intr. and Gradual			
43r-54r	Propers: All. verses			
54rv			All. verse (JW)	
55r-57v	Propers: All. verses			
57v-61r	Tr.			
61v-83r	Sequ.			
83rv	Propers: Offer. and Com.			
84r-89v	Credo			
90v-95v		Ordinary and Proper sections		
95v-96v			All. verses (JW)	
97r-105v	Office chant: nocturns			
105v				Propers: Assumption of BVM
106v-110v		Ordinary and Proper sections		
110v-112r				Propers: Assumption of BVM
112v-119v			Mass for Dead (printed insert)	
120rv			(JW, JM c.1599)	

The Rorantists' Liturgy and Plainchant Repertory

As for the Mass Propers, the Rorantists' Gradual has only one extended mass cycle. This consists of the Introit 'Rorate Caeli' (fol. 42rv), the Gradual 'Tollite portas' (42v-43r), the Offertory 'Ave Maria' (fol. 83rv) and the Communion 'Ecce virgo concipiet' (83v). Sandwiched between the Gradual and Offertory are twenty Alleluia and verse settings,[21] three Tracts and ten Sequences. With these, one should include one further Alleluia and verse (item 79) and two Sequences (items 78 and 89), inserted after the initial phase of copying into free space elsewhere in the manuscript. Of the Alleluia and verses, the first fifteen (items 39-53) have Marian texts. They do not have identifying titles; instead, most have the note 'Aliud' or 'Item aliud'. Nevertheless a comparison with the *Missale Cracoviensis* of 1532 reveals that the majority of these texts are appropriate to the votive mass of the Blessed Virgin Mary throughout the year. The next six Alleluias (items 54-59) break away from the Marian orientation of the earlier group, and their titles indicate use during Easter and Pentecost. Three tracts follow, providing suitable replacements for the Alleluia and verse during Lent. (See Table II.3 below.) As for the Sequences, eight have titles indicative of

Table II.3: The Alleluia and verses and Tracts of the Rorantists' Gradual and the seasonal designated use of the texts as found in the *Missale Cracoviensis*, 1532

Seasonal designation *Missale Crac.* 1532	Alleluias (Tracts) of the Rorantists' Gradual
Advent - Christmas	All. Prophete sancti (39); All. Ab arce siderea (41); All. Angelus ad virginem subintrans (43, 52), All. Angelus ad virginem Christi subintrans (46, 51)
Purification - Easter	All. Ave Benedicta (40); All. O Maria rubens (42); All. Ave plena gratia (47); All. Ave virgo Maria (48)
Lent	(Tracts:) Ave Maria gratia plena (60), Gaude Maria Virgo (61), Laus Tibi Christe (62)
Easter	[Easter Saturday:] All. Haec dies (54); [Sundays after Easter:] All. Pascha nostrum (55); [Ferial days after Easter:] All. In die resurrectionis (56)
Ascension	All. Ascendit deus (57)
Pentecost	All. Veni Sancte Spiritus (58); All. Emitte Spiritum Tuum (59)
Trinity - Advent	All. Ave Benedicta (40); All. O Maria rubens (42); All. Ave plena gratia (47); All. Ave virgo Maria (48)

their use: Annunciation (items 63-5), Assumption (item 67), Christmas (item 69), Easter (items 66, 70), Pentecost (item 71). The other two (items 68, 72) were for general use, as indicated by their title 'quando placet'.

This extended cycle comprised the votive mass of the Annunciation celebrated daily in chapel as set out in the founding act of 1543. In practice, the single Introit, Gradual, Offertory, and Communion were always sung, one of the numerous Alleluia and verse was chosen according to the season of the liturgical year, an individual feast-day, or even specific day of the week. On more important feasts the Alleluia was also followed by one of the Sequences.

The last section of the Gradual was set aside for Matins (items 84-5). Chants for Matins and the other canonic hours, of course, are usually found in Antiphoners. However, since the college was obliged to recite Matins, or, as the founding act states, 'Vigils of the nine lessons', for the salvation of the founders only on the first ferial day of every month, there was no point producing a separate manuscript just for this purpose, and so the appropriate chants were copied into the Gradual. This comprises the three Nocturns of Vigils and Lauds from the Office of the Dead, and is followed by special prayers for the founder.[22]

The work of the editor Mikołaj of Poznań and the sources used for the Gradual

According to Gradual's title-page, Mikołaj of Poznań was responsible for the content of the manuscript. Indeed the actual term used, 'collectus', is indicative of his work here, since he chose the chants from the manuscript Graduals belonging to the cathedral. Whilst we do not know exactly what he had at his disposal during early 1543, the holdings of the cathedral were listed in the inventory of 1563, and it is unlikely that the corpus of manuscripts changed over this time. Amongst the liturgical books listed on fols. 79v-80v, four manuscript Graduals were recorded.[23] The first was the three-volume Olbracht Gradual, described as being an extraordinary manuscript ('Opus regale', 'praeclarum'). The other three were Graduals intended for everyday use ('quotidianum').[24] Judging by their description, these were old manuscripts and all of them were in need of repair. Of the four listed in the 1563 inventory, two are still preserved in the cathedral archive: the three-volume Olbracht Gradual (Kk 42, 43, and 44), and one of the other three 'everyday' Graduals (Kk 45).

Whilst both the extant Graduals have concordances with the Rorantists' manuscript, the similarities with the three-volume Olbracht Gradual are of particular significance and deserve closer attention. It was the largest and most substantial Gradual of the cathedral and thus the prime source for Mikołaj of Poznań. The manuscript was commissioned at the beginning of the sixteenth century by King Jan Olbracht.[25] The first volume, the Temporale (Kk 44), was produced in 1500 and a year later the second, the Sanctorale (Kk 43), was finished.

The third volume (Kk 42) contains votive masses, in particular Marian cycles, and was completed in 1506. Each volume is complete in itself, with a Kyriale preceding the proper cycles. The Kyriale sections of the three volumes are not identical, although there is a substantial amount of duplication in the three volumes.

As one might expect, it is the Marian volume (Kk 42) which is most closely related to the Rorantists' Gradual. The whole of the votive mass of the Annunciation of the former (fols. 39v-51r) was copied into the latter in two parts: the first and largest encompasses the Introit, Gradual, and all nine Alleluias and verses; the second comprises the Offertory and Communion. Between these two parts, additional Propers are inserted for practical use. This material was drawn from various places throughout the Marian volume. Several of the Alleluias and verses and Tracts were taken from the votive mass of the Blessed Virgin Mary in its different forms throughout the liturgical year and the majority of these also include their original title. The ten Sequences located within the Gradual's votive cycle, as well as the other two subsequently inserted (items 78 and 89), were all taken from the large corpus of Sequences at the end of the Marian volume. Six of these (items 63-6, 67 and 78) were copied exactly (fols. 143r-152r, 185r-188v, 182r-184r). The seventh, 'Verbum Dei Deo natum' (item 68) is a shortened version of the original (fols. 209r-213r). The other five (items 69-72, 89) have only the melody taken from the source manuscript (fol. 152r-158v, 181r-184r). Their texts are unique; Pikulik has suggested that they are of local production and possibly written by the Rorantists themselves.[26] If the information on the first page of the Gradual concerning its production is taken literally, in particular the phrase 'opera et industria', one might further suggest Mikołaj of Poznań as their author. Assuming the Marian volume was indeed the source for the Mass Proper cycle, a comparison of the fixed sections (Introit, Gradual, Offertory, and Communion) reveals the Rorantists' manuscript to be a close copy, with only occasional alterations in the chant. The first part of the Gradual 'Tollite portas' is shorter by a final melisma on the last syllable of the last word, 'glorie'. In the Offertory 'Ave Maria gratia plena', the melisma on the first syllable of the word 'dominus' is also slightly shorter than the original. Furthermore, the Marian volume has an additional verse, 'Quomodo, inquit', which was not copied.

The Mass Ordinary settings of the Rorantists' Gradual display a wider use of the Olbracht Gradual,[27] though the Marian volume still provided the largest number of suitable settings for the votive mass of the Rorantists. The first setting of the Kyrie, for instance, also appears at the beginning of the Marian volume. The Rorantists' copy is exact, and includes the trope text 'Kyrie Virginitatis'. Likewise, the Kyrie and Gloria settings for Saturday (items 5-9) were probably also copied from here (fols. 4v-11v). Further breadth of settings was gained from the Sanctorale volume, including the Kyrie 'de apostolis' (item 32), 'de martyribus' (item 33), and 'de confessoribus' (item 35). Other sections were taken regardless of their original use, and arguably these were chosen on the merit of the chant itself. Such sections rarely retained their original title. The Sanctus and Agnus Dei 'De Corpore Christi' taken from the Temporale volume (fols. 19r) became 'Aliud Feriis Quintis' in the Rorantists' Gradual. A significant number of the others were given descriptive titles by Mikołaj of Poznań, or possibly the scribe: 'pulchrum' (item 15), 'decorum' (items 22, 29), 'naydobne' ('noble', item 23), 'Roskoschne' ('beautiful', item 25). Only four settings of the Mass Ordinary contained in the Rorantists' Gradual (items 10, 11, 28, and 30) cannot be found in the Olbracht Gradual, or indeed any extant Polish source. One can only speculate whether they were copied from another source, now lost, or perhaps written specifically for use in the Rorantists' chapel.

The chants for the Nocturns of Matins located towards the end of the Rorantists' Gradual were most probably copied from another manuscript preserved in the cathedral archive, namely the Gosławski Cancionale of 1498 (Kk 58, pp. 339-57). The first verse and psalm of the first nocturn is a tone lower in the Rorantists' copy; otherwise the two are identical.

Later additions to the Gradual

Following the work of Mikołaj of Poznań and Walentyn of Jastrząb, the Rorantists' Gradual remained unaltered for fifty years. It was only after the introduction of the Roman Gradual in 1597 that further additions were entered into the Gradual. The three Alleluias and verses, inserted by Job of Wiślica into the main part of the manuscript (items 53, 81, and 82), belong to the Tridentine votive mass of the Virgin during Advent. The date of these additions can be reduced to a four-year period between the edict of 1597 and Job's death in 1601. One other important aspect of the 1597 edict had an effect on the composition of the Gradual, namely the ban on singing troped texts in the Mass Ordinary. It was probably at this time that many of the troped texts of the manuscript were scratched out or obscured by white paint.

There are a handful of subsequent additions which need to be mentioned here for completeness. The first is the response for Septuagesima 'Media vita', entered by Job of Wiślica on the verso of the last folio of the manuscript. The accompanying note indicates that it was copied in 1599 and sung as a petition for salvation from the plague: '1599 tempore pestis'. Beneath this is a hymn 'Sanguine proprio', copied most probably by Jan Mirmicus (prebendary 1595/7-1622/3). According to a note entered in one of the Rorantists' inventories, Stanisław Zając bequeathed a certain amount of gold and silver to the college,[28] for which it was obliged to sing this hymn after the elevation during mass every Friday. There is a Gloria (fol. 41rv), entered on 10 February 1658 by Maciej Miskiewicz (then the prefect of the chapel), and a whole Mass Proper cycle for the Assumption of the Blessed Virgin Mary (items 86, 87, 93-6) inserted in available spaces close to the end of the second section of the manuscript. There is, finally, the printed extract, comprising pages 210-24 of a Gradual, containing the Office for the Dead, and which was inserted after the chant for Matins, thus becoming fols. 112v-119v. It has not been possible to identify this printed excerpt, though probably comes from a post-Tridentine source and thus would have replaced the earlier written Matins for the dead.

The Gradual and its use

The presence of such a manuscript, containing as it does all plainchant for the daily votive mass throughout the liturgical year, seems somewhat of a problem, since the college was obliged to sing this mass in polyphony. One can only suggest that on occasion, polyphony was not sung, be it the whole mass or perhaps individual sections, and thus the college sang plainchant taken from this Gradual. It is worth remembering that the prefect himself was obliged to celebrate mass on Christmas, Easter, and Pentecost, feasts on which the college was exempt from celebrating their communal mass of the Annunciation.[29] This would explain the inclusion of certain non-Marian sections specifically suitable for these feasts in the manuscript. The Nocturns at the end of the manuscript need no explanation, given the Rorantists' monthly duty to sing Matins for the founder. Finally, it should be said that the Gradual was, judging by its condition and in particular the state of the bottom corners, a much-used manuscript and it remained in use well into the seventeenth century, possibly even later.

THE COLLEGE LITURGY: CONCLUSIONS

By way of conclusion, one can point to the dual aspect of the Rorantists' liturgy. The first was the continuation of the local Use in the chapel, and this can be substantiated by the presence of the printed Kraków Missals used, no doubt by the prebendaries for their weekly recited masses. The second, and by far the most significant for this study, was the unique liturgical practice which arose from the specific requirements of the whole college set out in the founding act, namely, the celebration of the daily votive mass. The plainchant repertory for this mass was taken from the local tradition and resulted in what might best be called a hybrid Mass Proper cycle, the votive mass of the Annunciation, which was peculiar to the Rorantists, and which became their hallmark. The introduction of the Tridentine Rite in 1597 did affect the college liturgy, although clearly the content of the original votive mass was preserved. As will be seen in the next chapter, these liturgical considerations also had great implications for the polyphonic repertory of the college.

NOTES

[1] A published annotated transcription of this manuscript can be found in Bochnak, *Inwentarz*. The references to the list of books come from this edition.

[2] A transcription of the section dealing with the Rorantists' chapel has already been published in Bochnak, 'Mecenat Zygmunta Starego', pp. 131-301.

[3] Ibid., pp.159 and 161.

[4] These mistakes take the form of a pair of duplicated phrases or words within a short distance of each other, the first of which is crossed out. These could have been the result of the scribe missing out a line of the original text and starting to copy the next line. When he noticed the mistake, he crossed out the offending phrase and returned to the appropriate line.

[5] Piotr Tomicki was Bishop of Kraków 1523-35.

[6] It was at Bishop Piotr Tomicki's request that in 1531 Michał Wechter of Rymanów undertook the publication of a Missal for the Kraków diocese, the Missal in question. Wechter was also given a royal privilege, giving him a monopoly to publish and sell this Missal for ten years. See J. Ptaśnik, *Cracovia impressorum*, p. 93.

[7] The chapel's consecration is discussed in detail in Chapter I.

[8] The manuscript has only 'Zygmunt' written here, although it can only be Zygmunt I Stary, since his son is referred to as 'Zygmunt August'.

[9] Kk Inv. 67, p. 65: 'Graduał pargaminowy'.

[10] The Pogoń was Lithuania's emblem; it depicted a warrior on horseback brandishing a sword.

[11] A copy of this document was inserted into the cathedral calendar of special observances, Kk 239, pp. 26-7. Excerpts of this can be found in Appendix VII.

[12] This transfer is recorded in *1563*: 'translati cum suis oneribus et apparatibus'. See Bochnak, *Inwentarz*, p. 158.

[13] Fryderyk Jagiellończyk (1468-1503), sixth son of King Kazimierz Jagiellończyk, was bishop of Kraków (1488-1503) and Cardinal and Archbishop of Gniezno (1493-1503).

[14] See Ptaśnik, *Cracovia impressorum*, p. 37, n. 1.

[15] The Gloria was, of course, also omitted from the mass during the seasons of Advent and Lent.

[16] A slightly different description of the manuscript can be found in J. Pikulik, 'Analiza źródłoznawcza MS 46 z Biblioteki Kapitulnej na Wawelu', in J. Pikulik (ed.), *Muzyka religijna w Polsce: materiały i studia*, ii (Warsaw, 1978), pp. 16-17.

[17] Pikulik, 'Analiza', pp. 15-16.

[18] See Chapter I for a full account of the chapel's establishment.

[19] Kc MS 1033, p. 56.

[20] A full description of the Gradual's notation can be found in Pikulik, 'Analiza', pp. 19-22.

[21] Two of these Alleluia and verses are incomplete due to a missing folio between fols. 47 and 48.

[22] There is a second set, which takes the form of a printed insert.

[23] Pikulik has suggested that one further Gradual dating from the middle of the 15th century, currently in the possession of the Jagiellonian University library, MS 1267, may have originally belonged to the cathedral. See J. Pikulik 'Sekwencje polskie' (Musica medii aevi, 4; Kraków, 1973), p. 15. The presence of certain Propers used specifically in the Kraków diocese, such as the cycle of the Conception of the Blessed Virgin Mary, are indicative of the manuscript's local origins, although there is no proof that it actually belonged to the cathedral.

[24] See Bochnak, *Inwentarz*, pp. 109-10: 'Inventarium librorum. Graduale de tempore amplum Bik dictum, circumferatum cum armis ternis Regni, per serenissimum Ioannem Albertum. Opus regale. Graduale de sanctis Islowka, praeclarum, cum illuminatura. Graduale paulo minus Kliescz dictum, etiam praeclara manu scriptum et illuminatum, sumptu Ioannis Albertis, regis, et opera Ioannis Iordan, zupparii, cum armis Regni. Libri solemniorum festivitatum. Graduale quotidianum feriale, non ita pridem renovatum, sed cute iam attrita et lacera, indiget reformatione. Graduale etiam commune minus, antiquius, in cute glauca, indiget clausura. Graduale intonatorium quotidiana dictum Pękacz, indiget clausa et reformatione . . .'.

[25] As with the Rorantists' manuscript, all three volumes of the Olbracht Gradual have title-pages with information on the manuscript's date and purpose.

[26] Pikulik, 'Sekwencje polskie', p. 25.

[27] Pikulik's discussion of the Mass Ordinary sections focuses primarily on a comparison with those of the modern *Liber Usualis*. See Pikulik, 'Analiza', pp. 35-42.

[28] Kk Inv. 67, pp. 43-5: '. . . A na to iest obligatia, w kaplicÿ Cantandę odprawuiącz po elewatÿ spiewać, Sanguine proprio redemisti nos Deus etc. a to ma bÿć tÿlko wpiątek spiewano perpetuis temporibus . . .'. ('. . . And for this there is the duty of singing the 'Sanguine proprio redemisti nos Deus' after the elevation in chapel. And this is to be sung only on Fridays, for all time. . .').

[29] The section in the founding act relating to those days on which the college was exempt from celebrating mass mentions Christmas and all Sundays, and as such, includes both Easter and Pentecost which invariably fall on a Sunday. See p. 26.

III

The Rorantists' Polyphonic Repertory as found in their Manuscript Partbooks and Prints

Amongst the colleges established at the cathedral on Wawel Hill, the Rorantists were unique in their use of polyphony. Initially confined to the daily votive mass of the Virgin Mary celebrated in their chapel, the college later provided music for High Mass at the main altar of the cathedral on the Marian feasts, as well as Christmas, Easter, and Pentecost. This chapter will focus on the college's polyphonic repertory from its inception up to the end of the sixteenth century. It will first examine at the contemporary inventories to determine the corpus of manuscripts and prints which belonged to the college at this time. The main part of the chapter will deal with the extant manuscripts, in chronological order. It will include basic palaeographical descriptions of each manuscript, relevant information on their production and date, a liturgical survey (hitherto neglected by musicologists), and an evaluation of the music itself. However, the aim here is not to present an analysis of every composition; this is neither possible nor desirable. Instead, a representative cross-section of compositions will be examined, together with other compositions of particular interest. The last part of the chapter will look at the printed music belonging to the college.

THE RORANTISTS' REPERTORY RECORDED IN CONTEMPORARY INVENTORIES

There are two sixteenth century inventories which contain information on the Rorantists' polyphonic repertory. The first, the cathedral inventory of 1563 (Kk Inv. 29), has just one item of interest in its description of the Rorantists' chapel: 'Cantionale quattuor vocum in papyro notatum et pulchre concinatum pro officio Beatae Virginis solemniter decantando comparatum'.[1] This choirbook is not mentioned in any subsequent inventory or list and does not exist today. The record of a manuscript containing settings of mass cycles for four voices is hardly surprising in view of the nature of the college's duties, although given the predominant use of partbooks by the Rorantists, the choirbook format of this manuscript is unusual.[2] The absence of any other manuscripts or prints in this inventory does not necessarily mean that the college's repertory was restricted to this one manuscript; as will presently be seen, not all the music books were kept in the chapel, or indeed used there. The second inventory, the college inventory of 1599 (Kk Inv. 67), prepared by Job of Wiślica (prebendary, 1577-1601) at the request of Jerzy Radziwiłł, Bishop of Kraków, is a comprehensive description of the Rorantists' chapel, their communal house, and their contents. The Rorantists maintained a library in their house, and it was here that the polyphonic music was kept at that time. The library (entered on pp. 31-7 of the inventory) contained 163 volumes in all, most of these being theological, philosophical and practical ecclesiastical books. The last seven items (on pp. 36-7) are music books.[3] (See Table III.1.)

Table III.1: Kk Inv. 67: List of musical items found in the Rorantists' library in 1599

Page	Item	Original entry	English version
36	[1]	Libri aliquot at cantú pertinen vulgo dicti partesy, nullus usui.	Several books for singing, commonly called partbooks, no longer used.
37	[2]	Cantionale in folio Officiorú Lutetiæ impressum Anno dñi 1557	Choirbook in folio for the Mass, printed in Paris in 1557
	[3]	Cancionale aliud simile huic Anno dñi 1558 impressum	Another similar choirbook to this [the former] printed in 1558
	[4]	Partes quōr vocum æqualium, Introituum	Parts [partbooks] for four equal voices, [with Mass] Propers
	[5]	Partes Quinque Vocum Officiorum	Parts [partbooks] for five voices for the Mass
	[6]	Partes Quinque Motetarum Orládi impresś Anno dñi	Five parts [partbooks] of motets by Orlando [di Lasso] printed in [nodate]
	[7]	Cancionale in folio motetarú Josqn.	Choirbook in folio [containing] motets by Josquin

The first item of the inventory encompasses an unspecified number of manuscript partbooks which by 1599 were no longer in use. It is impossible to say with any certainty what this item included, since no such manuscript partbooks survive. The second and third items are books of masses, printed in Paris ('Lutetiæ') in 1557 and 1558 respectively. Given the format and the distinctive note 'Lutetiae', the books can only be the work of the Parisian firm of Adrian Le Roy and Robert Ballard. Judging by the subsequent inventories, it would appear that these were composite volumes containing several prints, with the date of the first in each being recorded to distinguish the two. The inventory of 1647, in Kk Inv. 67 (henceforth *1647*), does not list these items separately; presumably the two volumes were included in the entry describing three large printed music books: 'Partessow 3 wielkie drukowanych in folio'.[4] The inventory of 1834 (Kk Inv. 68, henceforth *1834*) presents one item, albeit in four books, by various composers ('variorum praestantiss. author.') and in parentheses lists the names of six composers: Cadéac, Hérissant, Goudimel, Certon, Maillard, and Sermisy. In his introduction to the first volume of editions of early Polish sacred music, Surzyński presented a list of ten separate prints by Le Roy and Ballard which he found in the cathedral archive on Wawel Hill, claiming that they had formerly been the property of the Rorantists.[5] These ten prints are also included in a list of items published by Chybiński in an article of 1910, which found their way from Kraków to Dresden prior to 1905.[6] (See Table III.2.) The same author reproduced this list almost identically in his monograph on the Rorantists.[7]

Table III.2: Le Roy and Ballard prints listed in Surzyński, *Monumenta musices sacrae* (1885) and Chybiński, 'Zbiory muzyczne' (1910)

> Missæ tres Claudio de Sermisi. Regii Sacelli Magistro . . . cum quatuor vocibus, ad imitationem modulorum (1558a)
> Missæ Tres a Petro Cadeac, Ioanne Herissant, Vulfran Samin, cum quatuor vocibus condite (1558[1])
> Missæ tres Cadeac prestantissimo Musico Auctore . . . cum quatuor vocibus, ad imitationem modulorum (1558)
> Missæ tres a Claudio Goudimel prestantissimo musico auctore . . . cum quattuor vocibus, ad imitationem modulorum (1558)
> Missæ tres a Claudio de Sermisy, Ioanne Maillard, Claudio Goudimel, cum quatuor vocibus conditæ (1558[2])
> Missæ tres Petro Certon pueris simphoniacis sancti sacelli parisiensis auctore . . . cum quatuor vocibus ad imitationem modulorum (1558b)
> Missa ad imitationem moduli (M'amie vn iour) Auctore Ioanne Maillard cum quatuor vocibus (1559)
> Missa ad imitationem moduli (Panis quem ego dabo) Auctore Nicolao de Marle cum quatuor vocibus (1558)
> Missæ ad imitationem moduli (Le temps qui court) Auctore Petro Certon: cum quatuor vocibus (1558c)
> Missa pro defunctis Auctore Petro Certon: cum quatuor vocibus (1558a)

The date 1557, which appears in the first entry in the 1599 inventory is problematic, since all the prints listed above date from 1558 and 1559. It is possible that this first volume was lost, and the ten prints listed above represent the contents of second volume alone, a volume containing 207 folios. However, given that *1834* presents four books of masses by these French composers, it is also possible that the two original volumes recorded in *1599* became fragmented by the nineteenth century, and a smaller number of prints, including the unknown 1557 print (or prints), were lost. As for the reference to the year 1557, the volume could have included one or more of eight prints published by the Parisian firm in this year,[8] of which only three would have contained suitable music for the college: *Missæ Tres Iacobo Archadelt . . . cum quatuor & quinque vocibus . . . , Missa ad imitationem Missae Virginis Mariae Io. Maillard cum quinque vocibus*, and *Missa ad imitationem moduli, (Ie suis desheritee) Auctore Nicolao de Marle: cum quatuor vocibus.*[9] Whatever the case, one can argue that all ten prints listed by Surzyński belonged to the Rorantists either in one or both of the volumes. This is corroborated by manuscript copies of several of these masses found in the Rorantists' partbooks, the first of these being Certon's 'Le temps qui court' mass, copied by Job of Wiślica into Kk I.1 about 1580.[10]

The fourth item of the 1599 inventory is described as a set of partbooks for four equal voices containing Mass Propers: 'quatuor vocum aequalium introituum'. The manuscript Kk I.4 best fits this description: it indeed contains a selection of Propers, and significantly not whole mass cycles. The fifth entry names a set of five partbooks containing mass cycles.[11] It most probably identifies Kk I.1, the only manuscript produced by the college in the sixteenth century which is known to have had a five partbooks. Furthermore, the manuscript consists predominantly of mass cycles.

The next item is a printed set of partbooks with five-part motets by 'Orlando', undoubtedly Orlando di Lasso. The entry does not provide the date of the publication despite including the phrase 'impressum anno d[omi]ni'. *1834* recorded Lasso's *Primus liber modulationum quinis vocibus* (Le Roy and Ballard, Paris, 1571[c]) with a near copy of the title and there is a note stating that the set currently comprised just four partbooks (Superius, Tenor, Contratenor, Bassus), since the Altus partbook was missing. It is possible that, like the choirbook prints discussed earlier, this item was a composite volume, recorded only by its first print. Chybiński's monograph of 1910 provides a list of eight prints by Lasso, and four by the firm of Le Roy and Ballard, including the above-mentioned first book of motets for five voices.[12] (See Table III.3 below.) There is a strong possibility that these four publications refer to the Lasso item originally belonging to the Rorantists.

Table III.3 Orlando di Lasso prints listed in
Chybiński, *Materjały* (1910)

Moduli quinis vocibus (Le Roy & Ballard, Paris, 1571a)
Primus liber modulorum, quinis vocibus constantium (Le Roy & Ballard, Paris, 1571c)
Secundus liber modulorum, quinis vocibus constantium (Le Roy & Ballard, Paris, 1571e)
Tertius liber modulorum, quinis vocibus constantium (Le Roy & Ballard, Paris, 1573c)
Novem Quiritationes Divi Job. (Le Roy & Ballard, Paris, 1572f)
Selectissimae Cantiones (C. Gerlach Nuremberg, 1587e)
Altera pars selectissimae Cantiones (C. Gerlach, Nuremberg, 1587f)
Fragment (c. 1580) [no title page, though Chybinski suggested that the print was Italian]

The final item in the 1599 inventory is a choirbook containing the motets of 'Josquin'. This item is absent from the later inventories and unfortunately has not survived. There is little doubt that the composer in question is Josquin des Prez, as he was commonly referred to by just his first name in manuscripts and prints alike. Although the entry does not stipulate whether the item was a print or a manuscript, given it is not described as 'impressum' (a term found in all entries which are prints), it was probably a manuscript. Furthermore, there is no known print of this format which contains solely the motets of the composer, and only one anthology, *Liber selectarum cantionum ... sex, quinque et quatuor vocum* (Grimm & Wyrsung, Augsburg, 1520[4]), which includes his music. Given this state of affairs, one can only speculate as to the contents of this volume.

The inventory of 1599 is an important record of the repertory available to the Rorantists at the end of the sixteenth century, doubly important in the case of the Josquin choirbook and all the prints, since these items have been lost. Marked by its absence from *1599* is the earliest extant manuscript Kk I.3, though given its daily chapel use, it may not have been kept in the library with the other music. It would appear that the Rorantists possessed a modest collection comprising three sets of manuscript partbooks in current use, a manuscript choirbook and an unspecified number of unused partbooks, together with three volumes of prints. By this time, the 'Cancionale' containing the masses for the Blessed Virgin Mary recorded in the 1563 inventory was no longer in their possession and a number of partbooks had become obsolete, though still preserved. It is, of course, possible that other manuscripts produced and used may have been discarded by this time. Finally, one further manuscript, Kk I.5, should be mentioned here. Kk I.5 is a composite manuscript comprising a number of smaller manuscripts, some of which were produced by the Rorantists at the turn of the sixteenth century. The late date of production, together with the fact that the respective manuscripts were bound in the nineteenth century, might well explain its absence from the 1599 inventory.

THE MUSIC MANUSCRIPTS

There are four manuscripts produced by Rorantists in the sixteenth century which are extant: Kk I.3, Kk I.1, Kk I.4, and Kk I.5 (in part). Each one had its specific use within the changing liturgical duties of the college: the earliest set, Kk.I.3, provides music for the daily votive mass of the Annunciation of the Blessed Virgin Mary in the chapel. The next two manuscripts, Kk I.1 and Kk.I.4, were produced following the subsequent acts of 1552 and 1584 to provide the appropriate music for High Mass at the main altar of the cathedral. These three manuscripts were intended to be complete in themselves, providing all the necessary music. They did, nevertheless, contain space for further additions to be made, and a number of compositions were indeed entered, such as those copied at the end of the century to bring the manuscripts in line with the introduction of the Tridentine Rite. The last manuscript, Kk I.5, differs from the others in that it seems to be a collection of supplementary sources probably used in conjunction with the other three.

Before embarking on the survey, some procedural points need to be mentioned. When dealing with a particular set, the partbooks will be referred to by their name, be they given on the covers, or deduced from the annotations within the manuscripts themselves. Due to the problems with the numbering system adopted by the various editors in the published catalogues *(Musicalia Vetera)*, a new numbering system has been provided for each of the manuscripts, and this system will be used throughout the text here. Complete catalogues of these manuscripts can be found in Appendix IX, which also includes information on the scribes responsible for the production of the partbooks.

Kk I.3: THE EARLIEST EXTANT MANUSCRIPT BELONGING TO THE RORANTISTS

The earliest surviving manuscript produced by the Rorantists is the incomplete set Kk I.3 (*olim* Poznań, Mickiewicz University Library, MS Ch. 202).[13] Three books are extant: the Discantus, Tenor, and Bassus, and it is the Altus partbook which is lost. Although the original covers have long been lost, the names of the partbooks can be derived from annotations within the books themselves.[14] Until recently, the books were bound in brown cardboard covers dating from the nineteenth century,[15] and in this state were made available to me for detailed examination. In 1988 the partbooks were rebound. They were given new spines and modern hard-back covers, unfortunately without the appropriate conservation required for such old books; fortunately, the original manuscript block (measuring 21 cms x 16.5 cms) was not trimmed.

Looking at the composition of the manuscript, Kk I.3 has two distinguishable layers. The first and main layer of the manuscript (now Discantus, fols. 9-82 and 119-46; Tenor, fols. 8-62, 86-9 and 92-103, and Bassus, fols. 6-80 and 119-40) is made up of paper produced in Kraków (or Poznań) dating from the early 1540s.[16] The initial repertory consists of complete mass cycles (Ordinary and Proper), one complete Mass Ordinary cycle, a number of individual sections and three tracts. The second layer (now Discantus, fols. 83-118, Tenor, fols. 63-85, 90-1, and Bassus, fols. 81-118) is made of paper dating from the 1540s, and originates from Poznań, Brześć, or Vilnius.[17] This layer is most probably a near contemporary to the first. It contains music appropriate for votive masses during the seasons of Easter, Pentecost, and Christmas, and was inserted after the tracts of the first layer, thus preserving the manuscript's liturgical sequence. Following the incorporation of this second layer, Mass Ordinary and Proper sections were subsequently entered into the manuscript. At an early stage of the manuscript's history, additional folios were incorporated at the beginning and the end of each partbook (Discantus, fols.1-8, 147-65; Tenor, fols. 1-7, 105-26 and Bassus, fols. 1-5, 141-57), and, presumably, the books were bound. The initial folios were utilized for polyphonic settings of mass responses.

The original production of this manuscript was clearly a collaborative effort. On a number of occasions, more than one scribe was responsible for entering compositions into the extant partbooks. The second mass of the Annunciation, is one such example: the Tenor book was copied by Scribe II, while the Discantus and Bassus books alternated between Scribes B and II. (See Table III.4.) Many of the titles are written in Gothic letters, most probably by Walentyn of Jastrząb.[18] Such a division of work suggests that part of Kk I.3 was copied from an earlier source no longer extant, and this can be further substantiated by the fact that a number of additional 'correction' slips were inserted into the partbooks. These corrections, written by Mikołaj of Poznań, comprise a section of music several bars in length, each possibly containing a whole line of the original music omitted by the copying scribe.

Table III.4: Scribal analysis of the Second Mass of the Annunciation (item 6)

Incipit	Discantus	Tenor	Bassus
Rorate caeli	II(28v-29v)	II(21v-22r)	II(25v-26v)
Kyrie eleison	II(29v-30r)	II(22rv)	B(26v-27r)
Et in terra	B(30r-32r)	II(22v-24r)	B(27r-29r)
Tollite portas	II(32v-33r)	II(24r-25r)	II(29r-31r)
Alleluia. Prophete sancti	II(33r-34r)	II(25rv)	II(31r-32r)
Mittit ad virginem	II(34r-36r)	II(25v-26v)	II(32r-33v)
Ave Maria gratia plena	II(36r-37r)	II(27rv)	II(34r-35r)
Sanctus	B(37r-38r)	II(27v-28r)	B(35rv)
Agnus Dei	B(38rv)	II(28r)	B(36rv)
Ecce virgo concipiet	II(38v-39r)	II(28v)	II(36v-37r)

In his initial description of Kk I.3, Chybiński suggested that the manuscript dated from the middle of the century,[19] and this has been subsequently repeated by all musicologists who have referred to the manuscript.[20] A more precise dating is now possible through a scribal analysis. Given the predominance of work carried out by Scribe B, probably Walentyn of Mieścisko (prebendary, 1543-8) or Szymon Radomski (prebendary, 1543-8),[21] and the titles by Walentyn of Jastrząb (d. 1547), it would seem that the bulk of the manuscript was produced in the initial five years of the college's activity, 1543-8.

The musical notation

White mensural notation is used throughout the Discantus and Bassus partbooks, and for part of the Tenor partbook. However, a significant portion of the Tenor book (fol. 8r-31r and 34r-39v) is written in Gothic notation, not unlike that of the Rorantists' Gradual (Kk 46). Here each of the notes assumes the value of a semibreve of the white notation, though final notes sometimes need to be expanded to a breve. Not only is the presence of such notation a clear indication of the source of the music in this partbook, it is also indicative of the nature of polyphony contained in the set.

Layout and liturgical content

The original portion of the Kk I.3, produced primarily by Scribe B, has a simple and practical layout. (See Table III.5.)

Table III.5: General layout of Kk I.3

Item	Content
1	Mass responses
2-3	*(later additions)*
4-6	Mass cycles of Assumption and Annunciation (Proper and Ordinary)
7	Mass Ordinary cycle
8-15	additional Ordinary sections
16-40	additional Proper and Ordinary sections
41	Mass cycle of the Annunciation (Proper and Ordinary)
42	additional Ordinary sections
43-52	*later additions (Ordinary and Propers)*

The first item in the manuscript comprises a set of polyphonic mass responses with two alternative settings of the preface response, and the titles of the latter indicate their specific use on ferial days ('Mediocris') and feast-days ('In festo solenni'). The main part of the manuscript begins with the three mass cycles, one for the Assumption (item 4) and two for the Annunciation of the Blessed Virgin Mary (items 5 and 6). The first of these mass cycles, that of the Assumption, is exceptional since there is nothing in the original founding act to suggest that the college had to celebrate the mass with polyphony. It is unlikely that this entry postdates the 1552 foundation, which obliged the college to adorn the masses on all of the Marian feasts with polyphony; in any case, of the music for the Marian feasts (including a different setting of the Assumption Mass), can be found in another manuscript, Kk I.1. As the Rorantists' chapel was dedicated to the Assumption of the Blessed Virgin Mary, one can only assume that this polyphonic cycle was prepared for a special dedication mass, celebrated by the Rorantists in their chapel on the feast of the Assumption (15 August).

The backbone of the Rorantists' early repertory were the two polyphonic settings of the Annunciation mass. Both are complete in themselves and include the Ordinary and Proper sections. The contents of the Proper cycle correspond to the votive mass of the Blessed Virgin Mary during Advent as found in the *Missale Cracoviensis* (1532), and are similar to the cycle presented in the Rorantists' Gradual. However, the contents of the ordinary of the two settings are not identical, since only the second setting includes a Gloria. Thus the two cycles of Kk I.3 are not alternative settings; rather, the first was used for ferial days and during Advent and Lent, while the second was suitable for feast-days and Sundays.

Following the votive mass cycles come additional settings of the Mass Ordinary. The first of these is a complete cycle, including a Credo, and was intended for solemn feasts ('Solenne') (item 7). The Kyrie of the mass has two troped texts: the first of these, 'Kyrie Virginitatis' is original, and the second, 'Deo fons bonitatis', was added at a later date.[22] With this complete mass there are individual sections: three Kyrie and Gloria pairs, designated respectively 'per octavas' (item 8), 'Sabbativis' (item 9), and 'Kyrie Virginitatis' (item 10), one Credo (item 11) later provided with the unusual title 'Ungaricum',[23] and finally four pairs of Sanctus and Agnus Dei sections: the first (item 12) without title, 'Angelicum' (item 13), 'Sabbatis' (item 14), and 'de electa' (item 15). The title of this last mass is not original, but added later, possibly by Jan Mirmicus (prebendary, 1595/7-1623).[24] These additional Mass Ordinary settings, as their titles indicate, provided suitable polyphony for the votive mass on solemn feasts and their octaves, as well as for Saturday, a day associated with special devotion to the Blessed Virgin.

The next portion of the manuscript contains additional Proper sections for the votive mass, appropriate for specific feasts and seasons of the liturgical year. There are three tracts which replaced the Alleluia and verses during Lent: two settings of the 'Ave Maria' (items 16 and 18),[25] the former designated for

Saturdays ('Sabbatho'), and 'Laus Tibi' (item 17). After a setting of the Kyrie and Gloria designated for Easter ('Paschale', item 19), there follows a series of Alleluias and Sequences for Easter, Pentecost, Advent, and Christmas (items 20-33, 36-7 and 40). Several of the Propers are set twice: 'Alleluia. Angelus intulit' (items 20 and 21), 'Alleluia. In die resurrectionis' (items 23 and 24), 'Alleluia. Veni Sancte Spiritus' (items 27 and 29), as are two Sequences 'Nunctiemus nunctius iocundum' (items 32 and 33) and 'Venit caeli nunctius' (items 28 and 40). One of the Alleluia and verse settings (item 26) is provided with two verse texts for Pentecost: 'Ascendit Deus in iubilatione' and 'Emitte spiritum tuum'. Judging by the spacing of the two texts beneath the stave, it is clear that both are contemporary in spite of being written out by two scribes (one of whom was Scribe B). Towards the end of this portion, there are also additional settings of the Mass Ordinary: a third 'Kyrie Virginitatis' with Gloria (item 34), a Credo (item 35) labelled 'Furmańskie'[26] and a Sanctus and Agnus Dei 'per octavas' (item 38).

The last composition entered by Scribe B was a complete mass cycle for the Annunciation (item 41), similar in content to the first (item 5), thus intended for ferial days. Following this, only one pair of Mass Ordinary sections, Sanctus and Agnus Dei 'Quinta feriis' (item 42), was copied in Kk I.3, by Scribe A. In this state, the manuscript remained virtually unchanged for the rest of the century. The one exception is the insertion of a second text, 'Surrexit pastor bonus', to the 'Alleluia. Angelus intulit' (item 21), albeit only into the Tenor partbook.

At the turn of the century, a final group of compositions was entered into the manuscript by Jan Mirmicus. The latter's contribution includes Mass Ordinary sections (items 43-4, 51) and further Propers for the votive mass: the 'Alleluia. O Maria ancilla' (item 45) and four Sequences 'Ave salvatoris Mater' (item 46), 'Rex caeli et terra' (item 48) designated for Wednesdays ('Prosa pro feriis Quartis'), 'Mittitur archangelus' (item 49) for Tuesdays ('Prosa pro Feria Tertia'), and 'Uterus virgineus' (item 50).

From this description of the items, a general picture of the manuscript's contents emerges. The whole manuscript, with the exception of the mass cycle of the Assumption, was orientated towards the daily votive mass of the Annunciation. The basic units were the three complete mass cycles, suitable for ferial and festal days. These were complemented by a selection of additional Ordinary and Proper sections, which replaced those of the set cycles on specific occasions. There were a small number of Propers set more than once; and their presence can only be explained on musical grounds.

The musical content

Although only three of the four partbooks of Kk I.3 are extant, parts of the Kyrie 'Sabbativis' (item 9) and the Sanctus and Agnus Dei 'Sabbatis' (item 14) can be reconstructed with the help of a later copy, made by Józef Pękalski, most

The Rorantists' Polyphonic Repertory

probably during his tenure of the prefect's post between 1739 and 1761.[27] The manuscript in question, Kk I.32, consists of four bi-folios, one for each voice, and contains the above-mentioned sections, together with a totally different setting of the Gloria. The complete sections of these 'Sabbati[vi]s' or 'Saturday' mass settings provides the starting-point for our analysis of the musical style of the manuscript. (A transcription of the Sanctus 'Sabbatis' is presented in Appendix XIV.1.)

The music of these mass sections is basically in a falsobordone style: there is a long-note plainchant cantus firmus in the Tenor, and a simple harmonization provided in the other three parts. The readings of the cantus firmi are close to those of the chants of the Rorantists' Gradual, and their treatment here seems to be quite rigid: the whole of the chant is used, with few melodic or textual deviations. It is placed in the Tenor part in semibreves, though the ultimate note of a given section is usually elongated.[28] Each note of the Tenor chant is harmonized in the other three voices, which results in straightforward homophony. Imperfect mensuration is used, and the note-values of the harmonizing parts are restricted to semibreves, breves and longs. All four parts enter and cadence together, there are no rests whatsoever, nor are there any reductions or pairing of voices. The harmony is predominantly consonant, with dissonances restricted to correctly prepared and resolved suspensions. Symptomatic of this consonant harmony is the lack of smooth voice-leading, with occasional awkward melodic lines and the frequent crossing of voices, although the latter is not unusual in such close harmony. The opening of the Kyrie 'Sabbativis' (Ex. 1) is typical of this sonorous, if unrelieved texture.

Example 1. Kk I.3, item 9a. Anon., Kyrie 'Sabbativis', bb. 1-12

Example 1, continued

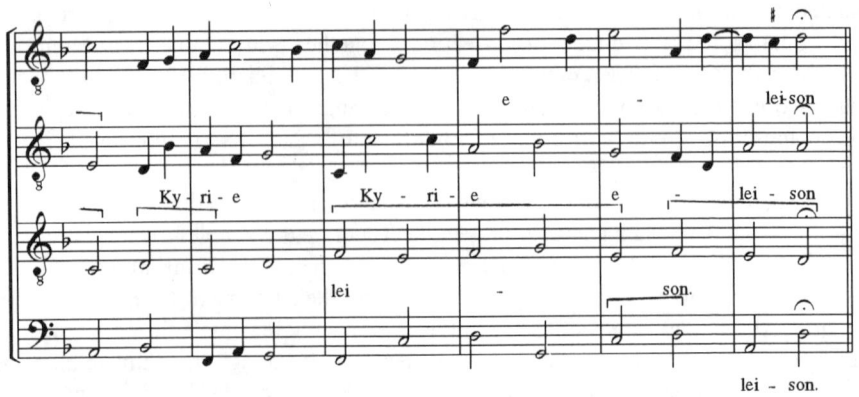

Repetition of the chant melody is variously treated. Some phrases reproduce the accompanying polyphony, such as bars 25-41 of the Sanctus 'Sabbatis', which are repeated two further times (bars 42-57 and 58-73). Elsewhere, repetitions in the chant are provided with a different setting. However, given the rigid presentation of the chant and the falsobordone style, the harmonic variations in such places are limited. An example can be found in bars 74-81 of the Sanctus 'Sabbatis' (item 14), which correspond to bars 34-41.

Judging by the three extant parts of the other compositions, the majority of Kk I.3 is in this falsobordone style: the Assumption mass (item 4), the second Annunciation mass (item 6), the complete Mass Ordinary cycle 'Solenne' (item 7), the Mass Ordinary sections (items 9-15) and most of the additional Proper sections (items 16-7, 21, 23-9, 30-1, 33, 35 and 37).

A number of compositions are more ambitious. These include the first Annunciation mass (item 5), the second 'Kyrie Virginitatis' and Gloria (item 34), the Kyrie and Gloria for Easter (item 19), and one further Kyrie setting (item 40).[29] The Tenor in these pieces is presented no less rigidly than in the simple falsobordone settings and each note is usually harmonized. Nevertheless, the other parts are more independent and florid. Voices do not always enter or cadence together and there are a few rests. Likewise, some overlapping of voices appears and consequently the text underlay is not vertically aligned. Typical too is the appearance of the unaccented passing note between two harmonized notes a third apart, often presented in a dotted-rhythm pattern. This appears in many forms, including long series in one voice, in parallel thirds or tenths between the Discantus and Bassus, or in contrary motion. The 'Caeli enarrant' of the first Annunciation mass displays many of the points mentioned above, and the extent to which it goes beyond the falsobordone style (see Ex. 2 below). Also of note here is the treatment of the intonation of the cantus firmus: the harmony is not static, rather, the setting alternates a few chords consonant with the Tenor note.

Example 2. Kk I.3, item 5a. Anon., 'Rorate Caeli', psalm 'Caeli enarrant', bb.1-18

Finally, there are some compositions which introduce an element of imitation: the third mass for the Annunciation (item 41); the tract 'Ave Maria' (item 18); the Alleluia verses 'Alleluia. Angelus Intulit' (item 20), 'Alleluia. Veni Sancte Spiritus/Ascendit Deus in iubilatione' (item 29), 'Alleluia. In die resurrectionis (item 22), 'Alleluia. Pascha nostrum' (item 36), and the Sequences 'Venit caeli nunctius' (item 40) and 'Nunctiemus nunctius' (item 33). All but the 'Alleluia. Pascha nostrum' (item 37) are second settings of texts already set in falsobordone style in the manuscript. In the majority of cases the imitation is limited to the opening of the composition or section. The initial notes of the plainchant provide the motif which is usually imitated in the other parts.[30] The imitation is straightforward, as in the opening bars of the second setting of the 'Venit caeli nunctius' (item 40) (see Ex. 3). Following the initial entry, compositions usually revert to a florid harmonization of the cantus firmus.

Example 3. Kk I.3, item 40. Anon., 'Veni caeli nunctius', bb. 1-6

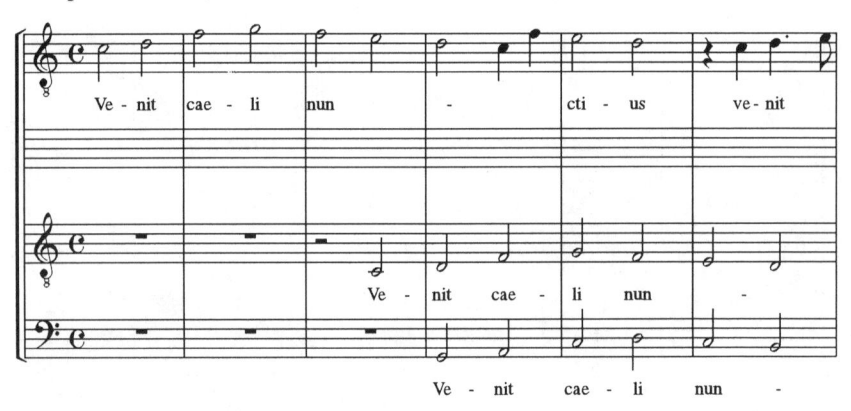

Also noticeable in these settings is the less rigid approach to the cantus firmus. Although the chant still serves as the underlying structural basis and appears in the usual long notes in the Tenor part, some modification of the cantus firmus does appear or freely composed melodic material is interpolated between sections of the chant. An example of this can be found in 'Alleluia. In die resurrectionis' (see Ex. 4). In these compositions, the emphasis has clearly moved from a straightforward harmonization of the rigid cantus firmus to a more contrapuntal composition, within which the plainchant plays an important structural role. The result is a more fluent harmonic movement, less restricted and awkward than in the previous groups of compositions. Furthermore, rests, voice reductions, and even voice pairings are used more consistently, articulating melodic phrases, and making the texture more transparent.

Example 4. Kk I.3, item 22. Anon., 'Alleluia. In die resurrectionis', bb. 26-31

Authorship and assessment

There is finally the question of authorship of the music preserved in Kk I.3. All the compositions are presented anonymously here, and not a single work can be found in any other earlier or contemporary source. Whilst there is no actual proof, circumstantial evidence suggests that the repertory was produced for, if not by, the Rorantists themselves, probably during the initial years of their activity. There does not appear to be any obvious external source from which music could have been taken. None of the other pre-existing cathedral foundations on Wawel Hill was required to sing polyphony, and the cathedral inventory of 1563 records polyphonic music only in the Rorantists' college entry. The royal court, and more specifically the royal chapel, can also be excluded as a source, since the earliest chapel capable of performing polyphony was established by Zygmunt August in 1544.[31] Not only does this post-date the Rorantists' foundation, but Zygmunt August's chapel was active in Vilnius, where it remained until 1549; thus any sharing of music between the two before this date would have been highly unlikely.[32] Also, there is no known print which pre-dates the creation of the Rorantists which contains suitable music.

For a manuscript produced in the fifth decade of the sixteenth century, the musical content of Kk I.3 is relatively archaic, and on the whole bears the hallmarks of musicians of limited technique. However, the Rorantists' specific situation should be taken into consideration when assessing the music. With no polyphonic tradition at the cathedral, the Rorantists had to produce a corpus of music within a short period of time and to the best of their abilities. Also, as a liturgical institution, the emphasis may well have been to accentuate the plainchant within the polyphony in this rigid form. The result was the corpus of falsobordone settings of the first two votive masses of the Annunciation and additional Ordinary and Proper sections contained in this set. One might point out that there seems to be little stylistic distinction between settings designated for festal and ferial days, though the former are usually longer due to the length of the cantus firmus plainchant. Next to these, the third setting of the votive mass and the second settings of certain Ordinary and Proper sections stand out stylistically: they may well have been composed slightly later, and this would explain their more ambitious character.

Kk I.1: MUSIC FOR THE HIGH ALTAR OF THE CATHEDRAL

The second set of partbooks, Kk I.1, was produced in response to Zygmunt August's foundation of 1552, and thus contains music suitable for the celebration of High Mass at the main altar of the cathedral on the main Marian feasts. This manuscript has attracted more interest from Polish musicologists than any other manuscript produced by the Rorantists during the sixteenth century, primarily due to the fact that a number of compositions are attributed to local composers, most of whom were members of the college at some stage.

Given its precarious history over the past century, it is fortunate that Kk I.1 has survived. In the early 1880s Józef Surzyński found the partbooks at the cathedral with the help of the archivist Ignacy Polkowski.[33] In 1885 Surzyński published editions of some four-voice compositions by Polish composers, and in an article of 1889 he provided a selective list of the manuscript's contents.[34] However, within two decades of its discovery, the set disappeared from the cathedral. At the beginning of this century, three of the four partbooks, the Cantus, Altus, and Bassus, appeared in Bertling's bookshop in Dresden, together with other music manuscripts and prints from the cathedral. The fourth book of the set, the Tenor, was presumed to be lost. Following a report on the three books by a Polish correspondent in 1907,[35] they were purchased by the so-called Conservationists' Association of West Galicia (Grono Konserwatorów Galicji Zachodniej), a cultural association of Poles active in the southern part of Poland which was at that time under Austrian control.[36] The books were deposited in the main city archive in Kraków (later the State Archive in Kraków), with the call numbers D. 25-27. These three books were recorded by Chybiński in his monograph of 1910, providing a more comprehensive list of the manuscript's contents than did Surzyński (though still not complete); he also suggested that it was produced between 1570 and 1580.[37] During the subsequent decades, Chybiński published a number of articles which dealt with individual Polish composers whose music was to be found in this set.[38] From these articles alone it was evident that the fourth partbook of the set (Tenor) was not lost, and that Chybiński had access to it. We now know that it belonged to Aleksander

Czołowski. Following Czołowski's death in 1944, this fourth book was acquired by Chybiński and incorporated into the collection of manuscripts from Wawel on loan to the Music Department of Lwów University, which was, during the war years, in his care. At the end of the war, Poland's boundaries were substantially altered, the eastern territories being taken by the Soviet Union, and Lwów was no longer in Poland. Chybiński moved with his library of manuscripts to Poznań, where he became Professor of Music at the University, and on his death in 1952, all of the 'Wawel' manuscripts, including the Tenor book in question, were transferred to the University's main library.[39] During the 1960s these manuscripts were catalogued, and this Tenor partbook was given the call number Ch. 192.[40] The last episode of the manuscript's history ended in 1982, when all four partbooks were returned to the cathedral on Wawel Hill, deposited in the cathedral archive, and given the present call-number.

The question of completeness

Before turning to the partbooks themselves, the question of the set's completeness should be addressed. The 1599 inventory records a set of five partbooks ('Partes Quinque Vocum Officiorum'), which identifies Kk I.1. All the literature refers to the set as being incomplete, lacking a fifth partbook. Indeed the manuscript itself includes some titles indicating five-part scoring, and since the additional part was not included in any of the extant books, a fifth partbook must have been produced, which is now lost. However, it will become apparent that it is the 'Quintus' partbook which is missing, and that the five-part compositions are few in number. Thus whilst the set is technically incomplete, the vast majority of the music is for four voices and therefore complete. As for the five part compositions, some can be reconstructed through later copies.

Description of the manuscript, its layout and content

The four partbooks are bound in brown leather covers and each measures approximately 16 x 20 cms. Immediately noticeable are the two contrasting layers of the covers: the older front-pieces, with embossed borders, the royal crest in the centre, and the name of the voice part above the crest (Cantus, Altus, Tenor, and Bassus), and the newer spines, made from a lighter brown leather. This difference in the layers of the covers suggests that the manuscript was rebound at some stage, and this may have been done to extend the size of the manuscript. Indeed the manuscript itself has distinguishable layers; both the watermarks and the sequence of scribal hands point to the production of an original manuscript, and a secondary manuscript, which was incorporated at a later stage (see Table III.6 below).

Table III.6: Layers and contents of Kk I.1
(dates of entry are provided in brackets)

Item	First layer - original manuscript	Second incorporated layer
1	Responses (later additions)	
2-6	Mass Ordinaries (1552-5)	
7	Mass: Josquin des Prez/Borek (c. 1556-72)	
8-10	Mass Propers (early 17th c. additions)	
11		Credo
12-13		Mass Ordinaries: Borek (c. 1573)
14		Mass Ordinary: Certon (c. 1577-80)
15-16		Mass Propers (17th-c. additions)
17-28	Mass Proper cycles: Visitation, Assumption, Nativity of BVM (c. 1552-5)	
29	Mass Proper (early 17th-c. additions)	
30-41	Mass Proper cycles: Conception and Purification (c. 1552-5)	
42	Responses (?later addition)	
43-7	Mass Propers (including cycle of dedication of church) (c. 1573)	
48	Mass Ordinary: Szadek (c. 1578)	
49		Mass Ordinary: Szadek (c. 1580)
50-4		Mass Propers of Tridentine Rite (c. 1597-1601)
55-6		Mass Ordinaries
58		Mass responses (17th-c. additions)
59		Mass Proper (17th-c. addition)
60-1		Mass responses (17th-c. additions)

The first layer, which now forms approximately the first and third quarters of each partbook, constituted the original manuscript. It was made from two paper types: the first dates from about 1549 and originates from Poznań, the second dates from 1547-56 and was produced in Kraków.[41] Characteristic of this paper is its printed staves,[42] with four staves on each page. This original manuscript was organized into two sections, the first containing settings of the Mass Ordinary (items 2-6), the second containing Marian Mass Propers (items 17-28, 30-41).[43] In both sections, a whole series of compositions was copied by just one scribe, namely Scribe E. This scribe was responsible for entries into the *Elenchus* between the years 1551 and 1554,[44] and the probable candidates are Andrzej Żmygród (prebendary, 1544-55) and Sebastian of Książe (prebendary, 1548-65).[45] Of these two, Żmygród seems the more likely candidate, in view of the fact that the entries in the account-book stop just before his death. Given its liturgical use, and the above information regarding its scribe, the manuscript can be dated between 1552 and 1555, two decades earlier than previously thought. Following Żmygród's work, only one addition was made to the original manuscript, namely the 'Mater Matris' Mass Ordinary cycle (item 7), copied by Krzysztof Borek into the first section immediately after the Mass Ordinary settings. The time of this entry can be confined to his membership of the college from 1556 to 1573.

The second layer of Kk I.1 now makes up approximately the second and fourth quarters of each partbook. There is little doubt that it was not part of the original manuscript, although it was incorporated by 1580. The layer was made from two types of paper. The first, which constitutes only the first gathering, was made from paper produced between 1546-63 originating most probably from Kraków.[46] The staves on this paper were drawn by hand, and this feature distinguishes it from the printed paper of the first layer. The rest of this layer (over fifty folios in each part),[47] was made with paper originating from the mills belonging to the Kraków Cathedral Chapter, and dates from about 1550-64.[48] The paper has printed staves, with four staves per page, however it has the unusual number of six lines per stave. This second layer was not attached to the end of the original manuscript, but divided into two near equal halves and inserted in two blocks. The first was inserted after the Mass Ordinaries of the original manuscript, presumably on account of it already containing a setting of a Credo (item 11).[49] The second part, undoubtedly still completely blank at this time, was appended to the end of the original manuscript, after the Mass Proper sections.

This second layer was used for further compositions, principally settings of the Mass Ordinary. These include two masses by Krzysztof Borek (items 12 and 13). It has not been possible to identify the scribes of either, although as Perz and Zwolińska have pointed out, neither was copied by the composer himself.[50] The second mass does have a date, 1573, which appears at the end of the composition in the Cantus, Altus, and Bassus partbooks. Since Borek died in February 1573, it is unlikely that this represents the date of composition, but is probably the date of entry. The scribe of this second mass was also responsible for a Mass Proper cycle, that of the dedication of a church or chapel (items 43-6), which he entered after the original Marian Mass Proper cycles of the manuscript. The presence of such a cycle is liturgically out of character with the rest of the manuscript, and it is not possible to say for what occasion it was intended.

The next stage in the manuscript's production was the work of Job of Wiślica. From one of the college's two choirbook volumes of Le Roy and Ballard prints, he copied Pierre Certon's mass 'Le temps qui court' (item 14),[51] immediately after the two Borek masses.[52] Assuming that the two layers had by now been amalgamated, there were only six to eight folios in the partbooks between the end of the Certon mass (item 14) and the first Mass Proper section of the original manuscript (item 17). Job did not have sufficient space for the next composition and turned to the first free pages after the Mass Proper cycles, thus breaking the ordered layout of the manuscript. Here he entered two masses by Tomasz Szadek (items 48 and 49),[53] one in the first layer and the other in the second layer. The dates which appear with the composer's name in the titles, 1578 and 1580 respectively, most probably refer to the dates of their composition and not their entry into the manuscript.

The next part of the manuscript, containing several Mass Propers (items 50-4), were entered by Job of Wiślica and Jan Mirmicus, on account of the introduction of the Roman Missal and Gradual in 1597. Presumably, these Propers were entered soon after 1597, and certainly before 1601, in which year Job died. Two further items, both Mass Ordinary settings, were subsequently copied by Mirmicus. The first mass is a Sunday mass ('Dominicale'), and contains all five movements; the second is designated for 'Feria tertia' (Tuesday), and as such includes just the Kyrie, Sanctus and Agnus Dei.

The later compositions entered into the manuscript should at least be mentioned here, if only because some of them were inserted into free space throughout the manuscript and need to be differentiated from the original part of the manuscript.[54] Only two items correspond to the original liturgical character of the manuscript: the Offertory 'Assumpta est Maria' (item 15, Tenor only) and the Communion 'Optimam partem' (item 16), providing alternative settings of the Propers for the feast of the Assumption. The others are most probably occasional compositions. Three five-voice Propers were inserted by Mirmicus amongst the original Mass Ordinary cycles: 'Rorate caeli' by Marcin Paligon (item 8), the Antiphon for the feast of St Adalbert (St Wojciech in Polish) 'Per merita Sancti Adalberti' by Walentyn Gawara (item 9), and 'Quoniam rex noster' (item 10); and the fourth, 'Sanguine proprio' (item 29), also for five voices, amongst the Mass Proper cycles. These four items can be reconstructed through a later complete copy, namely, Kk I.360. Towards the end of the manuscript, one further Proper was added, 'Vos qui secuti' (item 59), the Communion for the feast of St Matthew.

Finally, entered throughout the manuscript are mass responses, ranging from two to five parts. There is a three-part 'Deo gratias' inserted at the beginning of the manuscript (item 1), a second setting for two voices following the Mass Proper cycles (item 42), and three sets of responses for the preface at the very end of the manuscript, two for four and one for five voices (items 58, 60-1).

The musical content of the original manuscript of 1552-55

The musical content of the original manuscript conveniently falls into the two liturgical groups defined above: the Mass Ordinary settings and the Propers. The first portion of Kk I.1 contains five Mass Ordinary settings. They are all anonymously presented, although some do have titles. The fifth mass has already been identified by Głuszcz-Zwolińska, namely Morales' 'Missa Ave Maria'.[55] From an examination of the prints which contains this mass, it has been possible to identify the other four, since they all come from one publication, *Missæ cum quatuor vocibus paribus decantandae, Moralis Hispani, ac aliorum Authoribus*... (Scotto, Venice, 1542³).[56] This print does not appear in any of the Rorantist inventories; however, a book of masses by Morales is known to have been in the possession of the Zygmunt August's household chapel.[57] It is therefore most probable that the print was made available to the Rorantists by the latter during its residence in Kraków during the early 1550s.

The choice of masses taken from the print was determined by practical considerations: all of those copied were for low voices and thus suitable for the college; the 'Vulnerasti cor meum' mass by Morales was excluded due to the treble range of the Cantus part. The altered order of the masses in Kk I.1 is difficult to account for; perhaps the Rorantists intended this order of masses to be sung on the successive Marian feasts in the liturgical year (see Table III.7).

Table III.7: Copies of masses from *Missae cum quatuor vocibus paribus... (Scotto, Venice, 1542)* found in Kk I.1 (with item number)

Print: in order of appearance	Kk I.1: title (and item number)
C. Morales: Ave Maria	Ave Maria gratia (6)
C. Morales: Vulnerasti cor meum	[not copied] -
Anon: [no title]	[no title] (3)
Jachet of Mantua: Quam pulchra es	Quam pulchra es (4)
Anon: Gaude Virgo Mater Christi	Gaude Virgo mater christi (5)
V. Ruffo: Alma Redemptoris Mater	Alma redemptoris mater (2)

Looking at the masses copied into Kk I.1, it would seem that the scribe reproduced the music accurately.[58] The text is similarly copied, even the incorrect alignment of the textual underlay is reproduced. However, some significant changes were introduced into Kk I.1. First of all, there is the presentation of the final Agnus Dei sections of the masses by Ruffo, Jachet, and Morales, which are all for six voices. In the Ruffo mass, the print contains the Altus Secundus in the Tenor partbook, and the Tenor Secundus in the Altus partbook. Kk I.1 has all six, but the two Altus and two Tenor parts are together in their respective partbooks on facing pages. In Jachet's mass, the additional voices, found in the Tenor and Bassus partbooks, are reproduced in Kk I.1 with no change. The Morales mass is more problematic. The fifth voice is in canon with the Tenor and as such is not written out but indicated through entry signs given in the Tenor partbook, and the sixth voice is also printed in the same partbook. In Kk I.1, the Tenor voice with the appropriate sign is presented in the Altus partbook, however, there is no sixth part copied here, in spite of the note 'sexta pars', nor indeed is it present in any of the other partbooks. One therefore has to conclude that the sixth part was copied into the lost fifth manuscript partbook.

More substantial changes were made to the anonymous 'Gaude Virgo Mater Dei' Mass, namely the addition of newly composed parts in three sections originally for a reduced scoring. The 'Crucifixus' of the Credo, a duo for Cantus and Altus, is supplemented by a new Bassus part, whilst the ensuing 'Et resurrexit', originally scored for Tenor and Bassus, has an additional Cantus and Altus part. These additions were entered at the end of the mass, with a note 'Vide in fine post Agnus' inserted in the appropriate place.[59] (A transcription of the two versions is presented in Appendix XIV.2.)

The second part of the first layer contains a number of Marian Propers. Although they were not given titles or rubrics, indeed, with such a small number such annotations were not necessary,[60] a comparison with the *Missale Cracoviensis* of 1532, identifies them as the vast majority - if not all - of the Propers for the Marian feasts of the Visitation, Assumption, Nativity, Conception, and Purification. (See Table III.8.)

Table III.8: Layout of Mass Propers in Kk I.1 and their liturgical use

Kk I.1		Designation in *Missale Cracoviensis, 1532*				
Item	Text incipit	Visitation	Assumption	Nativity	Conception	Purification
17	Gaudeamus omnes	Intr.	Intr.	Intr.		
18	Audi filia	Grad.		Grad.		
19	All. Ave stillans melle	All.				
20	Ave verbi Dei parens	Sequ.				
21	Diffusa est gratia	Com.		Com.		
22	Propter veritatem		Grad.			
23	All. Assumpta est		All.			
24	Congaudent angelorum		Sequ.			
25	Dilexisti iusticiam		Com.			
26	Diffusa est gratia		Offer.			Offer.
27	All. Nativitatis gloriosae			All.		
28	Stirpe Maria			Sequ.		
30	Egredimini et videte				Intr.	
31	Qualis est dilecta				Grad.	
32	All. Veni regina nostra				All.	
33	Festum Maria celebramus				Sequ.	
34	Gloriosa dicta				Com.	
35	Hortus conclusus				Offer.	
36	Suscepimus Deus					Intr.
37	Suscepimus Deus					Grad.
38	All. Post partum virgo					All.
39	Laetabundus exultet					Sequ.
40	Audi filia					Tr.
41	Responsum accepit					Com.

The layout of this section is clear. The first cycle, that of the Visitation, was entered complete, with individual Propers of the subsequent cycles of the Assumption and Nativity added as necessary. In this way, Propers common to more than one cycle, such as the Introit 'Gaudeamus omnes', are entered only once. The cycles of the Conception and Purification were also entered complete since they are altogether different. Missing from the collection are the Offertories for the Visitation and the Nativity, which, according to the *Missale Cracoviensis*, are 'Ave Maria' and 'Beata es virgo' respectively. Assuming that the manuscript was complete in itself, one can conclude that one of the other Offertories was designated for both these cycles, most probably the 'Diffusa est gratia' (item 26).[61] Noticeable by their absence are the Propers for the feast of the Annunciation (25 March). Since the 1552 foundation required the college to adorn all of the Marian feasts, including that of the Annunciation, one can only assume that the Rorantists used one of the votive cycles of the Annunciation - together with one of the Tracts or Alleluias - found in Kk I.3.

There are certain structural and stylistic parallels between the Mass Propers of this manuscript and the majority of Kk I.3. First and foremost, they have a long-note plainchant cantus firmus placed invariably in the Tenor part. As with the Annunciation Mass cycle of Kk I.3, the plainchant of the feasts of the Purification, Visitation, Assumption, and Nativity were most probably taken from the three-volume Olbracht Gradual. The fifth cycle, that of the Conception, is exceptional. The Rorantists adopted a special cycle of Propers for this feast, which was observed at the cathedral on Wawel Hill in Kraków.[62] Surprisingly, this plainchant cycle does not appear in the Olbracht Gradual, nor in any manuscript preserved on Wawel Hill. It can, however, be found in a manuscript Gradual now in the possession of the Jagiellonian University Library (MS 1267),[63] which according to Pikulik,[64] may well have been produced and used at the cathedral. Although a direct link between this Gradual and the Tenor partbook of Kk I.1 cannot be established conclusively, there is a strong similarity between the readings of the two manuscripts, and thus one can confirm the local character of the Rorantists' setting.

The treatment of the chant in all the Propers is consistently rigid, much in the same way as the majority of compositions in Kk I.3. The whole of the plainchant is reproduced, both melody and text. The melody is invariably presented in semibreves, often in two-note ligatures,[65] with the exception of the last note of a composition or section, usually augmented to a long, which in practice is held until the other voices cadence. The other three parts, generally provide what might best be called non-imitative counterpoint, in similar or faster note-values than the Tenor. Indeed, the most distinctive feature of these pieces is the florid writing which permeates the texture of the majority of the compositions. Whilst the compositions or sections usually begin and end together, within sections the parts are not vertically aligned but overlap, maintaining the flow of the composition until the final cadence. As a result, the textual underlay is rarely aligned. Also characteristic are the rests which separate the subsequent melodic phrases of individual voices.

The harmony is predominantly consonant in these compositions: the harmonic pace is determined by the Tenor cantus firmus, although where the other three parts are more florid, harmonic changes occasionally occur over individual tenor notes. There appears to be distinct emphasis on full triads, often at the expense of the melodic line. Interest is introduced through numerous suspensions, passing notes, both unaccented and accented, and scalar passages. On the whole, suspensions are conventionally prepared and resolved; these usually appear in the upper two voices, especially the Altus part, less often in the Bassus part. Unaccented passing notes are common, often appearing in a dotted minim - crotchet pattern or in series of crotchet runs. At the beginning of 'Egredimini et videte' (Ex. 5), such movement is in juxtaposition to slower-moving falsobordone style writing.

Example 5. Kk I.1, item 30. Anon., 'Egredimini et videte', bb. 1-6

Only two of the compositions introduce an element of imitation, the Offertory 'Diffusa est gratia' (item 26) and the Sequence 'Laetabundus exultet' (item 39). The points of imitation are based upon the cantus firmus, but the imitation does not pervade the whole of the composition. Instead, the long-note Tenor is surrounded by short points of imitation in the other three parts. Such imitation appears only at the opening of 'Laetabundus exultet' (Ex. 6) and sporadically throughout 'Diffusa est gratia'. ('Diffusa est gratia' is presented complete in Appendix XIV.3.)

Example 6. Kk I.1, item 39. Anon,. 'Laetabundus exultet', bb. 1-5

In assessing the style and standard of the Mass Propers, the nature of these compositions should be considered. Like the contents of Kk I.3, these Propers are most probably of local production, composed for, if not by, the Rorantists themselves.[66] The presence of the specific cycle of the Conception, peculiar to the cathedral in Kraków, confirms this argument. The compositional procedure of using the pre-existing plainchant and setting it to polyphony is likewise similar to the earlier manuscript. The polyphony here is not without its awkward melodic lines, incorrect passing notes and consecutive perfect intervals; nevertheless, the general standard is more accomplished than that of Kk I.3.

The work of Krzysztof Borek

Krzysztof Borek, formerly the Master of the Boys at the court of Queen Bona and Rorantist prefect from 1556 to 1572, made a small but important contribution to the Rorantists' repertory, all contained in this manuscript: he copied a Mass Ordinary setting and was the composer of two further masses. Borek's first contribution to Kk I.1 was a copy of an adaptation of the 'Missa Mater Patris', attributed to Josquin des Prez.[67] The manuscript does not record the composer's name, and has a slightly modified title, 'Missa Mater Matris',[68] though it was identified by Głuszcz-Zwolińska in her thematic catalogue. In a subsequent article, she presented some basic information about the original mass and its authorship, and discussed the mass adaptation of Kk I.1, looking in particular at the Kyrie section.[69] Whilst it is not known how Borek came across the Josquin mass and in which version, it is likely that the original mass was available in print form, most probably in his third book of masses, first printed by Petrucci in 1514, and that Borek himself was responsible for the adaptation. The adapted mass uses practically the whole of the original four-part mass, with only a few minor omissions. The 'Pleni sunt caeli' and 'Benedictus' sections of the Sanctus have been removed, and the respective texts inserted into the remaining sections of the Sanctus. Also, the second Agnus Dei for two voices and the third for five have both been omitted.[70]

As for the nature of the adaptation, there are three distinct, though interrelated, features: the newly composed material, changes to the text underlay, and the re-assigning of the parts to the four voices. The original mass contains much voice reduction, this being characteristic of Josquin's music. In these places, the Rorantists' version often has a third and even a fourth part. A large portion of these new voices are simple melodic lines providing non-imitative counterpoint, consonant with the existing parts. Other lines produce a sequence of parallel imperfect intervals with a pre-existing line, usually thirds, sixths, or tenths. It has to be said that these lines are very much in keeping with the character of the original composition (Kyrie, bars 7-12, 70-5, Credo, bars 156-61, for instance). The addition of these lines had serious implications on the text underlay, thus the second aspect of the adaptation was the re-setting of these texts, at times introducing phrase repetitions. The latter in turn resulted in a more syllabic setting. The third feature was the re-assigning of the parts by pitch range to the Cantus, Altus, Tenor, and Bassus partbooks in descending order. Indeed this work was carried out primarily, though not exclusively, as a result of the newly interpolated lines to avoid unnecessary crossing of parts. Example 7a and b provide an illustration of these three aspects of the adaptor's work.

Example 7a. Josquin des Prez, 'Missa Mater Patris', Gloria, bb. 31-42.

The Rorantists' Polyphonic Repertory

Example 7a, continued

Example 7b. Kk I.1, item 7b. 'Missa Mater Matris', Gloria, bb. 31-42

Some of the newly composed lines of the adaptation play a part in the actual imitation. Given Josquin's predilection for transparent textures and reduced scoring, the mass provided ample opportunities for such additional voice entries. The final section of the Gloria 'Cum sancto spiritu', is one such case (see Ex. 8a and b). Here, the new Tenor part provides the third entry of the imitative point, which is quite strict; it subsequently resorts to parallel movement against the Bassus part.

The Rorantists' 'Mater Matris' mass is substantially different from the original model. The original transparent character of Josquin's music, particularly the voice reductions and the contrast between sections, has been lost. In its place we have a more continuous four-part texture, which was much more in character with the general musical style of the Rorantist's repertory.

Example 8a. Josquin des Prez, 'Missa Mater Patris', Gloria, bb. 94-9

Example 8b. Kk I.1, item 7b. 'Missa Mater Matris', Gloria, bb. 94-9

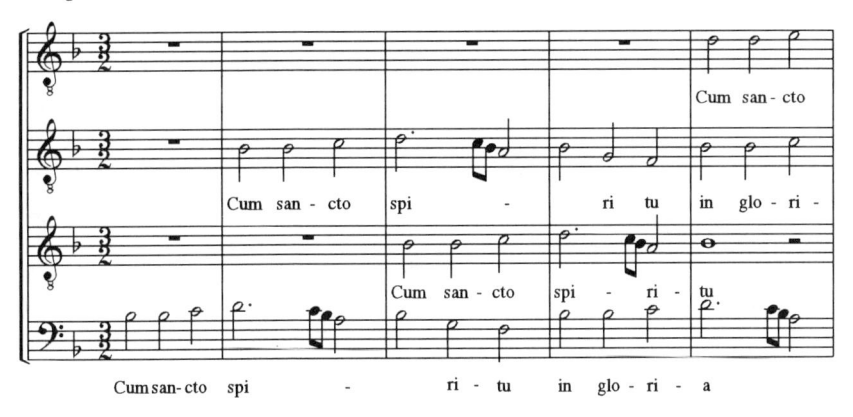

[musical notation]

Krzysztof Borek has been credited with the composition of two masses in Kk I.1: one without a title (item 12) and the 'Te Deum laudamus' Mass (item 13). It is not known when Borek composed these masses; they could have been written during his time as the Rorantists' prefect, or earlier whilst still in the service of Queen Bona. The date 1573, found in conjunction with the second mass, should be treated with caution: it is located at the end of the mass and probably refers to the time of copying, rather than the actual date of composition. Before turning to the music, the presentation of these masses in the manuscript, and their titles in particular, deserves comment. The first mass has no original annotations; Borek's name and the note '5 vocum' are entered by a different scribe, possibly inserted at a later stage. The title of the second mass was entered by the original copyist: 'Te Deum laudamus' (all four books), the date 1573 (all but the Tenor), and the initials 'CB' (Altus and Bassus),[71] which undoubtedly refers to 'Christopherus' Borek. A second copy of both masses was made by Job of Wiślica, of which only the top voice has survived.[72] In both the literature and in the modern editions,[73] the two masses have been regarded as five-part compositions. There is, however, nothing in the sources themselves to suggest that the 'Te Deum laudamus' Mass was written for five voices. Furthermore, the annotations of the first mass are not original, thus the grounds on which this scoring is based are also questionable. This issue will be addressed again after the discussion of the music itself.

The first mass consists of four sections of the Ordinary, the Kyrie, Gloria, Credo, and Sanctus. It is based on a cantus firmus, as yet unidentified, and all four sections begin with a similar imitative point. Borek's overall compositional approach is relatively straightforward. The Kyrie and Sanctus are predominantly contrapuntal and melismatic. The Gloria and Credo are multi-sectional, and are more homophonic and syllabic, with only a limited number of imitative or contrapuntal passages. The important phrases of the text, such as 'Jesu Christe' of the Gloria, are set to slower homophony, as was standard at the time. The overall texture of the mass is full, with only isolated voice reductions and pairing. Movement, especially in the Gloria and Credo, is maintained by partial cadences and overlapping phrases, punctuated by intermittent rests (see Ex. 9). The imitation is simple and short, and is usually taken up by all four voices. Furthermore, the points are rarely developed beyond their first statement.

Example 9. Kk I.1, item 12b. Krzysztof Borek, Mass, Gloria, bb. 23-8

Returning to the initial question of completeness, the lack of a fifth voice is neither evident nor obvious from the music here. The points of imitation always begin in one of the four extant voices, and although the imitation is not particularly strict, there do not appear to be any serious defects. The occasional incorrect voice-leading and dissonant intervals may be compositional traits, not necessarily the consequence of a missing part. Indeed in the modern edition of the Sanctus, Szweykowski states that the reconstruction of a fifth part presents fundamental difficulties in the imitation.[74] In the homophonic sections the four parts provide full triadic harmony almost consistently and likewise do not need a fifth part. As for the '5 vocum' noted in the manuscript, this may have been a simple mistake, possibly based on the incorrect assumption that the second copy of the Cantus part inserted into the Cantus partbook of Kk I.1 before the original, was a fifth part.

The second mass by Borek (item 13) is a paraphrase mass based on the plainchant hymn of thanksgiving 'Te Deum laudamus' (Solemn Tone).[75] The mass, comprising all five sections of the Ordinary, displays a selective and flexible use of the hymn material. The chant is used relatively economically, with just two or three excerpts for each section, and the composer took those passages of the chant which have a direct textual link with the Ordinary sections. The phrase 'Tu ad dexteram Dei sedes in gloria Patris', for instance, is used against with the words 'Qui sedes ad dexteram Patris, miserere nobis' of the Gloria. Each excerpt of the chant is presented in the Tenor with the original text, and mostly in long notes, though it is altered both melodically and rhythmically to suit the needs of the counterpoint. The other three parts, as well as the Tenor when not presenting the chant, continue in a mixture of imitative and non-imitative counterpoint and simple homophony. As in the first mass, the imitation is of a simple construction; the points are short and are rarely developed. Some of the imitation is based on melodic fragments of the chant they accompany, although the former is usually faster-moving than the latter (see Ex. 10).

Example 10. Kk I.1, item 13b, Krzysztof Borek, 'Te Deum' Mass, Gloria, bb. 60-70

Example 10, continued

[musical notation]

The Gloria and Credo are multi-sectional and within these, phrases are punctuated by partial cadences, though some imitative phrases do overlap. There are some awkward harmonic progressions found in the mass, as well as certain intervals which were currently regarded as dissonant, these resulting from an emphasis on voice-leading. One such example can be found in bars 113-15 of the Credo (see Ex. 11). On the whole, the texture is full, with only occasional voice reductions and pairing.

Example 11. Kk I.1, item 12c. Krzysztof Borek, 'Te Deum' Mass, Credo, bb. 108-19

[musical notation]

Example 11, continued

Both these masses show Borek to have been a composer of modest ability, with a reasonable grasp of contemporary contrapuntal technique. It is difficult to point to any direct influences by specific composers, or to show which earlier masses may have served as models, though certain general characteristics of Josquin's generation can be observed in Borek's music. The paraphrase technique was standard in the early part of the sixteenth century. The predominance of relatively long-note cantus firmi against faster-moving outer voices, the use of short sections with little or no variation, and contrapuntal lines in parallel movement can be observed in the masses of Jacob Obrecht. Short phrases and full sonorities through the use of all voices following a point of imitation were typical of Jean Mouton.

The two masses of Tomasz Szadek

Kk I.1 contains two masses by Tomasz Szadek (*c.* 1550-*c.* 1611). Like Borek, Szadek was also employed at the royal court prior to his membership of the Rorantists' college. He was recruited as a young singer in Zygmunt August's chapel in 1569,[76] and remained a member until the court's dissolution in 1574. By this time, he had already begun his association with the Rorantists' college, acting as a substitute, possibly as a clerk, for a period of nine months (last two quarters of 1572 and the first quarter of 1573).[77] In 1575 Szadek became a full member of the Rorantists' college; presumably by this time he had taken at least lower clerical orders. He held a prebend for only three years, leaving the college for an unknown reason in 1578. He nevertheless remained on Wawel Hill, first as a castle vicar ('vic. castrensis') (*c.* 1580),[78] and later also a confessor at the cathedral ('Pœnitentiarii Ecclesiae Cathedrali et vicarii') (*c.* 1600).[79] According to Chybiński, Szadek died in or after 1611.[80]

The first mass by Szadek in Kk I.1 has the title 'Officium Dies est laetitiae' (item 48). The mass was composed in 1578, and as he was a member of the college at that time,[81] one can presume it was written specifically for it. The copy here contains four movements of the Mass Ordinary, the Kyrie, Gloria, Credo, and Sanctus. There is no setting of the Hosanna or Agnus Dei. The mass is based on the Christmas carol 'Dies est laetitiae', which gives the mass its name. This carol seems to have been popular both in Poland and abroad since the fifteenth century. A version with a Polish translation appears in a Protestant songbook compiled by Walentyn of Brzozów: *Kancjonał albo księgi chwal boskich* (Aleksander Aujezedecki, 1554),[82] and a four-part setting with the carol in the Tenor was composed by Wacław of Szamotuły, printed separately as 'Pieśń o narodzeniu Pańskim' (Mateusz Siebeneicher, Kraków, 1558). The melody used by Szadek for his mass is identical with that found in the Tenor of Wacław of Szamotuły's setting. Chybiński suggested that Szadek's mass is a parody mass of Wacław's four-part setting of the song.[83] It is indeed possible that Szadek knew this setting, and there are individual moments where the two are alike. However, the correspondence is too slight for the mass to be regarded as a parody.

The 'Officium Dies est laetitiae' is essentially a paraphrase mass. In the outer movements, the melody is paraphrased in the Tenor, and is either imitated by the other voices or harmonized contrapuntally. In the Kyrie, for instance, each line of the song is presented in succession: the first two lines and their repeat in the Kyrie I, the next three lines in the Christe, and the final three in the Kyrie II. A similar approach seems to have been applied to the Sanctus. The first section paraphrases the first six lines of the melody, with the eighth appearing in the Benedictus. The seventh and last lines of the melody are not used, but would logically fall into the two Hosanna sections, which, as already mentioned, the copy does not have. Assuming that Szadek was not thoughtless, one can presume that the Hosanna sections were composed, but for an unknown reason were not copied into the manuscript.[84] Both the Gloria and Credo, in addition to the imitated paraphrase technique, present the whole carol as a long-note cantus firmus with the original Latin text. In the Gloria, it is located in the Altus part beginning at the 'Qui tollis' section. In the Credo, the cantus firmus is found in the Tenor part, beginning at the 'Crucifixus' section', and underlaid with the second verse of the text. Here the cantus firmus is accompanied by a mixture of imitation and simple homophony in the other three voices. Rarely are the imitative points based on the cantus firmus; instead, a new point is superimposed around the carol melody. The imitation found in this mass is usually simple and short, with the voices entering in close succession, and the imitation is rarely developed or repeated beyond its exposition. Momentum is maintained by the constant overlapping of phrases and partial cadences. This is also true of the Gloria and Credo, where the respective lines of the carol and the other three parts never cadence together (see Ex. 12). Text-setting does not seem to have been important for Szadek: little emphasis is placed on correct accentuation of the words, and the texts of the voice parts are rarely aligned vertically. Homophony is used only sporadically in the Gloria and Credo, and even then it is limited to individual text phrases.

Example 12. Kk I.1, item 48b. Tomasz Szadek, 'Officium Dies est laetitiae', Gloria, bb. 108-13

Szadek's second mass, the 'Officium in melodiam motetae Pisneme', is a parody mass based on a five-part chanson 'Pis ne me peult venir' by Thomas Crecquillon.[85] According to the additional information given in the partbooks, Szadek composed this mass in 1580,[86] and although he had already left the Rorantists, it is likely that the mass was also composed specifically for the college; there was no other ensemble at the cathedral capable of performing polyphony, and the royal chapel was no longer based in Kraków. For his mass, Szadek focused principally on the four lower voices of the chanson, the range of these voices (alto, two tenors, and a bass) clearly being the most suitable for the voice ranges of the Rorantists' chapel. The highest voice of the chanson (Superius) is not totally discarded; some phrases are used by Szadek, though these are altered and inevitably transposed down an octave. The mass displays a standard approach to parody technique. The opening phrase of the chanson appears at the beginning of each of the five sections, slightly modified each time; elsewhere, material is drawn upon to varying degrees and woven into the fabric of the composition. In the Kyrie, Szadek presents an almost complete exposition of the chanson, with only minor alterations. The first half of Kyrie I comes from the initial nine bars of the chanson. The rhythm of the second and the third notes of the Tenor is nevertheless changed to a dotted crotchet - quaver, making the opening word 'Kyrie' much more uniform in all of the voices. Bars 11-16 of the chanson make up the second part of the Kyrie I (see Ex. 13a and b). Here Szadek composed the top voice of the mass from the Superius part and the Quintus part transposed up an octave, with the Contratenor, Tenor and Bassus parts reproduced in the three lower voices.

Example 13a. Thomas Crecquillon, Chanson, 'Pis ne me peult venir', bb. 11-16, *Vingt et six Chansons Musicales*, T. Susato, Antwerp, 1543[15])

Example 13b. Kk I.1, item 49a. Tomasz Szadek, 'Officium Pisneme', Kyrie, bb. 9-14

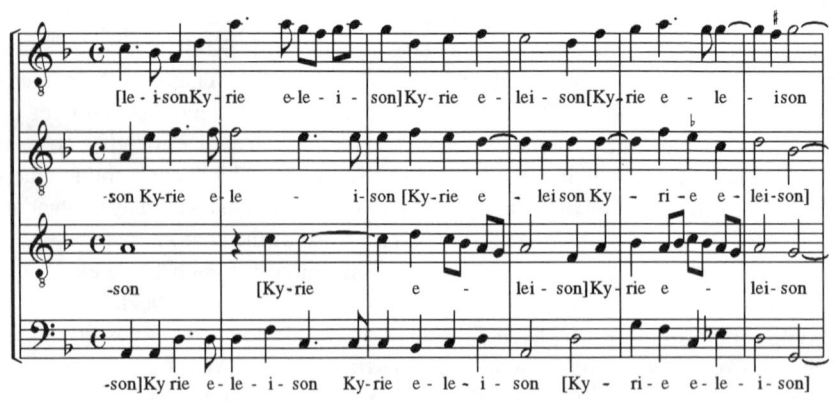

The other sections of the mass involve some manipulation of the chanson material, which is interwoven between newly composed music. Key motifs or melodic lines are extracted and used either as new points of imitation or otherwise are simply harmonized. The chanson's opening subject proved most fruitful for Szadek, with several adaptations inserted throughout the mass. One particular cadential figure of the chanson (bars 15-16) is also used persistently in its various permutations. As in the first mass, the newly composed imitation is simple and rarely developed. Phrases persistently overlap, with few clean breaks within sections. Likewise, in both the Gloria and the Credo, there are only sporadic homophonic passages, as in bars 117-25 of the Credo (Ex. 14), which are usually sandwiched between contrapuntal passages.

Example 14. Kk I.1, item 49c. Tomasz Szadek, 'Officium Pisneme', Credo, bb. 117-125

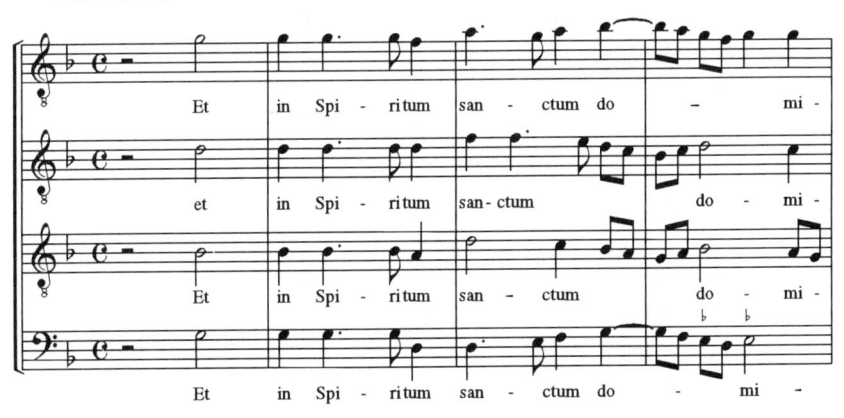

Both masses by Szadek show him to have been a competent composer, though not exceptional. The masses are undoubtedly more accomplished than those by Borek; this is true of both the structure of the compositions, as well as the style of the music itself. No doubt the time spent in the musical establishment of Zygmunt August at the beginning of his career was significant. Here, more than anywhere else in the country, he could have become acquainted with contemporary musical developments through the foreign prints belonging to the chapel,[87] and it was probably here that he came across Crecquillon's 'Pis ne me peult venir'. Szadek was also influenced by the mid-century masses of French composers, of which the Rorantists' college had a significant number in print.[88] This is evident in both the structure adopted in the second mass, and the style of writing in both. The imitation is short and simple, with little or no development of individual ideas. There are few extended melismas, and musical expression is limited. Similarities can also be observed in the text-setting, and in particular the lack of correct word accentuation, a trait typical of the French masses.

The propers of the Tridentine Rite c. 1597

The Tridentine Mass Proper cycles of the Marian feasts differed quite significantly in content from those originally adopted by the Rorantists. In particular, the former cycles of the Conception, Visitation, and Nativity were replaced by one cycle suitable for all three. The introduction of the Roman Gradual in 1597 therefore necessitated new settings of the appropriate Propers, and these additions were subsequently entered into Kk I.1 by Job of Wiślica and Jan Mirmicus. (See Table III.9.) The Offertory 'Beata es virgo Maria' was not included and one can only presume that a pre-existing Offertory was used. The lack of a Sequence here is not surprising since the vast majority of Sequences, were excluded from the new Gradual. The new Purification cycle differed only in the Alleluia verse, and in this case the original section 'Alleluia. Post partem' (item 38) was provided with the new text 'Alleluia. Senex puerum'. The cycle of the Assumption remained unchanged, and so the original Propers were kept.[89]

Table III.9: Additional Marian Propers of Kk I.1
and their use in the Tridentine Gradual

Item	Incipit (Composer)	Designation (in Roman Gradual)
50 and 52	Salve Sancta parens	Introit
51	Benedicta et venerabilis	Gradual
53	Beata viscera	Com.
54	Alleluia. Felix es sacra (Sebastian of Felsztyn)	Alleluia and verse

Stylistically, these new Propers are archaic, not unlike those of the first layer of the manuscript (items 17-41). They are plainchant cantus firmus compositions: the chant is reproduced in the Tenor in long notes and the other voices provide faster-moving harmonic accompaniment. Imitation is introduced in both settings of the 'Salve sancta parens'; the cantus firmus is accompanied by simple imitation in the other three voices, albeit only at the beginning.

Of note here is the presence of 'Alleluia. Felix es sacra' by Sebastian of Felsztyn (fl. 1507-44).[90] It is one of three Propers by the composer to be copied into the Rorantists' manuscripts in the last quarter of the century. Given that none of his polyphonic music was printed,[91] one can only speculate how the Rorantists came upon Sebastian's music approximately half a century after the composer's death. It is possible, that Sebastian had personal links with certain members of the college, as Chybiński suggested, and that the music was given to them directly.[92] The piece may well have been initially copied into another manuscript which no longer exists, such as the choirbook containing Marian mass cycles recorded in the 1563 cathedral inventory,[93] and only later copied into this set of partbooks. In style, 'Alleluia. Felix es sacra' is very much in keeping with the other Propers of Kk I.1,[94] and it is undoubtedly for this reason that the composition was now entered into the manuscript.

Conclusions

Kk I.1 contains a much more diverse collection of music than does the earlier manuscript, Kk I.3. Stylistically, the music falls into two convenient groups: the Mass Proper and the Mass Ordinary settings. The Propers are archaic and continue the conservative plainchant cantus firmus tradition established in Kk I.3; this is true of both the original set of 1552, as well as the individual items added at the end of the century. Nevertheless, the general standard of Propers is here more accomplished than in the earlier manuscript. As with Kk I.3, it is likely that these works are also of local production, if not actually by the Rorantists themselves, the one notable exception being the Alleluia and verse by Sebastian of Felsztyn. However, it is in the Mass Ordinary settings that the real interest in this manuscript lies. Kk I.1 contains several foreign masses, including settings by Morales, Ruffo, Jachet and Certon, as well as an adaptation of a mass by Josquin des Prez, all composers of international fame. The manuscript also contains settings by Poles and members of the Rorantist college: two each by Borek and Szadek. Although not as accomplished as the foreign masses, they constitute a departure from the earlier falsobordone settings. Finally, it is important to remember that Kk I.1 was used by the college not for the early morning votive mass in the private chapel, but for the High Mass of major Marian feasts celebrated at the main altar of the cathedral, which was a more public event. This change in location may well have been the main factor behind the introduction of Mass Ordinary settings by foreign composers and further settings by local composers in a more contemporary idiom, as well as more ambitious Mass Propers.

Kk I.4: ADDITIONAL MUSIC FOR USE IN CHAPEL AND AT THE HIGH ALTAR OF THE CATHEDRAL

The third manuscript produced by the Rorantists is the incomplete set of partbooks, Kk I.4 (*olim* Poznań, Mickiewicz University Library, MS Ch. 191). In many ways, Kk I.4 is a problematic manuscript. Two of the four books are missing and the two extant books have folios lacking. Furthermore, the manuscript was produced over a long period of time and underwent major repairs in the second half of the seventeenth century, losing some of its original character. The available literature has not provided a satisfactory description of the manuscript, and several important problems have not been adequately resolved, not least that of dating. The thematic catalogue prepared by Zofia Surowiak does have a general description of the manuscript in the introduction, and some of her points are pertinent; nevertheless, it is not comprehensive, and some of her scribal identifications are incorrect (these in any case contradict her dating of the manuscript).[95] Some work has been done on the actual music, most notably by Chybiński;[96] however, musicologists have focused primarily on the attributed compositions, particularly those few works which can be reconstructed with the use of later copies. Kk I.4 demands a thorough palaeographical examination, and in particular the various stages of its production need to be established. Only then can the repertory be assessed.

Basic description

The two surviving books of Kk I.4, the Discantus and Tenor partbooks, have 87 and 77 folios respectively. They are bound in brown leather and measure 17.5 x 25 cms. Each contains the name of the partbook, the initials 'S S' (referring to the Rorantists' chapel 'Sacellum Sigismundi' - Zygmunt's chapel)[97] and '1576', presumably the date of the manuscript's binding. The manuscript has two numbering systems. The earlier is a letter system written in ink in the bottom right-hand corners of the recto, similar to that found in contemporary printed books: the first four folios of the gathering were given a letter, the second four left free, and so on. Significantly, this system is incomplete both at the beginning and the end of its sequence. The second is a modern foliation written in pencil. There is little doubt that Kk I.4 originally comprised four partbooks: complete copies of individual compositions are preserved in other manuscripts, also, there are occasional annotations of voice reduction to three parts and augmentation to five and even six parts. It is not known when the other two books were lost.

Kk I.4 has two distinct layers. The first and original layer consists of at least eleven gatherings, each containing four bi-folios. The paper used cannot be identified exactly, although there are some similarities between the watermarks here and paper produced in Poland in the second quarter of the sixteenth century.[98] At some stage, the manuscript was damaged: both surviving partbooks lost four bi-folios at the beginning (the lettering system begins with B[1]), as well as at the end to varying degrees. Subsequently, the manuscript was repaired. New folios of paper, dating from the third quarter of the seventeenth century and possibly originating from Vilnius,[99] were added as a second layer to the existing gatherings. The manuscripts were also rebound, with the original front-pieces mounted onto new leather. In this process, however, some mistakes were made. The Tenor partbook has one gathering misplaced (fols. 65-9 should be located between fols. 59 and 60),[100] and the Tenor manuscript block is bound in such a way that the covers are upside down and back to front.[101] In this study, the original order of the manuscript as presented in the Discantus partbook will be used, and not that found in Surowiak's thematic catalogue, which follows the Tenor partbook. Table III.10 presents an overview of the manuscript, showing the contents of the set, the layers of the partbooks, and the scribes.

Table III.10: Overview of Kk I.4

Date	Contents		Discantus			Tenor	
		layer	fol.	scribe	layer	fol.	scribe
?1576-84	lost [Votive Propers]		missing fols.			missing fols	
c. 1576-84	Votive Propers [Discantus incomplete]	I	1r-3v [fols. missing]	SZ	I	1r-6v	SZ
c. 1584	Easter and Pentecost		4r-25v	SZ		7r-28v	SZ
c. 1584-97	additional Propers		26r-34v	SZ		29r-37v	SZ
c. 1597	Tridentine settings		35r-69r	J.M		38r-59v, 65r-69v, 60r-62v	JM
17th c.	additional Propers		69v-80r	JB, ?	II	70r-76r	MP
		II	81r-86r	MP			

Scribal analysis

The majority of the first layer of Kk I.4 was prepared by two scribes. (See Table III.10.) The first of these was almost certainly Stanisław Zając (prebendary, 1553-76, prefect 1576-1601). The textual underlay here closely resembles his handwriting in the *Elenchus*. He was the only member of the college active between the time of the manuscript's binding (1576) and the mid-1580s,[102] at which time some of the music was undoubtedly entered. Furthermore, it may be no coincidence that the date on the covers is the year in which Zając was elected to the prefect's post. Assuming, then, that he was the scribe in question, Zając was responsible for approximately half of the original manuscript (items 1-29). The second scribe, Jan Mirmicus, entered a whole series of compositions (items 30-50) within a few years of joining the chapel, and certainly before 1601. This can be deduced from titles of several of these pieces which were entered by Job of Wiślica (d. 1601).[103] Mirmicus later entered three further compositions: a Tract in 1606 and two masses, the second of these in 1611.[104]

Following Mirmicus's work, a number of compositions were entered into the original layer during the seventeenth century. It is impossible to say exactly how many were entered because the layer comes to an abrupt end, and at different places in the two partbooks (Discantus, fol. 80, Tenor fol. 62, remembering also that fols. 65-69 originally preceded fol. 60).[105] The Discantus book contains nine compositions entered by four scribes (items 54-62), while the Tenor book has just the first of these compositions. Only one of these scribes can be identified, Jan Borimus (prebendary, 1602/7, prefect, 1619-24); he entered two compositions (items 54, 57) following the mass of 1611, and before 1624, the year in which he died. In both books the first layer ends in the middle of a composition, and is followed by the initial folios of the second layer. This second layer was presumably added to rectify the lost part of the original manuscript, and one scribe was responsible for this work, namely, Mikołaj Pieszkowicz (prebendary, 1671/2-85, prefect, 1685-94). Remembering that the two books were damaged to a different extent, the scribe completed the last composition in the Discantus ('Sub tuum praesidium', item 62), and in the Tenor book he copied (or reconstructed) all nine of the missing compositions (items 54-62).[106] A further eleven compositions appear in both surviving partbooks (items 63-73). As Surowiak has suggested,[107] these are probably copies of compositions initially entered into the original layer. This argument is strengthened by the fact that two of these, 'Vir inclite Stanislae' (item 70) and 'Deus noster' (item 71), are attributed to Annibale Orgas, and may have been entered during the latter's time as chapel prefect from 1628 to 1629. In addition to completing the compositions in Kk I.4, Pieszkowicz was responsible for inserting many annotations into the first layer of the Kk I.4, mostly titles indicating their use.

Layout and liturgical content

Kk I.4 can be divided into several clearly definable sections (see Table III.10). The first encompasses the initial Marian Propers suitable for the daily votive mass. These could have been copied in the late 1570s - remembering the manuscript was bound in 1576 - and early 1580s. In its present state, Kk I.4 begins with a tract

'Ave Maria' and two sequences, 'Nunctiemus nunctium' and 'Ab arce siderea', all three seemingly miscellaneous Propers suitable for the votive mass of the Annunciation.

The second section, which includes Propers and Mass Ordinary settings for Easter and Pentecost, was produced soon after Anna Jagiellonka's foundation of 1584, to enable them to fulfil their new duties introduced therein. Unlike Kk I.3 and Kk I.1, Kk I.4 does not contain whole mass cycles, but just a selection of Propers for Easter and Pentecost, together with a number of Mass Ordinary sections (See Table III.11a and b). Absent also are any Propers for Christmas.

Table III.11a: Propers for Easter in Kk I.4

Introit	Resurrexi et adhuc tecum (item 5)
Gradual	- [*Haec dies quam fecit Dominus (item 31 added later)*]
Alleluia and verse	Alleluia. Pascha nostrum (item 8)
	Alleluia. In die resurrectionis (item 11)
Sequence	Virgini Maria Laudes (Sebastian of Felsztyn) (item 9)
Offertory	-
Communion	- [*Pascha nostrum immolatus (item 32 added later)*]

Table III.11b: Propers for Pentecost in Kk I.4

Introit	Spiritus domini replevit (item 16)
Gradual	-
Alleluia and verse	Alleluia. Veni Sancte Spiritus (item 17)
Sequence	Venit caeli nunctius (item 15)
	Veni Sancte Spiritus (item 18)
Offertory	-
Communion	Factus est repente de caelo (item 19)

The third section encompasses a selection of Propers. Five of these (items 24-8) are for the votive mass of the Annunciation, and a further five for saints' days, all foreign to the liturgy set out in the foundations: two are for the feast of St Margaret, 'Alleluia. Margerita quae decreta' (item 20) and the sequence 'Margeritam pretiosam' (item 21); an Introit for the mass of a Martyr-Bishop, 'Sacerdotes Dei' (item 22); the Gradual from the Common of a Martyr not a Bishop, 'Beatus vir' (item 23), and finally 'Alleluia. Qui creavit omnia' (item 29) for the feast of St Catherine. There are no indications as to why these Propers appear in the college's polyphonic repertory.

The fourth section of the manuscript contains settings of the Propers of the Tridentine votive mass and the Annunciation Mass together with two mass Ordinary settings. The introduction of the Tridentine Missal and Gradual in 1597 created a major problem for the Rorantists. The founding act of 1543 stipulated that the college was required to celebrate a daily 'Rorate' votive mass of the Annunciation: '... Missam Rorate de Annunciatione Beatissime Virginis Mariae ...',[108] the name of the mass being taken from the Introit 'Rorate caeli'. As was explained in full earlier in this chapter, the basic mass cycle formula adopted at the outset was a compilation of Propers from the Annunciation Mass and the votive mass of the Blessed Virgin Mary during Advent. Following Zygmunt August's foundation of 1552, this mass cycle of Kk I.3 was also used for High Mass at the main altar of the cathedral on the feast of the Annunciation (25 March). However, the mass cycle of the Annunciation of the Tridentine Missal was not the same as that previously used by the Rorantists, as it had a different Introit, Gradual, and Tract. It also included an Alleluia verse for use when the feast fell after Easter. (See Table III.12a and b.)

Table III.12: The Pre-Tridentine and the Tridentine cycle of the Annunciation and the Votive Mass during Advent

a) Propers for the feast of the Annunciation

	Local Pre-Tridentine (*Missale Crac. 1532*)	Tridentine (*Graduale Romanum*)
Introit	Rorate caeli	Vultum tuum
Gradual	Tollite portas	Diffusa est gratia (Eastertide: Alleluia. Ave Maria)
Tract	Ave Maria	Audi filia (Eastertide: Alleluia. Virga Jesse)
Offertory	Ave Maria	Ave Maria
Communion	Ecce virgo concipiet	Ecce virgo concipiet

b) Propers for the Votive Mass during Advent

	Local Pre-Tridentine (*Missale Crac. 1532*)	Tridentine (*Graduale Romanum*)
Introit	Rorate caeli	Rorate caeli
Gradual	Tollite portas	Tollite portas
Alleluia	Alleluia. Prophete sancti (and others)	Alleluia. Ave Maria
Sequence*	Mittit ad virginem	Mittit ad virginem*
Offertory	Ave Maria	Ave Maria
Communion	Ecce virgo concipiet	Ecce virgo concipiet

*Though the Marian Sequence was suppressd in the Roman Gradual, its continued used was sanctioned in Poland.

These differences caused a direct conflict between the requirements of the founding act of 1543 and the new liturgy, since the 'Rorate' Mass cycle, previously used by the Rorantists on a daily basis in chapel, was no longer the actual mass of the Annunciation. This next part of Kk I.4 (items 32-51) appears to be the Rorantists' solution to the problem (see Table III.13). The sequence here combines Propers for the Annunciation Mass and the votive mass for the Blessed Virgin Mary during Advent of the Tridentine Rite in one amalgamated block. First come the initial Propers specific for the Annunciation feast (items 32-5), followed by those for the daily votive mass (items 36, 37, 41-2), and finally those common to both (items 44 and 46). The sequence was completed by a selection of Mass Ordinary settings, positioned appropriately between the Propers. By adopting the votive mass of the Blessed Virgin Mary, the Rorantists retained their 'Rorate' Mass for daily use in chapel. They nevertheless adopted the new Annunciation Mass cycle on the feast itself at the main altar of the cathedral.

Table III.13: Sections of the Mass for the feast of the Annunciation and the daily Votive Mass in Kk I.4

item	Title/Annotation	Incipit
32	Introitus Annuntiationis BMV	Vultum tuum (T. Szadek)
33	Graduale Annuntiationis BMV	Diffusa est gratia
34		Gloria Patri et Filio
35	Tractus in Festo Annuntiationis BMV	Audi filia
36	Alleluia. ad Rorate	Alleluia. Ave Maria gratia plena (Sebastian of Felsztyn)
37		Rorate caeli
38		Kyrie eleison
39	[Missa]	Kyrie. Et in terra
40	[Missa Paschalis]	Kyrie. Et in terra
41		Alleluia. Ave Maria gratia plena
42		Alleluia. Virga Jesse floruit
43	Lubelskie	Patrem omnipotentem
44	Offertorium	Ave Maria gratia plena
45	Angelicum	Sanctus. Agnus Dei
46	Communio	Ecce virgo concipiet
47		Rorate caeli
48	[Missa]	Kyrie. Et in terra
49		Alleluia. Ave Maria gratia plena
50	Prosa	Mittit ad virginem
51	Tractus de BMV	Gaude Maria virgo

These changes resulted in a new nomenclature being adopted in the manuscripts: henceforth, the daily votive mass was referred to as the 'Rorate'

Mass, distinguishing it from the mass of the Annunciation celebrated on that feast-day. Several additional points should also be made here. The 'Alleluia. Ave Maria' (item 36), whilst being designated for the 'Rorate' Mass, also has a place in the Annunciation mass cycle, replacing the Tract when this feast fell after Easter. There is no Gradual 'Tollite portas' for the votive mass. Why this Proper was not included cannot be explained, although it is possible that the Annunciation Gradual 'Diffusa est gratia' may have been used. By contrast, two Propers are set more than once, offering alternative settings: the 'Rorate caeli' twice and the 'Alleluia. Ave Maria' three times. Finally, the presence of the sequence 'Mittit ad virginem' needs to be mentioned. Although this sequence (together with the vast majority of sequences) was generally excluded from the Tridentine liturgy, its continued use in Poland was allowed.[109] The other items entered into the manuscript by Mirmicus include the Gradual and Communion for Easter (items 30 and 31), which have already been discussed earlier,[110] and finally two settings of the Mass Ordinary (items 52-3), which were subsquently designated for the Wednesday ('Feriis Quartis') and Friday ('Feriis Sextis'), both presumably alternative settings for the daily votive mass.

The rest of the manuscript, various Propers copied during the seventeenth century, can be grouped together. These items do not belong to the original liturgical pattern of the college and fall outside the compass of this survey.[111]

The completeness of the manuscript

The present state of the manuscript raises two important questions: what was contained in the original four bi-folios which were lost, and why were the cycles for Easter and Pentecost incomplete? The first question is impossible to answer conclusively, though there are several possibilities. The 1599 inventory records Kk I.4 as containing Mass Propers 'Introituum'. Since such descriptions were usually based on the initial compositions of a set, one might infer that the missing part contained such sections. However, it is from the first items of the extant manuscript produced by Zając that the most probable contents of the missing folios, a whole Annunciation mass, can be argued. Only this position would explain the presence of the miscellaneous Propers for this mass and would make the manuscript complete. Since the manuscript contains music for Easter and Pentecost, it is possible that the lost section also included some music for Christmas, making the set appropriate for the three main feasts introduced in the 1584 foundation.[112] Like Kk I.3 and Kk I.1, this manuscript may have contained some polyphonic responses. As for the Easter and Pentecost cycles, one can only speculate why they were incomplete, and indeed how the Rorantists adorned the sections of the liturgy not covered in the manuscript. It is possible - though unlikely - that the college used a secondary manuscript or a printed source of polyphony; otherwise, the propers would have been sung to plainchant.

The musical content

Though incomplete, some of the compositions of Kk I.4 can be reconstructed through other extant copies; moreover, some information on both the structure and style of the other compositions can be ascertained from the surviving two books. On the whole, Kk I.4 continues the archaic plainchant cantus firmus tradition observed in both Kk I.3 and Kk I.1. The vast majority of Propers fall into this group. The plainchant is customarily placed in long notes in the Tenor, mostly without any breaks or rests. In all the compositions which can be reconstructed, the other three voices are faster moving, very similar in nature to the Propers of the earlier manuscripts: they display a full four-part texture, relieved only by short rests between phrases in the individual voices. Indeed, a number of the Propers found in Kk I.4 were copied directly from Kk I.3 and Kk I.1, some with their original text others with a new one.[113]

Three of these Propers are ascribed, two to Sebastian of Felsztyn and one to Tomasz Szadek. It is not surprising to find Sebastian of Felsztyn's Sequence 'Virgini Mariae laudes' (item 9),[114] and the 'Alleluia. Ave Maria gratia plena' (item 36) copied here; although composed half a century earlier, both are stylistically in keeping with the other Propers in this manuscript. More interesting is the Introit for the Tridentine Annunciation Mass, 'Vultum tuum' (item 32), composed by Tomasz Szadek presumably at the end of the century. Whilst our understanding of the piece is limited to the two extant parts, the Tenor does maintain a rigid plainchant cantus firmus, and the Discantus has long and uneven melodic phrases, not unlike the other pieces in this manuscript (see Ex. 15). Since we have already seen in the earlier masses of Kk I.1 that Szadek was an able composer, capable of writing in contemporary forms and idioms, one can only conclude that the 'Vultum tuum' was intentionally archaic, composed in the Rorantists' particular cantus firmus style.

Example 15. Kk I.4, item 32. Tomasz Szadek, 'Vultum tuum', bb. 1-6

A number of Propers copied into Kk I.4, whilst maintaining the plainchant cantus firmus, appear to introduce an element of imitation, not unlike the examples in both Kk I.3 and Kk I.1. The 'Alleluia. Margerita quae decreta' (item 20), 'Alleluia. Angelus intulit' (item 28), the two Sequences 'Nunctiemus nunctium iocundum fratres' (item 2) and 'Margeritam pretiosam (item 21) all fall into this category. The Tract 'Gaude Maria Virgo' (item 51) is more ambitious. This last composition can be reconstructed from a copy in Kk I.7. The contrast between the long-note Tenor and the short note-values of the other three parts is immediately noticeable. The imitation at the beginning is not based on the cantus firmus, and appears in quasi-canon in the other three parts at short displacement (see Ex. 16). Furthermore, the plainchant cantus firmus is very melismatic and this results in both textual repetition and even more melismatic writing in the other three voices.

Example 16. Kk I.4, item 51. Anon. 'Gaude Maria Virgo', bb. 1-6

The 'Fabricii' mass

Perhaps the most interesting composition copied into Kk I.4 is the mass with the annotation 'Fabricii' (item 13). It was Chybiński who in 1932 attributed the mass to one Jan Fabricius of Żywiec on account of the title 'Fabricii' which appears in both the Discantus and Tenor partbook, as well as a similar note in a later copy of the Bass part (Kk I.110).[115] Jan Fabricius was an occasional chapel substitute from 1634, and from 1663 (possibly 1661) to 1665 he held a college prebend.[116] Whilst Chybiński's attribution has not subsequently been questioned in musicological literature,[117] it is incorrect. The mass was copied into the manuscript by Zając together with the Pre-Tridentine Propers for Easter and Pentecost during the mid 1580s and undoubtedly before the Tridentine Propers inserted at the end of the century. This precludes the possibility of the mass being composed by Jan Fabricius of Żywiec, in favour of a composer active at least half a century earlier. Furthermore, the annotation 'Fabricii', on which Chybiński based his whole argument, is not original, but was added by Pieszkowicz in the late seventeenth century, and as such is of questionable value.

The 'Fabricii' Mass consists of all five sections of the Mass Ordinary. It was set for four voices, with the second Agnus Dei for five voices, and the third for six.[118] The mass has not survived complete, although in addition to the Discantus and Tenor parts, the Tenor book has the 'Quinta vox' of the Agnus Dei II and III. Furthermore, a single-leaf manuscript Kk I.110, which dates from the second half of the seventeenth century, contains the Bassus part of the Kyrie, Gloria, and the beginning of the Credo. This provides three parts for much of the composition. (The Gloria of this mass is presented in Appendix XIV.4.)

As Chybiński pointed out, the composition is a parody mass based on Wacław of Szamotuły's four-voice motet 'In te Domine speravi',[119] published in the anthology *Tomus quartus psalmorum selectorum quatuor et plurium vocum* (J. Montanus, Nuremberg, 1554).[120] It is in style and form a typical mid-century parody mass. The motet material is used extensively throughout the mass. First and foremost, the opening phrase of the motet appears at the beginning of all five movements of the mass, albeit slightly modified both rhythmically and melodically each time. Appropriately, the Benedictus of the Sanctus is based on the first phrase of the second section of the motet with the words 'Quoniam fortitudo'. Within the mass sections, other fragments of the motet are used, and here too these are not copied note for note, but altered to suit the needs of the new text or the overall musical plan. Only occasionally are phrases used for specific textual or melodic reasons. One notable example can be found in bars 56-61 of the Credo (see Ex. 17a and b). Here the falling melodic line of 'commendo spiritum meum' in the motet provided the ideal musical motif for the words 'descendit de caelis'.[121]

Example 17a. Wacław of Szamotuły, 'In te Domine speravi', bb. 136-40

Example 17b. Kk I.4, item 13c. Anon., 'Fabricii' Mass, Credo, bb. 56-61

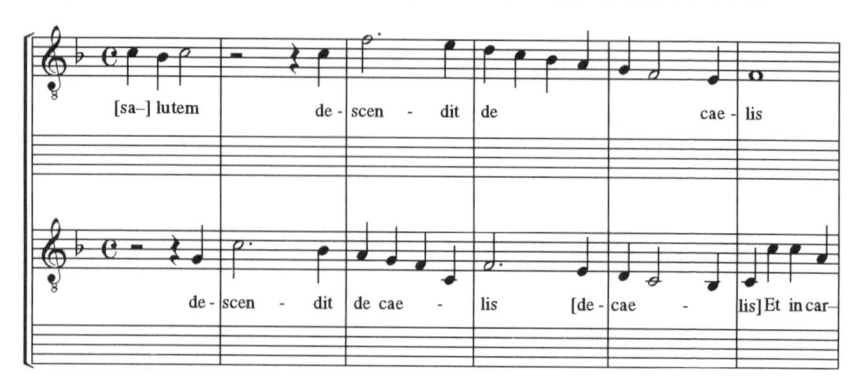

[sa-] lutem de - scen - dit de cae - lis

de - scen - dit de cae - lis [de - cae - lis] Et in car-

Apart from the use of actual melodic material, the mass resembles the motet in overall style. The mass is predominantly imitative, with the occasional use of homophony, particularly in the Gloria and Credo sections. On the whole, each line of the text is provided with new melodic material, be it taken from the motet, or newly composed. Phrases do not always overlap; instead, successive points start on or just following the cadence of the previous phrase (see Ex. 18).

Example 18. Kk I.4, item 13b. Anon., 'Fabricii' Mass, Gloria, bb. 29-32

[ni-]po - tens Do- mi - ne fi - li u - ni - ge-

[ni-] po - tens Do- mi - ne fi - li u-

[ni-] po - tens Do - mi - ne fi - li u - ni-

As the mass is not complete, it is difficult to discuss its texture with any certainty, although some passages suggest the composer employed voice reductions and voice pairing, bars 118-22 of the Credo (see Ex. 19) being one such place.

Example 19. Kk I.4, item 13c. Anon., 'Fabricii' Mass, Credo, bb. 118-22

There is finally the question of authorship. Although there is no conclusive evidence, it is tempting to suggest that the mass was composed by Wacław of Szamotuły. He is known to have composed several masses, including at least one for four voices,[122] and it was common for composers to base a mass on their own models be they motets or madrigals. The quality of the music - or at least what can be ascertained from the extant parts - is indicative of a composer of Wacław's standard, and surpasses that produced by Borek and probably Szadek. Last, but by no means least, the stylistic similarities between the motet and the mass discussed above are strong. Indeed, had it not been for the ascription found in the manuscript by which Chybiński felt bound, he himself would have credited Wacław of Szamotuły with the mass's composition.[123]

Conclusions

In many ways, Kk I.4 continues the musical traditions of the Rorantists' college. The Propers exhibit the archaic cantus firmus style of both Kk I.3 and Kk I.1. Szadek's contribution here is of special significance: it testifies to a conscious choice of this style over a more contemporary musical idiom. Likewise the mass ordinary settings contain much more modern music, and in particular, the 'Fabricii' mass, probably the work of Wacław of Szamotuły, is undoubtedly the most musically progressive composition of local origin, not only in this set, but in the whole of the Rorantists' repertory so far.

Kk I.5: A COMPOSITE MANUSCRIPT CONTAINING MUSIC FOR USE IN CHAPEL AND AT THE HIGH ALTAR OF THE CATHEDRAL

The final manuscript discussed in this survey is the single partbook, Kk I.5 (*olim* Poznań, Mickiewicz University Library, MS Ch. 58),[124] the Discantus from a set of four partbooks. It has been generally neglected by musicologists on account of its incompleteness, and due to the fact that few of the compositions can be reconstructed. Nevertheless, Kk I.5 should not be dismissed altogether, since it is provides an insight into the chapel's growing repertory at the turn of the sixteenth century.

The liturgical and musical contents

In its present state, the Discantus book has 51 folios. It measures 17 x 21 cms and has cardboard covers which date probably from the nineteenth century.[125] Although now bound as one manuscript, Kk I.5 has six distinguishable layers which may well have originally been separate manuscripts. Several factors suggest this: the arrangement of the paper in gatherings, their watermarks, the voice annotations within the manuscript itself,[126] as well as the fact that each layer is complete in itself, with no composition overlapping folios of successive layers (see Table III.14). It is not possible to say when the individual sections were bound into one manuscript; given its absence from the 1559 inventory, this presumably took place at a later stage, possibly even in the nineteenth century. Likewise, it is not known when the other partbooks of the set were lost.

Table III.14: Layers of Kk I.5, with their watermarks, scribes, and principal contents

Layer	Fol.	Watermark (date)	Scribe	Principle contents (item no.)
1 a	1-6	Czap 228 (1580)	?	Mass Ordinary of 1585 (1) and responses (2)
b			JM	additional mass sections (3-4)
2 a	7-11	Czap 376 (1585)	?	responses and hymn (5-6)
b			JW	Mass cycle of Annunciation (7-12)
3 a	13-17	Czap 228 (1580)	?	Mass by Scandello (13)
b	18-33	Briq 2337 (1590)	JW	Masses by Borek, anon., Palestrina and Klabon (14-17)
4	34-7	unidentified	JM	Mass [by Asola] (18)
5	39-44	MCh XI 1739 (1600)	JM	Mass by Baviera (19)
6	45-9	MCh XI 1614 (1599)	JM	Mass (21)

The first layer, fols. 1-6, contains a setting of the Mass Ordinary and a set of mass responses which appear not to have been produced by, or even for, the Rorantists. The scribe can neither be identified, nor was he responsible for other compositions in any of the college manuscripts. There is an annotation at the end of the mass: 'Niepolomiciis Anno Dni 1585 in Maio' (fol. 4v). Given that King Stefan Batory is known to have been residing in his villa in Niepołomice in May 1585 with his court,[127] it is more logical to assume that the mass was written at this time and place for use by his household chapel, and not for the Rorantists' college, which did not leave the confines of the cathedral on Wawel Hill. Furthermore, the part is written in a G clef for the treble range. It was therefore suitable for the king's household chapel, which did have boy choristers, and not the Rorantists. It is not known how the layer came to be in the Rorantists' possession; nevertheless, the final free pages were utilized by Jan Mirmicus to enter a setting of the 'Agnus Dei' (item 5) and a Communion 'Ecce virgo concipiet' (item 6), and this may explain the layer's inclusion in this partbook.

The second layer, fols. 7-12, was prepared by Job of Wiślica. It consists of just one gathering of six folios, and contains an anonymous pre-Tridentine mass cycle of the Annunciation (items 7-12). The paper dates from the mid-1580s, so one can confine the time of this manuscript's production to between 1585 and the introduction of the Tridentine Rite in 1597. Whilst it is difficult to assess the style of the music from just one part, the Discantus part of some of the sections can be superimposed over the long-note cantus firmus Tenors found in earlier settings of Kk I.3 quite adequately; thus the Rorantists' archaic falsobordone style may well have been adopted here too.

The third and largest layer of Kk I.5 (fols. 13-33) is made up of paper identical to that used for the first layer. It contains five Mass Ordinary settings. The first is a four-voice mass by Antonio Scandello, and, like the first layer, appears not to have been produced by or for the Rorantists. The scribe cannot be identified, and only this one item copied by him is preserved. The presence of a mass by Scandello in a Rorantist manuscript is itself somewhat intriguing since he is not known to have composed a four-part mass. It may have come from the music collection belonging to the household chapel of Zygmunt August, which we know included some music by Scandello,[128] or possibly a version of his lost six-part mass published in 1588.

The other four masses in this layer were entered by Job of Wiślica during the last decade of the sixteenth century.[129] The first of these, Borek's 'Te Deum' Mass (item 14), was almost certainly copied from Kk I.1 (item 13).[130] Since Kk I.1 was produced specifically for use on the Marian feast at the main altar of the cathedral, it is logical to conclude that this second copy was prepared for chapel use, or possibly even for the feasts of Christmas, Easter, or Pentecost in conjunction with Kk I.4. Job also made a copy of the other mass by Borek found in Kk I.1, and this almost certainly belonged here in this layer of Kk I.5.[131] However, this copy became separated and was incorrectly inserted into the Cantus book of Kk I.1 (fols. 65r-68v), just before the original. The second mass, which is anonymous, is problematic. It has no title and there is no other copy. It therefore cannot be credited to a local composer, or easily identified as a foreign composition. Although musical discussion is limited to one part, the awkwardness of the melodic line and text underlay is immediately noticeable. This is certainly true of the opening of the Kyrie (see Ex. 20). It is possible that the work is a parody mass based on a secular chanson or madrigal.

Example 20. Kk I.5, item 15a. Anon., Kyrie, bb. 1-5

[musical notation: Ky-ri-e e - lei - son Ky-ri-e e—]

The third mass (item 16) is clearly ascribed and titled 'Auctore Jo: Pe[traloysio] Prænestino. Papæ Marcelli'.[132] The copy here is not Palestrina's original six-part 'Papae Marcelli' mass published in his second book of 1567, but the four-part version, which appeared in his *Missarum cum quatuor vocibus. Liber primus.* (J. Vincenti, Venice, 1590).[133] This print comprises three of Palestrina's masses, the reduced 'Papae Marcelli' mass, the 'Sine nomine' mass, and the 'Missa Brevis', both presented in their original four-part form. The four-part version of the 'Papae Marcelli' mass in the 1590 publication is more than just a simple voice reduction of the original six-part work: whilst it maintains the overall character of the original mass and its voice range, some melodic lines are altered, and truncations do occur, most notably in the Kyrie, Sanctus, and Agnus Dei sections.[134] Job's copy of the top voice in Kk I.5 is quite accurate, although it is transposed down a fifth, making it more suitable for the college's vocal range.

The fourth and last mass copied by Job was the 'Officium Sancta Maria' by Krzysztof Klabon (item 17). Klabon spent his whole career at the royal court, initially as a choirboy in Zygmunt August's chapel, later as the prefect of the royal chapel created by Stefan Batory (1576-86), a post which he also held for the first fifteen years of Zygmunt Vasa's reign (until 1602).[135] This mass was therefore composed whilst he was still at the head of the royal chapel, and most probably intended for its use. Judging by the voice annotations in the partbook,[136] the mass was for five voices. The top part here is well within the alto range; however, it is impossible to say if it is presented here in its original pitch, or if, like the Palestrina mass, it was transposed to make it suitable for performance by the Rorantists' college.

The final three layers of Kk I.5 (now fols. 34-7, 39-44, and 45-50), were copied by Jan Mirmicus, some time during the first quarter of the seventeenth century.[137] Each consists of a single gathering containing one Mass Ordinary setting.[138] The first of these is the 'Octavi toni' mass (item 18). This mass was copied into a later set of Rorantists' partbooks (Kk I.6), which has survived complete. The 'Octavi toni' mass is not ascribed in either copy, although it can be identified as Giovanni Matteo Asola's mass on the eighth tone, first published in *Secundus Liber... missae octonis compositae tonis* (A. Gardane, Venice, 1581ª). The second mass (item 19) is puzzling. It has the title 'Missa quinque [vocum] supra Intravit Jesu'. At the end of the mass in the right-hand margin, Mirmicus entered the name 'Caspar Baviera' (fol. 44r). In the published catalogue, Surowiak suggests that this may be the name of the composer.[139] Due to the location of this note at the end of the mass and not at the beginning with the title, this proposition is questionable. In any case, no composer or musician of this name is known today. The title 'supra Intravit Jesu' indicates that the mass was based on a pre-existing melody or composition, as yet unidentified, and indeed all the sections (save the Gloria), begin with a similar motif. There is no information on the final mass (item 21): Mirmicus provided neither the name of the composer nor a title. There is no other extant copy of the mass, and little can be said on the basis of this single part.

Conclusions

In spite of the problems linked with Kk I.5, its purpose and significance within the overall Rorantists' repertory appears to be clear. Kk I.5 is a composite manuscript, which during the sixteenth century was still in separate sections. These individual manuscripts were clearly used as supplementary sources of polyphony to be used in conjunction with the other manuscripts which were geared towards specific chapel or cathedral duties. This is certainly true of the third layer, comprising Mass Ordinary settings. The copy of Borek's mass (from Kk I.1) corroborates this argument. Kk I.5 is therefore an important record of the continuing growth of the chapel's repertory at the end of the century, particularly the mass ordinary settings, and points the royal chapel as the principal source of the latter.

THE RORANTISTS' PRINTED REPERTORY

The printed repertory of the Rorantists' college at the close of the sixteenth century - those items recorded in the 1599 inventory - consisted of two bound choirbooks of masses and a set of five partbooks containing the motets of Lasso.[140]

The two choirbook volumes of masses by the Parisian firm of Le Roy and Ballard were in the possession of the college by the late 1570s.[141] Whilst we do not know their precise contents, it is likely they contained the ten separate prints of masses recorded by Surzyński in 1885,[142] and probably at least one further book of masses from 1557 by the same firm. Taken together, these gave the Rorantists a significant source of 23 four-voice Mass Ordinary settings by French composers of the mid-sixteenth century, most of these being short-scale parody masses based on a motet or a chanson.[143] It is not possible to say with any certainty whether or not the prints were actually used by the Rorantists to sing from during the liturgy. Given the copy of Certon's mass in Kk I.1, it is unlikely the prints were used for the High Mass on the Marian feasts. They may have been used in the chapel - in conjunction with other manuscripts - for the votive mass, perhaps on more special occasions.[144]

The set of partbooks with Lasso motets may well have also been a composite volume, possibly comprising the four five-voice motet books published by Le Roy and Ballard in the early 1570s listed by Chybiński in 1910.[145] However, the volume's usefulness to the Rorantist's college should be questioned on two counts. First, the volumes contain no music appropriate for the college's specific liturgical duties. Secondly, the vast majority of the music includes parts for the Treble voice, which the Rorantists did not have. Given the standard five-part scoring from Treble to Bass, transposition of the music was not possible. Clearly this volume was not acquired for the college with their liturgy in mind; instead, it may have found its way into the college library by chance, perhaps was left there by one of its members.

THE RORANTISTS' POLYPHONIC REPERTORY: CONCLUSIONS

The Rorantists' college possessed a modest collection of manuscript partbooks. These manuscripts were practical and functional, each covering a particular set of liturgical duties. Within a given set, there was little room for choice. Looking first at the daily votive mass in chapel, Kk I.3 contained just two complete mass cycles, one suitable for festive occasions, the other for ferial days and during Advent and Lent. The majority of the additional Ordinary and Proper sections were intended for use on a given feast, weekday, or during a specific liturgical season. In the first fifty years of the college's activity, just two further complete mass cycles were produced, one added to Kk I.3, the other originally a separate manuscript, is now incorporated into Kk I.5. As for the polyphony used at the main altar of the cathedral, Kk I.1 contained the propers for the respective Marian feasts, and Kk I.4 incomplete sets of Propers for Easter and Pentecost (perhaps originally also those for Christmas). The first of these manuscripts had a relatively large selection of mass ordinary settings, which further increased in number over the decades. Several other smaller manuscripts, now amalgamated into Kk I.5, were also used, possibly in conjunction with the other manuscripts.

The manuscripts provide a clear picture of the musical development of the Rorantists' repertory in the first half century of the college's existence. Their earliest extant music was in a simple falsobordone style in four parts, with the plainchant cantus firmus in the Tenor part, and with predominantly consonant movement in the other voices. This style may not have been the most modern, but the settings did underline their strictly liturgical function. With the introduction of the duties at the main altar of the cathedral in 1552, two distinctive branches of musical repertory emerge. The first encompasses the Mass Propers, which remain very much in the same archaic cantus firmus style of the original music. The second, including the majority of Mass Ordinary settings, was in a more contemporary idiom. This began with the copying of foreign masses into Kk I.1, and expanded to include settings by both foreign and local composers in Kk I.1, Kk I.4 and Kk I.5, some of which include five- and even six-part scoring. The majority of foreign music chosen by the Rorantists was taken from relatively recent publications. In the early 1550s, they took several masses from one print, published just ten years earlier, *Missae cum quatuor vocibus paribus* . . . (Scotto, Venice, 1542). In the late 1570s Job copied Certon's mass of 1558, and in the last decade of the century the same scribe copied the four-part version of Palestrina's 'Papae Marcelli' mass, published in 1590. As for the contributions by Polish composers, Tomasz Szadek, the anonymous author of the 'Fabricii' mass (possibly Wacław of Szamotuły), and, to a lesser extent, Krzysztof Borek, produced polyphony of a commendable standard. It is significant that all three of these were employed at the royal court prior to their membership of the Rorantists' college, and their contact with a wider variety of music here, especially in foreign prints, may well explain the quality of their work.

As one might expect, the range of the music was determined by the specific size and make-up of the college.[146] In spite of fluctuation in membership, the Rorantists were able to perform the four- and even five-part music contained in their manuscripts with one (and at times two) voices per part. As for the music itself, the range of the predominantly four-part settings fluctuated from what might now be described as one alto, two tenors, and one bass, to two tenors and two basses.

One should finally underline the Rorantists' impact on the liturgical and musical life of the cathedral on Wawel Hill. It introduced one more element to the cathedral's already busy daily liturgical timetable, at once further developing the Marian cult there. At the time of the college's creation, the cathedral did not yet have a permanent choir capable of performing polyphony. The Rorantists therefore introduced polyphony there on a daily basis, albeit in one of its side-chapels, and subsquently provided polyphony at the main altar of the cathedral for the major feasts of the year. They continued to be the sole provider of polyphonic music here until 1619, when Bishop Marcin Szyszkowski founded a secular choir and instrumental ensemble to provide music on a more regular basis (on certain feast-days and every Sunday). This new establishment did not make the Rorantists redundant, since on the three major feast-days of the Lord and the six Marian feast-days, the two were expected to join forces.

NOTES

[1] Kk Inv. 29 fol. 114v. See Bochnak, *Inwentarz*, p. 162.

[2] The term 'Cancionale' denoting choirbook format can be found in Polish sources in the Rorantists' inventory of 1599 (Kk Inv. 67) (see below), and the Jasivcicz inventory of 1572 (see Appendix XIII).

[3] This list of music books (in its original form) was published by A. Chybiński in an article on new material on the Rorantists' chapel: 'Nowe materjały do dziejów królewskiej kapeli rorantystów w kaplicy Zygmuntowskiej na Wawelu', *Księga pamiątkowa ku czci Oswalda Balzera* (Lwów, 1925), p. 147.

[4] Kk Inv. 67, p. 65.

[5] J. Surzyński (ed.), *Monumenta musices sacrae in Polonia* 1 (Poznań, 1885), p. iv, footnote 14.

[6] A. Chybiński, 'Zbiory muzyczne na Wawelu', *Przegląd Muzyczny* (1910), no. 1, pp. 1-4, and no. 2, pp. 5-6.

[7] Chybiński, *Materyały*, pp. 39-40.

[8] See F. Lesure and G. Thibault, *Bibliographie des éditions d'Adrian Le Roy et Robert Ballard (1551-1598)* (Paris, 1955), pp. 68-70.

[9] In 'Nowe materiały', Chybiński suggested that the 1557 print was the *Canticum Beatæ Mariæ Virginis (quod Magnificat inscribitur) octo modis* (1557^8). Such a book of Magnificat settings was of no use to the Rorantists, as they were not obliged to sing Vespers. Nevertheless, if the volumes were purchased already bound, such a print may have been discarded some time after the 1599 inventory. Surprisingly, in a second article written three years later, 'Stosunki muzyczne Polski z Francją w XVI stuleciu', *Przegląd Muzyczny* (1928), no. 4, p. 5, Chybiński presented a version of Surzyński's list of ten prints, although it included this print *Canticum Beatæ Mariæ Virginis (quod Magnificat inscribitur) octo modis* (1557^8), but not Certon's *Missa pro defunctis* which is found in Surzyński's original list.

[10] These masses are discussed in J. Kłobukowska, 'Msze francuskie w repertuarze kapeli roranckiej' *Muzyka*, 16 (1971), no. 3, pp. 85-6.

[11] Within the Rorantists' manuscripts, the term 'Officiorum' is used for mass cycles, including those with both ordinary and proper sections, and those with the ordinary only.

[12] Chybiński, 'Zbiory', p. 6. Chybiński's monograph on the Rorantists also presents an almost identical list of prints by Lasso (*Materyały*, p. 40), the exception being the omission of the fragment which does not have a title.

[13] Z. Surowiak-Chandra, Introduction to *Collections of Music Copied for Use at Wawel*. Vol. I, fasc. 3 of *Musicalia Vetera*, ed. Z. Szweykowski (Kraków, 1976). Here the author presents an adequate historical and palaeographical description of the manuscript. At that time, however, the set was still in the possession of the Main Library of the Adam Mickiewicz University, Poznań (MS Ch. 202). The books were returned to the cathedral archive on Wawel Hill, Kraków in the early 1980s.

[14] Cues in the form of the letters 'd', 'a', 't', and 'b' appear on the stave at the beginning of several compositions, informing the given voice of the entry note of the other voices.

[15] Surowiak-Chandra, Introduction (1976), p. 12. The author claims this was the work of I. Polkowski, the cathedral archivist in the 1880s.

[16] G. Piccard, *Wasserzeichen Werkzeug & Waffen*, IX.1 (Stuttgart, 1980). See watermarks nos. 331 and 326-32.

[17] G. Piccard, *Wasserzeichen Verschiedene Vierfüssler*, XV.3 (Stuttgart, 1987). See watermarks nos. 93-4, 101. As a useful point of reference, this paper was used by the royal treasury for books of payments for the years 1549 (RK 162a) and 1551 (RK 158).

[18] This can be concluded from his work on the Rorantists' Gradual.

[19] Chybiński, *Materyały*, p. 37: 'Z pierwszej połowy XVI stulecia (do roku 1550 lub bezpośrednio po nim) . . .' ('From the first half of the 16th century (up till 1550 or immediately after)').

[20] This includes the Surowiak-Chandra's dating, Introduction (1976), p. 18.

[21] This scribe was responsible for several unsigned receipts for the years 1546-8 in the *Elenchus* (fols. 3rv, 9r, 14r, and 18rv), which, excluding the known prebendaries, reduces the possible candidates to these two.

[22] This can be deduced from the scribes responsible for the text underlay.

[23] This term appears in several of the manuscript Graduals, including the Rorantists' Gradual and the Olbracht Gradual, and its meaning is uncertain.

[24] The *Elenchus* does not have any payment records for the years 1595-7, so it is not possible to say exactly when Mirmicus was accepted into the college. His name does appear from 1597 on the usual list of prebendaries.

[25] The first of these was given the title 'ad Officium in Sabbatho' most probably in the seventeenth century, in line with the alterations introduced with the Tridentine Gradual in 1597.

[26] It has not been possible to ascertain the meaning of this term.

[27] A. Chybiński, *Słownik muzyków dawnej Polski do roku 1800* (Kraków, 1948), p. 96.

[28] In the case of the Gothic notation, the notes assume similar values.

[29] The plainchant version in Kk 46, fol. 2v, which was used for the cantus firmus here, is designated 'In duplicibus festis'.

[30] In many cases, the initial entry of the missing Altus part can be reconstructed, especially when it is the first voice that enters, introducing the point of imitation.

[31] E. Głuszcz-Zwolińska, *Muzyka nadworna ostatnich Jagiellonów* (Kraków, 1988). Here the author states that the four chaplains employed at the court of Zygmunt I Stary were not capable of performing polyphony.

[32] See Chapter IV on the musical establishment at the royal court.

[33] E. Głuszcz-Zwolińska, Introduction to *Collections of Music Copied for Use at Wawel*. Vol. I, fasc. 1 of *Musicalia Vetera*, ed. Z. Szweykowski (Kraków, 1969), p. 12.

[34] J. Surzyński, 'Muzyka figuralna w kościołach polskich od XV do XVII wieku', *Rocznik Towarzystwa Przyjaciół Nauk Poznańskiego*, 16 (1889).

[35] See Głuszcz-Zwolińska, Introduction (1969), p. 20.

[36] From the end of the eighteenth century until 1918, Poland did not exist as a separate state, but was divided up between its three neighbours Austria, Russia, and Prussia.

[37] Chybiński, *Materyały,* pp. 38-9. No doubt this suggestion was made on the basis of the three dates 1573, 1578, and 1580 which appear in the manuscript.

[38] These will be referred to within the main discussion of the manuscript, and can all be found in the bibliography.

[39] This information was given to me by Professor Z. Szweykowski.

[40] In Z. Szweykowski (ed.), *Muzyka w dawnym Krakowie* (Kraków, 1964), the manuscript has no call-number. By the time of Zwolińska's catalogue of 1969, this call-number was used.

[41] The first watermark here most closely resembles no. 956 in Briquet's catalogue, namely, a shield divided into quarters, with an eagle and chequers in alternate fields. See C.M. Briquet, *Les Filigranes: Dictionnaire historique des marques du papier de leur apparition vers 1282 jusqu'en 1600* (Leipzig, 1923), no. 956. Similar paper was also produced in Legnica in Silesia (c. 1549) and Gorlitz in Bohemia (c. 1548-57). As for the second watermark, see G. Piccard, *Wasserzeichen Lilie*, XIII (Stuttgart, 1983), watermarks nos. 1201-17.

[42] This can be deduced from the recurring arrangement of breaks in the lines.

[43] Some additional folios of paper were needed for the Cantus, Altus, and Bassus partbooks to complete the final mass cycle of the Purification. This paper, according to Briquet, was produced in Poznań from about 1570, although it is possible that it was produced elsewhere in Poland before this time.

[44] These entries, unlike the receipts discussed in relation to Kk I.3, are titles and neat copies of payments.

[45] In 1551 there were only four prebendaries, of which the scripts of other two, S. Radomski and A. Słomniki, have been identified.

[46] Piccard,*Wasserzeichen Lilie*, XIII. See watermarks nos. 1085-1103.

[47] Now Cantus, fols. 74-98 and 155-85, Altus, fols. 71-94 and 150-90, Tenor, fols. 69-90 and 132-66, Bassus, fols. 69-93 and 145-83.

[48] G. Piccard, *Wasserzeichen: Die Kronen*, I (Stuttgart, 1961). See watermark no. 241.

[49] This can be concluded from the fact that the Credo is located on the first folio of the second layer, and not on the preceding pages of the first layer, which were blank at the time. These blank spaces were utilized by Jan Mirmicus at the end of the century, or in the first decades of the next.

[50] The Cantus partbook contains a second copy of the top voice (fols. 65r-68v), prepared by Job of Wiślica on paper which dates from the 1580s. Its presence here cannot be easily explained, though it is possible that a second copy was needed for performance, and was subsequently added to the Cantus partbook before the original copy (fols. 69r-75r).

[51] 'Auctore Petro Certon' appears in the Cantus, Tenor, and Bassus partbooks; the Altus has just 'Certon'.

[52] This item is discussed earlier in this chapter in the section dealing with the 1599 inventory (item 3).

[53] In the first mass, Job was responsible for copying the Altus and Bassus parts; the scribe of the Cantus and Tenor cannot be identified.

[54] These can usually be detected through scribal hands, liturgical content and inappropriate location in the manuscript.

[55] E. Głuszcz-Zwolińska: 'Supplement' to first volume of *Musicalia Vetera* (n.p., n.d.).

[56] This title appears only in the Cantus partbook; the other books have an abbreviated form: *Missarum cum quatuor vocibus paribus canendarum*.

[57] The Jasivcicz inventory of 1572 has two entries which may refer to the print in question: 'Item Officia moralis w papierze klÿonem 4' ('Masses [à] 4 [by] Morales stuck [i.e. bound] in paper') (item 61) and 'Item Parthessow ad pares voces 4' ('partbooks for equal voices') (item 16). See Appendix XIII.

[58] The notation is similar, although the diamond heads of the print are rounded in the manuscript.

[59] Similar changes were made by Stanisław Zając later in the last quarter of the century. These are all located at the end of the Altus partbook and take the form of an additional part or parts which created a four-part texture of original three- and even two- part texts of some of the masses (items 3-6). Details are given in Appendix IX.

[60] The titles were added in a different hand, presumably at a later stage.

[61] This Offertory was also suitable for the Common of Virgins (*Missale Cracoviensis*, fol. 316v).

[62] *Missale Cracoviensis*, fol. 196v: 'Alia officium proprium quod edidit Sixtus papa quartus et quod tenet ecclesia cathedralis Cracoviensis'.

[63] Kj 1267, fol. 233-237.

[64] Pikulik, 'Sekwencje polskie', pp. 7-125. Here Pikulik refers to W. Wisłocki, *Katalog rękopisów Biblioteki Uniwersytetu Jagiellońskiego* (Kraków, 1877), p. 320, which characterized this manuscript as originating from the cathedral.

[65] Exceptionally, 'Egredimini et videte' (item 30) begins with a breve, Tenor, fol. 102v.

[66] In the article on an incomplete set of partbooks originating from the town of Olkusz, 'Rękopiśmienne partesy olkuskie', *Muzyka*, 14 (1969), no. 2, pp. 18-44, M. Perz suggests that 'Sebastian X', scribe and composer of 'Cantate Domino' (1587), can probably be identified as Sebastian of Książe who held a prebend from 1548 to 1565. If this was the case, Sebastian would be a possible candidate for some of the polyphony here in Kk I.1.

[67] E. Głuszcz-Zwolińska, 'Missa Mater Matris z repertuaru rorantystów wawelskich', *Muzyka*, 15 (1970), no. 3, pp. 73-7.

[68] The Tenor partbook did have the original 'Patris', though this was altered to conform with the other three partbooks.

[69] Głuszcz-Zwolińska, 'Missa Mater Matris'. The author also discusses the question of authenticity of the Josquin mass.

[70] Ibid., p. 76.

[71] There is also a mark 'MR' (or 'NR') which precedes this date. No conclusive explanation of this has been presented. It may have been a mark made by the scribe, though most probably not his initials, since no member of the college is known to have had such initials.

[72] The copy of the first mass was inserted here into the Cantus partbook of Kk I.1 (fols. 65r-68v) just prior to the original, while the second now forms part of the single partbook, Kk I.5 (fols. 18r-21v).

[73] These include Poliński, *Dzieje*, p. 81; Z. Jachimecki, *Wpływy włoskie w muzyce polskiej*, i: *1540-1640* (Kraków, 1911), p. 91; Chybiński, *Słownik*, p. 11, and most recently, E. Zwolińska, 'Borek', *Encyklopedia Muzyczna PWM*, i (Kraków, 1979), pp. 364-5. Editions: Szweykowski (ed.), *Muzyka*, p. 331, and H. Feicht (ed.), *Muzyka staropolska* (Kraków, 1966), p. 382.

[74] Szweykowski (ed.), *Muzyka*, p. 331.

[75] LU, p. 1832.

[76] Chybiński *Słownik*, pp. 122-3; Chybiński deduced the approximate date of Szadek's birth from the fact that in all of the payments he is found under the heading 'adolescentes cantores'.

[77] Kk Inv. 65, fol. 79r. Here Szadek is referred to as 'Thomae Clerico SMR' ('Clerk of His Royal Highness'). There are, however, no indications in the royal account-books that he was a clerk in the king's chapel, thus it is possible that he held the clerk's post in the Rorantists' chapel.

[78] Kk I.1, Cantus partbook, fol. 152v.
[79] Kk I.4, Discantus partbook, fol. 35r.
[80] Chybiński, *Słownik*, p. 122.
[81] The Cantus and Bassus partbooks include 'Tomae Szadek 1578' and 'Thoma Szadek eiusd. Capelae Pb.' respectively.
[82] J. Nowak-Dłużewski (ed.), *Kolędy polskie* (Warsaw 1966), i, p. 230; 11, pp. 30, 36, 56, 75, and 201.
[83] Chybiński's views are summarized by Z. Szweykowski, 'Rozkwit wielogłosowości w XVI wieku', in Z. Szweykowski (ed.), *Z dziejów polskiej kultury muzycznej*, i: *Kultura staropolska* (Kraków, 1958), p. 99.
[84] Likewise the Agnus Dei section could have been composed, but was not copied into the manuscript.
[85] Crecquillon's 'Pis ne me peult venir' first appeared in *Vingt & six chansons Musicales & nouvelles à cinque parties* (T. Susato, Antwerp, 1543[15]), and judging by the number of subsequent publications in which it is found, was a popular chanson.
[86] Kk I.1, Cantus partbook, fol. 152v: 'Thomas a Szadek Vic. Castrensis fecit' and '1580'. In the introduction to the WDMP edition of the mass, Feicht suggests that Szadek was a vicar at the cathedral; however, the term used here, 'castrensis', specifically refers to the castle, and not the cathedral.
[87] See Appendix XIII.
[88] Given the Certon mass appears before Szadek's first mass of 1578 in this manuscript, there is little doubt that the Le Roy and Ballard prints were acquired prior to this date, and thus available to the composer while he served with the college.
[89] The cycle of the Annunciation was not included in Kk I.1, and will be discussed in due course.
[90] In his article 'Do biografii Sebastjana z Felsztyna', *Kwartalnik Muzyczny* (1932), nos. 14-15, pp. 594-8, Chybiński presented all the known biographical information on the composer. The first mention of Sebastian dates from 1507, when he enrolled at the University in Kraków; two years later he gained a bachelor's degree in the liberal arts. By 1515 Sebastian had been ordained and held a benefice in Felsztyn. He later acquired a benefice in Sanok, and by 1536 became the rector of the church there. Sebastian of Felsztyn wrote several music treatises for pedagogical use, ranging from the theory of music, *Opusculum musices* (J. Haller, Kraków, 1517), to methods in accentuating chant, *Modus regulariter accentuandi lectiones* (Kraków, 1518). The exact date of his death is not known, although presumably he died towards the middle of the century, at some stage following the publication of his last treatise, *Directiones musicae* (H. Wietor, Kraków, 1543).

[91] Sebastian is known to have had a set of hymns published in 1522, *Aliquot hymni ecclesiastici . . . Vario melodiam genere editi* . . . (Kraków, 1522), now lost; there is, however, nothing to suggest that this print contained polyphony, or included Alleluia and verse settings.

[92] Chybiński, *Słownik*, p. 30.

[93] In the local Pre-Tridentine Rite, the 'Alleluia. Felix es sacrae' was suitable for the votive mass of the Virgin Mary from the feast of the Purification to Lent and Trinity to Advent.

[94] S. Łobaczewska, 'O utworach Sebastjana z Felsztyna (XVI wiek)', *Kwartalnik Muzyczny* (1929), no. 3, pp. 227-44 and no. 4, pp. 347-65. In the analysis, Łobaczewska points to the conservative character of all three compositions of Sebastian.

[95] Z. Surowiak, Introduction to *Collections of Music Copied for Use at Wawel*. Vol. I, fasc. 3 of *Musicalia Vetera*, ed. Z. Szweykowski (Kraków, 1974), pp. 10-32.

[96] Chybiński, *Materyały*, p. 38; 'Jan Fabrycy z Żywca (XVII wiek)', *Kwartalnik Muzyczny* (1932), no. 16, pp. 665-70, and 'Walentyn Gawara-Gutek', *Przegląd Muzyczny* (1927), no. 11, pp. 1-3.

[97] Chybiński, 'Walentyn Gawara Gutek', p. 1-3.

[98] Piccard, *Wasserzeichen Lilie*, XIII. See watermarks nos. 993-1003.

[99] Surowiak, Introduction (1974), p. 26. In the Tenor partbook, two folios of a different paper (now fols. 63-4), were added to the last folio of the original layer. Neither the date nor the place of production of this paper has been determined.

[100] This can be deduced from the incorrect sequence of the lettering.

[101] Although this fact was mentioned by Surowiak in her introduction, the catalogue itself does not take this into account, and follows the altered and distorted order of the Tenor partbook.

[102] Andrzej Słomniki is the one exception, though he can be excluded on account of his own entries in the *Elenchus*.

[103] Job also copied a 'Gloria patri' (item 34).

[104] These dates appear at the end of the respective compositions.

[105] This fault in the manuscript is discussed earlier.

[106] Since the last composition of the first layer, 'Sanguine proprio', was incomplete, and was misplaced due to the incorrect insertion of one gathering, the scribe wrote out the whole composition on the first folio of the second gathering.

[107] Surowiak, Introduction (1974), p. 20.

[108] Kk dyp. 1184, p. 11.

[109] In the *Graduale Romanum . . . Illustrissim. Rev. D. D. Mathiæ Łubieński* published in Poland (c. 1620), the rubric for the votive mass has the following note: 'Sequentia iuxta consuetudinem approbatam, Mittit ad Virginem'.

[110] See the section on the mass cycles for Easter in relation to the new duties of 1584.
[111] It is possible that they postdate 1619, the year in which the cathedral *cappella* was created. This *cappella* was required to provide music for the major feasts of the liturgical year, and the relevant acts mention the co-operation between the *cappella* and the Rorantists' chapel.
[112] The location of such Christmas music before that for Easter would be logical from a liturgical point of view. The Marian Propers which are to be found at the opening of the extant manuscript would therefore have to be seen as subsequent additions entered into space originally left between the Christmas and Easter sections.
[113] The catalogues in Appendix IX provide all the concordances.
[114] The composition is presented anonymously here, though it is ascribed in a later copy, Kk I.335.
[115] A. Chybiński, 'Jan Fabrycy z Żywca (XVII wiek)', *Kwartalnik Muzyczny* (1932), no. 16, pp. 665-70.
[116] Ibid., p. 665.
[117] This includes Surowiak, Introduction (1974) and Z. Surowiak-Chandra, 'Fabricius', *Encyklopedia Muzyczna PWM*, iii, p. 55.
[118] This can be derived from the annotations 'quinque vocum' and 'sex vocum' in both the Discantus and Tenor partbooks.
[119] Chybiński, 'Jan Fabrycy', no. 16, p. 669.
[120] This motet has been edited by M. Szczepańska, WDMP 9 (4th edn., Kraków, 1977).
[121] This falling motive is by no means original; it was a trait used by Josquin des Prez in the Credo of the 'Missa Mater Patris' (A. Smijers (ed.), *Werken von Josquin des Prés*, 12 (Amsterdam, 1950), p. 11, bars 60-3. As already discussed, an adapted version of this mass was copied into Kk I.1.
[122] The inventory of Jurek Jasivcicz of 1572 records several masses composed by Wacław. See Appendix XIII.
[123] Chybiński, 'Jan Fabrycy', p. 670: 'Chwilami nie można oprzeć się wrażeniu, że mamy przed sobą własną kompozycję Wacława z Szamotuł . . . Nazwisko kompozytora jednak jest w naszym rękopisie podane wyraźnie: 'Fabricij'. ('At moments, one cannot but be under the impression that we have in front of us an actual composition of Wacław of Szamotuły . . . [However] the name of the composer is clearly provided in the manuscript: 'Fabricij'.).
[124] As with the other manuscripts discussed above, this partbook was returned from the University Library, Poznań to the Cathedral Archive on Wawel Hill in the early 1980s.
[125] Surowiak, Introduction (1974), p. 20.
[126] The note 'Disca[n]t[us]', for instance, is written in red letters on fol. 8r.

[127] Davies, *God's playground*, p. 432.

[128] The inventory of 1572 mentions an eight-part mass by Scandello; see Appendix XIII.

[129] The paper itself dates from 1590, and the music may have been copied out at any time up until Job's death in 1601.

[130] Item 13.

[131] The paper type used by Job for the two Borek masses, as well as the Scandello mass, is identical.

[132] Kk I.5, fol. 25r.

[133] This set was also published by Simon Tini in Milan with the same title and in 1590. However, it is less likely that the Rorantists used this particular print for their copy, since the mass here is presented without a title.

[134] Some more information on the 1590 version can be found in H.J. Busch, *Giovanni Francesco Anerio and Francesco Soriano: Two Settings of Palestrina's Missa Papae Marcelli* (Recent Researches in the Music of the Baroque Era, 16; Madison, 1973).

[135] At this time, an entire musical ensemble arrived from Italy, and Klabon, along with the whole of the Polish chapel, was demoted. See A. Szweykowska, 'Przeobrażenia w kapeli królewskiej na przełomie XVI i XVII wieku', *Muzyka*, 13 (1968), no. 2, pp. 3-21.

[136] The note 'Quattuor' appears in front of the 'Crucifixus' and the 'Benedictus'.

[137] The paper used for the fifth and sixth layers dates from 1605 and 1599 respectively. See Surowiak, Introduction (1974), pp. 28-9.

[138] One additional composition was entered after the mass of the fifth layer, namely a short 'Veni Creator Spiritus' (fol. 44r).

[139] Surowiak, *Collections of Music Copied for Use at Wawel*. Vol. I, fasc. 4, card no. 93.

[140] The identification of the prints has been discussed at the beginning of this chapter which deals with the Rorantists' inventories.

[141] See n. 88, p. 123.

[142] Surzyński (ed.), *Monumenta*, p. iv, n. 14.

[143] One of the exceptions here being Certon's Requiem mass.

[144] Had any of the masses been used on a more permanent basis, one might expect them to have been copied into the respective manuscript.

[145] Chybiński, 'Zbiory', no. 2, pp. 5-7.

[146] This does not include the portions of Kk I.5 which were clearly not produced for this college.

Part II

The Musical Establishment at the Court of Zygmunt II August (1543-1572) and the Music of the Royal Chapel

IV

The Musical Establishment at the Court of Zygmunt II August

In his early years, Zygmunt August did not possess his own separate court, but was allocated a few personal servants from his father's court. When in the summer of 1543 he travelled from Kraków to Vilnius, he was given a small entourage, comprised mostly of his father's courtiers and servants and paid from the royal treasury, and this entourage included just one chaplain, three trumpeters, and six pipers. It was only in October 1544, when Zygmunt I transferred control of Lithuania to his son, that Zygmunt August gained his own treasury, comprising the income paid by his new Lithuanian subjects, and was therefore able to create a much larger court. Like his father, Zygmunt August surrounded himself with educated courtiers and artists, including some of the most notable figures of the Polish Renaissance: Jan Kochanowski, the father of Polish vernacular poetry, the writer Łukasz Górnicki,[1] the historian Marcin Kromer, and Bishop Stanisław Hozjusz, one of the presidents of the Council of Trent in 1563. He also created a new musical establishment, comprising a chapel of singers and several groups of instrumentalists. This chapter provides an account of this musical establishment, the initial formation of the royal chapel and the different instrumentalist groups, as well as their activities over the three decades of the court's existence. It will examine musical and non-musical factors which influenced the establishment, and will provide details of individuals' employment as well as payments made to them (taken from source material preserved in Main Archive of Old Acts in Warsaw (Wagad), henceforth RK),[2] since this information is relevant to their function and status within the establishment.

THE ROYAL CHAPEL

The chapel structure

Zygmunt August's chapel, as presented in the register of courtiers and servants (RK 110), was to comprise a prefect, a composer, a number of chaplains, including one clerk, some young singers, and four boys.

At the head of the chapel was the prefect ('Praefectus sacelli'). The prefect, in addition to holding an ecclesiastical post, was a practical and financial administrator and a musical director. He was the master of the boys, responsible for their singing tuition as well as their welfare. Judging from the register, the prefect was placed in charge of a household which accommodated himself, the composer, the boys, and possibly a cook. His own salary was set at 60 florens a year, with a clothing allowance of 10 florens for his surplice. He also received an annual sum of 44 florens, which constituted the salaries of the composer and cook, with a sum to cater for the needs of the boys. Finally, the prefect drew a weekly food allowance of 2 florens and 15 groszy for all those in his household.

The post of composer ('componista') in Zygmunt's chapel was not as prestigious as it was elsewhere in Europe. The terms of employment show him to be subservient to the prefect, from whom he also received his modest salary of 20 florens per annum.[3] In addition to his responsibility for providing music for chapel use, he was also expected to assist with the boys' singing tuition ('. . . Quos [i.e. the boys] componista, et ipse [i.e. the prefect] docebunt canere').[4]

The main body of the royal chapel was made up of chaplains ('sacellani') and a clerk ('clericus'). The register does not stipulate the actual number of chaplains to be employed, providing only the details of their individual remuneration. Each was to receive an annual salary of 20 florens, a clothing allowance of 8 ells of purple cloth, and a weekly food allowance of one floren.[5] The post of clerk was to be given to one of the chaplains, and for this additional function he received an extra 8 florens per annum and a supplementary measure of cloth (7 ells) for a cloak.[6] Although the clerk's duties are not described in the register, he was no doubt assigned the clerical duties linked with the functioning of the chapel. Payments made to the clerk indicate that he was responsible for the liturgical books,[7] the chapel fabric,[8] and especially candles used for services and ceremonies.[9] The clerk also acted as a financial intermediary between the treasury and the other members of the chapel.[10]

Provisions were also made for junior members of the chapel. There were to be a number of young singers ('adolescentes cantores'),[11] and as with the chaplains, the register does not stipulate their number. Each young singer was to be given clothing and a food allowance similar to that of a chaplain, and received an annual stipend of only 12 florens. With these were four boys ('pueri cantores'), placed in the care of the prefect.[12] The boys received no salary as such, though, as mentioned above, money was set aside for their general upkeep. In particular, the register mentions that they were to be provided with clothes and shoes when necessary.[13] Finally, the household cook was also responsible for cleaning and repairing their clothes.[14]

The court organist should also be mentioned here in spite of the fact that the sources are unclear as to his precise orientation within the musical establishment. The organist's terms of employment, although entered amongst the instrumentalists in the register, resemble those given to members of the chapel in both salary and, perhaps more significantly, in the allotment of distinctive purple cloth.[15] It is therefore probable that his duties were partly if not wholly linked with the royal chapel.

The formation of the chapel in Vilnius, 1544-1547

The actual formation of the chapel and its early development can be traced with some degree of precision through the payment records, and a certain amount of background information can be given on a few of the key members. Zygmunt August established an initial chapel sub-unit on 2 February 1544 whilst in Olita (a town not far from Vilnius),[16] comprising the prefect, presumably with the boys, and the composer.

The post of prefect was given to Jan Wierzbkowski, the only member of the new chapel who was already in Zygmunt August's service. Wierzbkowski had previously served at the cathedral in Kraków as a vicar from 1528 at the latest,[17] and from 1537 as a prebendary in the chapel of the Holy Trinity and a sub-dean of the cathedral.[18] On 29 April 1540 the cathedral records refer to him as 'Sacrae M[aiesta]tis Regie Capelanus',[19] a title which would not be inappropriate for a prebendary of the Holy Trinity chapel. In 1543 Wierzbkowski entered the service of the Zygmunt August as a chaplain, with an annual salary of 20 florens and a clothing allowance (8 ells per annum).[20] In August of that year he departed with Zygmunt's entourage for Vilnius, having resigned from his prebend at the cathedral in Kraków three weeks earlier (27 July).[21] Although it is not certain that Zygmunt August intended Wierzbkowski to be the prefect of his chapel choir from the outset, the facts do seem to point to this. First of all, he was the only member of the new chapel already in Zygmunt August's service. Also, his previous status at the cathedral made him a good candidate for such a position of authority, the five years in the chapel of the Holy Trinity gave him the necessary liturgical experience for the post, and finally, the proximity of his resignation from the prebend and his departure for Vilnius seems too close for coincidence.

Next to nothing is known about the first chapel composer Władysław. He was appointed on 2 February 1544 together with the prefect, and by the time of the first payment, covering the period from November of that year, he had already left the chapel, having served for less than ten months.[22] After this, the post lay vacant for two and a half years.

The register does not provide dates for the engagement of the other members of the chapel: the chaplains, the clerk, the young singers, and the organist. Given they are not on the list of servants receiving cloth at Easter 1544,[23] but do appear on the earliest extant quarterly payment (November 1544 to February 1545),[24] one can confine the time of their employment to between April and November 1544. It is, of course, probable that they were employed in

October, when Zygmunt gained his own treasury. Initially, there were five chaplains: Maciej Raszek, Jan Jaszcz, Szymon of Lelów, Jan of Gamrat, and Marcin of Iłża, who was also given the clerkship. It is clear, however, that Zygmunt August was aiming at a larger corpus of chaplains for his chapel. By the summer of 1545 a further four were employed: Jakub of Piątek (14 December 1544) and Daniel Mazowita (3 April 1545), both employed in Vilnius, Franciszek of Poznań, taken from the Rorantists' chapel on 2 July 1545 during Zygmunt August's visit to Kraków,[25] and Sebastian Strzeszkowski, whose name appears in the account-books in August 1545.[26]

With the first chaplains, two youths were recruited, Klemens of Sandomierz ('Klimek') and Jurek Jasivcicz ('Jurek'),[27] as well as the organist Sobek (short for Sebastian). It may be no coincidence that all three were given the same terms of employment and that they were referred to by a diminutive of their name. It is therefore likely that Sobek was also quite young, if not still an adolescent. One further fact corroborates this hypothesis. In February 1545 Sobek's salary was increased from 12 to 20 florens,[28] and in May of that year, the two 'adolescentes cantores' received a similar rise,[29] giving all three terms of employment identical to the chaplains'.

One final appointment to the chapel was made on 6 May 1547, namely that of the composer Wacław of Szamotuły. Wacław's terms of employment differed from those given to the previous composer Władysław; also, his name and the details of his contract were not entered underneath those of the original 'componista' in the register, but onto a fresh page in the register after the chaplains and young singers. It would appear that he was not part of the prefect's household; rather, he was to be treated more like one of the chaplains.[30] He was given an annual salary of 30 florens a year (which he received directly from the treasury and not from the prefect), together with an allowance for food and clothing similar to that of a chaplain. Not only was this a substantial improvement on the circumstances of his predecessor, but it also set him above the other chaplains, second only to the prefect.

By the summer of 1547 the formation of Zygmunt August's chapel appears to have been complete: prefect, the newly appointed composer, nine chaplains, two youths, and now six boys in the prefect's care.

Brief mention should be made of the court of Zygmunt August's first wife, Elizabeth Habsburg, if only for later comparison. Elizabeth had two chaplains in her service: Adam and Paulus, both employed on 3 October 1544,[31] and from the beginning of 1545 a clerk called Mathias.[32] These three do not appear to have been linked with the royal chapel. Their terms of employment were inferior, and their names and terms were not entered in the register of courtiers and servants, but instead were inserted into a volume of payments for the year 1543-4.[33] Furthermore, they were not re-employed by Zygmunt August after the death of Elizabeth on 15 June 1545, but were paid their due wages and dismissed on 28 August, four days after the queen's funeral.[34]

The transfer of the court to Kraków and the early years there (1548-1554)

The initial period of formation was followed by three years of disruption, caused by the death of King Zygmunt I Stary, and more specifically, the drawn-out and fragmented transfer of Zygmunt August's court from Vilnius to Kraków during 1548 and 1549. It should be mentioned that the documentation for this period is incomplete, and the precise movement of individuals is at times difficult to ascertain.

When Zygmunt August travelled to Kraków in May 1548 to assume the Polish throne, he took with him only a few of his chaplains, possibly just two. The main part of the chapel remained in Vilnius. Four of its members were allocated to the recently formed court of Zygmunt's second wife, Barbara Radziwiłł: Szymon of Lelów, Jakub of Piątek, Mazowita, and finally Jasivcicz, who was also appointed clerk to her court.[35] In Kraków, Zygmunt August paid his father's courtiers and servants (24 June) and the court was dissolved.[36] Of the late king's five chaplains, only the clerk, Maciej of Poznań, was re-employed by Zygmunt August, retaining his clerkship.[37] A month later, one further chaplain was employed, Stanisław of Szamotuły (19 July).[38] By the time of Zygmunt August's first session of Parliament as king in Piotrków (December 1548-February 1549), several more chaplains arrived from Vilnius, taking their number to nine.[39] The next portion of the chapel, the four chaplains allocated to Barbara, appeared in Kraków in March 1549, shortly after her arrival in the capital.[40] This left just the prefect (Wierzbkowski) and two chaplains in Vilnius. Only the first of these journeyed to Kraków, at the beginning of September.[41] Wierzbkowski remained in Kraków for just two months, and returned to Vilnius on 10 November.[42] On his departure, he was given the sum of 30 florens 'de gratia M[aiestatis] R[egie]'. This payment refers to him not as chapel prefect, but as the king's chaplain and canon of Vilnius - 'D. Ioanni Vierzbkowski Capelano M. R. Canonico Vilnensis' - suggesting that he had been relieved of his function as master of the chapel.

There is finally the question of the boys. They are last mentioned at Easter 1548 when the whole choir was still in Vilnius.[43] It is possible, though improbable, that they came with Wierzbkowski in September 1549; during his short stay, he received the full weekly food allowance for the whole household, including a sum for the boys. Even if this had been the case, there is no evidence to suggest there were any boys in the chapel following Wierzbkowski's departure in November. They would have been placed in the care of another member of the chapel choir and an appropriate note recorded into the register. No such entry was made and no subsequent payments can be found for the upkeep of the boys.

During the first years in Kraków, the royal couple shared the chapel's resources - composer, twelve chaplains, and one youth.[44] All the chaplains were primarily employed by the king, though the four who had come with Barbara's entourage in 1549 remained attached to her court and a note to this effect was entered next to their names in the register: 'Apud M. Reginalem'.[45] The arrangement was a practical one: when the king travelled alone, his chaplains accompanied him, while those allocated to the queen remained with her in Kraków. Following Barbara's coronation on 7 December 1550, the queen gained a new chaplain, Benedykt of Stryków (2 February 1551), and at about the same time Klemens of Sandomierz (Klimek), previously a young singer ('adolescentem cantorem'), was also assigned to her court as a chaplain.[46] On the death of Barbara on 8 May 1551, all her chaplains assumed their former membership of the king's court.[47] Thus by the summer of 1551, Zygmunt August's chapel bore little resemblance in form or size to the model established in Vilnius less than a decade earlier: it had developed into a single body of fifteen chaplains, including the former youths, the composer Wacław of Szamotuły, and the three clerks. There was no prefect and no boys.

A turning-point for the chapel came in 1552. The recent session of Parliament in Piotrków had discussed and approved the proposed marriage between Zygmunt August and Catherine Habsburg. Perhaps the forthcoming arrival of a new bride and the plans for the wedding celebrations rekindled the king's interest in his chapel after a period of apparent neglect. The recruiting began there and then, with the employment of a second composer Johannes (also called Josquin) Baston on 8 March 1552.[48] Very little biographical information exists on Baston. He was, according to the register, a Netherlander ('Flander'), and may have spent some time at the court in Vienna before his arrival in Poland.[49] Furthermore, it is uncertain whether Baston came on Zygmunt August's invitation or was a passing visitor to Poland, though his first payment includes a travelling allowance, ('. . . pro expensis per eum in itinere fac . . .'),[50] which would have been in order had he been invited. Baston's appointment was extraordinary since the chapel's original constitution made no provisions for a second composer. He was given a very high income of 12 golden florens per month (equivalent to about 240 Polish florens a year), plus an additional weekly food allowance of 15 groszy for his apprentice, Bernard Raizaber.[51] Excluding Raizaber's allowance, this gave Baston about three times the total income of Wacław of Szamotuły, previously the best-paid member of the chapel. The difference in the two composers' pay did not go unnoticed for long. Less than two months later, the day before departing for the north on his tour of Royal Prussia (1 May 1553),[52] the king raised Wacław's salary from 30 to 50 florens and granted him an additional measure of damask for a cloak.[53]

The other new appointments included two new chaplains, Bartłomiej of Wyszogród (16 April in Piotrków) and Stanisław Zagorski (5 June in Margenberg, now Malbork). The actual number of chaplains rose only by one to fifteen, due to the death of Daniel Mazowita.[54] Two young singers were also recruited in line with the original foundation: Wojciech Odoliński (27 December 1551 in Vilnius), just prior to Zygmunt August's departure for Piotrków, and

Stephanus Lesser (19 June 1552). Lesser is described in the register as coming from Styria ('Stiirus'),[55] at that time part of the Austrian Empire of the Habsburgs.

The absence of the boys since the establishment of the royal court in Kraków was rectified on 8 June 1552 with the recruitment of three boys during the king's visit to Toruń. However, the original provisions for the boys - which depended on the presence of a prefect and cook/house servant - were no longer suitable and more appropriate terms were devised and entered into the register.[56] Although no new master of the boys was formally appointed, the three were placed in the care of the clerk Jurek Jasivcicz ('Hi commissi sunt Georgio clerica').[57] For the moment, Jasivcicz was responsible only for the material needs of the boys, for which he did not receive an additional salary. Each boy was now allocated the sum of 20 groszy per week for food and 4 groszy per month for his shoes, as well as clothes 'whenever necessary' ('vestium pro libitum M R'). A small sum of money was also given every month to a cleaner for the washing and maintenance of their clothes (6 and 8 groszy respectively). As for the boys' music tuition, this was probably carried out by Wacław of Szamotuły, in accordance with the original duties of the composer.

Finally, another organist, Marcin of Jędrzejów (Andreopolitanus), was employed on 18 April 1552. Like the first organist Sobek, Marcin was not technically a member of the chapel, but his duties were clearly linked with it. The king intended Marcin to be the resident organist in Kraków and this is quite clearly stated in his terms of employment in the register. He was, however, expected to travel with the royal entourage at the king's request: 'Quamuis Cracć manere debet tamé qńdocumque per M. R. vocatus fuerit debet venire in expeń et vectore Regio. quam vero ex necessitate M. R. illum in Curia habere voluerit obligatus erit manere'.[58]

With the chapel now reformed, Zygmunt August further enlarged it, albeit only temporarily, for the festivities linked with the royal wedding and Catherine's coronation as Queen of Poland on 29 and 30 July 1553 respectively. The number of boys rose from four at the beginning of the year to eight on 28 April.[59] A sixteenth chaplain, Marcin of Drohiczyn, was employed (24 April), and even Jan Wierzbkowski, the former prefect of the chapel, was present at these royal celebrations.[60] According to Stanisław Orzechowski's published description of the marriage, it was Wierzbkowski who lead the choir in the singing.[61]

Shortly after the celebrations and before the departure of the king from Kraków to Knyszyn in September, the chapel was partially streamlined. The first to be dismissed was Johannes Baston on 6 September, after only eighteen months in the king's employ.[62] The number of boys was reduced by three ('16 Sept. . . . Georgio clericae fl 1 et pueris 5 quia 3 dimissi . . .'),[63] and stabilized at five thereafter. Although no chaplains were dismissed at this stage,[64] the king did not replace departing members for the next three years, and by 1556, their number had fallen from sixteen to thirteen. One possible reason for these reductions can be deduced from a document of 1553 (RK 319, fol. 244r), which describes the growth in the size of Zygmunt August's court since the death of his father, including the increase of chaplains and instrumentalists, and how this expansion was straining the resources of the royal treasury. It is therefore feasible that the reductions were made for financial reasons and not by choice. Indeed, it may have been no coincidence that the highest-paid member of the chapel, Johannes Baston, was the first to be dismissed.

As with the late queen, Zygmunt August now allocated some of the chaplains to Catherine's court: the clerk Jurek Jasivcicz, Ambroży of Bełdrzychów, Stanisław Zagorski, and the newly appointed chaplain, Adam of Bełżyce (22 August). By virtue of Jasivcicz being allocated here, the boys too were deemed members of the queen's court.[65] However, this arrangement did not last for very long. The payments distinguish between the king's and queen's chaplains only until Easter of 1554,[66] after which all are referred to only as the king's chaplains. Moreover, no specific annotations denoting the division were entered into the register as had happened before, underlining the brevity of the arrangement. Catherine did have some of her own chaplains, including Krzysztof Leopolita and Antonio ('verbi Dei ministro M Rlis'),[67] but their names were not entered into the register, nor were they mentioned in connection with the royal chapel in any of the payments.

A decade of decline, 1554-1564

Having reached its zenith by the year 1553, the chapel entered a period of decline during the years 1554-64. The late 1550s and early 1560s were difficult years for Zygmunt August. His marriage to Catherine Habsburg had failed, neither annulment nor divorce was possible, and no heir to the Polish throne had been produced. In his capacity as king, he divided his time between his residence in Vilnius and the various sessions of Parliament (eight in this ten-year period) held in Piotrków, Lublin, Warsaw, and Parczew. In 1557 he spent several months camped with his army on the Polish-Livonian border during the early stages of internal unrest in Livonia and and Muscovite hostilities towards that country. Following Livonia's submission to the Polish crown in 1561, Zygmunt August was faced with a war against the Muscovites which the Senate refused to finance. As a result, most aspects of life at the royal court were affected, not least the chapel. This is evident from the account-books, with servants paid at irregular intervals for long periods of service.[68] The source material for this period is not complete, but the extant payments do reveal that the royal chapel, or at least part of it, followed the king on most of his journeys.[69] Indeed, the new mobile character of the chapel may well have played a part in its decline. In 1559 - significantly the year in which the king left Kraków for the last time - the chapel lost five of its members, with only seven chaplains travelling from Kraków to

Vilnius in the king's entourage in May of that year.[70] In all, eleven chaplains left during the decade in question, five of whom we know remained in Kraków, supporting themselves on cathedral benefices previously granted them by the king,[71] and a further four died. Against this loss, only a handful of new chaplains were employed during this decade: Adam Żmigród (16 May 1556), a former member of the Rorantists' chapel and chaplain to Queen Bona until her departure from Poland;[72] Mikołaj Kochanowski (29 April 1558), a former member of the Rorantists' college and more recently chaplain to Catherine ('a Mté Reginali acceptus');[73] Albert Francuz ('Frenchman'), who served for only fourteen months (1 July 1560 - 9 September 1561) during the king's stay in Vilnius;[74] Marcin Brzykowski of Sieradz, recruited on 13 March 1563 during a session of Parliament in Piotrków,[75] and finally Marcin Leszczyński, whose name was not entered into the register, but who was paid regularly together with the other chaplains from 1558 to 1566.[76] As a result of this high turnover in chaplains, membership fell from fifteen in 1554 to just six in 1564.

The decreasing number of chaplains during the late 1550s and early 1560s was counter-balanced, if only partially, by an increase in the number of young singers. Following the loss of Stephanus Lesser in 1554 and Odoliński's promotion to a clerkship that same year, the number of young singers rose to four: Piotr of Bodzentyn, recruited 16 May 1556 (in Vilnius) from the disbanded court of the queen mother following her departure to Italy;[77] Szymek (the diminutive of Szymon), employed on 28 October 1558 in Warsaw; Tomek of Sącz on 24 April 1559 in Kraków,[78] and finally, on 1 August 1562, Teodolski, formerly one of the chapel choirboys.[79]

At this time, the chapel also lost its composer, Wacław of Szamotuły. References attest to his presence at court till June 1555, prior to his journey with three other chaplains to Warsaw, and his last salary payment covered the period of May to November 1555, which he received in 1557.[80] It is uncertain whether he was actually dismissed from the court, as there is no note to this effect in the register, though there is little doubt that he ceased to be a permanent member of the chapel after 1555. Wacław spent the last years of his life in Vilnius, in the service of Mikołaj Radziwiłł, Zygmunt August's brother-in-law.[81] There is a note in the register recording Wacław's death, suggesting that he continued to be in the service of the king, if only nominally and without a salary.

Also at this time, on 9 August 1554, Jurek Jasivcicz was appointed the music tutor to the boys of the chapel. This duty, according to the original foundation, was previously fulfilled by the composer, Wacław of Szamotuły. Since Wacław had been absent from court for part of this year,[82] the boys would have been without a music teacher, and this may have prompted the king to appoint a new tutor. According to the register, Jasivcicz was required 'to instruct the boys in the art of music' ('... quod pueros cantores M R exercet in arté Musices ...'),[83] a task which seemed somewhat broader than the original duty of the prefect and composer to teach the boys to sing ('quos componista et ipse [i.e.

prefect] docebunt canere').[84] For these new responsibilities, the king granted Jasivcicz a supplementary salary of 10 florens a year, a second floren per week for food,[85] and an additional measure of damask for a cloak which replaced his cotton surplice.[86] This last item is not unimportant; damask had previously been granted only to the former composer, Wacław. Jasivcicz's duties as a chapel clerk now become questionable, in spite of the fact that this label nearly always accompanies his name in the sources. Judging by his payments during the 1550s, he was concerned almost entirely with the boys and their upkeep. Those duties usually associated with the clerkship were now taken over by Albert Odoliński, previously one of the young singers.[87]

Following the departure of Wacław of Szamotuły in 1555, the post of composer lay vacant for several years until the appointment of Marcin of Lwów on 1 May 1560. However, Marcin's engagement was short and, judging by the sources, somewhat unusual. His name is entered into the register together with the other chaplains as 'Martinus compositor cantus', with no special terms of employment. There is only one payment (dated 29 September 1561) which refers to him, incorrectly naming him Albert,[88] and the 27 florens, 27 groszy and 6 denari which he received was for the fifteen months' service since his appointment. Marcin's yearly salary, therefore, was 20 florens, significantly less than that of Baston or Wacław of Szamotuły, but corresponds to the amount allocated to the composer in the original foundation of 1544. Due to the absence of his name on subsequent lists of payments, one can assume that Marcin left the chapel towards the end of 1561, possibly on the king's departure from Vilnius in November of that year.[89]

Three other composers are mentioned in the accounts. The first of these is Johannes Wircker, who 'had sent a manuscript to the king containing a Te Deum laudamus, and then had himself come to Piotrków to the King',[90] and for his labour, the king granted him 11 talars. The second composer, Johannes Neubaur 'Megalburgen', was likewise given 10 talars for the writing of some motets or chansons ('cantiones') on 20 July of the same year.[91] It would appear that both composers were looking for employment at the Polish court; there seems no other reason for them to have offered their own music to the king. However, neither was employed. The same may be true of the third composer, Johannes of Vienna, who in 5 July 1568 received a payment of 5 florens, at the request of Jurek Jasivcicz.[92]

The reorganization of the chapel and its final years, 1565-1574

By the end of 1564 the chapel had reached a critical state. The departure of Jakub of Piątek reduced the number of chaplains to a mere five, and one of the young singers, Theodolski, died in Warsaw.[93] Most of the boys had now reached adolescence,[94] and this further reduced the chapel's capacity for performing polyphonic music. What followed at the beginning of 1565 was essentially a structural reorganization of the chapel. No new chaplains were employed: on this occasion, all the changes and new recruiting took place in the other sections of the chapel: the young singers ('adolescentes cantores') and the boys.

The most important event was the formation of a new group of singers, the 'cantores', which was to replace the former 'adolescentes cantores'.[95] The new group embraced the two remaining 'adolescentes cantores', Tomek of Sącz and Szymek, the recently appointed Laurencius of Pabianice (recruited 18 November 1564), and three new singers: Bartłomiej Zinger, Leonard Jankowski (6 January 1565), and Marcin Wartecki (10 February).[96] Their terms of employment differed little from those of the former group: the salary of 20 florens and the weekly floren for food remained unchanged. However, the yearly allotment of cloth previously given to the 'adolescentes cantores' was substituted by a payment of 10 florens 'pro omni vestitu'.[97] Financing the new group did not pose a problem, since money was available due to the declining number of chaplains ('Stipendium vel ex beneficys bonorum spiritualium vel ex pensionis eorundem').[98] One other point deserves comment here. The entries of both Pabianice and Wartecki include a clause making them payees of Jasivcicz ('Stipendium . . . a domino Georgio Clerica'), suggesting that these two, if not all the new singers, were under Jasivcicz's direct supervision.[99]

On 6 January of this year, four of the choirboys (Krzysztof Klabon, Stefan Reder, Szymon Trubicki, and Bartłomiej Kicher), presumably on reaching adolescence, were assigned to the wind-players as junior members or apprentices ('assignatus ad numeri fistulatorum').[100] For the moment, they were not totally removed from the chapel but remained in the care of Jasivcicz, from whom they received their salary ('Stipendium ex pensionibus a domino Georgi Clerica').[101] In due course, all four left the chapel and became full members of the wind group ('translatus ad Fistulatores maiores'), with an appropriate salary.[102]

In their place, the king recruited a new group of boys for the chapel and made totally new provisions for them in order to remedy the inadequacies of the old arrangement.[103] The actual number of boys was set at six. Their weekly food allowance was raised from 20 to 24 groszy each. Specific quantities of cloth and individual items of clothing were allocated to them on a regular basis,[104] in contrast to the earlier more arbitrary method of granting clothing 'as needed'. An annual sum of 24 florens was also allocated for their general upkeep.

In the final six years of Zygmunt August's life, the chapel stabilized and even increased in size. Against the loss of only one chaplain and three singers ('cantores'), it acquired three chaplains, six singers, and three further boys, and by 1572 the chapel consisted of Jasivcicz (the master of the chapel), nine chaplains, nine singers, and nine boys.[105] During this period, the king was no less occupied by matters of state and continued to travel extensively. However, the chapel was not constantly at his side, as had previously been the case. Towards the end of 1567 Zygmunt August spent several months surveying his army in the district of

Mińsk,[106] and most of 1569 was taken up with the session of Parliament which led to the historic Polish-Lithuanian union. On both occasions, the chapel resided in Kraków and afterwards travelled to Knyszyn and Warsaw respectively, to rejoin the king. While in Kraków in 1569, Jasivcicz recruited several new members: one chaplain, Stanisław Robatyn (27 August), together with four singers, Nicolaus Klaus (9 January), Tomasz Szadek (25 June), Jakub Bronowski (13 August), and Jan Ramułt (27 August).[107] There is no information in the sources to show that on this occasion Jasivcicz acted on the king's instructions, although previous payments, which refer to him as acting on the king's request,[108] make this a strong possibility. During the last two years of Zygmunt August's life, which he spent in Warsaw, the chapel was again given leave to return to Kraków in autumn 1570, spring 1571, and in spring 1572.[109] This last leave coincided with the final departure of the king from Warsaw, due to an outbreak of the plague, and his death in Knyszyn on 7 July 1572.

The royal chapel was not disbanded after Zygmunt August's death: it still had to fulfil its final duty of attending the king's funeral, which took place on 11 February 1574. By this time, however, the composition of the chapel had changed quite substantially. Jurek Jasivcicz, master of the chapel, died on 31 June 1572;[110] the number of chaplains and singers had fallen to eight and six respectively;[111] and following the death of Jasivcicz, the boys disappear from the records altogether.[112] The king's funeral cortège which left Tykocin near Knyszyn on 10 September 1573 included only the eight chaplains.[113] For the actual burial service on Wawel Hill, the whole of the chapel was present: ten chaplains (the additional two being Piotr Bodzeniec and Sebastian Danikowski) and the six singers 'cantores'.[114]

Shortly afterwards, on 21 February 1574, Henry Valois of France was crowned king of Poland. During Henry's short reign of just 118 days, Zygmunt's chapel was neither disbanded nor re-employed by the new monarch. Instead, the chapel was maintained until at least May of that year, keeping its autonomy as the 'late king's chapel' ('Krola Je. M. zmarlego') and paid by the royal treasury.[115] In the interregnum between Henry's departure on 19 June 1574 and the coronation of Stefan Batory on 1 May 1576, the small corpus of account-books make no references to the chapel. One can therefore assume that the chapel was disbanded in the summer of 1574 or soon after. As for the musical establishment created by King Stefan Batory, his chapel included three of the young singers previously in Zygmunt August's chapel: Krzysztof Klabon, now the choirmaster, Jan Skiczki, and Jan Ramułt.[116]

THE GROUPS OF INSTRUMENTALISTS

The instrumentalists at the court of Zygmunt August are best considered as separate groups: the trumpeters and drummers, the wind-players, two separate and independent troupes of instrumentalists, and finally the soloists. Presenting a clear picture of these groups is not easy due to the nature of the sources. The nomenclature used in the records is at times confusing and inconsistent. Furthermore, the payments often classify individuals according to their terms of employment regardless of their musical specialization.

Trumpeters and drummers

Throughout Europe, trumpeters were employed by monarchs, dukes, and wealthy magnates to fulfil festive and annunciatory functions, both outdoors and in. To a certain extent, the size of the group reflected the greatness and importance of the employer. This was certainly true of Zygmunt August, who throughout his public life, first as crown prince, then Grand Duke of Lithuania, later King of Poland, and finally King of the Polish-Lithuanian commonwealth, employed an increasing number of trumpeters. Though the activities of the trumpeters may have been musically limited, they themselves were musically literate: they possessed partbooks and presumably played from them.

On his departure from Kraków in 1543, Zygmunt August had only three trumpeters in his entourage: Maciej Ciemiorka, Jenczy, and Irzyk. All three were previously members of his father's court. The terms offered to these trumpeters comprised a yearly salary of 20 florens, an allotment of cloth ('Lundinen') for a uniform, and a weekly food allowance of 20 groszy. (Ciemiorka was not offered the salary on account of the life pension worth 40 florens per annum granted by Zygmunt I, he nevertheless received the same yearly cloth and weekly food allowance.) For the first year in Vilnius, the prince had to be content with this small number of trumpeters, utilizing the wind-players to assist them when necessary, particularly during meals and banquets.[117] On special occasions, Zygmunt August hired additional trumpeters, although this occurred infrequently.[118]

Soon after gaining his own treasury, Zygmunt August set about establishing a self-sufficient group of trumpeters. On 10 March 1545, and not insignificantly a few days after the death of Jenczy, Zygmunt August sent Ciemiorka to Silesia and Kraków to recruit a number of instrumentalists, including four trumpeters.[119] These four, together with the existing two, would have given Zygmunt August a troupe of six players. Ciemiorka's assignment was only partly successful, since only two trumpeters were engaged: Joachim Spangel (28 March) and Tomek Krakowczyk ('of Kraków') (25 April). There is evidence to suggest that Zygmunt August's drive for a complete troupe was not to be made at the expense of quality. On one occasion in December 1545, he dismissed a prospective candidate on the grounds of incompetence: 'Casparo Tubicinatori ... Quia vero non erat in hac arte peritus dimissione ...'.[120] It may have been for a similar reason that one of the new recruits, Spangel, was also dismissed after only a few months' service.[121] The required number of six trumpeters was reached, but only two years later, with the employment of Stanisław Doidzwon (19 July 1546),[122] Hanzel Ibrol (10 December 1546), previously in the service of the bishop of Wrocław,[123] and Stefan Ząbek (18 October 1547), a civic trumpeter in Vilnius.[124]

Two apprentices ('socii tubicinatores', or 'adolescentes tubicinatores') were assigned to the trumpeters: Stanisław Krasowski (a trumpeter), and Stanisław Kot (a drummer). These appear on the account-books from January 1545:[125] they were not given a stipend, but did receive a modest food allowance.[126] In the spring of 1545 they were joined by a second drummer, Andrzej Dusza, possibly recruited by Ciemiorka from Zygmunt Stary's court.[127] These apprentices were assigned to Ciemiorka: he was responsible for their daily needs as well as teaching the two Stanisławs in their respective instruments, and was occasionally paid for his trouble.[128] Only on 28 July 1546 did the king decide to give Ciemiorka a regular payment of 20 florens per year, granting him a further 10 groszy to his weekly allowance for the boys' food.[129]

As with the chapel, the drawn-out process of moving the court to Kraków brought disruption to the group of trumpeters. On his journey to Kraków for the funeral of his father in May 1548, Zygmunt August took with him Ciemiorka and Stanisław Doidzwon, as well as all three apprentices. These also travelled with the king to Piotrków for the session of Parliament in October of that year. Here Doidzwon died towards the end of 1548,[130] and Stanisław Krasowski was promoted to full trumpeter (10 November 1548).[131] The other four trumpeters who had remained in Vilnius together with Barbara - Irzyk, Tomek Krakowczyk, Hanzel Ibrol, and Stefan Ząbek - subsequently arrived in Kraków in February 1549, presumably in her entourage.[132]

Following the dissolution of his father's court, Zygmunt August re-employed four of his trumpeters on 4 June 1548: Jenik Czech, Paweł Lancz, Georgius Chromi, and Stanisław Racławski.[133] The last was initially employed as a timpanist, but a month after the death of Chromi on 11 January 1549, he too became a trumpeter (10 February). This wave of recruiting ended on 27 April 1550, with the employment of Paweł Josko,[134] giving the king a troupe of ten trumpeters. Zygmunt August aimed at maintaining this number of trumpeters over the next decade, 1550-61, although their actual number oscillated between eight and ten. The main problem seems to have been the relatively high death-rate (five between 1553 and 1560) and the difficulty in finding appropriate replacements.

During the 1560s the ranks of the trumpeters were further expanded. The king, boosted by the submission of Livonia to the Polish crown in 1561, began recruiting more new players. Among those recruited were Maciej Lubelczyk, Wojciech Żelazowski, and Jan Goniwiecha, all employed in Lublin on 16 April 1564 during a session of Parliament,[135] Andrzej Kołakowski and Błażej Kościelski on 19 June 1567 and 2 July 1568 in Grodno,[136] and Mikołaj Sokół, employed on 2 July 1569. Sokół was not employed directly by the king, but was enlisted in Kraków, probably by Jurek Jasivcicz, who at that time and place was recruiting singers for the royal chapel.[137] By 1569, the year of the Polish-Lithuanian Union, Zygmunt August had sixteen trumpeters in his employ. Following this peak, the number of trumpeters declined slightly to fourteen towards the end of the king's reign, and in 1572 a further five players died, possibly of the plague.

Closely associated with the trumpeters were the drummers. The two youths recruited in 1545, Stanisław Kot and Andrzej Dusza, were promoted in May 1549 and given a modest salary of 12 florens and a weekly food allowance of 15 groszy. Two years later, this was improved to 20 florens and 20 groszy respectively, placing the drummers on equal terms with the trumpeters. Both drummers served until the late 1550s. In 1558, Dusza joined the ranks of the trumpeters, and his place was taken by a new drummer, Stefan Pieniajecz.[138] A year later Kot died, and he was replaced at the beginning of 1560 by Maciej Tudesco. It would seem that both of these new drummers were apprentices, since they were originally granted a salary of 12 florens (11 February 1560), comparable to the original youths, and only several years later were their terms improved to match those of the trumpeters (4 February 1567).[139] With the number of trumpeters in the king's employ gradually rising in the mid-1560s, the present two drummers may have been insufficient, and on 30 August 1565 a third, Maciej Janowicz, was recruited. Zygmunt August's court included one further timpanist, Johannes Korybut (engaged 6 July 1548, died 7 April 1554). He was employed for the specific purpose of playing the Turkish timpani ('Qui pro turcica debet servare laicellum perfectum').[140] It is not known whether Korybut (occasionally referred to as 'Surmacz') played with the other drummers in conjunction with the trumpeters or with the wind-players.[141]

Although there seems not to have been a hierarchy within the ranks of this group of instrumentalists, two were given preferential terms of employment, indicating their distinction. Maciej Ciemiorka, possibly the head trumpeter, was the most senior player and longest-serving trumpeter employed at Zygmunt August's court. He had already been granted a life pension by Zygmunt I of 40 florens from the royal salt-mines ('ex zuppis') in the 1530s; thus he entered the service of Zygmunt August with an income double that of the others. In the early years in Vilnius he was charged with recruiting new instrumentalists. Ciemiorka was entrusted with the tuition of the apprentice trumpeter and drummers and was given an extra payment for this duty; he continued to receive this sum even after the apprentices were promoted and presumably no longer taught by him. Hanzel Ibrol, also a favoured trumpeter, was employed in 1548 on terms similar to the others. Shortly after the transfer of the royal court to Kraków, Ibrol was granted the salary of a wind-player ('sicut fistulatoribus'),[142] which was considerably better than that of the trumpeters. Ibrol had a young apprentice in his care, 'Joannes Ragoszka puer', albeit for only about two years (1550-52), and was responsible for his tuition.[143] Finally, as a mark of gratitude, the king granted him a life pension in 1559 worth 40 florens from the royal salt-mines.[144]

The wind-players: Fistulatores (Fistulatores Germani)

Generally speaking, wind-players provided entertainment in the royal chambers, especially dance music. Zygmunt August, according to contemporary accounts, was proficient in the art of dancing from an early age;[145] it is therefore not surprising that he invested funds in this section of his musical establishment throughout the period of the court's existence. He granted the wind-players with money for their music,[146] and provided them with new instruments on a number of occasions. From some of the references in the payments, we know that the group played on both reed instruments and flutes.[147]

On his departure from Kraków in 1543, Zygmunt August was allocated the relatively large number of six wind-players ('fistulatores') for his entourage: two from his father's court, Claus Brugner and Jurek Wilhelm, and four new players, Hanus Rheder, Hanus 'Tenorista' Wilhelm, Thomas Georg, and an unnamed sixth player. When in 1544 Zygmunt August established his new court in Vilnius, all but the last of these were formally employed. Each was given a salary of 40 florens and a fixed amount of various cloth for his garments. Their food allowance was set at 20 groszy per week, though they received an extra 10 groszy, since they were required to assist the trumpeters in providing music at the king's table.[148] It is not certain who the sixth player was, or why he was not employed with the other five. It may have been Silvestro, who appears sporadically on the royal payments, even in connection with the other *fistulatores*. A replacement for this sixth player was undoubtedly sought by Zygmunt August for his group. As already mentioned, Ciemiorka was sent by him to Silesia and Kraków in March 1545 in search of instrumentalists, which included one wind-player,[149] although on this count, Ciemiorka was not successful.

The wind-players had two boy apprentices, Mikołaj Gomółka and Andrzej Pieniążek, who appear on the records at the beginning of 1545. They were placed in the care of Claus ('duo pueri discipuli Claus') and were presumably taught by him.[150] As with the 'sociis Tubicinatores', they received no stipend, but just a food allowance of 15 groszy each per week.[151]

Following the death of Zygmunt I in May 1548, none of the wind-players accompanied Zygmunt August to Kraków. Instead, they remained in Vilnius with Barbara until the New Year and arrived in Kraków at the beginning of March 1549.[152] In the early years in Kraków, the group not only acquired a sixth player, Joachim Kepel (20 December 1549),[153] thus completing the originally planned troupe, but two further players. The first of these was Mikołaj Gomółka, who advanced from apprentice to what might best be described as an intermediate 'adolescent' stage on 22 August 1550, with a salary of 25 florens, before finally becoming a full player on 20 February 1555.[154] The second was Carolus, employed on 7 May 1556.[155] It is not known what became of the other apprentice, Andrzej Pieniążek; he is last mentioned in October 1549,[156] and presumably he left the court or was dismissed soon afterwards.

On 8 May 1560, Zygmunt August reorganized the group of wind-players, giving them totally new terms of employment.[157] The 'Fistulatores Germani', as they were now called in the register, consisted of six of the eight former 'Fistulatores': Brugner, Rheder, Hanus Wilhelm, Georg, Kepel and Carolus. Jurek Wilhelm had died a year earlier, and the eighth player, Mikołaj Gomółka, was not included in the new line-up. Given that the *fistulatores* played six-part music,[158] there may not have been any reason to have a seventh player; Gomółka nevertheless continued to be employed at the court on the terms previously granted him. The salaries of these 'German' players, which had become unequal in 1553 through the granting of life pensions to the five original wind-players, was now amended. Those with pensions still received their 40 florens 'ex zuppis'.[159] They were given a further sum of 56 florens from the treasury for clothing, stable costs, and other expenses, which had originally been given in kind. The sixth player, Carolus, was granted a salary of 96 florens from the treasury, thus equal to the income of the others. Claus - the leader of the group - nevertheless continued to receive an extra 50 florens per annum which the king had given him the previous year. The food allowance of all six was increased from one to two florens per week. Apart from the salaries, the king allocated a wagon with two horses to the group for the transportation of their instruments.

Five years later, on 6 January 1565, Zygmunt August assigned four of the choirboys, presumably on reaching adolescence, to the wind group as apprentices: 'translatus ex pueris ad numerum fistulatorum'.[160] Only one of these, Krzysztof Klabon, was given a salary of 56 florens plus a weekly food allowance of one floren. The other three - Stefan Rheder, Szymon Trubicki, and Bartłomiej Kicher - were given a food allowance similar to the new choirboys of the chapel (24 gr.). Furthermore, they remained in the care of Jasivcicz. Why had this development taken place? By 1564, Hanus Rheder and Thomas had died and only one new player was recruited, Laurentius Margoński (13 February 1564), thus the promotion of Klabon alone would have regained the required number of six players. As for the introduction of three further apprentices, two possible explanations can be offered. First, the king may have been concerned about the future of the wind group, and more specifically, some of the players were well on in years: Claus had been employed at the royal court since 1533 and Jurek Wilhelm since 1538. By introducing the boys now, the succession of players would be maintained and the future of a complete troupe assured. Secondly, it is possible that the king intended to expand this group of instrumentalists, and this did indeed happen. One by one the four were promoted to full wind-players ('ad fistulatores maiores') and were given the appropriate salary: Krzysztof Klabon on 4 February 1567, Stefan Rheder on 5 August 1570,[161] and both Szymon Trubicki and Bartłomiej Kicher in February 1572.[162] One further singer of the chapel, Szymek Muzyk, was moved to the wind-players on 5 August 1568. He did not undergo a period of tuition or apprenticeship as had the others, but became a full member immediately.[163] Thus by 1572, the year of Zygmunt August's death, the number of wind-players, taking into account Brugner's death in October 1571, had risen to nine.

The 'Musici Fistulatores' and the 'Musici Itali'

There were two additional troupes of instrumentalists who appeared at the royal court during the 1550s. The first of these, previously in the service of Bishop Maciejowski of Kraków, was active in the early 1550s. The second troupe came from Antwerp in Flanders, and was employed from 1556 to 1560/1. The two groups were undoubtedly literate musicians; this can be deduced from numerous references to both in the payments as 'Musici Itali', a title reserved for educated musicians (not necessarily Italian).[164] For the purpose of this study, the two groups will be referred to as 'Musici Fistulatores' and 'Musici Itali' respectively,[165] the collective names given to them in the register of courtiers and servants.

The 'Musici Fistulatores' were a troupe of five Italian musicians, Stephanus, Joannes ('Dziano') Bali, Theodoricus, Hugo, and Antonius Ruffo, formerly in the service of Samuel Maciejowski, Bishop of Kraków and Zygmunt August's vice-chancellor. Little is known of the court of Samuel Maciejowski, or how these Italians came to be in his employ. They were in the bishop's service by the mid-1540s, and were known to Zygmunt August, since they received money from the royal treasury, probably for performing before the king.[166] Furthermore, Theodoricus was sent to Italy at Zygmunt August's request in 1549, and with Stephanus to Flanders in the following year.[167]

When Bishop Maciejowski died on 20 October 1550, Zygmunt August employed all five musicians almost immediately (29 November 1550), giving them terms similar to the wind-players (Fistulatores).[168] The title given in the register, 'Musici Fistulatores', is probably the most appropriate: we know that Joannes Bali was an organist, and the other four were almost certainly wind-players.[169] Whether or not they played on other instruments cannot be determined from the sources, although this possibility should not be ruled out in view of the fact that they are also referred to as 'Musici'. Likewise, it is not possible to say with any certainty if these wind-players formed an independent musical unit at

Zygmunt's court, or if they performed with the other wind-players. Whatever their precise role at the court, their service as a group was short-lived. Stephanus and Theodoricus were paid their salaries in August 1552,[170] and do not subsequently appear on the account-books. Ruffo and Hugo left the court (or died) in August 1553 and Easter 1555 respectively,[171] leaving only the organist Joannes Bali in the king's employ.

The second group of instrumentalists who came to the court in 1556 comprised four musicians, Guido Hoberean, Arnoldus Veracter, Philipus Mansart and Paulus Baninch. The register of courtiers and servants, while collectively giving them the title 'Musici Itali', individually describes the first three as Flemish and the fourth, as a native of Antwerp.[172] The manuscript further indicates that the group entered Zygmunt August's employ on their departure from Antwerp: 'suscepti in servicium M.R. et inscripti iussu M sue a die 10 Novembris 1556 quo egressi ex Anthwerbia', suggesting that they had been invited to Poland by the king.

At the court, they were granted terms far superior to those of the other instrumentalists. Each received a salary of 150 talars (just over 160 Polish florens), which included their food allowance and clothing. Some of the payments refer to them as 'Cytaredis', thus they were string-players, and probably formed a separate musical ensemble. Their appearance at the Polish court was no doubt a notable addition to the already flourishing musical establishment. However, like the previous troupe, the activities of the 'Musici Itali' at the Polish court were short-lived. Baninch died on 29 January 1560, on 3 July Veracter drowned, and the other two were dismissed the following summer (7 August 1561).[173]

SOLOISTS

The last category of instrumentalists does not comprise an integral musical unit, but encompasses the soloists employed at the court. These include the string instrumentalists, Mikołaj Gomółka, and the organists. Like the wind-players, the soloists provided music for the various chambers of the king's residence. Nearly all these musicians were given terms of employment identical to the wind-players (at least initially) and more often than not, their entries in the register contain a note to this effect ('salarium et vestium ac diaria equalia sicut fistulatores habent').[174] Consequently, the account-books often list them under the term 'Fistulatores', in spite of the fact that all of them, save Gomółka, were not wind-players. After the disintegration of the Flemish group, the term 'Musici Itali' was adopted for the soloists, suggesting that they were all literate musicians.

String players

Against the large number of trumpeters and wind-players, Zygmunt August required the services of only a few solo string-players. The first of these soloists was a harp-player, Dominicus de Verona, recruited in Vilnius on 20 December 1545.[175] Dominicus served at the court for just four years, accompanying the king on most of his travels.[176] After the arrival of Bakfark in 1549, Dominicus remained at the court for only a few more months before being dismissed on 26 April 1550.

Bálint Bakfark[177] (1506/7-1576) was undoubtedly the most famous musician to be engaged at the Polish court. The Hungarian-born lute-player was educated in Buda, at the royal court of John Zapolya, Zygmunt August's brother-in-law. He had spent some time in the late 1540s in Paris prior to his appointment at the court in Kraków on 12 June 1549. Initially, Zygmunt August granted him the standard salary of the wind-players ('fistulatores'). However, following a leave of absence (1552-4), during which he travelled to Germany, France, and Italy, the king increased his income by 50 florens, and again by a further 60 florens in 1558.[178] Bakfark was well known and highly respected in Poland: his virtuosic lute-playing was recorded by several contemporary writers including Jan Kochanowski and Łukasz Górnicki. He was also an able composer, with several printed collections of lute music to his name. One of these, *Pannonni harmoniarum*, was published in 1565 by Ł. Andrysowic in Kraków and dedicated to his patron, King Zygmunt August. Ironically, in the year of this publication, Bakfark's fame and fortune in Poland came to an abrupt end: his house in Vilnius was plundered by soldiers, and he himself fled the country. The causes for these dramatic events are not known, although two possible reasons have been suggested by Polish musicologists. We know that Bakfark corresponded with Duke Albert Brandenburg of Prussia from about 1552, and that his letters to the Duke included information on the state of affairs of several European countries. It is possible that Bakfark was also passing confidential information on the events at the Polish court to the Duke, and this was discovered. Such collaboration between Bakfark and the Duke seems more probable in view of the fact that the latter had interceded on the former's behalf with Zygmunt August on a number of occasions, urging the king to improve his salary.[179] The second possibility is that the lutenist had become involved in the internal intrigues of the court and had gained the displeasure of the king.[180]

On 28 July 1553 a string-player was employed, the violinist Franciscus Italus 'Lyricen'.[181] His appearance at the court coincides with the arrival of Catherine Habsburg in Poland. It is tempting to suggest that Franciscus came in Catherine's entourage, possibly having been recruited during her time at the Gonzaga court in Mantua, although there is no archival evidence to substantiate this. his name was entered beneath those of the 'Musici Fistulatores', and he was given similar terms of employment. Franciscus served at the royal court for almost ten years, until the latter part of 1562,[182] after which his name disappears from the account-books. After a break of several years (1565-70), during which time no string-player was employed at the royal court, one final string soloist appeared, the harpist David König. His name was not entered into the register, but according to payment records, he was employed on 18 June 1569 and remained in the king's service until his death in December 1571.[183]

Mikołaj Gomółka

The discussion of Mikołaj Gomółka's presence amongst the soloists is hampered by the lack of detailed source information. As already mentioned above, he joined the royal court as a boy wind-player in 1545, became an apprentice from 1550, and was subsequently appointed a full player in 1555. He was not included in the new line-up of six wind-players in 1560; perhaps the king wanted to make more of Gomółka's talents as a solo performer than within a consort setting, although it is impossible to say exactly what sort of music he performed and on what instrument. Gomółka remained at the royal court for three more years before being dismissed on 19 August 1563, after which he returned to his home town of Sandomierz to pursue a career on the civic council. Today, Gomółka is remembered primarily for his *Melodiae na psałterz polski* of 1580, which comprises a polyphonic setting of all 150 psalms, translated into Polish by Jan Kochanowski.[184] Undoubtedly the time spent at the royal court, almost twenty years, provided him with a sound musical education and brought him into contact with a variety of music, performed there on a regular basis.

Organists and keyboard players

In all, four keyboard-players, principally organists, were employed at the royal court. Their appointments were staggered throughout the time of the court's existence, and each had his own individual career. Nevertheless, their activities did overlap for a six-year period between 1555 and 1561. The payments portray the organists essentially as instrumentalists, but, as argued earlier in this chapter, their activities were linked at least in part with the music of the royal chapel.

The first two organists, Sobek (employed 1545-65) and Marcin of Jędrzejów 'Andreopolitanus' (employed 1552-72) have already been mentioned in connection with the royal chapel. However, additional payments testify to their secular music-making. As early as May 1545, when Sobek was still the sole organist at the court, the king engaged an organ-builder called Józef from Kraków to repair 'a regal and some other instruments' ('Regalis Simphonilis M R et instrumenti Mtas').[185] Also, Marcin possessed his own regal,[186] and this instrument accompanied him when he travelled with the royal court.[187]

The appointment of the third organist, Joannes Bali, has also been discussed in the section on the 'Musici Fistulatores'. He was the longest-serving organist, active for more than twenty years from 1550 until 1572. He was also the best paid. Apart from his salary of 40 florens, the king granted him a pension 'ex zuppis' in 1554, worth 100 florens per year.[188]

The fourth organist, Pawlik, entered the royal court together with the 'Musici Fistulatores' in 1550 as an apprentice to Bali. His name was not initially entered into the register, although his presence can be confirmed by individual payments made to Bali intended for him.[189] Three years later, on 20 December 1553, Pawlik's name was inserted into the register; however he was still referred to as a boy in Bali's care: 'puer qui Apud Dziano est', and granted a weekly food allowance of 20 groszy.[190] Pawlik was promoted on 16 November 1555 and given the same terms of employment as the other 'Musici Fistulatores', remaining at the court until 1561. He was not only an organist, but also played another keyboard instrument. In 1555, he received money for some brass strings for an instrument, possibly a clavichord.[191]

THE MUSICAL ESTABLISHMENT: CONCLUSIONS

It is evident that Zygmunt August was a very musically inclined patron, and fostered the musical establishment as far as he could, or finances permitted. Whilst this chapter discussed only those singers and musicians permanently employed at the court, one should at least acknowledge the fact that others did receive money from the royal treasury, for enlarging the musical establishment on special occasions, or for performing before the king.

Looking first at Zygmunt August's chapel, in its initial form it comprised a prefect, a composer, nine chaplains, two young singers, and four to six choirboys. Such a chapel may not have been exceptional by European standards; by Polish standards, it was quite innovatory, not only in its overall size and inclusion of the younger members, but also for the presence of a composer. The chapel's fortunes fluctuated quite significantly, though the two periods of decline were followed by renewed interest of the monarch and structural reorganization within the chapel. The composer's post perhaps deserves further comment here. In the early years, Zygmunt August encouraged the composition of music in his chapel; this is clear from the service of Wacław of Szamotuły (1547-55), not to mention the appearance of a second composer, Johannes Baston, in the early 1550s. Following Wacław's departure from the court in 1555, the post lay vacant except for a short period of time in 1560-1. Whilst it is possible that the king had lost interest in musical production later in life, it seems more probable, in view of the small payments made to little-known foreign composers for their submitted works, that he could not secure a suitable composer to come and work at his court.

As for the instrumentalists, there seems to have been what might best be described as 'core' and 'occasional' groups. The first of these, the trumpeters and drummers, the wind-players 'Fistulatores Germani', and the organists, were permanent features of the court, constantly maintained and supported by the king. The second, including the 'Musici Fistulatores', the 'Musici Itali', and the other soloists, were employed on an occasional basis, depending on availability. Here, individuals were not replaced, and consequently their activities as groups were short-lived. The different nationality of the various instrumental groups seems to have been a feature of the musical establishment at the Polish court: the 'German' wind players, the Flemish and the Italian troupes of musicians.

As one might expect, the respective parts of the musical establishment developed quite separately over the period in question; nevertheless, some of the organizational changes affected more than one section. The most notable example is the transfer of four choirboys to the wind-players on reaching their adolescence in 1565. With this in mind, the youthful character of the establishment should also be mentioned. Many young singers and players were recruited, especially in the early years in Vilnius, and the instrumental groups had their pupils or apprentices. There may have been financial reasons for such an arrangement, also, competent musicians may not have been always easy to find. Whatever the case, the royal court undoubtedly offered the best musical training in Poland, and this approach did secure longer-term stability for the respective groups.

It is evident that non-musical factors played a significant role in shaping of the musical establishment. The increasing financial capacity of the king's treasury was reflected in general expansion of all sections, though at times this process was curtailed. Another important factor was the mobility of the king. The various journeys on the one hand caused the fragmentation of the musical establishment, but on the other resulted in the recruitment of a large number of new members. Many of the trumpeters, for instance, were employed during Zygmunt August's time in Lithuania, and a number of singers were enlisted into the chapel during the king's tour of Royal Prussia and Gdańsk in 1552. Other specific non-musical factors include the festivities linked with the wedding of Zygmunt August to Catherine Habsburg and her coronation in 1552-3, for which the chapel was re-formed and enlarged, as well as the historic Polish-Lithuanian Union of 1569, which saw a peak in the number of trumpeters.

Following the death and burial of Zygmunt August, the musical establishment was disbanded. Poland subsequently experienced two lengthy interregna and a four-month reign of French monarch who was little interested in preserving continuity at the royal court. Only after several years did the monarchy, under Stefan Batory, gain some stability. In the mean time, the musical establishment created by the last Jagiellonian, together with its traditions, faded away almost without a trace.

NOTES

[1] Ł. Górnicki was the author of *Dworzanin polski* (Kraków, 1566), the Polish version of B. Castiglione's *Il Cortegiano*.
[2] Individual volumes of payments are preserved in other libraries in Poland (Wrocław, Ossoliński Library (WRo) and Kraków, Czartoryski Library (Kc)).
[3] RK 110, fol. 875r.
[4] Ibid.
[5] Ibid., fol. 902r.
[6] Ibid., fol. 902r.
[7] RK 156, fol. 80r; RK 152, fol. 133r; RK 137, fol. 55r.
[8] RK 152, fol. 142r.
[9] Ibid., fol. 311v.
[10] RK 124a, fol. 41r; RK 145, fol. 39r; RK 159, fol. 42v; RK 162a, fol. 31r.
[11] RK 110, fol. 902r.
[12] Ibid., fol. 875r.
[13] Ibid: 'Pannú vero et pellicea pro vestita istoŕ pueroŕ dabit M. R. de grá et arbitrio suo singlis annis, ac pro Jopulis et caligis'.
[14] Ibid. The cook received an annual sum of 24 florens for her services.
[15] Ibid., fol. 939r.
[16] Their terms of employment were initially recorded in the current book of payments (RK 114) before later being duplicated in the register.
[17] Kku Offic. Crac. 47, p. 43.
[18] Kk Capit. Crac. 3, fol. 184r.
[19] Kku Episc. Crac. 18, fol. 311r.
[20] Initially he served as chaplain; RK 114, fols. 54r, 55r.
[21] Kku Episc. Crac. 20, fol. 253r.
[22] RK 124a, fol. 91r. The first sum given to the prefect excluded the wage of the composer: 'Domino Wierzbkowski defalcatis flor. 5 pro componista . . .'.
[23] RK 114, fol. 93r.
[24] RK 124a, fol. 91r.
[25] RK 110, fol. 903r.
[26] RK 124a, fol. 115r.
[27] Jasivcicz is mistakenly known as Jasińczyc in the musicological literature.
[28] RK 110, fol. 939r.
[29] Surprisingly, the *cantores* do not have an appropriate note made in the register, although their upgraded salaries are consistently paid out from May 1545 (RK 124a, fol. 116r).
[30] RK 110, fol. 904v.
[31] RK 114, fols. 83r-84r.

[32] RK 124a, fol. 97v.
[33] RK 114, fols. 83r-84r.
[34] RK 120, fol. 77v: 'Item personis 3 p expedicione. a Curia post morté olí Mtis Rlis eod anno p ulńs 16 videlicet ulńs 48'.
[35] A payment for prefect, composer, and the youth (RK 137, fol. 209v), and allotment of cloth for funeral attire made to the three chaplains: Szymon of Lelów, Daniel Mazowita, Jakub of Piątek and Jurek Jasivcicz cleric (RK 140, fol. 279a) were both made in Vilnius after the departure of Zygmunt August.
[36] RK 149a, fols. 95v-97r contain the appropriate payments made to the chaplains and instrumentalists.
[37] RK 110, fol. 903r. It should be said, however, that three of the others had been promised vicarial posts by Zygmunt I, and may not have sought re-employment: RK 149a, fol. 95v: Kasper in Soliecz, Walentyn Submontanus in Radoszicze, and Walentyn of Sieradz in Kuczanów. Nothing is known of the fate of the last chaplain, Adam of Środa.
[38] RK 110, fol. 903r.
[39] RK152, fol. 256r. This included the composer Wacław of Szamotuły.
[40] RK 150, fol. 89v.
[41] RK 150, fol. 253v. Wierzbkowski received his usual food allowance of 1 floren and 25 groszy from 7 September.
[42] This is the date given on the payment in RK 151, fol. 137v, although according to RK 150, fol. 300v, he received his weekly food allowance until 23 November.
[43] RK 140, fol. 226v.
[44] Ambroży of Bełdrzychów was employed on 8 April 1549, although probably to replace Jan of Gamrat, who does not appear regularly on the payments. Jan is on the list of 30 April 1549 (RK 145, fol. 101v), but is absent from that of 12 May (RK 159, fol. 143r). A week later one of the clerks, Marcin was given a payment of 4 florens for him, possibly for medicine (RK 145, fol. 39r), and on 3 June Franciszek of Poznań was given 3 florens for the cost of his burial (RK 145, fol. 53r).
[45] RK 110, fol. 903r.
[46] Ibid., fol. 903v.
[47] Maciej Raszek, who died in April or May of that year, was replaced by a new chaplain, Andrzej of Opoczno, on 23 May, just a day before the departure of the funeral cortege from Kraków to Vilnius for the burial of Barbara.
[48] RK 110, fol. 906v.
[49] A. Dunning, 'Baston', *New Grove Dictionary of Music and Musicians*, ed. S. Sadie (London, 1980), ii, p. 282.
[50] RK 164, fol. 59v, this payment was made in the second half of October 1552.

51 Ibid.
52 The details of Zygmunt August's travels is provided in Gąsiorowski, 'Itineraria'.
53 RK 110, fol. 904v.
54 The sources do not provide the precise date of his death. The register notes only that he died in Vilnius 'mortus Wilne' (RK 110, fol. 903r), and the last recorded payment made to him was the quarterly payment of February 1552, which is the only extant quarterly payment from that year (RK 164, fol. 142v).
55 RK 110, fol. 904r.
56 Ibid.
57 Ibid.
58 Ibid., fol. 948v.
59 RK 170, fol. 42v '... Georgio clerico M. R. Clientulis musicis 4 ... et alys 4 pueris noviter 28 Aprilis susceptis ...'.
60 Ibid., fol. 107r. Wierzbkowski's name appears on the list of chaplains who received a supplementary allotment of clothing (perhaps for the wedding ceremonies) sometime during the spring or summer of that year.
61 S. Orzechowski, *Panegyricus Nuptiarum Sigismundi Augusti Poloniæ Priore correctior & longe locupletior* (Łazarz Andrysowicz, Kraków 1553), fol. Fij v: 'Et cum illi sacramentum Christi Dei noster Archiepiscopus communicasset, illud sacrum nuptiale fuit peractú. quod Ioanne Virbkouio chori regij magistro, tanto uocum concentu a symphoniacis modulatum fuit, ut non Iosquini modo Belgici: neque Adriani cantores Gallici, sed Musæ ipsæ nouem suo cum Apolline ad cantum illorum siluissent oblitæ cytharæ plectrique. Fecerat autem modos Venceslaus Samotulinus regius Musicus. cui ad summam artis præstantiam nihil præter uicem defuit.'
62 RK 170, fol. 142r.
63 RK 169, fol. 203r.
64 One change did take place, namely the replacement of Szymon of Lelów by Adam of Bełżyce on 22 August 1553. Szymon's name appears in the quarterly payment of 10 August 1553 (RK 171, fol. 126r), but not on the next, dated 7 February 1554, which covers two quarters' wages (RK 173, fol. 43r), and since no intermediate payment was made to him, one can assume that he left the chapel soon after being paid in August. Szymon was elected to a prebend in the chapel of the Holy Trinity 'Sancte Trinitatis' in the cathedral on Wawel Hill on 4 June 1557 (Kk, AA 5, fol. 268v) and retained the post until his death early in 1565. During this period of time at the cathedral, he received some money from the royal treasury, in spite of not being a member of the chapel (RK 161, fol. 37v, dated 5 May 1559).
65 RK 173, fol. 66r, 70r.
66 Ibid., fol. 56r, 'Panni ... R et Rlis pro Pasche die 25 Marcii 1554'.

[67] Ibid., fol. 52r.
[68] This was the case in 1559 and 1561 (RK 183, fols. 42r-45r).
[69] For short visits, the king would take only some chaplains with him, the rest remaining at the royal residence of the previous location.
[70] Wagad V, vol. 3, fol. 79r: Jurek Clerika Kro. ieo. m. wzialem na 7 Capellanow ktorich kro ieo m z obozem do wilna szlie . . . Datum Cracouiae 16 May Anno 1559'.
[71] Sebastian Strzeszkowski - altar of St Zygmunt, second ministry; Szymon of Lelów - prebend in the chapel of the Holy Trinity; Franciszek of Poznań - altar of Sts Zygmunt and Erasmus, martyrs, third ministry; Andrzej of Opoczno - prebend in the chapel of St Michael; Stanisław of Szamotuły - prebend in the chapel of St Michael, later prefect of that chapel.
[72] RK 110, fol. 903v.
[73] Ibid., fol. 904v.
[74] RK 183, fol. 42v.
[75] RK 110, fol. 904v.
[76] RK 182, fol. 61r, RK 213, fol. 34r.
[77] RK 110, fol. 903v: 'Suscepti a M Rli seniori 16 may 1556 Vilne'.
[78] Ibid.
[79] Ibid. 'Translatus ex pueris cantoŕ inter adolescentes . . .'.
[80] RK 180, fol. 18v.
[81] Z. and A. Szweykowscy, 'Wacław z Szamotuł - renesansowy muzyk i poeta. Szkic biograficzny', *Muzyka*, 9 (1964), no.1, p. 7.
[82] This can be deduced by his absence from the interim quarterly payments.
[83] RK 110, fol. 905r.
[84] Ibid., fol. 875r.
[85] This was actually granted later, i.e. 29 October 1554 (RK 110, fol. 904r).
[86] RK 110, fol. 904v.
[87] RK 173, fol. 51v. The first payment which refers to Odoliński as clerk post-dates 25 March 1554. The second, RK 173, fol. 51v, not dated, is a payment of 12 florens for the cleaning of ecclesiastical vestments: 'Odoliński clericus. Ratione ablutionis vestium ecclesiarum fl. 2'.
[88] RK 183, fol. 42v. In this payment, the scribe mistakenly wrote 'Alberto compositori' instead of 'Marcin Compositori' in anticipation of the next singer, Albert Francuz. This undoubtedly refers to Marcin, as he was the only composer in the chapel at that time, and the date of employment corresponds to that given in the register.
[89] RK 183, fol. 75v; 1561 (no precise date given).
[90] RK 161, fol. 55v: 'Die 16 [April] 1563 Nieiakiemu Musicowi Wirkier Compositorowi: Z Wrocllawia. ktory byll iego k. m. posllall darować xiągi wielkie pargaminowe, na których bylla notowane te Deum laudamus. potym

sam, do Piotrcowa do kro: iego m. przyiechal. Zllaski iego kro m przes Jurka Clerykæ K.J.M. dali taĺ 10 fac mon. pol fl. 11/-'.

[91] RK 192, fol. 9v: 'Ioanni Neubar Megalburgen Musico. Die 20 Julii Eidem iussú sacræ Mtis Regie speciali dedi offerenti sac. M. Regiae quasdam propriae industria confectus cantiones . . .'.

[92] Ibid., fol. 152r: 'Ianowi de Wienna Compositor Niemczo: . . . za wlasznym Kro Io Mćźi roskazanim ÿ za opowiedzenim pana Iurka Cleriki Kro. Ieo Mczi'.

[93] RK 110, fol. 903v. Only the year and place of his death is given.

[94] This can be deduced from their subsequent move to the young singers and the other sections of the musical establishment.

[95] This can be concluded from the fact that both Tomek of Sącz and Szymek were re-entered into the register together with the four new singers and given similar terms of employment.

[96] RK 110, fols. 907v-908r.

[97] Ibid.

[98] Ibid., fol. 907v.

[99] Ibid., fol. 908r.

[100] Ibid., fol. 907v.

[101] Ibid.

[102] Ibid., fol. 935v.

[103] Ibid., fol. 905v: 'Mtas Regie constituit hanc inferius speficatam solvendi methodum'.

[104] This cloth consisted of 'Lundinen' 34 ells, 'veluti' 15 ells; 'carasia' 18 ells, 'Telle nigrae' 3 ells.

[105] RK 234, fol. 60rv. Only Szadek and Bronowski are stated as being recruited by Jasivcicz in the register 'per Georgi Clerica', but it is highly improbable that the others were recruited by anyone other than Jasivcicz.

[106] Gąsiorowski, 'Itineraria', p. 272.

[107] RK 110, fol. 908rv.

[108] RK 192, fols. 3v-4r.

[109] Wagad V, vol. 4, fol. 430r (6 December 1570) and fol. 744 (2 July 1571). Both these are receipts signed by Jasivcicz in Kraków for money given for the choir's travelling expenses to Warsaw. ASK V, vol. 5, fol. 39 (29 July 1572) is a receipt signed by Jasivcicz for food allowance for the period of 7 April to 29 July 1572.

[110] RK 249, fol. 21v.

[111] Petronius and Żmygród left or died in February 1573. The number of chaplains was reduced by one only due to the employment of Paweł Rostok in November 1572 and the promotion of one of the singers, Leonard Janikowski, to

chapel clerk. Of the other singers, Klaus died in 1572 and Przeworsko died or left in 1572.

[112] The last payment including the nine boys was made prior to Jasivcicz's death, as the money was given to him 'in manis D. Georgii', RK 234, fol. 61r.

[113] RK 249, fol. 26r.

[114] WRo MS 9789, fol. 307r.

[115] RK 238, fol. 1r, RK 249, fol. 1r and 26rv.

[116] RK 252, fol. 33rv.

[117] RK 110, fol. 937r: '. . . debent [i.e. fistulatores] he se submiserút omnes Claus excepto, semper cum tubicinatoribus ad mensam Regiá tubis caneré, vltra officia sua fistulatoria'.

[118] Various payments were made to such trumpeters in the early part of 1544: Stefan 'Tubicinatori Civitatis Vilneń.' (RK 124a, fol. 27r), 'Casparo Tubicinator' (RK 124a, fol. 29r and 33r) and 'Tataris Tubicinatores' (RK 124a, fol. 39r).

[119] RK 124a, fol. 236r: 'Mathie cziemiorka Tubiciátori. Die 10 Marcii eidem Vilnae de mandato M R missus Slesiam et Nisam et Cracoviam ad acquiren. et convenień Tubicinatores 4 et Fistulatoré unú . . .'.

[120] RK 124a, fol. 29r.

[121] Spangel's name does not appear on the payments made in August 1545 (RK 124a, fol. 135r).

[122] RK 110, fol. 943r.

[123] Ibid., fol. 943v: 'Susceptus in seruicium M R ab ea diæ qua dimissionem actepit a seruicio Domi episcopi wratislawień vczt a die 10 decembris anno domini 1546'.

[124] Ibid., fol. 944r.

[125] RK 124a, fol. 27r.

[126] 74 groszy for both of them per month.

[127] A reference to 'the old king's timpanist who came to the king [i.e. Zygmunt August]' which comes immediately after the payment made to Ciemiorka of 6 May following his return from Silesia and Kraków, may well refer to Andrzej Dusza.

[128] RK 124a, fol. 71r: '. . . ab instructione adolescentes in timpana unius et alterius in tuba . . . fl. 6' (21 October 1545).

[129] RK 110, fol. 940r: 'Die 28 Julÿ 1546 vilnæ M: R. ex eo ą iuuenes in tubis et timpanis docere dżt constituit pro annuo solario fl 20. ft' sinǵliś qŕtualibus fl 5. Preterea racione diariorum illi addidit gr 10 itaque singulis septimanis habebit fl 1.'.

[130] The register provides only the day and year of his death (18 and 1548 respectively), but not the month. Since the king was in Piotrków from 17 October, Doidzwon presumably died in the last quarter of the year.

[131] RK 110, fol. 947r.

[132] The weekly food allowance dated 2 March 1549 (RK 150, fol. 63rv) includes these trumpeters for the first time, noting that they had arrived from Lithuania ('qui venerunt ex Lithuania').

[133] All four are labelled in the register as coming from the old king's court ('ex servicium M R senioris') (RK 110, fols. 945r, 945v, and 946r). However, only the names of the first two, Czech and Lancz, are to be found on the appropriate payments. Georgius Chromi may well be the Jurek Sliezak in the old king's employ, but whose name was changed to differentiate him from an existing trumpeter of the same name. Thus the Latin Georgius was used instead of the Polish 'Jurek', and the surname 'Chromi' replaced by 'Sliezak' ('from Silesia'). Likewise, Stanisław Racławski served Zygmunt I under a different surname, Cygan (Polish for gypsy).

[134] RK 110, fol. 948r.

[135] Ibid., fol. 946v.

[136] Ibid., fol. 948r.

[137] Ibid., fol. 949r. 'Susceptus die 2 July 1569 Crac.'

[138] Pieniajecz is not named to begin with, but referred to as Dusza's boy-apprentice.

[139] RK 110, fol. 929r.

[140] RK 110, fol. 944v.

[141] Ibid.

[142] Ibid., fol. 943v.

[143] Ibid.

[144] WRo MS 180 II, fol. 105r. A transcript of this document is presented in Appendix XI.

[145] This is discussed in the early part of this chapter.

[146] RK 192, fol. 137r: 'Odwiazania 12 partessow . . . 3/- . . . Odwiazania drugich partessow 6 malych fl -/ 22$^{1}/_{2}$' ('for the binding of 12 partbooks . . . 3 florens . . . For the binding of other 6 small partbbooks . . . 22$^{1}/_{2}$'groszy').

[147] RK 161, fol. 16v: 'die 10 [Octobris 1552] Pisscckom k ie⁰ m. na trzinæ do pissccallek Jurkowi Altiscie' ('10 October 1552, For the wind-players of his royal highness for reeds for the instruments [for] Jurek Altista'); RK 161, fol. 30v: '11 nov. [1558] w Krak. Hanussowi Pissccckowki Tenoryscie za Pissccallki nowe flietnie zroskazania kro. iego mosci dat tal. 12' (' 11 November [1558] in Kraków, to Hanus wind-player tenorista for new pipes, [that is,] flutes at the king's command, 12 talars given').

[148] RK 110, fol. 937r. This was granted by Zygmunt August on 21 October 1543. Brugner was exempt from this duty, although he too received the 10 groszy.

[149] RK 124, fol. 236r.

[150] RK 110, fol. 938r.
[151] Ibid.
[152] They received their first food allowance in Kraków on 9 March. RK 150, fol. 69r.
[153] RK 110, fol. 938r.
[154] Ibid., fol. 938r.
[155] Ibid.
[156] RK 150, fol. 271r.
[157] RK 110, fol. 930r.
[158] This can be presumed from the references in the sources to six and twelve partbooks, RK 192, fol. 137r.
[159] WRo MS 180 II, fols. 46v-47r. A transcription of this document is presented in Appendix XI.
[160] RK 110, fol. 907r.
[161] Ibid., fol. 930v.
[162] The dates for these two are not given in the register, although they can be deduced from the payments in RK 235, fols. 22v and 26v. The first, dated 6 February, differentiates them from the other *fistulatores* as having inferior salaries, the second, dated 23 February, does not.
[163] RK 110, fol. 930v.
[164] Perhaps the best-known example of this term is to be found in the preface of Gomołka's *Melodiae na psalterz polski* (Kraków, 1580), fol. iir, which states that the metrical psalm settings were intended 'not for Italian [educated musicians] but for Poles, for . . . simple home-folk' ('Nie dla Włochów, dla Polaków, Dla naszych prostych domaków').
[165] In Głuszcz-Zwolińska, *Muzyka nadworna*, p.37, the author refers to the two groups as 'Musici Itali' ('Fistulatores Itali') and 'Fistulatores Flandri'.
[166] RK 162a, fol. 37v.
[167] Ibid., fol. 106v: 'Theodoricus Italo musico. ult. Dec. 1549 musico R. dni. epi. Crac. in Italiam misso ex Niepolomice ad lra M. R. . . .'. RK 162a, fol. 86v: 'Stephano et Theodorico 2 Musici Italis cuntibus [?] visendi de gra. patriam solet [?] 29 Julii [1550] pro illium emento salario quart. 1 ad 11 Augusti terminati . . .'.
[168] RK 110, fol. 936v,
[169] This can be concluded from the constant reference to them as 'fistulatores', and in one case 'Pisczkom' ('for the wind-players') (RK 319, fol. 78v).
[170] RK 164, fol. 137r.
[171] This can be concluded from the disappearance of their names from the appropriate quarterly payment: RK 170, fol. 137r and RK 171, fol. 136r.
[172] RK 110, fol. 936r.

[173] RK 110, fol. 936r.
[174] Ibid., fol. 938v.
[175] Ibid.
[176] RK 144, fol. 50; RK 150, fol. 45r.
[177] Known also as Valentinus Greff Bakfark.
[178] RK 110, fol. 939r.
[179] A. Chybiński, 'Bekwarek. Lutnia i polityka', *Przegląd Muzyczny* (1918), no. 6, pp. 1-3.
[180] P. Poźniak, 'Bakfark', *Encyklopedia*, i (Kraków, 1979), pp. 170-1.
[181] RK 110, fol. 936v.
[182] RK 183, fol. 82r. This payment, up to 7 August 1562, is the last he received.
[183] RK 235, fol. 22r.
[184] See M. Perz, *Mikołaj Gomółka. Monografia*, 2nd rev. edn. (Kraków, 1981).
[185] RK 124a, fol. 18v.
[186] Kk, Capit Crac. 7, fol. 46v.
[187] The king granted him the use of a wagon with two horses and two servants to assist him in the transportation of his instruments. A transcription of the respective document, WRo MS 180, fol. 87v-88r, together with other relevant documents pertaining to Marcin of Jędrzejów, is provided in Appendix XI.
[188] WRo MS 180, fol. 59v. A transcription of this document is provided in Appendix XI.
[189] RK 162a, fol. 21v: 'Dziano Musico Italo die 22 Mai [1551] in manus dati quod exposuit in expensas omnes Pawlikowi puero organiste post morté Rmi olim Epi. Crac. usque ad ho. tempus per 30 [groszy] fl.14'.
[190] RK 110, fol. 936v.
[191] RK 161, fol. 28r: 'Pawlik Organiscie mallemu na struny mosiądzowe do instrumentu . . .' ('For little Pawlik the organist for brass strings for an instrument . . .').

V

The Music of Zygmunt II August's Chapel

This chapter focuses on the polyphonic repertory of the royal chapel of Zygmunt August. The source material for this study is relatively slim. None of the actual prints or manuscripts belonging to the chapel are known to be extant, though the later were recorded in an inventory of 1572. With this are a small number of extant compositions by Wacław of Szamotuły which survive in print. Taken together, even this small amount of source material can provide an informative, if not entirely comprehensive, picture of the music repertory of the royal chapel, and allows a discussion of the quality of the music by its principal composer. The first and by far the largest part of this chapter will be devoted to Jurek Jasivcicz and the inventory of music books from 1572, the repertory of the chapel, and possible modes of acquisition of the music. The second part will cover the extant compositions of Wacław of Szamotuły.

JUREK JASIVCICZ AND THE INVENTORY OF MUSIC MANUSCRIPTS AND PRINTS OF 1572

Jurek Jasivcicz spent the whole of his career at the royal court in Poland. Recruited as one of the original young singers of Zygmunt August's newly established chapel in Vilnius in 1544,[1] he became a clerk in 1548,[2] and was placed in charge of the boys of the chapel in 1552 before becoming their music tutor two years later.[3] This made Jasivcicz, in effect, the master of the chapel, although the sources refer to him by this title ('magister sacelli') only from about 1561.[4] In addition to his position in the chapel, Jasivcicz had some authority over other members of the musical establishment at the court. Following the reorganisation of the chapel in 1565, he was placed in charge of the boys allocated to the wind-players as apprentices.[5] On several occasions in the 1560s and 1570s Jasivcicz was evidently responsible for the transfer of the musical establishment from its base in Kraków to the king at his various residences.[6] During the final years of Zygmunt August's reign, he also acted as an intermediary between the treasury and all the singers and instrumentalists, being entrusted with large sums of money which constituted their salaries, food allowances and travelling expenses.[7]

The sources give little direct information as to when Jasivcicz took charge of the chapel's music books. In the early years in Vilnius, the music was probably held by the prefect Jan Wierzbkowski, or possibly by the clerk Marcin of Iłża, who is known to have received additional payments for the repair of liturgical books.[8] Following Wierzbkowski's departure from court in 1549 and Jasivcicz's promotion to music tutor in 1554, one might expect that the music books were put in his charge. By this time Zygmunt August had begun to travel extensively; on many occasions the chapel accompanied the king, and Jasivcicz would have been responsible for transporting the music. Certainly on one such journey, a royal excursion to Rudnik in February 1561, some music was apparently forgotten, and one of the boys in his care was sent back to Vilnius to collect the appropriate partbooks.[9] Presumably, Jasivcicz remained in charge of the music for the rest of his life; judging by the inventory, he kept the volumes in chests at his home in Kazimierz (a separate municipality neighbouring Kraków), and took the appropriate music books for each trip. The last of these, to Warsaw, covered a period of less than one year between August 1571 and the spring or early summer of 1572. Afterwards, the king travelled on to Knyszyn and allowed the chapel to return to Kraków. It was here, on 30 June 1572, that Jasivcicz died. Three weeks after his death, an inventory of the items found at his house was made, and this included several hundred music manuscripts and prints. These were all listed, and according to the final colophon, returned to the royal castle.

The source of the inventory: Kpa K 446

The Jasivcicz inventory is to be found in a manuscript book of inventories now preserved in the State Archive in Kraków (Wojewódzkie Archiwum Państwowe w Krakowie), formerly the Archive of the City and Province of Kraków (Archiwum Miasta i Województwa Krakowskiego), with the call-number of K 446 (*olim* Acta Casimir. Hipot. 960, henceforth Kpa K 446).[10] The manuscript measures approximately 18 cms x 45 cms and consists of paper pages bound in leather and has the title *Liber officiosum Inventariorum coram offitio scabinorum conscriptem Anno Domini Millesimo Quingentessimo septuagesimo primo* (fol. 1r). It is a civic document originally belonging to the municipality of Kazimierz,[11] and contains inventories from the years 1571-3. The book is written in a mixture of Latin, used invariably for the opening paragraphs and longer legal texts, and Polish, used quite consistently for the lists of items themselves. Inventories of this type usually recorded the belongings of a deceased person, and were made at the request of a widow or a descendant where there was more than one claim to an inheritance, if there was no inheritor at all, or - as in Jasivcicz's case - where a will needed to be executed. Jasivcicz's inventory is to be found on pp. 26-37 of the manuscript. According to the opening paragraph, which refers to the deceased as 'Georgij Jazwÿcz', the inventory was requested by Tomasz Postekalski (the vice-procurator of the castle on Wawel Hill), Ludwik Decius (the procurator of Kraków), Jan Szelmiczki, and Jan Miernik, all executors of Jasivcicz's will. The actual inventory was produced on 19 July 1572 in the presence of Jasivcicz's nephew George and two municipal officers, Andrzej Naczowicz and Bartłomiej Biegłowski, one of whom was probably the scribe.[12]

The composition of the inventory and the scribe's method of notation

The inventory is a concise list of identifiable items found in all the rooms of his house, including the kitchen and wash room, as well as the entrance hall. Amongst the furniture, domestic articles, clothing, and personal items, there were three chests containing music. The first two chests were found on the first floor in a front room overlooking the street, and consisted almost entirely of music books. The first of these also contained some writing utensils and more specifically pens and rules ('rastra') for copying music.[13] The third chest, a travelling chest, stood together with another travelling chest in the entrance hall. In addition to the music books, this third chest contained some quilt covers, bed linen, table cloths and some napkins (which are at the beginning of the listed items), and a harp and cittern (entered at the end). (An annotated transcription of the relevant items is provided in Appendix XIII.)

The lists of music books do not seem to follow a specific order; presumably, each item was recorded as it was found in the chest. In line with the inventory's purpose, the scribe recorded every musical item separately. The format is mentioned, be it a choirbook or a set of partbooks, and in the case of the latter, the number of parts of a set is given. Many entries include an external description, including the material and the colour of the covers, though relatively few mention the size or the age of a given item. Other entries include particular features or distinguishable details, such as gold borders or gilded sides, an embossed royal emblem, book ties, and clasps.

Not all the entries record distinctive external bindings: some clearly had paper or plain parchment covers, or were found in a folder; others presumably had no cover whatsoever. In many such cases, the scribe turned to the contents of the item for some distinguishable feature to record. In the case of a print, the scribe usually utilized the information given on the first page. Prints dedicated to an individual composer are usually recorded by their name; often some information on the genre of music they contained is also given. Anthologies are recorded by the title, either in full or in an abbreviated form. A small number of entries have a composition incipit: these volumes may well have lacked a distinctive title-page, and the scribe therefore recorded the first composition of the volume. One such entry, 'Parthessij w czervonei skorze o regem caeli' ('partbooks in leather 'o regem caeli', item 110), can be identified as the *Primus liber cum quattuor vocibus||Motetti del fiore* (J. Moderne, Lyons, 1532). All but the superius partbook have an abridged form of the title, *Primus liber cum quattuor vocibus*, and faced with this, the scribe recorded the first composition of the set, namely 'O regem caeli' by Andreas de Silva. By contrast, the manuscripts were clearly more problematic to record: only five entries provide a composer's name and genre of the composition, seven mention the genre only, and a further six give just an incipit, presumably of the first composition.

Problems of terminology and identification

Although the scribe's work was probably comprehensive enough for its original purpose, the inventory contains a number of problems for the modern researcher trying to recreate the composition and contents of the collection. A number of entries provide only an external description of the item, from which little can be deduced. Even those entries which describe the contents of a print or manuscript do not always contain sufficient information to identify the item exactly. 'Parthessÿ Constancÿ porte voces 5' (item 17) is one such example. Being the only set by Costanzo Porta in the collection, it was listed without further detail. However, it is now impossible to determine which one of five possible print it referred to: the first book of motets of 1555, either of the two books of introits of 1566, or one of the first two books of madrigals of 1559 and 1569.

The inventory also contains a number of terminological difficulties, some of which may not have been the scribe's doing. One such term is 'officia' ('officium'), used on three occasions. The 'office' is generally understood to denote the services of the hours (as distinct from the mass), but it is also used to designate the introit to the mass or mass introits. In Polish sources, such as the Rorantists' partbooks for example, the term 'officium' usually refers to both the ordinary and proper of a mass for a specific feast or occasion, or even the ordinary alone. Such a usage would identify 'Officia moralis . . . [a] 4' (item 61) as Morales's second book of masses, published in partbooks by Antonio Gardane in 1544. Since the terms 'missa' and the Polish equivalent 'msza' were used more consistently throughout the inventory, it is possible that the term 'officia' appeared on the cover or first page, and was simply copied by the scribe. Another problematic term is 'na . . . Jezyk' which literally translates 'for/on a . . . tongue/language'.[14] This appears in eleven descriptions of books all located in the second chest. Given the various forms in which the term appears ('small', 'large', 'long'), a literal translation makes little sense. For the same reason, a looser translation 'for the voice' or 'for a voice part' is also unsuitable. One possibility compatible with all the entries is that the term refers to an external feature of the item, its binding or cover. This is substantiated more specifically by item 83, which records some printed Italian villanellas 'sewn on a tongue'. In this case, if not all the others, the 'Jezyk' might have been a strap or spine to which the music was attached.

One entry, 'Muteti drugie Adriani Jakieth 5' (Other motets [by] Adrian [and] Jachet 5 [partbooks]) (item 22), seems to be a scribal error, as no book of five-part motets by Adrian Willaert and Jachet of Mantua was published. Given that the previous entry refers to Jachet's first book of five-part motets, this entry probably refers to his second book, and the scribe mistakenly wrote Willaert's forename instead of Jachet's. Janequin's music also seems to have caused some trouble for the scribe. Several of his books of chansons have unusual titles, lacking the customary genre label. The entry 'Madrigal Jannequin' (item 10) undoubtedly refers to one such book, possibly one of the two books of *Inventions musicales* (1555), or the *Verger de musique* (1560).

The size of the music collection and its general composition

The inventory gives a good indication of the actual size of the collection. There are 136 separate volumes or sets of music described, of which only a few (a lute tablature and some 'fugi') may not have been used by the chapel. These, like the non-music books listed, may well have belonged to Jasivcicz himself. The general nature of 102 items can be established from their inventory entries: there were 73 prints - remembering that some of these volumes may have contained more than one print of which only the first was recorded - and 29 manuscripts. Of the 73 prints, it has been possible to identify 26 by correlating the information with extant prints preserved elsewhere,[15] and the possible identities of a further 19 can be given. The manuscripts, unlike the mass-produced prints, were nearly all unique and are much more difficult to identify. Of the 29 manuscripts, only one can be identified: a choirbook including Wircker's 'Te Deum' (item 104). A number of presentation manuscripts, including this composition, were produced by Wircker, and some of these are still extant.[16]

The musical contents

An analysis of the musical repertory of the chapel can only be based on those items identified, thus primarily the foreign prints. As this amounts to just a portion of the whole collection, one cannot claim that the picture that emerges is totally objective; nevertheless, it offers an interesting insight into a cross-section of the music belonging to the chapel. The chapel was active for three decades and music was undoubtedly acquired throughout this period: this is corroborated by the dates of the prints. For this reason, this section will deal first with the printed music in roughly chronological order, and then the manuscripts.

The chapel possessed a relatively small amount of music of Josquin des Prez and his generation, with just three anthologies identified: two choirbooks, *Liber quindecim missarum* (A. Antico, Rome, 1516[1]) and *Liber selectarum cantionum* (Grimm and Wyrsung, Augsburg, 1520[4]), and a third slightly later, though stylistically retrospective set of partbooks, *Liber decem missarum* (J. Moderne, Lyons, 1532[8]). This is hardly surprising: it is questionable whether such printed music was still readily available at the time of the chapel's establishment in the mid 1540s.

The chapel possessed a much more substantial amount of printed music by the post-Josquin generation of Franco-Flemish and other composers active in the second quarter of the sixteenth century, both in anthologies and in the newly emerging single-composer prints. Indeed, a newly created chapel would have needed an adequate corpus of music to function properly. The music found here reflects mainstream European musical tastes, and the established composers are well represented. The best represented individual here is Jachet of Mantua (1485-1558), an important composer and possibly one of the best-known of his time. The chapel owned copies of Jachet's first two books of motets for five voices from 1539 and 1565, as well as his book of masses for five voices (1554); it also possessed two collaborative books of psalms: the first (with Willaert) *I salmi appertinenti* (Venice, 1550[1]), scored for two antiphonal choirs, and the second (with Cipriano de Rore) *I salmi a quattro voci* (Venice, 1570), published after Jachet's death. Other individual compositions by Jachet can also be found in several anthologies. The chapel owned three books of music by Adrian Willaert (c. 1490-1562), one of the most versatile composers of the first half of the sixteenth century and now acknowledged as the founder of the Venetian school. In addition to the 1550 book of psalms produced with Jachet, one can find here his second book of four-part motets of 1539 and his *Musica nova* (Venice, 1559), containing motets and madrigals for three to seven voices. Only a small amount of Nicholas Gombert's music appears to have been available to the chapel, all in anthologies: three masses for five voices (1542[2]) and five motets, three for four voices (1532[10]) and two for six voices (1564[3]). Other music of this period found in the chapel's collection stands outside the Franco-Flemish tradition. The French school was represented by Clément Janequin (c. 1485-1558) and Dominique Phinot (c. 1510-55). There were two books of secular music by Janequin, possibly his *Inventions musicales* (1555), and *Verger de musique* (1560). Three further items are recorded as 'La bataglia', and presumably refer to Janequin's famous chanson: two of these were for four voices, while the third was an adaptation for five voices. Of Phinot's music, the chapel owned one of the two books of chansons for five voices (both published in 1548), his book of psalms for four voices of 1555, and two eight-part psalm settings which appeared in

Jachet and Willaert's publication of 1550. The one item of music by the Spaniard Cristóbal de Morales was his second book of masses for four voices mentioned earlier.

The third and largest group of foreign music loosely encompasses the generation of composers contemporary with the inventory itself. The chapel possessed a more ambitious collection of prints here, containing new music by both famous composers and those relatively unknown. The Venetian school is represented by two of Willaert's most famous pupils, Cipriano de Rore (c. 1516-65) and Costanzo Porta (c. 1529-1601). This includes two books of Rore's madrigals, for four and five voices, a number of four-part motets, and psalms. There was a book of five-part compositions by Porta, which, as mentioned above, could have been any one of several books of motets, introits, or madrigals for five voices. The chapel also owned masses by Vincenzo Ruffo (the book for four voices of 1557) and by Jacobus de Kerle (first book for four and five voices, 1562). Both these composers were closely associated with later sessions of the Council of Trent of the 1560s, which discussed the role of sacred polyphony and proposed reforms which were to be introduced in the church. It may be no coincidence that during the 1563 session of the Council, one of the presidents was a Polish delegate, Stanisław Hozjusz, Bishop of Warmia, whose name appears in the dedication of Kerle's *Preces* of 1562.

Concerning the two great masters of the second half of the century, the chapel possessed a relatively large amount of music by Orlando di Lasso and apparently no music by Giovanni Pierluigi da Palestrina. Of Lasso's work, there is one book each of his Magnificats, five-part madrigals, and three-part villanellas, not to mention his works in the anthologies. The reason for this preferential treatment of Lasso may lie in the greater availability of his printed music during the 1550s and 1560s. By the time of the inventory, almost a hundred different volumes of his music had been published, as opposed to just ten by Palestrina. The presence of so much of Lasso's music might also be explained by the fact that from 1556 he was employed at the neighbouring court of Duke Albrecht of Munich, with whom Zygmunt August corresponded.

Finally, there are a number of volumes of music by relatively unknown and younger composers of this generation: five-voice motets by Heliseo Ghibelli, Francesco Londariti, and Johannes Pionnier; madrigals by Bernardo Luppacino (à 4), Jacopo Corfini (à 5), and possibly also by Paulo de Magri, as well as three-part villanellas by Jean de Gero.

The collection possessed at least 29 manuscripts.[17] Most of the inventory entries reveal little of their contents, although their very presence is indicative of a significant production of local music, presumably original. Five entries record the music of Wacław of Szamotuły: two sets of Lamentations for four and five voices, masses ('Officia') for four and six voices, and one eight-part mass. We know two motets by Wacław were published in German anthologies; presumably the chapel possessed these compositions, either in manuscript or print, and it is probable that further motets by him were contained in other manuscripts.[18] These extant compositions will be discussed in due course. Finally, two further manuscripts contained Polish songs for four and three parts,[19] an indication that the chapel had at least some indigenous music.

The genres of music in the context of the chapel's duties

The Jasivcicz inventory sheds some light on the general duties of the chapel. As one might expect of a chapel choir of a Catholic monarch, its main duty was to adorn the daily liturgy with music. It is likely that the chapel was responsible for the actual liturgy, and although the inventory does not include any liturgical books, such books were usually located in the chapel itself. Likewise, it is probable that the chapel sang some plainchant; the inventory does record a psalter and a gradual. As for the polyphony, the largest portion of the identified items was intended for the mass. Twelve printed books of mass ordinary settings can be identified: eight anthologies and four single-composer prints (Jachet of Mantua, Vincenzo Ruffo, Jacobus de Kerle, and Rocco Rodio). Other settings included the two eight-part mass settings by Wacław of Szamotuły and Antonio Scandello, and an anonymous 'morrow' mass ('na hejnał' - literally 'on rising'), all three presumably in manuscript form. Six further entries, described as 'Officium', may well refer to mass ordinary settings: the printed volume by Cristóbal de Morales, two manuscript books by Wacław of Szamotuły, and three anonymous and unspecified items. In addition to the mass settings, one can include here the books of motets, of which there were at least twenty-five volumes, with whole prints dedicated to Jachet of Mantua, Dominique Phinot, Cipriano de Rore, Heliseo Ghibelli, Francesco Londariti and Johannes Pionnier. With these, one should include Adrian Willaert's motets published in his *Musica nova*, and possibly a book of motets or introits by Costanzo Porta. There were also numerous printed anthologies, although only three can be positively identified: the two old collections of 1520 and 1532 already described and *Thesaurus musici tomus tertius* (J. Montanus & U. Neuber, Nuremberg, 1564[3]). A second group encompasses polyphony for Vespers: the Psalms and Magnificats. Of the seven books of psalms, two included the music of a sole composer, namely, Phinot and Willaert; the next two were shared by a pair of composers, de Rore and Jachet, Willaert and Jachet; and the other three were anthologies. There were only two books of Magnificat settings, one by Lasso, the other an anthology including settings by Morales and Adam Rener.

The inventory records other types of sacred music which do not fit into the above two categories. The first comprises music for Holy Week, and seems to have consisted almost entirely of manuscripts of local production: three sets of Lamentations (two by Wacław of Szamotuły), two books of Passions, and a fascicle containing some Passion verses. The second includes 'German' books,[20] which by their very description suggest music for Protestant services. One final item of sacred music is Johannes Wircker's 'Te Deum', a hymn of praise sung traditionally during matins on Sundays and on all feast-days. Given that the entry refers to the composition as being written in a grand style ('na wielki mod[um]') it is possible that Wircker's setting was intended for more special occasions.

The presence of secular music indicates that the chapel members also provided secular entertainment at the court. Nine books of madrigals can be identified, with whole volumes by Jean de Gero, Cipriano de Rore, Dominique Phinot, Orlando di Lasso, Jacopo Corfini, and Adrian Willaert. There was a similar number of books of villanellas, all anthologies save Lasso's second book for three voices. There was most probably a handful of books of chansons, in spite of being described as madrigals in the inventory, including those by Clément Janequin. Finally, the inventory includes the two books of 'Polish' songs mentioned earlier, which, by virtue of their labelling, probably contained local settings of vernacular texts. Whilst one has to acknowledge that the chapel underwent a major transformation in the mid-1560s, introducing lay singers in the place of chaplains, the early dates of some of the secular prints, not to mention the 'old' manuscript containing four-part madrigals (no. 74), suggest that such secular music-making had been taking place long before the reorganization, if not from the beginning of the chapel's activities in the 1540s.

The acquisition of music

The composition of any musical library was determined to some degree by the availability of music and by the means of acquiring it. These issues are of particular importance in this case, due to the distance between the Polish court and the main centres of music and music-printing. Precisely how the majority of the foreign prints and manuscripts found their way into the chapel library is difficult to establish conclusively: the archival material contains only isolated references regarding the acquisition of individual items. We therefore have to use additional circumstantial evidence and examine all possible routes.

First, music could have been acquired by the agents in Zygmunt August's employ. On gaining his own treasury in 1544, Zygmunt August set out to create his own private library at his residence in Vilnius. In the late 1540s and early 1550s he sent two agents abroad, Andrzej Trzecieski (d. 1547) and later his son, also called Andrzej (d. 1584), in search of books. The royal payments reveal that the second of these travelled to Frankfurt in 1548, and purchased a number of books there.[21] It is known that by 1552, these two agents had bought 1273 volumes, which were first sent to Kraków for binding before going on to Vilnius. Whilst this channel of book-buying was principally focused on Zygmunt August's personal library, it is possible that during these early years music was also bought by these royal agents, perhaps at the annual book fair in Frankfurt.

From the mid-1550s the flow of books decreased, and the sources do not include any other sizeable payments for books bought abroad. Instead, the royal bookkeepers, Stanisław Koszucki (d. 1559) and Łukasz Górnicki (1527-1603), worked from their base in Vilnius (and later Tykocin), purchasing books in Poland, principally in Kraków.[22]

Foreign music prints could also have been purchased from booksellers active in Poland, and in particular in Kraków. However, it is evident from extant booksellers' inventories that the trade in music was somewhat limited to begin with, possibly due to market forces, and only improved during the second half of the century. The inventories of three businesses in particular, those of Szarfenberg, Thenaud, and Kesner, show the extent to which this was true. It should be remembered that the inventories were made on the death of the booksellers; thus they do not record all the books which would have passed through their hands, but list only the books left unsold at the time of their deaths. Also, the inventory entries are often incomplete, and do not allow exact identification. Nevertheless, all three have entries which can be associated with items recorded in the Jasivcicz inventory. The first of these booksellers, Maciej Szarfenberg, traded from 1520 to his death in 1547. His inventory (Kpa Advoc. Crac., vol. 142, pp. 515-26) contains only a handful of music items, which are not described in detail: some four-part Magnificats, antiphons, a 'registrum', and three unspecified partbooks for three voices. The second bookseller, Jan Thenaud of Bourges, settled in Kraków in 1563 and built up a business over the next two decades. Thenaud's inventory of 1582 contains over twenty musical items (Kpa Advoc. Crac., vol. 200, p. 121). It includes volumes of 'cantiones' by Willaert and Phinot, composers whose music was also to be found in the chapel collection. It also includes a copy of a *Thesaurus musicus* published by Montanus and Neuber in 1564, which may be the same as item 106 of the Jasivcicz inventory, recorded as 'Thesaurus partes 6'. The third bookseller, Zacheus Kesner, appeared in Kraków towards the end of the 1560s,[23] and his business flourished right up to his death in 1602. Although Kesner's trading in Poland barely overlaps with the activities of the royal chapel, one should not rule out the possibility that music for the chapel was purchased from him. The majority of the music books listed in his inventory (Kpa Advoc. Crac., vol. 226, 1602-3) post-dates the Jasivcicz inventory,[24] and only one entry, a book of madrigals by Lasso, appears in both.

Only a few individual acquisitions can be traced in the source material. The court composer Wacław of Szamotuły received money from the king for composing various motets in 1554.[25] The same is true of the three foreign composers who received money from the royal treasury, Johannes Wircker, Johannes of Vienna, and Johannes Neubaur. Another composer, Rocco Rodio, may have sent his *Missarum decem liber primus* (Rome, 1562) to Zygmunt August, since it contains a dedication to him, and this volume was almost certainly in the chapel collection (item 91). We know from a letter of Stanisław

Tarło to Duke Albrecht von Hohenzollern of Prussia, dated 15 May 1547, that Zygmunt August had received a book of masses ('Die gesangmessbucher') from the duke. This letter also revealed that Zygmunt August had ordered his chapel to become acquainted with the music therein.[26] This item is not closely identified in the letter, and may be any one of the prints of masses of the inventory which pre-date the letter, possibly one of the two items referring to 'German' books (items 47 and 50).

Some music books may have been purchased on an occasional basis. Music may have been bought during the king's stay in Gdańsk (Danzig) in 1552. Gdańsk was a prosperous city, with a developed civic identity; the book trade flourished here, as did the sale of music prints. Zygmunt August resided in Gdańsk for almost two months with his court, sufficient time for music to be purchased for the chapel.[27] Also, the sessions of Parliament which brought together the monarch, magnates, and the country's nobility were suitable occasions to hold book fairs. A few payments reveal that a number of books were bought in this way and directly at the king's request, though again, none explicitly describes music books.[28]

It would seem that the most obvious route for music to reach the court was through the musicians who travelled abroad, and foreign musicians employed at the court. However, such contacts between Poland and the rest of Europe were relatively limited and restricted primarily to the instrumentalists. In 1549 Zygmunt August sent Theodoricus to Italy, and the following year he and Stefanus were sent to Flanders. The purpose of both journeys is not revealed in the sources, although one cannot rule out the possibility that some music was purchased for the chapel. The lutenist Bálint Bakfark was given leave from the court between 1552 and 1554, during which he travelled to Frankfurt, Wittemberg, Rome, Lyons, Paris, and finally Venice. We know Bakfark toured Europe to look for a publisher for his compositions and transcriptions,[29] and possibly to find a more lucrative post,[30] but there is nothing to suggest that he collected music for Zygmunt August's chapel.[31] The 'Musici Fistulatores', the 'Musici Itali', and the individual soloists from Italy may all have brought music with them, though presumably this would have been for their own use. The royal chapel included just one foreigner, Johannes Baston, albeit for less than two years.[32] Baston may well have come to Poland in the spring of 1552 with a certain amount of music, if only his own compositions. However, all of this would have presumably also gone with him on his departure in 1554, and one can only speculate as to which of his extant works were copied for the chapel during his time at the court.

Looking at the whole of the period in question, different routes seem to have been more probable at different times. In the early years of the chapel's existence, the agents working abroad, especially in Frankfurt, appear the most effective in obtaining new music. In the later years, the local book trade improved, whilst at the same time few agents travelled abroad for the king. Thus the booksellers of Kraków became a much more likely source of music for the chapel. Their selection may not have been as varied as that of the traders abroad, but these booksellers would have presumably imported suitable music for their customers. Also, the purchase of prints from local traders was less arbitrary, possibly involving Jasivcicz himself.

Conclusions

Since the collection itself has not survived, the Jasivcicz inventory is of great importance. The volumes recorded here undoubtedly belonged to the royal chapel (and thus technically to the king) and not to Jasivcicz himself; this can be argued from the descriptions of some of the books which included the royal emblem on their covers, as well as the fact that the whole collection was returned to the royal castle. It is likely that this collection comprised the whole of the chapel music. One might expect the music books to be kept together and in the possession of the master of the chapel; also, the chapel was a mobile unit singing in the chapels and chambers of the royal residences in Kraków, Vilnius, Warsaw and Piotrków, thus it would be impractical to leave music in any one of these places. Finally, the inventory states that the music books were returned to the castle on Wawel Hill and 'deposited with the other instruments'. One can therefore assume that there were no other music books in the palace buildings, and that there was no specific place for them there.

Jasivcicz's inventory represents the size and state of the collection in 1572. Obviously, this was a 'cumulative' collection: only a small part would have been available to the chapel at the beginning, and with time and new acquisitions, some of the older items might have been discarded or lost, and not all the recorded items may have been in use at the end. As for the possible repertory in use in 1572, the actual location and arrangement of the music in Jasivcicz's house is surely relevant. Whereas the first two chests were found in one of the first-floor chambers, the third chest was one of two travelling chests located in the entrance hall. Both these chests contained clothing and bed linen, items which would have been taken on longer trips. Given that Jasivcicz had returned from Warsaw to Kraków not long before his death, these two travelling chests may well have constituted his recent travel baggage. If so, the forty-four items of music in this third chest - one-third of the whole collection - comprised the repertory used during this final period of time in Warsaw. The books, most of which have been identified, constitute an interesting and varied assortment of music. The masses are numerous, and include the oldest identified print of the collection, *Liber quindecim missarum* (Rome, 1516[1]), as well as one of the most recent acquisitions *Praestantissimorum divinae musices auctorum misse decem, quatuor, quinque & sex vocum* (Louvain, 1570[1]). This may be an indication of the predilection for the earlier masters as well as an interest in recent trends. Wacław of Szamotuły figures quite prominently here, an indication of this composer's respected position in the chapel. There is also a relatively large amount of secular music here, especially villanellas.

Exactly how foreign prints reached the chapel cannot be conclusively established from the sources, although the discussion on this question has shown that music was more probably purchased by book agents working abroad in the earlier years and via the Kraków booksellers in the later years. Whatever the case, it is apparent that music was purchased on a regular basis, since the chapel owned prints dating from almost every year from the late 1530s to the early 1570s. This pattern persists until the very end, with two anthologies published in 1570: *Di Cipriani et di Jachet i salmi a quattro voci* (C. da Correggio, Venice, 1570[2]) and *Praestantissimorum divinae musices auctorum misse decem* . . . (Phalèse & Bellère, Louvain, 1570[1]), just two years before the inventory was made.

Finally, one can make some observations about the chapel's repertory during specific periods of its activity, drawing on the information on the chapel's history presented in the previous chapter. In its initial years, the chapel was capable of performing four- and five-part music, and the majority of the prints which date from late 1530s and the early 1540s are for such a standard scoring. Following the transfer of the royal court from Vilnius to Kraków in 1548-9, the chapel lost its boys, the two youths were promoted to the ranks of the chaplains, and by 1552 it consisted of a group of fourteen chaplains. Thus Wacław of Szamotuły's Lamentations and Passion responses (composed 1550-2) may perhaps have been written for four lower voices out of necessity. The subsequent reorganization in 1552 and the enlargement of the chapel for the wedding of Zygmunt August to Catherine Habsburg in the summer of 1553 increased the chapel's potential for performing music. Wacław of Szamotuły's mass for eight voices could have been composed at this time, possibly even for the actual ceremony. Likewise the collection of eight-part psalms by Willaert and Jachet of 1550 may well have been purchased at this time. Following this peak, the chapel diminished in size slightly, but judging from the prints subsequently purchased, it was still capable of performing at least five- and six-part music.

WACŁAW OF SZAMOTUŁY

Wacław of Szamotuły was born c. 1520.[33] After primary education in his home town and later in Poznań (Lubranscianum), he moved to Kraków in 1538. It is known that he enlisted at the academy there,[34] although there is no evidence that he graduated. Wacław's first vocation seems to have been poetry: four panegyrical poems written by him appeared in print between 1539 and 1545, all relating to events at the royal court.[35] From the preface to the last of these prints it is known that by 1545, at the latest, Wacław was secretary to Hieronim Chodkiewicz, the castellan of Troki and member of the king's Lithuanian

Council. He probably remained in Chodkiewicz's service until 1547, when he was appointed composer in Zygmunt August's chapel (6 May). How and when Wacław received his musical education is not known. In a biographical article on the composer, Anna and Zygmunt Szweykowski have suggested that by the time of his appointment he had already proved himself a capable composer.[36] Whilst this may be true, it does seem strange that Zygmunt August did not employ Wacław until 1547, in spite of the fact that he knew him (if only through his poetry) and that the post of composer in the chapel had been vacant for two and a half years. It is therefore more likely that Wacław had only recently started composing, and that he developed his art as a member of the chapel.

The details of Wacław's employment at the royal court have been given in some detail in the previous chapter. He was an active member of the chapel for just eight years, from 1547 to 1555, and during this time his Lamentations were published in Kraków, and one of his motets appeared in a German anthology. After leaving the chapel, Wacław moved to Vilnius, to the service of the Calvinist Mikołaj Radziwiłł, Grand Hetman and Chancellor of Lithuania. This move may well have been in order to pursue his interest in the Reformation movement, which he may not have been able to do whilst at the royal chapel. Indeed, several settings of sacred songs in the vernacular by him have survived. According to Anna and Zygmunt Szweykowski, Wacław died in about 1560, possibly in Pińczów,[37] the 'Calvinist capital' of Poland.

Piecing together Wacław's polyphonic output is not easy. His *Lamentationes Hieremiae . . . quatuor parium vocum*, printed by Łazarz Andrysowic, Kraków, in 1553, is preserved incomplete with only two of the four partbooks extant (Cantus and Tenor).[38] From annotations in the print, we know that this music was composed between the years 1550 and 1552. There are two extant motets which were included in German anthologies: 'In te Domine speravi', in *Tomus quartus Psalmorum selectorum, quatuor et plurium vocum* (J. Montanus and U. Neuber, Nuremberg, 1554[11]), and 'Ego sum pastor bonus', in *Thesauri musici tomus quintus, et ultimus, continens sacras harmonias quatuor vocibus compositas* (J. Montanus and U. Neuber, Nuremberg, 1564[5]). There are also nine simple four-part settings of sacred Polish songs and psalms, which appeared in print, though these were intended for the reformed church-goers, and as such fall outside the scope of this survey. The 'Fabricii' mass, preserved incomplete in one of the Rorantists' partbook sets (Kk I.4) and discussed in Chapter III, should also be mentioned. However strong the similarities are between this mass and the extant motets, we do not have conclusive evidence to attribute the work to Wacław. One further composition, 'Nunc scio vere', found in a Polish organ tablature dating from the second half of the sixteenth century, has also been attributed to Wacław by Polish musicologists on account of the letters 'WS' entered next to the title.[39] Unfortunately, not only is the authorship of this composition questionable, but there are also problems with the source: even if it was originally a vocal work, one cannot be sure what changes were made on intabulation.[40] Other compositions by Wacław, recorded in the Jasivcicz inventory, are known to be lost:[41] an eight-part mass, masses ('offitia') for four and six voices,[42] and the Passion responses for five voices.[43] The first of these may have been written for the ceremonies linked with the marriage of 1553. Stanisław Orzechowski's published description of the marriage does state that some of Wacław's music was performed during the rite itself,[44] though this is likely to have been something other than the mass, probably a motet or hymn. We also know from the royal account-books that Wacław had composed 'various motets' for which the king granted him a sum of 50 florens in 1554.[45]

It is therefore only on the two motets which appear in the German anthologies that an assessment of Wacław of Szamotuły's music should be based. Both are available in modern editions[46] and have been the subject of study by several Polish musicologists, including Chybiński and Szweykowski.[47] Yet these compositions alone give an insight into the quality of his music. The first, 'In te Domine speravi', is the longer motet, and probably the better of the two. It is in two sections, the second beginning with the words 'Quoniam fortitudo mea'. The motet is imitative, with each line of the text provided with a new point. There is a tendency to pair the voices in imitation, with each voice of the pair entering in close succession; most of the points, excluding those opening sections, being on the up-beat. The imitation is generally quite strict, though some relaxations can be found, particularly in the repetitions of the text phrases. Successive phrases overlap each other, uninterrupted by strong cadences or pauses, giving the music a continuous flow. The setting is predominantly syllabic, with penultimate syllables of phrases usually furnished with an extended melisma. Wacław's treatment of the melodic lines is varied: some are expansive and extended over the four voices, others are short and compressed into a very short time span. As to Wacław's melodic inventiveness, there are some fine melodic phrases, especially those given to the top part (Cantus) over a full harmony in the lower registers of the other three voices. Examples of these can be found for the words 'In manus tuas domine' and 'commendo spiritum meum' (bb. 136-40, see Ex.17a pp. 109-10). The overall mood of the piece is uniform and there are no sudden or dramatic changes in the music. Light declamatory interjections do appear, such as for the word 'accelera', which suggest the composer did not have an altogether indifferent approach to text accentuation.

The second motet, 'Ego sum pastor bonus', is in one section, and the recurring 'Alleluia', set slightly differently after each line of the text, provides the composition with its main structural feature *(abcb'db'eb'eb')*. In many aspects it resembles the first motet; it is imitative, with each line of the text furnished with a new point, and voice pairing can be found, particularly in the Alleluias. These Alleluia sections also contain some stronger cadences, punctuating the text. There are likewise some fine melodic lines here, particularly for the words 'pro ovibus meis' (bb. 55-66). This second motet is, if anything, a little more melismatic.

Both these motets suggest Wacław was a capable and talented composer, belonging to the mainstream Franco-Flemish tradition of the post-Josquin generation. As to possible influences on Wacław, one could turn to the printed music recorded in the Jasivcicz inventory, some of which was undoubtedly available to the composer in the late 1540s and early 1550s. Most striking are the similarities between these two motets and the music of Jachet of Mantua, in particular the latter's first book of motets of 1539. The nature of the imitation is generally similar, as are the overall shape of the points, the time interval of voice entries, and the repetition and development of melodic material. Initial entries are usually in extended imitation and the sections end in a broad and decisive cadence, often including pedal points in one or more of the voices.[48] The actual counterpoint (predominantly note-against-note) is also a common characteristic. The use of voice pairing and short declamations is another typical feature of Jachet. It is true that none of these features found in Wacław's music is exclusive to Jachet; nevertheless, given the remoteness of the Polish court and the importance of imported prints used by the chapel, Jachet does appear to be the prime candidate, more so than other composers such as Gombert or Clemens non Papa.[49]

As to the quality of the compositions and their reception during the sixteenth century, one might underline the fact that both motets appear in the German anthologies, next to works by contemporary masters such as Gombert, Crecquillon, Clemens non Papa, and Lasso. They were obviously deemed worthy of inclusion in such collections. Moreover, there are a number of German manuscripts which contain copies of the two motets,[50] made presumably from the prints, and these further testify to their quality and continued use during the second half of the sixteenth century, beyond the confines of the royal chapel in Poland.

NOTES

[1] RK 110, fol. 902r.
[2] RK 137, fol. 209v.
[3] RK 110, fol. 904r.
[4] RK 183, fol. 42r.
[5] RK 110, fols. 907r-908r.
[6] There are several receipts for such journeys: Wagad V, vol. 4, pp. 221, 293, 430, 431.
[7] Wagad, V, vol. 4, p. 744; vol. 5, p. 39.
[8] These payments for the repair of liturgical books can be found in RK 156, fol. 80r, RK 152, fol. 133r, and RK 137 fol. 55r.

[9] RK 161, fol. 49r: 'Die 3 February [1561] pacholiaciu spiewakowi przy Jurku Cleryce, ktory sie byll wrocill ZRudnik do Wilna po parteski na odwiezienie f. 0/5' ('For the boy singer in Jurek the clerk's care, who returned from Rudnik to Vilnius for some partbooks, 5 groszy for the journey.')

[10] A. Chybiński, 'Krakowskie inwentarze muzyczne z XVI wieku', *Kwartalnik Muzyczny* (1912), no. 3, pp. 253-8. Here the author refers to the manuscript under its previous call-number, Acta Casimir. Hipot. 960.

[11] In the eighteenth century, Kazimierz was incorporated into Kraków, and all of the municipal documents were transferred to the Kraków archives.

[12] Kpa K 446, p. 26.

[13] Ibid., p. 27.

[14] F. Popławski (ed., vols. i-iv); M.R. Mayenowa (ed., vols. v-), *Słownik polszczyzny XVI wieku* (Wrocław, 1966-), ix, pp. 515-26.

[15] These have been ascertained through published catalogues, principally *RISM*. A small number of lost prints recorded in some older catalogues, or publishers' catalogues, are also mentioned.

[16] Extant copies can be found in D Dl; LEu; G. See C. Hamm and H. Kellman (eds. vol. i); H. Kellman (ed. vols. ii-v), *Census-Catalogue of Manuscript Sources of Polyphonic Music 1400-1500*, 5 vols. (Renaissance Manuscript Studies, 1; Neuhausen-Stuttgart, 1979-88).

[17] There are 34 items in the inventory which do not indicate whether the item was a manuscript or a print.

[18] There is a third motet, which is of questionable authorship, preserved in an organ tablature manuscript. This composition will also be discussed later.

[19] Items 75 and 129.

[20] See items 47, 50, and 107.

[21] A. Kawecka-Gryczowa, *Biblioteka ostatniego Jagiellona: pomnik polskiej kultury renesansowej* (Wrocław, 1988), p. 60.

[22] Ibid., p. 74.

[23] Ibid., p.105.

[24] The books presented here form only the first portion of the whole inventory recorded. The other two comprise books which arrived at his shop following his death in 1602, and although they are of great interest in themselves, are irrelevant to the survey here.

[25] RK 173, fol. 133r: [n.d.] 'Venceslao Compositori cantus Sac M R De grá Sac M Regie compensan. eidé laboré in componendis varÿs musices mutetis per ipsiú fetiú Parczowiæ dat . . . [no sum].' This payment dates from 25-6 September when the king was in Parczew. See: Gąsiorowski, 'Itineraria', p. 269.

[26] Kawecka-Gryczowa, *Biblioteka*, p. 34.

[27] Unfortunately, the appropriate account-books recording the expenses made during the tour, and possibly the purchase of music, have not survived.

[28] RK 161, fols. 31v, 34v, 57v.

[29] According to a letter of recommendation from Melanchthon to Leovitius Ciprianus, Bakfark had travelled to Germany to publish his works: 'Venit in Germaniam ut edat in officinis typographycis scripta sua arte et pecunia instructus est' (A. Koczirz, Introdution to Bakfark's compositions in Denkmäler der Tonkunst in Österreich, 37 (Jg. 18/2) (1911), p. 35). Although this failed, Bakfark succeeded in having his work published in Lyons by Jacques Moderne in 1553.

[30] On Bakfark's return to Poland, the prince of Prussia wrote to Zygmunt August on Bakfark's behalf, claiming that the latter had been offered employment by several patrons, including the pope and the king of France: 'commemoravit mihi, sibi a multis videlicet a Summo Pontifice et alijs ampla stipendia annuatim esse proposita, praecipue vero a Serenissimo Rege Franciae qui non modi ipsum viventem, sed heredes etiam illius magnis beneficijs ornare promiscerit . . .' in: O. Gombosi, *Der Lautenist Valentin Bakfark, Leben und Werke*, 1507-1576, ed. Z. Flavy (Musicologia Hungarica, Neue Folge, Veröffentlichungen des Bartók Archivs in Budapest, 1; Budapest, 1967 (repr. of Budapest, 1935 edn.).

[31] The first payment he received after he returned was for some new strings for his lute, but no mention of music of any sort.

[32] Of little or no significance were two further foreign chapel members, Albert Francuz ('Frenchman'), chaplain in Vilnius for just over a year (1560-1), and the youth Stefan Lesser from Styria in the Austrian Region of the Habsburg empire, employed between 1552 and 1554. It is doubtful that either was responsible for bringing prints into the country.

[33] A. and Z. Szweykowscy, 'Wacław z Szamotuł'. This has been deduced by the authors by dating Trzecieski's *De obitu Venceslai Samotulini* . . . , at about 1560, which states that the composer was 34 years old when he died.

[34] A. and Z. Szweykowscy, 'Wacław z Szamotuł', p. 11.

[35] *In nuptiis sereniss. Domini Ioannis, Hungariae Regis et sereniss. virginis Isabellae, sereniss. et invictiss. principis, Domini Sigismundi Primi Poloniae regis filiae, poema gratulatorium* ...(Ungler, Kraków, 1539); *In nativitate illustrissimi Domini Ioannis Sigismundi, principis Hungariae et Transilvaniae ... filii serenissimorum principum D. Ioannis regis et D. Isabellae reginae Hungariae. Poema gratulatorium* (Vietor, Kraków, 1540); *In nuptiis Serenissimi Poloniae regis magnique Lituaniae ducis, Sigismundi secundi Augusti et serenissimae virginis Elizabethae, gloriosiss. et invictis, principis Ferdinandi ... filiae Poema gratulatorium* (Ungler, Kraków, 1543), *In funere Serenisss. Principis et D: D. Elizabethae sereniss. Rom. Hung. Bohe. etc. Regis filiae, Potentiss. ac invictiss. Principis et D. D. Sigismundi II Augusti, Dei gratia Regis Poloniae, Magni Ducis Lithuaniae,* . . . *Coniugis multo amantissimae.*

Carmen lugubre VII die Augusti conscriptim Anno MDXLV (Ungler, Kraków, 1545). Only the last of these is extant.

[36] A. and Z. Szweykowscy, 'Wacław z Szamotuł', p. 18.

[37] Ibid., pp. 6-7. This they base on the lament on the composer's death by Trzecieski, *De obitu Venceslai Samotulini* . . . , written in Pińczów in or about 1560.

[38] I am indebted to Professor Z. Szweykowski for making the facsimiles of the extant partbooks available to me. Detailed work on the extant books is now being carried out by Dr P. Poźniak of the Jagiellonian University, Kraków.

[39] Only a copy of this survives; the manuscript itself was destroyed during the Second World War. A transcription of the whole tablature has been prepared by J. Gołos, *The Organ Tablature of the Warsaw Musical Society* (Antiquitates musices in Polonia, 15; Graz, 1968), pp. 231-323.

[40] A vocal arrangement has been prepared by Mirosław Perz in Feicht (ed.), *Muzyka staropolska*, p. 61.

[41] See the Jasivcicz inventory, Appendix XIII, items 109, 111, 113, 116 and 131.

[42] One of these may be the 'Fabricii' mass copied into one of the Rorantists' manuscripts, Kk I.4, in the 1580s. The mass is discussed in Chapter III.

[43] The four-part Lamentations and Passion responses also recorded in the Jasivcicz inventory can be presumed to be those published in 1553, which the chapel possessed either in print or possibly in an original manuscript form.

[44] See above, Chapter IV, note 59.

[45] RK 173, fol. 133r: 'Venceslao Compositori cantus sac. M. R. De grá Sac M. Regie compensari eidé laboré in componendis varys musices mutetis per ipsú fetiú Parczoviæ dat f. 50.'. This note is also recorded in Z. and A. Szweykowscy, 'Wacław z Szamotuł', p. 22.

[46] 'In te Domine speravi', (WDMP 9, 4th edn., Kraków, 1977); 'Ego sum pastor bonus', *Muzyka w dawnym Krakowie*, pp. 64-7.

[47] A. Chybiński, 'Ze studiów nad polską muzyką wielogłosową w XVI stuleciu', *Przegląd Muzyczny*, nos. 8-9, pp. 5-8. Z. Szweykowski, 'Rozkwit', pp. 102-4.

[48] G. Nugent, Introduction to *Jachet of Mantua, Opera omnia*, (CMM 54/4; Neuhausen-Stuttgart, 1982), p. xi.

[49] The influence of these two composers on Wacław's music has been generally accepted in the past by Polish musicologists.

[50] The manuscripts in question are **G** Rs MS 849-52; S L 8; **PL** WRo S 2 (lost); WRo S5 (lost); WRo S10 (lost). These last three items are known from E. Bohn, *Die musikalischen Handschriften des XVI. und XVII. Jahrhunderts in der Stadtbibliothek zu Breslau* (Breslau, 1890).

Conclusions

The royal court in Poland was arguably *the* main focal point of cultural life in the country during the sixteenth century; judging from the extant archival information, it was unmatched by any other court of the Polish magnates or bishops. Here, as elsewhere in Europe, the musical climate was determined very much by the personal interests of the monarch as well as his specific way of life.

Of the two establishments discussed in this study, it is Zygmunt II August's musical establishment that should take pride of place. Its creation in Poland is all the more praiseworthy in view of the fact that it superseded those of his predecessors. The chapel choir comprised a full complement of voices almost consistently, and included a composer for a number of years; there were also several independent groups of instrumentalists. The constant alterations and improvements made by the king, not to mention the salary rises of individual members, testifies to a real interest in music in its various forms. Whilst there are general similarities between this establishment and those of other European courts, there are a few important differences. Throughout Europe it was the permanent courts of the monarchs and dukes which were the most splendid; itinerary courts, for practical reasons, were more modest. In Zygmunt August's case, his apparent dislike for the capital Kraków, and his attendance at the sessions of parliament in their various locations made him a very mobile monarch. This did not prevent him from maintaining a sizeable musical establishment, which accompanied the king for the most part. Indeed, this mobility did have its advantages, since a significant number of members were recruited during the king's various travels. As for the repertory of the royal chapel, it has been shown to be both substantial and varied. The presence of such a variety of foreign prints as well as his encouragement of local music production is surely indicative of Zygmunt August's wide-ranging musical taste.

Next to the royal chapel, the Rorantists' college clearly looks pale by comparison, though given its specific nature, a direct comparison should not be made. Unlike the relative flexibility of the royal chapel, the Rorantists' college was restricted by the founding acts; its size and make-up (of ordained priests) was determined from the outset, and it was obliged to perform set duties. To a large extent, these constricting factors explain the college's modest repertory, much of which was locally produced and intended specifically for its use. The college did acquire a small amount of foreign music during the second half of the century, and some of this almost certainly came via the royal chapel. Nonetheless, the Rorantists' position within the context of the cathedral on Wawel Hill is noteworthy. They introduced polyphony on a daily basis in one of the building's side-chapels, and they were the sole providers of polyphonic music for the liturgy at the cathedral for the main feasts until 1619.

As for the relationship between the royal chapel and the Rorantists' college, the movement of individuals between the two during the period in question is revealing. On a number of occasions in the mid-1540s and early 1550s, chaplains moved from the Rorantists' college to the royal chapel. It is possible that Zygmunt August was creaming off the best talent for his own private chapel. By contrast, following the dissolution of Zygmunt August's court in 1574, several of the late king's chaplains, presumably with no other career prospects, resorted to benefices in the Rorantists' chapel.

Finally, it is interesting to observe the fate of the two institutions and their place in the overall development of music in Poland. The musical tradition built up by Zygmunt August, arguably the first pinnacle of musical splendour in the country, came to an abrupt end with his death and burial. There was no heir to continue or develop what he had created, and the remnants of the establishment faded away during the ensuing interregna. Likewise the vast music collection of the chapel perished almost without a trace. This is not to say that musical patronage at the royal court disappeared altogether; however, the next monarchs created their own establishments and introduced new elements to them. It was only at the very end of the sixteenth century that the next significant wave of royal musical patronage, under Zygmunt III Vasa, took place. He invited a whole troupe of Italian composers, singers, and instrumentalists to Warsaw,[1] where he made his main residence, and in so doing initiated a new era in Poland's musical history. By contrast, the Rorantists' college survived relatively unchanged for more than two centuries, and preserved an indigenous (if modest) musical tradition, developed and fostered by successive generations of Polish composers.

NOTES

[1] A. Szweykowska, 'Przeobrażenia w kapeli królewskiej na przełomie XVI i XVII wieku', *Muzyka*, 13 (1968), no. 2, pp. 3-21.

Appendices

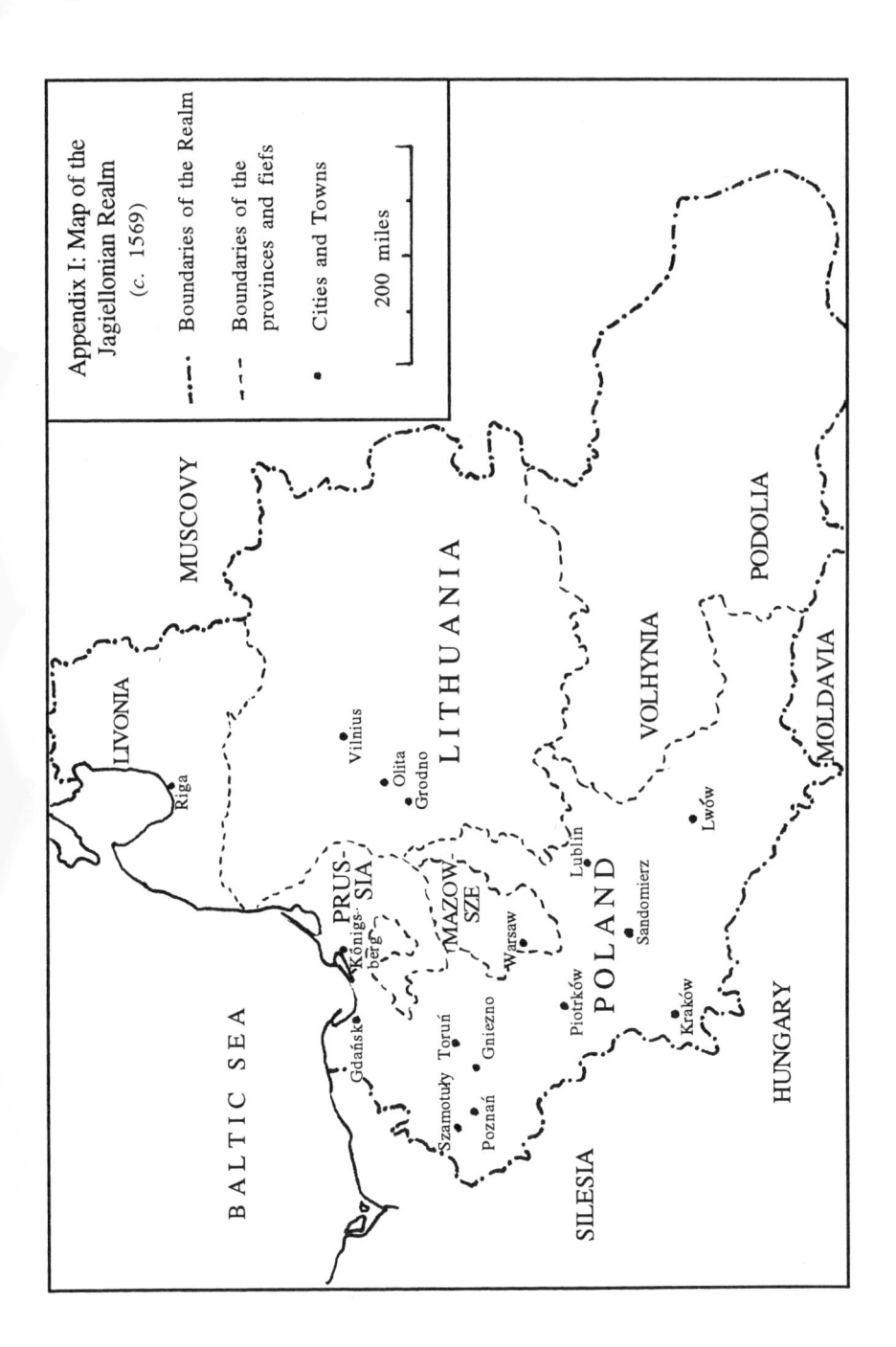

Appendix I

Appendix I: Map of the Jagiellonian Realm (c. 1569)

—··— Boundaries of the Realm
— — — Boundaries of the provinces and fiefs
  • Cities and Towns

200 miles

APPENDIX II: THE RORANTISTS' ACTS

This appendix contains diplomatic transcriptions of the Rorantists' founding acts, preserved in the cathedral archive on Wawel Hill, Kraków. The text has not been emended and all abbreviations and contractions are reproduced as closely as possible, the one exception being the symbol for '-que' which, due to technical difficulties in representing the symbol in the script here, has been expanded. For documents Kk dyp. 1184, Kk dyp. 1172, and Kk dyp. 1190, foliation or pagination is presented within the text in square brackets. Kk dyp. 1184 has two paginations, the earlier includes only the inner pages which has the text and a more recent pagination which includes the outer bi-folio. The latter has been adopted here. Kk dyp. 110 is a single folio document, with the text appearing only on the recto. Some editorial comments are provided within the text in square brackets, and additional notes and explanations are given as endnotes to the respective documents.

Appendix II.1

II.1: Kk dyp. 110, King Kazimierz III Wielki, 5 February 1430

IN NOMINE DOMINI AMEN. Per felices actus humanos fructus phennos carpiunt^ur, dum mat^er ecclia nouis ornata dotibus, a regeneratis populis adoratur. Igit^r tam pns etas nouit q^uam futura, Quod nos kazimirus dei gra Rex Polonie, Qui exmito legalitatis munificencias matris Ecclie, Adauge pmrs viribus decnentes, vt mrs tempibus ipa mat. Ecclia in cultu diuino aucta, felicibz inc^ementis tranquilla deuocone letet^ur, Nosque ab uberibus consolaciois eius saciati phenniter excultemus, Itaque Capllam fundacois nre in honorem glose Assumpcois Ste Maria in corpe Ecclie nre Cracov. Kathedralis ista dote adornantes, damus donamus et confimus dno Nicolao de Wercziczow, cui pmum cotulimus Capllam pnotatam, eiusqz succedaneis annis singulis tempibus ppetuis semp in quibuslibet quatuortpibus duas mrcas gross. annuatim pcipiendas in nro Theloneo Cracovien vendicone eiusd. Thelonei non obstante. Sic quod cum ipm. Theloneum ovendiderimus ante omia hy qui theloneu emerint semp possessori dte Capelle duas mr pdtas, vt pmissum e soluant in quibuslibz qt^ortpibus, et solue sint astricti. Nosque cultum diuinu p defunctis et viuis ibidem instaurare volentes cu efftu. exnuc decimam et decimas post aratra nra in Scepanow in Słomniki in Nagnoyouicze et in Winari, iungimus Caplle pnotate q^uisquidem decimas possessor eiusdem Capllé habeat ppetuo singulis annis eas pcipiens, a nobis vo et a nris successoribus in expensis et vna veste anno quolibet inppetuu pcurentur Nihilominus successores nros comuit^r et diuisim oms Regali iure astrigimus ad obsuaconem huius nre donaconis, contrarios ira Judicis etni ferientes sup eos glosa Vgine Maia supplicit inuocata. Hec ig^ur omia etne meorie commendantes ntro Regio insignio iussimus phennari Actum Cracouie, die bte Agathe Vg^is Anno dni M· CCC· xl. Pntibus hys Nobilibus nris Spicimio Castllo. Mistigneo Palatino Zbigneo Pposito et Cancellario Iaroslao Archid^no Cracouien, Pet^o nosal Sandomien Andrea Radom Casellanis et alys multis fidedignis, Datum p maus Cancelarij pnotati.

II.2: Kk dyp. 1184, Piotr Gamrat, bishop of Kraków, 28 August 1543

[3] IN NOMINE DOMINI NOSTRI IESU CHRISTI

Ad perpetuam rei memoriam, Est hoc proprium Episcoporum munus, ea quæ ad divinum cultum pertinent, diligenter providere, atque in eo quamplurimum elaborare, vt is quam maxime augeatur, Cuius autem liberalitate munificientiaque auctus fuerit literarum monumentis mandare, vt ea posteris quoque testata et illustrat́ esse queat. Et nos itaque Petrus Gamrath a Szowokląski Dei et Apostolicæ Sedis gratia Archiepiscopus Sanctæ Ecclesiæ Metropolitanè Gnesnēn, Sedis Apostolicæ Legat natus, et Regni Poloniæ primas, necnon Episcopus Cracovień, planum testatumque facimus Vniuersis et singulis quicumque in hæc ńra monumenta inciderint, Quod Serenissimus atque idem longe omnium religiosissimus Princeps, et dominus dominus Sigismundus eo nomine primus Dei gratia REX Poloniæ, Magnus Dux Lithuaniæ, Russiæ, Masoviæ etć dominus et heres, dominus noster clementissimus, maiorum suorum uestigia secutus, quos et ipsos pietate et religione habuit insignes, Divinum cultum in Ecclesia nostra Cathedrali Cracovień permultum auxit, idque eis temporibus quibus indormiscente nauclero ńro Christo, multa existunt heresum naufragia, multorumquè animi in fide fluctuant, vt apud vicinos populos magna ex parte imminutus, et [4] modo non penitus, sublatus Divinus cultus uideatur, Jis ipsis itaque temporibus tam miseris quibus in errorem inducuntur, etiam electi, uolens suam in prisce fide constantiá declarare, quod iuxta Pauli præceptum depositum fideliter custodierit, prophanas nouitates deuitauerit, neque se omni doctrinæ uento circumferri, atque ab eo quod uocauit in gratiam christi: in aliud Euangelium transferri passus sit, in ornandum templum Domini summa liberalitate usus est; persuasum enim sibi habebat (id quod res ipsa est) si quam aliam hanc ad Reges et Principes curam pertinere maxime, vt et ipsi Diuini cultus augendi sint studiosi, & quo sunt præ cæteris diuites, magnis et copiosi, hoc amplius de suis facultatibus impartiant, cum in alendos et sustentandos eos qui inuocænt nomen domini, et in Lege eius meditentur die ac nocte, tum in ipsa etiam templa ornanda, instauráda ac de integro etiá fabricáda in quibus interior homo qui secundum Deum creatus est, suam in Deum uoluntatem explicare, et quæ supplex ab eo petierit, ea, clementia illius et benignitate possit impetrare. Deinde vero gratum et memorem præstare se cupiebat eorum beneficiorum quæ a Divina Maie^te immensa acceperat: Illius enim benignitate praeterqm̄ quod filio auctus est se dignissimo, imagine anima et corporis sui, quem Regem coronatum cum Serrenissima domina Elizabeth Serenissimi et Excellentissimi domini Fœrdinandi Romanorum Regis filia matrimonium contraxisse vidit, multas de hostibus suis et eius insignes victorias et triumphos reportauit. Nam et Moschorum ac prope innumerabiles copias: parua manu memorabili prælio vicit: Et Tartarorum sepe magnos fudit exercitus: Et Valachos non vno prælio superatos adegit, Vt a qua desciuisse et quam contempsisse nisi erant ad eius authoritatem redirent. Prussiam uero totam sui Juris fecit: Et Masouiam absque armis sub

Appendix II.2 189

imperium & potestatem suam successorumque suorum subiunxit. Quæ sua præclara facts tum dona esse et beneficia Dei agnosceret, atque illius clementiæ: non suis ea Juribus tribueret, pro eo qua præditus est pietate et religione, tenere se non potuit princeps optimus, quin de tanta Dei in se beneficentia, grati sui animi, monumentum alioquod relinqueret: Neque satis dignum est arbitratus, cum sibi in Arce sua Cracouiensi magnificas ædes incredibili sumptu ędificasset, atque eas fortuito incendio magna ex parte absumptas, nouis et magnis impensis instaurasset: non aliquam eadem in Arce ædiculam fabricare in qua Deus pié coloretur: Itaque maiore quam credi queat sumptu, ac præclaro quodam artificio ædiculam eius modi in Ecclesia nra Cathedrali Cracouień e fundamentis erectam, colato lapide fabricatus est, vt non modo in Regno, sed ne in omnibus quidem terris, in quibus Maiestas eius summa cum potestate uersatur, nullam perinde visendum et memorandum opus extæt. Quamquidem ædiculam, siue Oratorium, aut Sacellum, vel Capellam, in Laudem et gloriam Dei optimi Maximi, Et in memoriam Sanctissimé Virginis matris Mariæ Assumptionis, ac Divorum Sigismundi Regis, et Barbaræ Virginis martiris ædificatam, a fabre admodum et lapide exornatam, multam Aurea & Argentea [5] supellectili, gemmis, et Lapidibus præciosis, multis etiam ornamentis Auro et Argento intextis copiose instruxit: Ac Sepulchrum inibi, in quo sua suorumque ossa conderentur, plane Regium extruxit: Collegium præterea Sacerdotum instituit, qui sempiternis temporibus psalerent Deo altissimo, praecationibusque et obsecrationibus iram a nobis eius auerterent, gratiamque et misericordiam consiliarent, cū matris misericordiǽ, tum aliorum Divorum intercessionem implorando. Numerus autem sacerdotum est, praepositus vnus, Prębendarii nouem, Clericus vnus, Quibusquidem et de habitatione commoda prouidit, domo illis in Arce Cracouiensi Lateritia non paruo impendio fabricata, et de victu sustentationeque corporis liberaliter prospexit. IMPRIMIS et ante omnia prouentus et obuentiones ad altare, Capellaniam, siue in eadem Capella ante illius nouiter factam per suam Maiestatem extructionem ut praemissum est fundatam et erectam ex antiquo spectań et pertineń, Praeposito ipsius Capellæ pro tempore existenti, ascribi et appropriari sua Maiestas uoluit, ita tamen: q̄d onera illi capellaniaé incubentia rita et recta[1] supportentur, iuxta ordinationem ac literarum desuper factarum uim, formam et continentiam. Fructus autem et prouentus ab antiquo ipsius altaris et Altaristæ sunt infrascripti, Imprimis videlicet in Zuppis Vielicień idem Altarista singulis Anni quartalibus ratione census percipit Marcas quatuor. Item de Theloneo Cracouień pro quilibet anni quartali habet Marcas duas latorum grossorum, alias marcas duas cum media, cum octo grossis communis monetæ modernæ; Item habet Decimam Prædialem in Oppido Szłomnẏkii, cuius valor secundum temporú qualitatem augetur uel minuitur. Item habet Decimam prædialem in villa Szczepanowicze a Schłomnẏkii versus Proschewicze in medio miliari distante, vbi non est Curia, tamen agri coluntur, et frumenta inde collecta ad prædium villae Crzissouycze inducuntur: quam uel quas Jure hereditario M[cus] d[ús] de Tharnow obtinet. Item habet Decimas Praediales in villis Posznachowicze siue Gorna Villa, et Vinari ad Castrum Dobczicze spectań, Quorum omnium fructus in numerum redacti Alteristæ pro tempore existenti efficiunt annis communibus marcas quadraginta tres. Demum pro Præbendariis Decimas manipulares omnis grani et seminis post araturas Villarum Kąskii, Czerwona Nywa, et Coszłowicze ad Ecclesiam parrachialem in Viszkithkii Dioecesis Posnamień, olim pertineń ab ea dismembratas, prout in literis R^{mi} in christo patris domini Sebastiani Branÿczki Dei gratia Episcopi Posnaniensis desuper confectis latius apparet contineri, quarum tenor sequitur, et est talis.

IN NOMINE DOMINI AMEN. Ad perpetuam rei memoriam SEBASTIANUS Branÿczki Dei gratia Episcopus Posnanień. Vniuersis et singulis pntēs nrās literas inspecturis, illis præsertim quibus interest, intererit, aut interesse, quosque infrascriptum tangit negotium, tangereque poterit in futurum, Salutem in domino sempiternam. De summis cœlorum ad ima descendens vnigenitus Dei filius, vt hominem de laqueo eriperet seruitatis, in quem ex suggestione serpentina impegerat, Vesté nostræ mortalitatis induit, ut aspersione sui Sanctissimi sanguinis, incendii perpetui cruciatus extingueret: ac nos ęterna morte depulsa, efficeter vitæ æternae possessores, antequam autem nostræ redemptionis misterium perficeret, nos omnes commone facere uoluit inquiens. Thesaurisate vobis Thesauros in cœlo etc. [6] Huc accedunt etiam præcelsa meritorum insignia, quibus Regina cœlorum virgo Dei genitrix gloriosa, sedibus preclari sÿderis quasi stella matutina prærutilat, quae cum devota consideratione perscrutamur, et dum etiam inter pietatis archana reuoluimus, quod ipsa, ut puta, misericordiæ mater, gratiæ et pietatis amica, humani generis consolatrix et peruigil, apud Regem quem genuit intercedit, dignum quinimo debitum reputamus, ut loca suo nomini dicata, sint a nobis merito ueneranda, Vt etiam eius piis adiuti suffragiis, æternæ tribulationis præmia consequi mereamur. Sane huiusmodi ac pari deuotionis ardore permotus, ac Diuino numine comonitus SERINISSIM' et Inuictissimus Princeps, et dominus dominus eo nomine primus SIGISMŨDVS Dei gratia REX Poloniæ', Magnus Dux Lithuaniæ', Russiæ', Prussiæ, Masoviæ etc', dominus et heres. Ecclesiæ' parrochialis in Wiszkithki, nostræ Dioeć Posnanień vnicus patronus, Capellam in Arce sua Cracouień, Sub inuocatione Assumptionis intemeratæ et gloriossimæ' Dei genitricis Virginis Mariæ, ex fundamentis, magnis sumptibus extruxit et exornauit, ac in ea præpostum & certum numerum præsbiterorum ad psallendum omnipitenti Deo, deputari et constitui, facere et dotare intendit, ac ut commodius sustentari ualeant, in dismembrationem Decimarum manipularium infrascriptarum, ad Ecclesiam parrochialem in Wiszkithkii ex antiquo pertinentium, ad eum effectum, quod huiusmodi Decimæ prædictæ Capellæ & communitati præsbiterorum in eadem Capella ad psallendum Diuinú officium statuendorum unirentur et incorporarentur, patentibus literis titulo et sigillo suæ Maiestatis comunitis, consentiendum duxit et consensit, alias ad id facień nobis facultatem concessit, prout in eisdem literis continetur, quarum tenor de uerbo ad uerbú sequitur & est talis: SIGISMVNDUS Dei gratia REX Poloniæ', Magnus Dux Lithuaniæ', Totius Prusiæ. Masoviæ etc

Appendix II.2

dominus et haeres, Significamus tenore præsentium quorum interest Vniuersis. Cum in laudem et gloriam Dei omnipotentis in Ecclesia Cathedrali Cracouień, Sacellum ingenti sumptu ædificassemus, in memoriam Assumptionis intermerate Virginis matris, visum est nobis Præpositum in eo et certum Sacerdotum numerum constituere: qui psallerent nomini Domini Altissmi, ac præcibus et Sacrificiis placatum nobi Deum reddere, et iram eius a nobis auertere conarentur: Quoniam uero, qui seruit Altari, ei uiuendum est de Altari, oper præcium existimauimus vt quos in sacello nŕo ministros Dei constituissemus, eis de victus ratione prospiceremus, Quam ad rem cum certam quandam vectigalium nostrorum patrem conuertissemus, quoniam ea nequaquam sufficere uidebatur, prochialis uero Ecclesia in Viszkithki Juris patronatus nŕi, tam uberes et copiosos fructus habebat, vt si pars aliqua eorum detracta esset, nihilominus in satis lauta et bene acta parte parrochus eius fructus esset: faciendum putauimus, vt certas Decimas ex parrochiali ecclesia in Viskithki in Sacelli nŕi sacerdotes alendos conuerteremus. Sunt autem Decimæ per nos assignate istæ. Omnes et singuleˊ Decimæ manipulares cuiuscumque grani et seminis ex Agris tam Kmethonalibus quam Prædialibus Villarum nostrarum Kąskii, Geruanÿowa, et Cozliuicze wulgariter dictæ, in Ducatu nostro Masouiæ et Districtu Sochaczouień consisteń prouenień. Has itaque Decimas ex parrochiali ecclesia in Wiszkithki detractas, et Sacerdotibus sacelli nostri sempiternis temporibus adiunctas, atque in eorum usum conuersas esse volumus, ita ut easdem præsentibus lŕis nŕis a parrochiali detrahimus, & sacerdotibus [7] sacelli nostri adiungimus, atque in eorum sempiternum usum conuertimus, Ea tamen lege & conditione, ut in Ecclesia Viszkithki parrochus non habeat necesse earum Decimarum nomine, quæ detractæ sunt, onera ulla sustinere: sed ad quos commodum, ad eosdem etiam onus perueniat: vt si queˊ erunt contributiones soluendæ, eas pro ratha sacerdotes nostri soluant. Parrochus autem non sit obligatus plus tribuere, quam quantum efficiunt Decimæ, in quarum possessione remansit. In quorum omnium fidem et testimonium hec scribi sigilloque nŕo communiri fecimus. Daẗ Cracouiæˊ feria sexta infra octauas Epiphaniarum. Anno domini Millesimo, Quingentesimo, Quadragesimo. R^{to} Reuereń in chŕo pr̃is domini Samuelis Maczieiowski Episcopi Chelmēń, et Regni Poloniæ Vicecancellarii. Fuimus tandem nomine Sacræ Maiestatis requisiti, quatenus ad huiusmodi dismembrationem et unionem respectiue decimarum prædictarum procederemus, literasque desuper necessarias concederemus. Nos igitur Sebastianus praedictus Epús huiusmodi piis Sacræ Maié^{tis} Regieˊ domini nŕi clementissimi desideriis et conatibus, paternæˊ annuentes, amplitudinique honori et cultui diuino in prænominata Ecclesia Cracouień augendo, quantum in nobis est, consulere cupień, ad ulteriorem sacræ Maiē^{tis} Regiæˊ domini nŕi clementissimi vnici patroni instanciam, accedente etiam Vene^{lis} domini Joannis Andreeˊ de Valentinis Præpositi Cracouień Regiæ M̃^{tis} secretarii et Phisici, ac præedictæ parrochialis in Viszkithki Rectoris moderni, expresso consensu coram nobis sponte ad id facto attendēń, quod prædicta parrochialis in Viszkithkii tantum habet, quod dismembratione infrascripta facta, parrochus ipsius seu rector modernus et tempore existens, commodissime de reliquo prouentum ipsius parrochialis sustentari possit et valeat, omnes et singulas Decimas manipulares cuiuslibet grani et seminis ex Agris tam kmethonalibus quam prædicalibus villarum Regiarum Kaski, Geruanijowa et Cosłouicze wulgariter dictarum, in Ducatu Mazouiæ' et Districtu Sochaczouień consistentium prouenientes, a prædicta parrochiali in Viskithkj duximus dismembrañ, prout dismembramus, et dismembratas, seperatas, et diuisas, perpetuis temporibus esse uolumus, easque cum omnibus Juribus, vsibus & emolumentis vniuersis, Præposito et communitati præsbiterorum in præfata Capella Regia constituent pro eorum sustentatione, in perpetuum exnunc Vnimus, incorporamus, et annectimus in Dei nomine per præsentes perpetuo et in euum, Ita quod liceat prædicto Præposito et præsbiteris alias Vniuersitati præsbiterorum dictæ Capellæ pro tempore existentibus, Decimas & proventus huiusmodi percipere et habere, ac in usus suos et dictæ communitatis præsbiterorum conuertere, et perpetuo obtinere, nr̃a aut successorum nostrum, necnon Regie' M^{tis} et Rectoris prædictæ parrochialis in Wiszkithkii pro tempore existentis licentia et consensu, super hoc alias minime requisito, iuxta statutũ & ordinationem ordinarii loci faciendam: Ita tamen ut satisfiat illi regulæ Juris, qui sentit commodum, ut idem sentiat onus, Vt parrochus Ecclesiæ in Viszkithkii non teneat^r ad ferenda onera ex parte Decimarum quæ sunt illi detractæ' sed illarum decimarum nomine omnia onera sustineant Sacerdotes Sacelli sacrae Regiae M^{tis}, atque pro ea parte decimarum quam possederint, contributionem soluere sint obligati, plebanus uero in Viskithkii non soluet, nisi pro ualore earum decimarum quæ sunt ei relictæ. QVOCIRCO Vobis Vniuersis et singulis personis Ecclesiasticis, Notariis, et Tabellionibus publicis, per Ciuitatem et Diocesim nostrum Posnanień constitutis, auctoritate nŕa [8] tenore præsentium sub pena excommunicationis Mandatum committteń, quatenus vos aut alter uestrum, qui super hoc fueritis requisiti, aut alter uestrum requisitus fuerit, præfatum Præpositum et Vniuersitatem præsbiterorum in corporalem possessione huiusmodi Decimarum per nos ut præmittitur unitarum, Juriumque et pertinentium ṕdictaŕ ponatis et inducatis vice nŕa, eiusdemque de prænominatis Decimas et prouentibus Vniuersis respondeatis, & faciatis quantum in uobis est plenarie' responderi. QUÆ omnia et singula præmissa, necnon præsentes literas et earum contenta, vobis omnibus & singulis supradictis ac uestrum cuilibet intimamus, insinuamus, et notificamus, ad uestramque et cuiuslibet uestrum noticiam deducimus et deduci uolumus per præsentes, ne de præmissis ignorantiam aliquam prætendere seu etiam allegare valeatis. In quorum omnium et singulorum fidem et testimonium præmissorum, præsentes literas scribi et per Notarium publicum infrascriptum subscripti et publicari mandauimus, nŕique sigilli iussimus & fecimus appensione communiri. Daȋ Cracouiæ in Curia Mag^{ci} domini Joannis a Thanczin Palatini Sandomirień in platea Castreń sitta. Anno a natiuitate domini Millesimo, Quingentesimo, Quadragesimo, Indicione tredecima, die Mercurii, quartadecima Mensis Januarii. Pontificatus Sanctissimi in chr̃o pr̃s domini, nostri Pauli diuina prouidentia Pape

Appendix II.2 193

tertii, anno SEXTO. Præsentibus Venerabilibus et Honorabilibus dominis Jacobo Vchanski Canonico Cracouień Regię Maiestatis Referendario. Bartholomeo Ganthkowski Cancellario Posnanień. Paulo Obrziczki Canonico Sancti Georgii in Arce Cracouień, et parrocho Dzierszkouień, Jacobo Riskowski Capellano nostro, Gnesnēń, Cracouień, Posnāń, et Plocēń Diōce Clericis, testibus ad præmissa vocatis et assumptis. Et quia ego Martinus Stanislai Naropinski de Naropna Clericus Gnesnensis dioć Notarius Sacra Auctoritate Apostolica publicus et coram supra scripto R^{mo} in christo patre et dño dño Sebastiano Branẏczki Dei gratia Epo Posnanień actus pntis scriba, præmissis dismembrationi Consensum præstitioni, et præsentiú decreto, omnibusque aliis et singulis, vna cum prænominatis testibus præsens interfui eaque sic fieri vidi et audiui, Ideo præsentis dismembrationis literas subscripsi, publicaui et consignaui, Sigillique memorati R^{mi} domini Episcopi Posnanień de mandato suæ p^{tis} $R^{mé}$, legittimá appensione cummuniui, in fidem et testimonium præmissorum omnium et singulorum. etc. Postremo centum marcas pecuniarum numeri et monetæ polonicalium, quadraginta octo grossos in quamlibet marcam computando, ad Magistrum montium Salinarum Zuppę Bochnēń olim pertinēń, sua Regia M^{tas} ære suo proprijs pecunijs comparat. Necnon domum latericiam præfatam penes portam Castri Cracouień in manu dextra sitt, impensa Sacræ M^{tis} Regię propria extructam et fabricam, simul eidem collegio præsbiterorum asscribi & incorporari voluit iuxta modum in lŕis desuper confectis, Quarum tenor de uerbo ad uerbum sequitur et est talis. IN NOMINE DOMINI AMEN. Ad perpetuam rei memoriam. Nos Sigismundus Die gratia REX Poloniæ, Magnus Dux Lithuaniæ, Necnon terrarum Cracouiæ, Sandomiriæ, Siradiæ, Lanciciæ, Cuiauię, Russię, [9] totiusque Prussiæ, Masoviæ, Culmēń, Elbingēń, Pomeraniæque etc dominus et heres. Significamus tenore præsentium quibus expedit Vniuersis et singulis præsentibus et futuris harum noticiam habituris, Quod nos maiorum nostrorum Serenissimorum Poloniæ Regum uestigia persecuti, qui cultus Diuini propagandi semper studiosissimi, in ecclesia uero Cathedrale Castri ńŕi Cracovień, cumprimis benefici fuerunt et liberales: Volentes et ipsi grati nostri erga Deum animi, et erga eandem illius ecclesiam studij nŕi monumentum relinquere, ac nostram in prisca fide et religione constantiam testatam omnibus facere, quo magis in ea diuinus cultus augeri possit et aplificari; Sacellum in ea magno sumptu nostro ædificauimus, ac certum Sacerdotum numerum, qui sacris operarēńt instituimus, qui ut tranquilliore animo omni alia cura posthabita, diuinis officiis uacare possent: Domum in castro nostro Cracovień latericiam, penes portam eiusdem Castri, inter domos duas Burgrabiales sittam Seip vulgo dici solitam, ex fundamentis extruximus, eiusdem domus partes duas immunitati Ecclesiasticæ adscriptas in tempora sempiterna Præposito, Mansionariis, et Clerico prædicti sacelii nostri Regij, in habitandum dedimus et donauimus, Quemadmodum damus et donamus præsentibus donatione irreuocabili, parte eiusdem domus tertia pro frumentis nŕis relictâ. Volent & constituen, ut in dictis duabus partibus domus nemo habitare possit uel audeat, præter Præpositum,

Mansionarios et Clericum sacelli nři prædicti. Quibus etiam pro victu, competenti præter Decimas a parochiali in Viszkithkii dismembratas, in Agris Villarum Caszki, Czeruona nÿwa, et Cosłowicze, dedimus et donauimus, ita ut damus et donamus ex prouentibus Salinarum nostrarum Cracouień Censum, Centum Marcarū numeri et monetæ Regni nři, a Magistro montium percipi quondam solitum, quem nos nosta[2] pecunia redemimus, et Præposito ac Mansionarÿs capellæ nostræ prædictæ assignavimus, ita ut ad singula quartalia Anni per marcas Viginti quinque ipsis soluendas et numerandas. Hanc itaque donationem nřam firmá et ratam esse uoleń sempiternis temporibus, successores etiam nostros ad eam ratam habend́ astringimus: Si quis autem contrauenire, et eam violare ausus fuerit, ei coram seuero Iudice Deo optimo maximo, diem dicimus, vt ad iustum illius tribunal primo quoque tempore, se sistat, et piǽ uoluntatis huius nřæ temerate causam dicat. Harum quibus sigilum nostrum est appensum testimonio literarum. Dat́ Cracouié Sabbato post diem festum sancti Jacobi Apostoli proximo. Anno domini Millesimo, Quingentesimo, Quadragesimo tertio. Regni uero ntři Anno Trigesimo septimo. Præsentibus Reuereń[mo] ac Revereń in chřo patribus dńis, Petro de Gamratis Archiepiscopo Gnesneń, et Episcopo Cracouień, Legatus Nato et Primate. Samuele Maczieiowski Episcopo Ploceń, et Regni Poloniǽ vicecancellario. Necnon Magnifico, Venerabilibus et Generosis, Petro Opalenski Gnesneń, et Serenissimi filii nostri char[mi] Curiæ Magistro, ac Olstinens et Costeń Capitaneo. Seuerino Boner Bieceń, & Zuppario, Burgrabio, et Magno procuratore nřo Cracouień, ac Bieceń, Osiączimeń, Zathorień, et in Oczietz Capitaneo Castellanis. Andrea Czarnkowskii Scolastico Cracouiensi, Mathia Drzeuiczkii Canonico Cracouień, Stanislao Hosio utriusque Juris Doctore Canonico Cracouień Hieronimo Staskowski coquine nře Magistro. Augustino Cothficz stabuli nostri præfecto, et aliis quamplurimis Dignitariis, Secretariis, [10] Officialibus, et Aulicis nostris fide dignis sÿncere nobis et fidelibus dilectis. Dat per manus præfati Reuereń in christo přis, domini Samuelis Maczieiowski Episcopi Plocensis, et Regni Poloniæ Vicecancellarii, Syncere nobis dilecti. Rło Reuereń in chřo patris domini Samuelis Maczieiowski Episcopi Ploceń et Regni Poloniæ Vicecancellarii. Quibusquidem prouentibus Maiestas sua Regia uoluit, et animo suo declarauit, ut collegium præsbiterorum constitueretur, quod habeat unum Præpositum perpetuum, Necnon nouem præbendarios, et unum Clericum manuales, et nulla cura animarum seu als aliis sacerdotiis oneratos, qui in eadem Capella perpetuis futuris temporibus domino Deo laudes decantarent, iuxta ordinationem nobis per Sacram Maiestatem Regiam traditam, et per nos inferius describeń et declarań, Postulatumque est a nobis eiusdem Sacræ Maiestatis nomine, quatenus[3] ad ordinationem et decretum huiusmodi cum opportuna confirmatione et approbatione omnīu et singulorum premissorum procederemus. Nos uero in talibus modum et formá seruare uoleń, ante omnia Citationis nre in vim Cridæ litteras contra sua communiter uel diuisim interesse putantium, et quos tangit præsens negotium, seu tangere poterit quomodolibet in futurum, duximus

Appendix II.2

præmitten prout in Dei nomine præmisimus ad Diem et terminum infrascriptum: Quibusquidem die et termino advenien comparuit coram nobis in Judicio, in loco solitæ nræ habitationis ac residentiæ, ad Jura reddendu et causas audiendum, pro tribunali sedēn Venerabilis vir dominus Benedictus Isdbienskii, Cantor Ecclesiæ nostræ, et Serenissimi ac Excellentissimi Principis, & dni domini Sigismundi Primi huius nominis, Die gratia, Regis Poloniæ, Magni Ducis Lithwaniæ, Russiæ, Prussiæ, Masouiæ étc dominus et heredis a secretis legitimus procurator, prout de suæ procurationis onera et mandato, manu legalis Matthiæ Joannis de Makolin Sacræ Apostolica auctoritate notarii publici, scripto et publicato plená ac indubiam per acta nostra facit fidem, et eo nomine procuratorio, nostra citationis in vim Cridæ literas, contra sua communiter uel diuisim per ædictum publicum in facie Ecclesiæ Cathdralis Cracovień, debite ut apparebat executis, facto realiter et in scriptis exhibuit et produxit, Cittatorumque sua communiter uel diuisim interesse putań: nec aliquid contra Capellæ prædicte dispositionem, ordinationem, Erectionem, latius inferius describeń, dicere, facere, contradicere uerbo uel inscriptis curań contumatiam accusauit et in eorum contumatiam, Collegium præsbiterorum, vczt præpositum cum nouem præbendariis et vno clerico in prædicto oraculo siue Capella constitui et ordinari: Fructusque et obuentiones superius nominatas, illorum communitati necnon immunitati Ecclesiasticæ asscribi et incorporari, et onere illis et cuilibet ipsorum imponi alias et alia fieri et decerni debita cum instantia petiuit et postulauit. NOS igitur Petrus Gamrath Dei gratia Archiepiscopus et Episcopus præfatus, attendeń dicti Serenissimi domini domini Sigismundi Primi Dei gratia Regis Poloniæ, etc, pium laudabile, et uere christianum in domino propositum, et Maiestatis suæ Regiæ uotis paterne annueń, ad Erectionem, fundationem, et ordinationem præmissorum, ad ulteriorum dicti Procuratoris Instantiam et petitionem, in contumatiam citatorum ut præfertur, et non comparentium, proceden [11] duximus in Dei nomine, in hunc qui sequitur modum. Imprimis et ante omnia Census, Decimas, prouentus, et obuentiones singulas superius designatas & expensas, necnó domum pro eiusdem Sacerdotibus donatam libertati et immunitati Ecclesiasticæ adscribimus, incorporamus, inuisceramus, necnon ad laudem et honorem omnipotentis Dei et Beatissime Virginis Mariæ matris domini nri Jesu christi, necnon Sanctorú Sigismundi Regis et Barbaræ Virginis Martyrum, et omnium sanctorum, Collegium præsbiterorum, vnum videlicet Præpositum, nouem præbendarios et vnum Clericum, ad psalendum domino Deo perpetuis temporibus. laudes in dicto Oraculo seu Capella ut præmissum est, per Sacram Regiam Maiestatem de nouo a fundamentis erecta et fundata: Constituimus, fundamus, et ordinamus, Quiquid Præpositus, Præbendarii, et Clericus, domum prædictam pro eorum collegio per Sacram Maiestatem Regiam ut præmissum est constructam et donatam simul inhabitabunt; et quod Præpositus quadraginta tres, seu alias omnes et singulos redditus, Decimas, Census, et obuentiones ad altare, antiquæ fundationis, in eadem Capella Regia ex antiquo pertineń seorsum et de per se singuli Præbendarii per Viginti. et clericus pro tempore existens, sedecim marcas pecuniarum annis singulis ex supranominata summa et prouentibus nomine dotis et pro illorum sustentatione habebunt et eorum quilibet habebit. Et quoniam Beneficium datur propter officium, Statuimus et ordinamus, ut Præpositus et Præbendarii dictæ Capellæ pro tempore existentes Missam Rorate de Anunctiatione Beatissime Virginis Mariæ in eadem Capella cantu figurato als na Szorth singulis diebus et perpetuis temporibus in continenti post missam: et ante primam: Mansionariorum omnibus temporibus Anni præterquam in Adventu: quæ max post missam Rorate, in choro a vicariis decantari solitam, in dicta Capella siue oraculo concinna et sonorosa uoce simul omnes vestibus decentibus induti et superpiliciati decantari, per se, & non substitutos, aut submissas personas debebunt et sint astricti. Et quia tempus aliquando non fert, ut officium iuxta fundationes suas proprias expleantur[?], quamobrem obmittere oportebit missam hanc nouæ fundationis, iuxta missas aliarum fundationum, puta missas Sanctæ Crucis, et Beate Virginis Mariæ Mansionarioru, potissimum hiis diebus in Adventu videlicet Dominicis diebus, die sancti Andreæ, Sancti Nicolai, Conceptionis Beatissimæ virginis, Thomæ Apostoli, Natiuitatis domini, Item Statuimus et ordinamus, quod quilibet dictorum Præbendariorum Missam unam de Assumptione Virginis Mariæ, cum impositione collectæ pro fundatoribus uiuentibus, et pro defunctis Alteram videlicet missam, similiter sub tribus Orationibus, pro fundatoribus, famula, et fidelium singulis septimanis legere, et ultra hoc singulis Kalendis, als primo die cuiuslibet Mensis, prædicti Præpostius et Præbendarii simul omnes vigilias nouem lectionum peractis prandiis, pro salute animæ fundatoris in eadem capella psalere et decantare perpetuis futuris temporibus teneantur et sint astricti, sub excommunicationis et mortalis pecati penis. Præpositus autem solus per se missam Rorate praedictam in maioribus festivitatibus, Videlicet Sacratissimo die Pasche, Penthecosten, Natiuitatis domini nri Jesu christi, singulisque festis gloriosissimec virginis Mariæ, cantare tenebitur et erit astrictus, per se et non per alium & hoc [12] cessante legitima causa et impedimento, Vbi tunc loco illius præbendarius ex ordine suo, pro eo officium huiusmodi missæ tenebit. Et ut ne circa missarum officium ex deffectu eorum quæ ad rem Diuinam pertinent aliqua negligentia committatur, pro cera in capella circa Diuina officia insumenda, decem marcas pecuniarum ex proventibus supra nominatis consignamus et decernimus. Vinum uero et panem ad huiusmodi sacrificium necessarium. ab ecclesia nra habere debebunt, prout alii sacerdotes eiusdem ecclesiæ hactenus habere sunt soliti. Volumus autem et ordinamus Præpositum Pro tempore existentem fore et esse perpetuum, Cuius præterea Officium erit, bono imprimis ordini circa Divina Officium diligenter intendere, re familiaris et domus curam habere, Proventus communes exigere. In præbendarios et clericum excessiuos: cum concilio tamen aliorum præbendariorum, seu alios senioris partis animaduertere, ac eosdem pro qualitate excessus mulctare, iuxta ordinationem et statuta domus quæ communi eiusdem Collegii consensu accedente ad similitudinem aliarum communitatum fuerint, et omnia alia tam i

Appendix II.2 197

Ecclesia quam in domo curare & ordinare, præbendarios uero et clericum uolumus esse manuales, nulla alia Beneficia ecclesiastica, et præcipue quibus cura immineret animarú habeń, Et ad nutú Præpositi et maioris, seu aĩs senioris partis eiusdem Collegii et communitatis præbendariorum ammobiles, Qui tandem non nisi ex legitima causa et intolerabili excessu remoueri, et in remoti seu remotorum locum alius vel alii magnis idoneus seu idonei constitui debebunt. Ad huiusmodi autem præbendas et clericaturam non nisi persone habiles[4] et idonei, actu præsbiteri, qui ex arte cantare et psallere sciant cum bona et sonorosa uoce, Aĩs prius et ante omnia examinatos et in proba ad instar uicariorum nr̃æ Cathedralis Ecclesiæc probatos atque idoneos repertos presentari et suscipi debebunt, quod si præsentatus per sufficiens examen et probam, minus abilis et idoneus ad Cantum et Officia huiusmodi subeunda repertus fuerit, extunc alius abilis et idoneus denuo præsentabitur, de cuius idoneitate et proba præpositus pro tempore existens relationem nobis et fidem facere debebit et tenebitur, cuius relatione habita nos et successores nostri huiusmodi præsentatum et probatũ, debebimus et debebunt ad huiusmodi. Præbendam, siue Clericaturam admittere absque aliqua alia institutione per nos facień. Clericum quoque deligendú statuimus fidelem et idoneum, qui simplex clericus et non in sacris existens gerere officium hoc poterit: Cuius officium erit vasa et uestes Sacras ac cętera ornaméta ipsius Capellæ seruare candida et munda tenere ac fideliter custodire: Præposito et Præbendariis aĩs omnibus et singulis præsbiteris, in eadem Capella circa rem diuinam seruire et ministrare: Qui si peritiam cantus et uocem ad psallendum aptam habuerit, aĩs abilis et idoneus ad præbendæ officium repertus fuerit, extúc ad unam ex præbendis proxime tunc siue per cessum uel decessum seu amotioné ac alias quocumque modo uacantem præbendam præsentari et ad huiusmodi præbendam admitti, et in eius locum alter clericus æque fidelis ac idoneus suffici et constitui debebit. Volumus etiam pariter et ordinamus quod Præpositus Præbendarii et Clerico prædicti in prænominata domo ipsis ut præmissum est per Sacrá Maiestatæm Regiam donata, simul habitare et communem mensam tenere debeant [13] & teneantur, pro quorum sustentatione necnon leguminibus, Butiro, Sale, Lardo spetiebus siue aromatibus ad cibos condiendos viginti quinque, pro lignis ad usum coquinæ et fornacis, decem marcas pecuniarum ex eiusdem prouentibus deputamus et concedimus. Quiquidem Præpositus et Præbendarii tenebunt in eadem domo communi aliquam mulierem maturam et honestam, quæ uestes Sacras et mensæ domus mundæt, ac abluat, et curam omnem ciborum pro communi mensa domus habeat, cui pro huiusmodi fatiga et servitiis quinque singulis annis marcas pecuniarum de prænominata summa decernimus et dari uolumus: seruitorem quoque domus dicti domini præpositi et præbendarii in eadem domo ad illis seruiendum habeant, cui in singulos annos nomine salarii tres marcas ex eadem summa dari volumus. Item statuimus et ordinauimus ex eadem summa pro reformatione et conservatione Capellæ et apparamentorum domus communis marcas decem esse retinendas et conseruandas, quibus id quod aliaquando refectione indigeret reficeretur. Item statuimus ordinamus et decernimus, vt reliquú summé prædictę quicquid solutis et completis oneribus superius nominatis et expressis quicquid resultabit omne illud in carbonam & in Thesauram eiusdem cappellé reponatur et fideliter conseruetur: Que quidem Carbona in eadem capella tenebitur et conseruabitur, et ab ea Præpositus unam et senior præbendarius aliá clauem habebunt, peccunæ uero si quæ resultabunt, non nisi pro reperatione Capellæ et domus communis, necnon apparamentorum necessariorum adauctione tolli et recipi debebunt, in quo Præpositi et Præbendariorum pro tempore existentium conscientias oneramus. Et si aliud et aliter quidpiam fecerint, anatematis uinculo uolumus teneri, et sententiam excomunicationis eos incurrere uolumus ipso facto, a qua non nisi satisfactione prænia absolvenos esse decernimus. Ad rationem autem et calculum accepti et expensi faciendum Præpositum pro tempore existentem uolumus omnino teneri, quem singulis annis conuocatis et in præsentia omniú præbendariorum facere semper debebit et tenebitur. Et ut id commodius et citra omnis suspitionis notam facere ualeat, habere debebit librum authenticum in quo proventus omnes conscribere, et de expositis rationem reddere possit. Iuspatronatus autem et præsentandi Præpositi præbendariorum et clerici prædictorum Serenissimæ suæ M[ti] Regiæ quoad Maiestas sua uixerit, atque utinam diu et in perpetuum uiuat et imparæt reseruandum duximus et reseruamus post mortem uero suæ Maiestatis ad Serenissimum principem et dominum dúm Sigismundum Augustum huius nominis secundum Regem Poloniǽ iuniorem, Magnum Ducem Lithuaniǽ, Russiǽ, Prussiǽ, Masoviæ, etc. dominum et heredem, suæcque Maiestatis Legittimos successores Reges Poloniǽ pro tempore existeń huiusmodi Iuspatronatus et præsentandi deuoluetur qui nobis et successoribus nostris Præpositum vacatione occurente præsentabunt abilem et idoneú ac præbendarios similiter habiles et idoneos, et qui uoces claras habeant, et bene psallere sciant, alias per Præpositum et alios Mansionarios probatos, ad instar ut præmissum est vicariorum eiusdem ecclesiǽ nostræ, per nos et pro tempore existentes Episcopos Cracovień, iuxta constitutionem et ordinem superius expressum Instituendum et inuestiendum Præpositum, qui quidem Præpositus pro tempore existens Mansionarios et clericum legitime probatos admittet et loca illis assignabit [14] non expectata alia a nobis instructione modo et forma superius expressis. Quia uero Sacra Maiestatis Regia Capellam siue Oraculum in Arce Cracouień penes coquinam sitt́, a suæ Maiestatis antecessoribus extructam et dotatam, in qua, vno sub titulo et inuocatione Sanctorum Foelicis et Aucti, et alia Sanctæ Mariæ Egiptiacæ præbende per eiusdem Maiestatis suǽ antecessores fundate et dotate & per nostros prædesessores Erectǽ fuerant circa ædificationem Arcis suæ Maie[tis] Cracouień tolli et demolliri fecerat, prout in effectu demollita est, et denuo illic commode locari non potest: Nos ad eiusdem Sacræ Regiæ Maiestatis domini nr̃i clementissimi postulationem et Instantiam, Præbendas huiusmodi, videlice Sanctorum Fœlicis et Aucti, cuius Vener[les] dńs[5]   et aliam præbendá scté Mariǽ Egiptiacæ, cuius Stanislaus Schlumowski Ecclesiæ nr̃æ Gnesner

Appendix II.2

Canonicus ad præsens possessores existunt, et quarum Maiestas Sacræ Regia patronatus est, ad prænominatam Capellam siue oraculum Assumptionis gloriossimæ virginis Mariæ, in Ecclesia ńra Cracouień transferimus, ponimus, et locauimus, et pro ornamento et decore eiusdem capellæ eosdem præbendarios in canonicos sanctæ Mariæ designamus, creamus et deputamus, ita quod deinceps futuris perpetuis temporibus earundem præbendarum possessores Canonici Sanctæ Mariæ nuncupentur, et onera illis ab antiquo incumbentia in eadem Capella per se vel per suos vicarios supportare debeant et sint astricti, saluis per omnia redditibus ad ipsos et eorum quemlibet ab antiquis temporibus spectantibus, quibus in nullo præindicare intendimus. Quæ omnia et singula præmissa videlicet fundationem, donationem, tuicionem, fructum, proventuum, et reddituum vniuersorum, Praeposito, Mansionariis, Clerico et aliis annexiōm Præpositi praebendariorum Clericique numerum et onerum impositioni ita fore et esse perpetuo statuimus et decernimus, Confirmamus, approbamus, ratificamus, assignamus annectimus, et incorporamus, inuisceramus libertati ac inúunitati ecclesiastice perpetuo asscribimus, roburque auctoritatis ordinariæ pariter et decretum apponimus, ac eandem Capellaniam in omnibus et per omnia fundamus, eregimus, in Die nomine per præsentes, Atque ea omnia et singula premissa omnibus quorum interest, intererit, seu interesse poterit in futurum intimamus, insinuamus, notificamus, ad ipsorumque noticiam deducimus et deduci uolumus per præsentes, decernentes perpetuis temporibus esse vualitura. Et nichilominus Honorabilem Nicolaum de Posnania Vicedecanum chori Ecclesiæ nostræ Cathedralis Cracoviensis nobis per Sacram Maiestatem Regiam ad Præposituram dictæ Capellæ patentibus literis præsentatum per manus nostræ ipsius capiti impositionem instituimus ac inuestimus, Instituimusque et inuestiuimus in Dei nomine in his scriptis, Curam administrationem spiritualium, regimen temporalium eiusdem sibi committeń, recepto præsentibus ab eodem d. Nicolao Præposito principali obedientiæ Juramento corporali, per ipsium in manibus nostris ad Sacrosancta Dei Evangelia præstitio, & q̃d Census et prouentus, Necnon bona ipsius Capellæ et Collegii, tam mobilia quá immobilia non alienabit, sed deifice et sanctæ iuxta traditum a nobis modum & ordinationem dispensabit, tenebit, et conservabit. Quare uobis Executoribus et uestrum cuilibet sub excommunicationis pena mandatus quatenus ubi et postquam [15] per præfatum Honorabilem Nicolaum Præpositum, ut præmittitur per nos institutum tenore præsentium fueritis requisiti, aut uestrum alter requisitus fuerit, ipsum in et ad realem actualem dotem præpositurae possessionem inducatis, facień ipsi de omnibus et singulis dictæ Præpositurae fructibus et redditibus universis per eos ad quos pertinet integre respondi. In cuius rei testimonium præsentes ńras Erectionis literas seu aľs præsens publicam fundationis et Erectionis Instrumentum, fieri, scribi, et per Notarium nostrum factique huiusmodi coram nobis scribam infrascripť subscribi, publicari, nostrique Sigilli iussimus ac mandauimus subappensione communiri

Et quia ego Maths Joannis Grzimala de Pokrzywnycza Clericus dioc Cracovien Sacris appostolica et Imperiali Autoritatibus notarius publicus: Causarum Curię cora Rmo in Chró patre et domió domió petro de Gamratis dei gra Archiepó Gnesnen. Epó Crać legato nato et Rgnj polonie p'mate scriba. p'missus omibus et singulis du' sic ut p'mititur agerentur et fierent una cum restibus p'nominatis presens interfui. Eaque sic fieri vidi et audivij Jdeo presentes Errectionis lraś manu alrius: me protúc alys occupat negotÿs scriptas: subscribsi: publicavi et in hanc forma publicam reredeji signoque ac nomis meis solitis ac consuetis una cum sigilli memorati Rmj domj subappésioń comunivi. In fidem et testimoniu' omium et singulorum p'missorum rogatus et requisitus.

Literarum Cridæ in vim Cittonis generalis ad effectum approbandæ supræ insertæ Erectionis emmanat tenor talis est.

Petrus Dei gratia Archiepus Gnesnen et Epus Cracovien Sedis Aplicæ Legatus Natus ac Regni Poloniæ Primas. Noverint vniuersi q cum sernus et Christianissimus Princeps Dnus nr Clementnus Sigismundus Dei graa Rex Poloniæ Magnus Dux Lithuæ Russiæ Prussiæ ec Dnus & hæres. Ad laudem et gloriam Oipotentis Die et in memoriam Sanctmæ Virgs Matris Mariæ Assumptionis ac Diuorum Sigismundi Regis Barbaræ Virginis Martyris Capellam in Eccla nra Cathli Cracovien e fundament elato lapide magno sumptu et præclaro quidem artificio fabricari fecisset. Atque in eade Capella Præpositum Vnum Perpetuum Præbendarios Novem et Clericum vnum manuales. Ad psallendum Dno Deo perpetuis temporibus Maiestas sua institui deliberasset, et pro illorum sustentatione certas obuentiones annuas designauit. Et Domum lateritiam pro eorundem Præpositi et Præbendariorum habitatione Serma sua Mttas perpetuo donavit fuimus pro parte eiusdem suæ Sermæ Regiæ Mttis petiti Quatts Capellam hmoi erigere. Præpositum et Præbendarios vna et Clericum instituere. Censum et obuentiones Collegio prædicto Presbyterorum designatos. Nec non Domum pro illis donatam immunitati Eccliacæ adscribere, ordine [16] et modum in psallendis Dno Deo precibus ponere. Et alia in talibus et circa talia necessaria facere dignitasset. Nos vo modum et formam in talibus diucius[6] solitos seruare cupien Lras Cride ante ota contra sua interesse putań decreuimus præmittendas et præmittimus in Dei noe perpfntes. QUOCIRCA vobis Executoribus in Virtte Sanctæ Obediæ et sub Excois pæna mands quats aliquo die Dnico aut alio festo publice proponeń seu ats per publicum edictum et affixionem pfntium ad valvas Ecclæ nræ Cathts Cracouien oes et singulos sua interesse putań. Citetis quos et nos pfntibus Citamus vt coram Nobis Crac: Feria Secunda post Dnicam Iubilate proxa. Ad Viden et audien Capellam hmoi erigeń decerni et errigi Præptum et Præbendarios ac Clericum institui Census et obuentiones eidem Capellæ incorporari et immunitati Ecclicæ adscribi. Inpsallendo et cultu Diuino peragendo modum et ordinem statuti et ordinari, Ac ats oibus præmissis authem Nram interponi. aliaque fieri circa talia necessaria et opportuna ltmé et peremptée' compareant. Certifican eosdé sic Cittań quod siue in terno hmoi comparuerint siue non Nos nihilominus ad Vlteriorem Sermæ Mttis Regiæ

Appendix II.2 201

Instantiam ad eaquæ Iuris et raōis exñt dante Dñō procedemus et procedi faciemus Contumaā seu absentia Cittōrum in aliquo non obstań. Datť. Cracoū die XXXVII Mĕsis Marty Anno Dni MDXLIII Nró Sub Sigillo Locus Sigilli Executionis tenor est eiusmodi Anno quo intro die solis XV Aprilis. Ego Andreas de Radomskie Ecclæ̃ Cathlis Crāc. Vicarius protunc Chori hebdomadarius parens Mandatis suæ Rnsdmæ P. ōēs et singulos sua interesse putañ per edictum puɓcum et per affixionem pnˉtium ad valvas Ecclæ̃ Cathedralis Citavi Ternumˉque eis assignaui iuxta vim et formam præsentis Mandati.

Literarum Intituōis primi Præ̃pti tenor hmōi est qui sequitur. Anno Domini Millesimo Quingentesimo Quadragesimo Tertio. Die Vó Sabbathi Vigesima Tertia Iuny. Ad Præposituram nouiter Erectam in Capella Regia Ecclæ̃ Cthlis̄ Cracovień ad præsentationem Serenissimi Principis et Dñi Dñi Sigismundi Dei graā Regis Poloniæ Magni Ducis Lithuæ̃ &ć eiusdem Præptūræ Vnici Patroni Venerabilem Dñūm Nicolaum a Posnania Vicedecanus Ecclæ̃ Cathlis Cracovień Rnsdˉmus Dnūs aˉls Cancells Curiæ suæ protunc Reuerendmæ̃ per manus capiti suo impositionem instituit et inuestivit curam administrōēm Spuālium et temporalium rerum sibi eiusdem commisit recepto tamen prius ab eo obedientia, reuerentia et non alienań a dicta Præ̃ptura bonis corporali Iuramento literas desuper necessarias dandas decreuit. Præsentibus Honorabili Bartholomao Siekierzecki Plebano in Wilczyna Petro Radwanowski Notarius[7] Curiæ testibus et Andrea Hincz Actus præsentis Scriba.

Ex Actis Rndsmˉi olim Chrō Patris Petri de Gamratis Archiepiscopi Gnesnensis Episcopi Cracovień Legati Nati et Primatis Regni Poloniæ. Sub Sigillo Perillris ac Rrmˉi Dni Nicolai Oborski Epı̄ Laodiceń Suffraganei Archidiaconi Vicarii in Spuālibus et Offıs̄ Gnalls̄ Cracovieṇ extractum. Locus Sigilli. Benedictus Zegota pubˉcus Sacra Authē̃ Aplicā et in absentia Actuary̋ Conŕus Crać Notriūs mpa.

NOTES

[1] Corrected to 'rite et recte', possibly by the same scribe.
[2] Later corrected to 'nostra'.
[3] Originally 'quatinus'.
[4] Originally 'abiles'.
[5] A space was left for the name, although none was entered.
[6] This is a later addition written over a word now illegible.
[7] 'Notarùs' in original.

II.3: Kk dyp. 1172, Andrzej Zebrzydowski, Bishop of Kraków, 10 December 1552

[2r] IN NOMINE DOMINI AMEN. Ad sempiternam rei memoriam Omnium rerum quæ sempiternæ sunt future. nulla cercior firmitudo excogitari potest, quam ea quæ fit lrárum monumentis prodita memoriæ posteritatis. Cætera enim facta humana quantum cumque memorabilia, aliis modis quam literis æternitati dicata. aliquot quidem seculorum decursu durare possunt. quæ uero literarum officio memoriæ mandantur, nunquam intereunt. ipsaque vetustate fiunt angustiora. Proinde Nos ANDREAS Zebrzidowski Dei gratia Epús Cracouieñ. Magnifestum facimus tenore presentium vniuersis et singulis, presentibus et futuris, harum noticiam habituris. Quod Serenissimus Princeps dominus Sigismundus Augustus Dei gratia Rex Poloniæ. magnus dux Lithuaniæ. Russię, Prussie, Masouie etč. dominus et heres. Volens in capella a Serenissimo sanctæ memoriæ patre suo diuo Sigismundo Rege Polonie. et magno Duce Lithuaniæ, Regio ac magnifico sumptu, in ecclesia nrá cathedrali Cracouień extructa. Preciosaque suppellectili aurea, argentea, uestibus sacris exornata. ac dotata. cultum Diuinum per eius paternam Regiam M[tem] institutum, æuo sempiterno duranturum firmare, adauxit ipse Serenissimus Rex Sigismundus Augustus dotem eiusipsius capellæ, ac ad priores redditus et prouentus eidem capelle iam antea a diuo Rege patre suo donatos, alios nouos fructus ac decimas omnis grani ac seminis, a Præpositura ecclesiæ collegiatæ Lanciciensis opulentur dotata; dismembratas videlicet in oppidis Pabiianicze, Rzgow villisque Gathka. Choczianouicze et Laszkowicze consisteń, per nos supradictæ Capellæ et eius Presbiteris ac ministris annecti et applicari. ordinationemque nouam pro meliori condicione eorundem per M[tem] eius factam approbari. ratificari. et confirmari authoritate nostra ordinaria postulauit. Eiusque dismembracionis decimarum a prepositura Lanciciéń per Reverendissimum in chŕo pŕem dominum Nicolaum Archiepḿ Gnesnensem Primatem ac Legatum natum factæ. et ordinationis suæ Regiæ nouæ, lŕas sub titulis et sigillis eorum, appensis exhiberi coram nobis per procuratorem suum mandauit. Quarum tenores sequutur et sunt de uerbo ad uerbo tales. IN Nomine Domini Amen. Quum statum rerum vniuersarum non modo temporalium. uerum etiam ecclsiasticarum pro temporum locorum et personarum necessitate, siue utilitate, uariari, aut quandoque mutari in melius et ordinari Divina et humana jura, maxime uero in his quæ ad augmentum cultus Diuini maiorem cedere dinoscuntur permittunt. Proinde nos Nicolaus Dzierzgowszki Dei gratia sanctæ eccleiæ metropolitanæ Gnesneń Archiepús, legatus natus et primas. Ad vniuersorum et singulorum presentium et futurorum noticiam deducimus. Quod cum non ita pridem Serenissimus princeps et dominus. dominus Sigismundus Augustus Dei gratia Rex Poloniæ magnus Dux Lituaniæ Russiæ. Prussie. Mazouiæ. etč. dominus et hæres, nobis exponi fecisset. Quomodo diuus olim suæ M[tis] parens, Sigismundus Primus Poloniæ Rex, magno sumptu, sacellum in ecclesia Cathedrali Cracouień extruisset. atque in eo mauseolum siue

Appendix II.3

depositum funeri suo uiuens ipse sibi posuisset. præpositarumque cum novem Sacellanis seu prebendariis ac clericum, consignatis illis certis proventibus et redditibus, erigi fundari et insitui authoritate ordinaria curauisset, ut singulis scilicet diebus. et temporibus perpetuis missam de incarnatione domini nŕi Jesu Christi concinerent, et cætera onera in literis erectionis lacius descripta, explerent. Quia uero redditus huiusmodi funda [2v] cionis dictorum præpositi et præbendariorum tenuiores,esse dinoscuntur, quam ut sustentari eis in hoc potissimus tempore difficili ualeant. Aque ita declarari et exponi nobis fecit sua M^{tas}, Quomodo præpositus ecclesiæ collegiate Lancicień tantum in decimis redditibus, censibus, et proventibus abundat. quod si uero certa pars decimarum manipulariu' ad eandem preposituram Lanciciensem spectań. vicżt in oppidis Pabiianicze. Rzgow. ac villis Gatka, Choczianowicze. et Laszkowicze. in territorio Pabiianicień sitt́. ab ea ipsa prepositura dismembrarentur, dictisque præposito et Prebendariis in eodem Sacello Regis Sigismundi ad teneń honesti eorum status incorporaretur. atque inuisceraretur. per hoc eidem preposito et prebendariis sacelli memorati plurimum consuleretur. Preposito uero Lancicień minime incommodaretur immo satis commode et honeste' prepositi Lancicień pro tempore existeń absque illis sustentari atque onera sua obire possent. Quare postulatum est a nobis pro parte M^{tis} Regiæ. pro parte uero memorati Prepositi, et prebendariorum sacelli nobis supplicatum, cum instantia. quatinus Decimas supradiptas, de expsso tam Revereń domini Andree Czarnkowszki Gnesneń et ipsius Lancicień ecclesiarum prepositi, ut et tanquam possessoris, præpositurae memoratæ Lancicien. quam etiam supradicti Serenissimi principis et domini. domini nostri Sigismunsi Augusti Regis Poloniæ ut et tanquam vnici ipsius prepositurae Lancicień patroni consensu, coram nobis, et Notario publico infrascripto præstito, et per patentes lrás suæ M^{tis} ac instrumentum publicum. manu et signo Legalis Stanislai olim Joannis Borziminszki clerici diocesis ploceń Aṕlica et jmperiali aucŧōtatibus notarii publici predict́. et coram nobis causam scribæ scriṕt ut apparuit et subscriptum. quod coram nobis ibidem facto. et inscriptis exhibitus est. tenoris inferius annotati adscribere. incorporare, et vnire dignaremur. Et licet nos attenderimus huiusmodi peticionem fore iustam. et consonam racioni. uoluimus tamen per nŕm aliquod celere dismembracionis. et incorporacionis. ac vnionis respectiue decretum, alicui in suo jure præiudicare. ante omnia lrás cittacionis in vim Cridæ. contra omnes et singulos sua communiter uel diuisim ad dictas decimas interesse putań. decreuimus premitten̄. prout pro certo infrascripto competenti termino præmisimus. Quorú quidem consensuum tam M^{tis} Regiæ. quam possessoris beneficii, de quibus supra fit mécio, tenores sequuntur. et sunt tales de uerbo ad uerbum et in primis tenor instrumenti IN NOMINE DOMINI AMEN. per hoc presens publicum instrumentum cunctis euidenter pateat et sit notum. Quomodo sub anno a nativitate eiusdem Millesimo. Quingétesimo. Quinquagesimo. Jndicione octava sede Romana per obitum Sanctissimi olim domini domni Pauli Diuina prouidencia papæ tercii vacań. die Lunæ Vigesima Septiá Januarii, Cracouiæ, in lapidea Illustris et Magnifici domini Andreæ Comitis a Gorka Castellani Posnanień. et Capitanei maioris Poloniæ. generalis sub acre Cracouień sití. et stuba superiori magna murata, uersus meridem iaceń hora uesperorum vel quasi. corá R^{mo} in chró pŕe domino domino Nicolao Dzierzgowszki Dei gracia Archiepó Gnesneñ Legato nato primate. meque Notario publico et testibus infrascriptis. Revereń dominus Andreas Czarnkowszki Gnesneń. et Lancicień prepositus non coactus, neque aliqua sinistra machinacione circumuentus, sed sponte. libere. gratis. et ex certa scientia et spontanea voluntate maturaque deliberatione et consiliis præhabitis in dismembracionem. seperationem. diuisionem et incorporationem decimarum ex oppidis Pabiianicze. Rzgow Necnó villis Gatka. Choczianowicze et Laszkouicze, in districtu Lancicień sití iaceń, pro prepositura Lancicień a primeua fundatione spectań. et pertineń. pro prebendariis Sacelli Regiæ Ma^{tis} in ecclesia Cathedrali Cracouień. nouæ fundationis Serenissimi olim Principis domini, domini Sigismundi Dei gratia Regis Poloniæ. etč. tituli assumptionis mariæ illorumque proventibus. et obuencionibus adaugeń. et locupletandis cedeń conuerteñ applicandarum. et ex illorum arbitrio disponendarum. idque non nisi post mortem měorati domini Czarnkowszki. uel quam diu præpositum dictæ præpositruæ agit: per [3r] quemcunque Judicem et signanter Reueren^m in chŕo patrem dominum. Dominum NICOLAVM Dei gratia Archiepm̃ Gensnensem Legatum natum primatem fień. cósensit. palam. expresse. et uiuæ uocis oraculo. ac per se quem consensum ratum et gratum habuit. admittique confirmari, aprobari. et eidem robur perpetuæ firmitatis pariter et decretum per Revern$^{\prime m}$ dominum Archiepm Gnezneń memoratum, apponi debita cum Instatia peciit, et postulauit. Super quibus omnibus et singulis predictus dominus Andreas Czarnkowszki prepositus Lancicieñ sibi a me Notario publico infrascripto, vnum vel plura, publicum seu publica fieri peciit. instrumentum seu instrumenta. Acta sunt hæc anno indicione. die. loco quibus supra. Pñtibus R^{mo} in chŕo patre. Magnificis. Reuereñ et Venerabilibus dominis Samuele Dei gratia Epó Cracouień. Regni Cancellario. Joańe Dzierzgowszki Palatino et Vicesgereń Ducatus Masouiæ, Sigismundo Parniczewszki Lancicień. Martino Zborowszki Calissień, Castellanis. Philipo Padnieuuszki Cantore Cracouiensi. Andrea Przeczlawszki Decano Posnanień. Stanislao Dambrowszki Gnesneń Wladislauiensi Canonicis. testibus circa præmissa. Et me Stanislao olim Joannis Borziminszki, clerico diod́ płoceń, Sacris Aṕlica et Jmperiali auctoritatibus notario publico, qui predicto consensui ad dictarum decimarum dismembracionem fień. aliisque omnibus et singulis præmissis cum dictis testibus interfui. eaque omnia et singula sic fieri uidi et audiui. Jdeo presens publicum Instrumentum manu mea scripsi. subscripsi. et signo consignaui rogatus et requisitus. Tenor autem consensus Regie M^{tis} talis est. Sigismundus Augustus Dei gratia Rex Poloniæ. magnus Dux Lituaniæ. Russie. Prussie. Mazouie etc. dominus et hęres. Significamus presentibus lŕis quorum interest vniuersis. Cum diuus parens noster magno sumptu Sacellum in ecclesia Cathedrali Cracouień extruisset, atque in ea prepositum nouemque capellanos seu prebendarios ac clericum institui curraset. ut

Appendix II.3

singulis dieb missam de incarnatione domini, quam Rorate uocant, concinerent. ac alia quædam onera in lris erectionis lacius perscripta explerent. eisque redditus certos assignasset redditus uero ipsis tenuiores essent. quam ut sustentari ex eis Sacerdotes, hoc difficili tempore, posset, Voleń nos Diui parentis nri in augendo cultu diuino studium prosequi egimus cum Vene[li] Andrea Czarnkowszki Gnesneń Lancicień Preposito. Scholastico Cracouień et secretario nostro. ut ex redditibus præpositurae Lancicień Jurispronatus nri decimas in oppidis Pabiianicze et Rzgow. ac villis Gatka. Choczianowicze. et Laszkowicze in territorio Pabiianiceń Venerabilis Capituli Cracouiensis consisteń detrahere. ac preposito prebendariisque Sacelli predicti Regii aßumpcionis Mariæ incorporare, et vnire permitteret. Quemadmodum coram Reueren[mo] in christo patre domino Archiepö Gnesneń Legato nato. et Regni nri primate publice in eam dismembrationem et incorporationem consensit. In quamquidem dismembrationem ac incorporationem, nos qui patronus tam prepositurae predicte Lancicień, quam prepositurae Prebendarumque, in Capella nra Regia sumus in dismembrationem predictam, incorporacionemque consensimus. ita ut consentimus presentibus lris. Hortamurque et requirimus R[m] in chro prem dominum Nicolaum Archiepm Gneznensem Legatum Natum. ut authoritate sua ordinaria decimas predictas a prepositura Lancicień dismembret, easque preposito et prebendariis capellé nræ predicte adscribet, et incorporet usibus eorum applicandas perpetuo et in euum. In cuius rei fidem manu nra subscripsimus. et Sigillum nostrum appendi iussimus. Dat Cracouiæ postridie Circumcisionis domini. Anno eiusdem Millesimo. Quingentesimo. Quinquagesimo. Regni nostri Vigesimo. Sigismundus Augustus Rex ffzt Quoquidem cittacionis termino adueniente Venerabili Bartolomeus Sziekiereczki, sancti Georgii in arce Gnesneń Canonicus dictorumque præpositi. et prebendariorum sacelli Regis Sigismundi, legittimus procurator prout de suæ procurationis mandato per certum constitucionis procurator jnstrumetum manu Legalis Petri de noua ciuitate, clerici dioć Gnesneń, Sacra auctoritate Aplica Notarii publici script. subscript et consignatum. legittimam fecit fidem. et eo nomine pro [3v] curatorio reproductis lris cittacionis in vim cridæ contra omnes et singulos sua communiter uel diuisim, interesse ad dictas decimas manipulares putań, legittime ut apparuit exequutis, contumaciam cittatorum non comparentium. neque quicquem uerbo uel in scriptis contra dismembracionem ipsarum decimarum a prepositum Lancicień. illarumque vnionem. et incorporacioém prepositurae. et præbendariis memoratis Sacelli Regis Sigismundi perpetit. dicere siue opponere curantium, accusauit, ipsosque contumaces reputari. et in eorum contumaciam decimas manipulares predictas. omnis grani et seminis post agros oppidorum predictorum Pabiianicze et Rzgow. necnon uillis Gatka, Choczianowicze. ac Laszkowicze. ab antiquo ad prepositurá ecclesiæ collegiatæ Lancicień spectań et pertineń. ab eadem prepositura Lancicień auctoritate ordinaria dismembrari dictisque preposito, et prebendariis Sacelli Regis Sigismundi pro eorum mensæ communis sustentacione. ascribi. vnire. et incorporari. ac inuiscerari, lrasque desuper neccessarias in forma solita sibi. partique suæ prefat.

per nos dari et concedi, debita cum instancia peciit et postulauit. Nos uero Nicolaus Archiepús memoratus, ad ulterioré eiusdem Bartholomei procuratoris instanciam et peticionem dictos cittatos legitime ut apparuit. et non compareń. neque quicquem uerbo uel inscriptis contra præmissa dicere siue opponere curań, licet diucius et ultra horam solitam espectatos, et non compareń. merito prout erant, reputauimus contumaces, Et in eorum contumaciam uisis ac diligenter inspectis consensibus præinsertis. eisque iuxta iuris formam. stillum, et obseruantiam per certos testes idoneos super hoc receptos et iuratos. mediis eorum iuramentis corporalibus. recognitis, Decimas manipulares supradictias, post agros oppidorum Pabiianicze Rzgow. Necnon uillarum Gatka. Choczianowicze. ac Laszkauicze prouenień. a prepositura memorata Lancicień dismembrań. et mensæ dictorum prepositi et prebendariorum Sacelli Regis Sigismundi modo prepetito cum omnibus eorum juribus et pertineń. asscribeń. vnień. et incorporań. atque annecteń perpetuo. et in euum auctoritate ordinaria, qua fungimur, in hac parte duximus. prout dismembramus respectiue asscribimus, vnimus, incorporamus atque annectimus. illarumque realem et actualem possessionem eis consignamus, et tradi decernimus tenore presentium. Per eosdem prepositum et prebendarios Sacelli Regis Sigismundi predicti. preseń et pro tempore existeń deciman'. percipień. venden'. et in usus suos beneplacitos converteń. Quæ omnia et singula præmissa. Vobis vniuersis et singulis signáter autem Decimas supradictas dantibus. uel dare et extradi obligatis. quibus interest. intererit. aut interesse poterit quomodolibet in futuram, intimamus, insinuamus, et notificamus, ac ad nrám et cuislibet vŕm noticiam deducimus. et deduci uolumus per pńtes, Decerneń et uolen'. ut de decimis memoratis in oppidis Pabiianicze. et Rzgow. ac uillis Gatka. Choczianouicze ac Laszkouicze, nemini alteri. quam supradictis preposito et prebendariis Sacelli Regis Sigismundi in ecclia cathedrali Cracouień sitt. respondeant. et illas plene, et integré extradant cum effectu. Vt autem premissa omnia et singula robur obtineant firmitatis, nec super illis ulla dubietatis uideat questio suboriri. pńtes lrás scribi. et per Notarium publicum et causarum, factique huiusmodi coram nobis Scribam, subscribi. Sigillique nri iussimus et fecimus appenssione communiri. Act et Dat Piotrkouiæ in curia nrá Archiepáli. Anno domini Millesimo Quingentesimo. Quinquagesimo. Indicione octava, die ⅹo mercurii tredecima mensis Junii. Pontificat Sanctissimi in chro pris et domini domini Julii Divuina prouidencia papæ tercii. Anno primo. Pńtibus tunc Veñe^{bus}. et Nobilibus dominis Stanislao Dambrowszki Gnesneń. et Wladislauień et Auditore causarum. Joanne Vithinszki Gnesneń. Canonicis Petro Volczowszki. Joanne Oszthrowszki. et Stanislao Borziminszki procuratoribus et Notariis curiæ nŕæ testibus ad premissa. Et quia ego Lucas Bilina Stephani Szathkowszki clericus dioc Plocień. sacra autôte Notarius publicus predictis decimar̄ dismembratióm earundemque incorporaroń annexioni possessioń assignacoń. et dereto Aliisque omnibus et singulis præmissis. dum sic fierent et agerentur. una cum prænominatis testib presens fui. Eaque omnia et singula premissa sic fieri vidi et audiui. Jdeoque hoc presens. [4r] publicum instrumentum. manu alterius

Appendix II.3

me tunc aliis negotiis occupato, fideliter scriptum subscripsi. signoque ut nomine meis solitis et consuetis consignaui et communiui in fidem et testimonium præmissorum rogatus et requisitus. Sigismundus Augustus Dei gratia Rex Poloniæ. magnus Dux Lithuaniæ. Russie. Prussiæ. Masouiæ. etc. dominus et hæres. Significamus pntibus lris quorum interest vniuersis. Et si diuus parens noster uolens, ut Præbendarii Sacelli sui assumpcionis gloriosæ virginis Mariæ in officio per eiudem felicis recordacionis parentis nostri memoriam instituti: fundarentur manuales, Nos tamen considerantes paucos esse, qui easipsas prebendas obtinere uellent. ob id quod metuant. ne ubi consenuerit, atque ad perferendos labores minus apti fuerint. ammoueantur. Consulere itaque illis atque de nra gratia speciali prouidere uolen, ut cantus in eo ipso sacello ex animi sentencia sanctæ memoriæ parentis nri institutus, recte et concinne perficiatur. consentiendum duximus, consentimusque pntibus lris ut R^{mus} in chro pater dominus Epús Cracouiensis. aut p eius Viccarius in Spiritualibus generalis Cracouviensis. nouam ipsorum prebendariorum erectionem faciat perpetuosque constituat Clerico duntaxat exepto. quem manualem esse volumus, ac pro arbitrio Præpositi ammouibilem. Nichilominus casus certi excipiantur in quibus per Reuern^m prem dominum Epm Cracouiensem alienari poterint. ubi per præpositum delati et conuicti fuerit. Inter quosquidem casus primum esse uolumus. Si quis præter voluntatem prepositi et per expressum consensum abfuerit, atque per seipsum officium suum exercere neglexerit, præter quod aliqua egritudine correptus fuerit. Deinde uero si quis preposito inobediens et rebellis fuerit, aut quietem et tranquilitatem aliorum prebendariorum contécionibus turbauerit, vel alioqui scandalosus fuerit. Volumus præterea ut idem prepositus Sacelli nostri omnem superioritatem in prebendarios predictos, et clericum iuxta debitam ordinacionem habeat. eosque instituendos debitam facultatem possideat. De prouentibus autem eorum et redditibus in priori erectione contentis ac de Decimis nuper a Prepositura Lancicien. concensu nro dismembratis. eorumque possessioni ascriptis et incorporatis responderi faciat. In cuius rei fidem et testimonium Sigillum nostrum presentibus est subappensum. Dat Cracouiæ feria Quinta post festa Penthecostes proxiá. Anno domini Millesimo. Quingentesimo. Quinquagesimo primo. Regni nri Vigesimo primo. Joannes Oczieszki R. p. Vicec ffzt R^{lo} Mag^{ci} Ioannis Oczieszki Regni Polo^e Vicecancellarii Succamerarii et Burgrabii Cracovien et Sanecen Olstinenque Capitanei. Postquarum quidem lrarum coram nobis exhibitarum presentacionem. postulatum a nobis fuit nomine Sacræ Regiæ Maiestatis. prefate. ut ad effectum. et executionem in eiusdem utrisque lris contentorum procedere uellemus. Nos vero modum et formam in talibus actibus seruare solitam, seruare uolentes, lrás cittacionis nostræ in vim cridæ contra omnes interesse habere se putań. præmitten duximus. prout in Dei nomine præmissimus. In quarum termino visis dicte Cridæ lris debitæ exequutis. nemineque ex adverso comparéte. neque contradicente in absencium contumaciam per procuratorem legitimum accusatá, ad earumdem Sacræ Regiæ M^{tis} et R^{mi} domini Archiepi lrarum executionem. postulacionemque Regiam processimus. et easipsas utrasque lŕas. tam uidelicet ordinationis nouæ per Sacram Regiam M^{tem}, quam dismembracionis decimarum a prepositura Lancicień per R^m D. Archiepm̄ factæ. in omnibus earum articulis et condicionibus authoritate nŕa ordinaria approbauimus. ratificamus. et confirmauimus. approbamusque ratificamus et confirmamus tenore præsentium lrárum nŕarum, Decimasque integras. siue vlla diminucione in oppidis Pabiianicze et Rzgow, ac in uillis Gathka. Choczianowicze et Laszkowicze omnis grani et seminis dioceis Gnesneń excrescentes, a præpositura Lancicień dismembratas supranominatæ Capellé Regiæ Præposito et prebendariis in ea institutis. eorumque usui ac proprietati appropriamus, ac ad priorem dotem per diuum Regem Sigismundum patrem collatam adiungimus. applicamus annectimus, incorporamus [4v] inuisceramus. et immunitati ecclesiaticæ ascribimus. per eosdem Prepositum. Prebendarios ac ministros dictæ Capellæ suprascriptas decimas decimań. colligendas. percipień. vendeń. et pre eorum arbitrio libere disponeń. et pecunias pro illis venditis collectas, secundum infrascriptam ordinacionem diuideń. et distribueń. hoc uidelicet modo quod prepositus eiusipsius Capellæ modernus honorabilis Nicloaus de Poznania idem Vicedecanus ecclesiæ nostræ Cathedralis Cracouiensis, et quilibet Prepositus pro tempore existens, ultra stipendium ex priore fundacione et datacione paternæ Regiæ Maie^{tis} designatum. habebit et percipiet perpetuo singulis annis ex vniuersitate omnium prouentuum pro sorte sua viginti marcas peccuniarum per Quadraginta octo grossos computatas. Prebédarii uero singuli. et quisque eorum seorsum. similiter ultra illud salarium in Priore dotacione designatum, habebit et percipiet. omni anno pro persona sua decem Marcas peccuniarum moneté et numeri Polonicaĺ. Clericus autem eiusdem capellæ auctius stipendium habebit et percipiet anno quolibet ultra salarium antea ei designatum quatuor Marcas peccuniarum per quadraginta octo grossos computatas. Sic uidelicet quod Prebendarii habebunt et percipient singulatim ex eadem utraque dotacione per marcas triginta pro seruicio et salario annuo. et clericus etiam habebit annuatim ex utroque salario predicto viginti Marcas peccuniarum pro seruicis suis. Qui omnes ideo sic, ut præmissum est. sufficienter prouisi sunt. ac dotati. vt curis Secularibus vacui et de certo victu securi: liberius Diuinarum rerum meditacione. Sacræ lectioni, deuocioni. Sacrificiis. oracionibus. Diuino cultui intendere ualeant ac debeant. Et quia in erectione supranominaté Capellé Regie perscriptum et constitutum est. ut pro reparacione eiusdem capellé. proque vestium sacrarum et aliarum rerum in ea existencium reformacione. ac etiam pro reparacione communis domus, quam prepositus cum dictis prebendariis inhabitant. non nisi decem Marcæ peccuniarum ex redditibus eiusdem capellæ ad corbonam seu ad thesaurum singulis annis deponerentur. Nunc postquam hæc ipsa capella auctiores redditus annuos consecuta est. Statuimus ex ordinacione Sacræ Regiæ M^{tis} ut ex vniuersitate omnium reddituum ex utraque datacione eidem Capellé assignatorum. et donatorum. Viginti marcé peccuniarum in Corbonam ipsam ad usus et necessitates, in erectione specificatas, annis singulis per prepositum et prebendarios reponantur. Ad cæram autem pro cereis et candelis.

Appendix II.3

usuque dicte capellæ, coemendam similiter ex vniuersitate reddituum utriusque dotacionis amborum Regum duodecim cum media marcas peccuniarum. Lotrici vestimentorum capelle marcam unam Servitori uero domus dictorum prepositi et prebendariorum salarium ei augen⁰ ad priores tres Marcas quartam ei marcam peccuniarum pñti nŕa ac Regiæ maie^{tis} ordinacione addimus. applicamus et ascribimus. Coca uero collegio eorum seruiens habebit etiam salarium quinque marcaŕ peccuniæ. et numeri Polonici. Cæterum expeditis Corbona. Preposito. Prebendariis. Clerico. Cæra. Coca. Servitore. ac Lotrice supranominatis in eorum salriis annuis secundum ordinacionem suprascriptam, de residuo peccunie ex vniuersitate prouentuum resultantis, sic statuimus et ordinamus ut id pro mensa communi domus et collegii prefatæ capelle cedat et conuertatur. De perceptis autem et expositis racionem et calculum præpositus annis singulis secundum prescriptum erectionis. collegio prebendariorum reddere et facere teneatur. Et quia beneficium datur propter officium Vt qui sentit commodum, senciat et onus. Id circo nos ex commisione et voluntate Sacræ Regiæ M^{tis} Statuimus et ordinamus ut ipse Prepositus cum omnibus Prebendariis dicte Capelle summam missam in festiuitatibus solennibus. Purificacionis Anunciacionis. Visitacionis. Assumpcionis. Natiuitatis. et Concepcionis gloriosæ virginis sanctæ Marie dominæ nostre, in ecclesia nŕa Cathedrali cantu figurato canant, et canere annis singulis tempore sempiterno teneantur. Iuspatronatus autem et præsentandi prepositum et presbiteros seu prebendari [5r] os cum clerico ad officia dicte Capellæ Sacre M^{ti} Regiæ domino nŕo moderno et Succe^{bus} suæ M^{tis} Serenissimus Regibus Poloniæ, tanquam ueris Patronis, et dotatoribus perpetuo reseruamus. sic quod quilibet Regum ipsorum, occurrente uaccacione, prepositum: virum maturum ecclesiasticum boni regiminis amantem, actu presbiterum, in cantu utroque chorali et figurato doctum et peritum et uoce bona ex arte canentem et ad regendum collegium dignum ac idoneum ad dictam capellam instituendum. Epö Cracouień pro tempore existeń presentabit Prebendarios uero quorum nouem sunt in erectione designati et constituti. et Clericum decimum ii idem Sere^{mi} Reges non iam Epo. sed soli duntaxat eiusdem Capellæ preposito presentabunt. Quos ipse prepositus per examen sufficienter probatos arte et voce bona vtrumque similiter cantum, canentes, idoneosque pro capella cognitos actu presbiteros authoritate sua uigore pñtium ei concessa, instituet. Atque ut uiri digni et idonei tanto auidius ad Capellam et collegium predictum confluant. Creamus eosdem prebendarios ex manualibus perpetuos, iuxta ordinationem Sacre Regiæ M^{tis} qui iam a modo et deinceps per omne vitæ eorum tempus a locis et prebeń suis. (exceptis casibus infrascriptis) amoveri non poterunt, nec debebunt. Clericus tamen iuxta priorem ordinationem ad arbitrium prepositi, manualis et ammouibilis erit. Qui nichilominus debet esse idoneus, et sufficienter in cantu figurato peritus. sic ut cum prebendariis capellæ missas cantare ualeat. ad aliaque omnia officia et onera illi incumbentia in erectione descripta, obligatus sit. et teneatur. Cui etiam prerogatiuam seu gratiam expectatiuam in eadem erectione designatam, salvam pñtibus reseruamus. Statuimus in super ex ordinatione Sacre modernæ Regiæ Maie^tis ut quilibet Prepositus dictæ Capellæ plenam superioritatem in eosdem prebendarios suos et Clericum habeat. et ea in illos fungatur. Decimas et redditus colligat, Salaria annua eis distribuat. et eos secundum ordinationes et instituta regat, et gubernet. Excessiuos. ac viciosos corrigat et puniat. Quorum si quis rebellis. ac inobediens preposito. statutisque fuerit si sine licencia prepositi se absentauerit. si per se ipsum officium suum exercere neglexerit, si quietem aliorum turbauerit: si rixas ac discordias in collegio seminauerit. aut si Scandalosus fuerit: et de iisdem excessibus, aut aliquo illorum delatus per prepositum apud nos et conuictus fuerit hunc nos. et alios similes corrigendi destituendi et ammovendi a collegio atque a prebendis facultatem nobis reseruamus. In euentu uero ubi aliquis eorundem prebendariorum senuerit aut in grauem egritudinem deuenerit. sic ut per se ipsum cantare officiumque suum facere non ualeret in eo casu licebit illi, seu illis de consensu prepositi pro tempore existentis. substitutos idoneos, et in cantu figurato doctos, et ex arte voce bona canentes. habere. et loco sui substituere. Quos tamen prepositus per examen probatos et idoneos repertos suscipere aut non suscipere si idonei non fuerint plenam haberit potestatem. In cæteris vero omnibus et singulis condicionibus ac institutis erectionem dictæ Capellæ ordinacionemque ac uoluntatem Sere^mi Regis patris defuncti, saluam et inuiolatam esse iubemus, et conseruamus. Huic autem presenti disposicioni, ordinaiconi, et constitucioni nræ authoritatem nram ordinariam pariter et decretum interponimus. eamque robur debitæ firmitatis æuo perpetuo duraturum habere decernimus tenore p̄ntium mediāñ. In quorum omnium et singulorum fidem et testimonium Premissor̄ hasce lŕas nŕas manu notarii publici infrascripti subscribi Sigillique nŕi iussimus et fecimus appensione communiri. Daŕ Cracouiæ in curia nra Eṕali. Anno domini Millesimo Quingentesimo. Quinguagesimo secondo. Indicione Decima Die deciā mensis Decembris Pontificāt Sanct^mi in chr̄o patris et domini Julii Diuina prouiden^a papæ tercii. anno secūdo. Pn̄tibus tunc Ven^bus dominus Joanne Korczbok Decano Gneznēń, Stani° Slomowszki Canō^cis Crāc. Jacobo Paczinszki Decano Wladvień. et Cancellario ńro. Stanislao Grotkowski prefecto curiæ nŕæ. Et alis testibus fidedignis. ad p̄missa vacatis atque rogatis.

[5v] Et quia ego Albertus Joannis Pruskowskj de Pruskowo. clericus dioć Posnanień. sacra aplića aucté norius´ publicus et coram memorato dńo Epō Cracovień. auctoru´ scriba. presenti ordinacioni census ad auctioni omnibusque et singulis ṕmissis, dum sic agerentur et fierent unacu´ prenominatis testibus presens interfuj eaque oia´ sic fieri vidj et audiuj. Ideo hoc pńs publicu´ instrumentu´ manu alterius. me tuć alÿs negocys occupato fideli´ scriptu´. subscripsi. singnoque et nomine meis solitus et consuetis, consignaui et comuniuy, in fidem et testimoniu´ præmissoru´ rogatus et requisitus.

II.4: Kk dyp. 1190, Piotr Myszkowski, Bishop of Kraków, 11 June 1584

[2r] IN NOMINE DOMINI NOSTRI IESU CHRISTI AD PERPETUAM REI MEMORIAM. Quum ea quæ sub tempore fiunt, tractu temporis de facili ab hominū memoria euanescunt, nisi apicibus litterarū testiumq; & sigillorū munimine roborentur. Proinde nos Petrus Myszkovvski Dei gratia Episcopus Cracovieñ notū testatumq; facimus vniuersis & singulis præsentibus & futuris, præsentes inspecturis, lecturis & audituris, & ad quorum hæ litteræ nostræ peruenerint notitiam. Quomodo Serenissimi Princeps, Domina, Dña ANNA Iagelonides Dei gratia Regina Poloniæ, & Serenissimi Principis, Domini Dñi STEPHANI Dei gratia Regis Poloniæ, Coniux desideratissima fœliciter moderna, zelo deuotionis ac pietatis accensa, maiorum suorum Serenissimorum Regum Poloniæ vestigia secuta, quos pietate & religione semper habuit insignes: & qui scientes se, iuxta Apostolicam sententiam, nihil in hunc mundum intulisse, nec inde auferre quid posse, thesauris auerunt sibi cautè thesauros æternos & incorruptibiles in cœlo: ac cum Psalmista decorem domus Dei diligentes, Ecclesias Christi cùm in diuersis Regni huius locis, tùm in hac Crac: Cathedrali Capellam Regiam, siue oratoriū, ad laudem & gloriam Dei Op. Max. & in memoriam sanctissimæ virginis matris Mariæ Assumptionis, ac Diuorum Sigismundi Regis, & Barbaræ virginis martyris, in qua olim Seren: Principes & Dñi nostri, Sigismundus Primus pater, & Sigismundus Augustus filius, frater germanus eiusdem Sere: Reginæ Annæ, in Domino sancte & piè defuncti sepuli requiescunt, extruxerunt, largis longe lateq̇; prouentibus & commodis dotauerunt. Ad imitationem eorundem igitur prouocata, cupiens ad priores eiusdem Capellæ dotationes suas quoq; nouas & recentes applicare, & ea pro amore Diuino augere & locupletare, præsertim cùm in ea ipsa Capella, seu oratorio, more maiorum suorum post obitum suum, piam & Ecclesiasticam sepulturam corpori suo iam constituerit, vt videlicet Sacerdotes Christi in eadem ipsa Capella ordinati, cultui Diuino liberaliùs vacare, & Creatoris sui clementiam in Altaris ministerio quotidiano, pro sua Serenitate, illiusq̇; Sere: antecessoribus salute, suppliciter exorare poterint: Villam suam propriam hæreditariam Szvvoszovvice dictam, in districtu Wislicieñ & Palatinu Sendomirieñ sittam, suis propriis peccuniis ad id specialiter apud Generosum dominum Hieronymum Konarski emptam, & coram officio terrestri Cracouieñ, Præposito & communitati Presbyterorum dictæ Capellæ in perpetuum de consensu Maiestatis Regiæ, ad hoc specialiter concesso, in augmentum prouentuum dictæ Capellæ perpetuò resignauit, & dono perpetuæ ac irreuocabilis donationis adiunxit, applicauit, incorpotauit & inuiscerauit. Ac insuper duorum Altarium seu Præbendarum ministeria, à suę Maiestatis antecessoribus in Basilica Craocuieñ certo modo erectorum & fundatorum, tituli vnius Sanctorum Fœlicis & Adaucti, alterius verò tituli Sanctæ Mariæ Ægiptiacæ, certo modo vacañ, cum suis oneribus & commodis, de speciali consensu S.M. Regiæ, tanquam dictorum Altarium vnici & legittimi collatoris, Capellæ prefatæ iuxta ordinationem

infrascriptam perpetuò vniuit & incorporauit, ordinationemą́: nouam huiusmodi fundationis & dotationis suæ, nihil tamen derogando anteriorum fundationum dictæ Capellæ, per olim sanctæ memo riæ parentem & fratrem suos Reges Poloniæ factarum, seu veriùs illius Capellæ fructuum & obuentionum quarumuis in eisdem fundationum litteris contentarum: quinimo easdem in suo esse conseruando, modo infrascripto constituit, posuit & descripsit. Cuius quidem Villæ prænominatę venditionis & emptionis ac resignationis, tum & consensus M. Regiæ, ac dictorum Altarium, de quorum titulis supra fit mentio, de consensu M. Regiæ, vnionis memoratæ, ac occasione præsentandi Præpositum [2v] Capellæ liberè electum, cautionis litteras sub titulis & sigillis eorum appressis & appensis exhiberi coram nobis per Procuratorem suum legittimum mandauit. Quarum tenores sequuntur & sunt de verbo ad verbum tales.

 Compares personaliter coram Iudicio & Actis præsentibus terrestribus Cracouień Generosus Hieronymus Konarski, bonorum Szvvoszovvice & sortium in Mekarzovvice & Korytho hæres, recedeń à terris, palatinatibus, districtibus, iuribus, iurisditionibusą́; suis quibusuis propriis & competeń, & se cum bonis omnibus successoribusą́; suis iurisditioni præsenti iuriq́; & iurisditioni cuiuscunque iudicii & ofricii, ad quod ratione infrascriptorum cittatus fuerit suią́; successores cittati fuerint, quo ad actum hunc totaliter incorporań & ad respondeń subiicień, fanus mente & corpore existens vsusą́; salubri amicorum suorum consilio, non compulsus nec coactus, & matura deliberatione intra se habita, palam, liberè, publicè, & per expressum coram eodem Iudicio terrestri Cracouień recognouit & fassus est. Quia bona sua hæreditaria, hoc est totam & integram Villam Szvvoszovvice cum prædio, & sortes totas & integras in villis Mekarzovvice & Korytho, in terra Sendomirień & districtu Wislicień iaceń, cum totali eorundem bonorum omniũ præfatorum hæreditate, ac cum omni iure, dominio & proprietate tituloq́; hæreditario, omnibusque & singulis dictorum bonorum vtilitatibus, fructibus, prouentibus, attineńq́; & pertineń vniuersis quomodolibet ad eadem bona antiquitus spectań & pertineń, nil iuris, dominii & proprietatis, ac quorumcunq; vsufructuum & vtilitatum in prædictis bonis pro se & suis successoribus reseruań seu excipień, sed ita latè, longè, circumferentilaiterq́; prout præfatorum bonorum hæreditates se in suis metis & limitibus extendunt & ab aliis sunt distincta & dislimilata, & prout eadem bona ipse tenuit, habuit & possedit, tenereq́; & possidere debuit. Nihil omnino excipień, sed in totum & plenarie, ita quòd specialitas si quæ esset, nihil deroget generalitati Serenissimæ Principi Dominæ Dñę ANNÆ Dei gratia Reginæ Poloniæ &c. Et eius Seren: Mtãtis successoribus legittimis dedit, donauit, prout dat, donat, & modo donatorio inscribit præsentibus, perpetuè & in æuum, irreuocabiliterque, & indicań coram Iudicio præsenti iudicialiter resignat perpetuis temporibus. Et iam exnunc prædictus Gñosus Hieronymus Konarski, prædictę Serenissimæ Principi Dominæ Dñæ Annæ, Dei gratia Reginæ Poloniæ, & suæ Mtãtis successoribus, in bona præfata taliter vt præmissum est, data, donata, inscripta, & resignata, dedit & admisit, datq́; & admittit præsentibus realem

Appendix II.4 213

intromissionem & actualem pacificamq̨; possessionem per Ministerialem terrestrem, quemcunq; sibi eligendum duxerit cum suis successoribus ad intromittendum per Iudicium præsens ad id additum. Quæ quidem bona modo præmisso data, donata, inscripta & resignata, prædicta Sere: Mtãs Reginalis cum omni iure, dominio & proprietate, tituloq̨; hæreditario, vtilitatibusq̨; ac attineñ vniuersis tenebit, habebit, possidebit, eisdemq̨; vtifruetur cum suis successoribus ac ea ipsa bona dare, donare, vendere, commutare, alienare, obligare, arendæ & quouis modo onerare, ad vsusq̨; quosuis alios beneplacitos liberè conuertere cum suis posteris poterit. Et debet ac tenebitur prædictus Gñosus Hieronymus Konarski eiusq̨; successores debent & tenebuntur, quos & se super omnibus bonis suis hæreditariis & obligatis, mobilibus & immobilibus, summisq̨; peccuniariis, quæ & quas ad præsens habet & post modum quocunq; modo & quiauis iuris ratione haberet & possideret, inscribit & obligat præsentibus, præfatæ Sere: Principi Dominæ Dñæ Annæ Deo gratia Reginæ Poloniæ & eius legittimis successoribus, eam ipsam Seren: Principem Dominam Dñam Annam Dei gratia Reginam Poloniæ & eius successores, in bonis præfatis taliter, vt præmissum est, ipsi datis, donatis, inscriptis & resignatis, & occasione eorundem bonorum omnium & singulorum tam in parte quàm in toto, ab omnibus & singulis iuribus, oneribus, debitis, vinculis, impedimetis, inscriptionibusq̨, prioribus & posterioribus tam perpetuis quam ad tempus factis, reformationibusq̨; dotum & dotalitiorum ac aduitalitat̃ quibusuis, necnon inscriptionibus recemptionalib. censibusq̨; ex eis emanatis & fundo bonorũ præfatorum annexis, super bonis præfatis vel aliqua parte eorum factis & facien, inscript̃ & inscribeñ; [3r] ac cuiq; personarum ex causa quauis & quocunq; iuris titulo seruieñ. Necnon à cittationibus, adcittationibus, concittationibusq̨; ad satisfacieñ & innotesceñ brachii Regalis & quærellarum quarumlibet in prædicta bona vel aliquam partem corum importat̃, & importañ. Lucris deniq; & perlucris vadiisq̨; lucratis tam pro interesse Capitanei quam partis instigantis, rumationibus, bannitionibus, & pro complicitate ad banniendum, tum processibus iuris quibusuis super bonis præfatis vel aliqua parte eorundem bonorum obtentis & obtineñ, per ductis & perduceñ, acquisitis & acquirendis, in quocunque puncto & gradu iuris existeñ & dependeñ, & ab omnibus propinquis & consanguineis, status, sexus, dignitatis, officii & præminentiæ cuiusuis existeñ. Necnon ab omnibus damnis, iniuriis, violeñ & impedimeñ violentaq̨; expulsione de bonis præfatis, ac ab ademptione eorundem bonorum valeñ per omnes præscriptiones terrestres, nulla præscriptione terrestri obstante, aut eadem auadeñ totiens quotiens opus & necesse fuerit in omni iudicio & officio Regni (non obstañ si Sere: Princeps Domina Dña Anna Dei gratia Regina Poloniæ ad euictorem suum non receperit suiq̨; successores non receperint, seq̨; pro præmissis omnibus & singulis ipsa cum suis posteris tueri & defendere inceperit, aut ei & eis dilatio ad euictorem data non fuerit) tueri, defendere, intercedere, euincere, eliberare, ac vbilibet indemnen & indemnes reddere: bonaq̨; ipsa donata tam in toto quàm in minima parte semper munda, libera, pacifica & quieta reddere, intromissionemq́ue cum possessione &

vsumfructum in bona præfata per se & per suas quasuis submissas & subordinatas personas non denegare, immò ipsam dare & libere admittere, datamq; & admissam non præpedire, nec ea ipsa bona tam in toto quàm in parte adimere, ac in eisdem bonis iniurias, damna & molestias aliquas non inferre, sub damnis terrestribus ad simplicem verbi assertionem sine corporali iuramento prædictæ Sac: & Sere: Dei gratia Reginæ Poloniæ, & suæ Sere: Mtātis successoribus per præfatum Gñosum Hironymum Konarski & eius successores ad soluendū succumbeñ. Pro quibus quidem damnis terrestribus præfatis, ratione præmissorum omnium & singulorum tam in toto quam in minima parte non completorum & non exequutorum, vt præmissum est, ad solueñ succubīt cittatus existens prædictus Gñosus Hieronymus Konarski suiáque successores cittati ad instantiam prædictæ Sere: Principis Dominæ Dñæ Annæ Dei gratia Reginæ Poloniæ, ad iudicium vel officiū Castreñ Capit. Crac. Extunc recedeñ a terris, districtibus, iuribus iurisditionibusq; suis qnibusuis [sic] propriis & competeñ illisq; renunciañac se successoresq; suos bonaq; omnia sua præfata illi iuri & iurisditioni, vbi cittabitur, incorporañ & subiicieñ in primo cittationis termino, quem sibi suisq; successoribus facit peremptorium, parere, stare, respondere, & pro damnis terrestribus præfatis ac cittatis totiens quotiens cittabitut, a iudicio seu officio non recedeñ, satisfacere. Et nihilominus solutis damnis terrestribus præfatis, hanc tam in toto quàm in parte, sub aliis damnis terrestribus similibus, complere & exequi debet & tenebitur, eiusq; successores debebunt & tenebuntur. Terminū ipsum primum & alios consequeñ causæ terminos semper peremptorios vera vel simplici infirmitatibus & actione pro maiori non differeñ. Exceptiones, controuersias, dilationes, motiones, appelationes, ac earum prosequutiones per adcittationes quasuis nullas facieñ. Ad quietationem quoq; tam de re principali quam de perlucris in quouis puncto vel gradu iuris, etiam in exequutione rei iudicatæ, ac in vltimo puncto bannitionis, dilationem sibi nullibi recipieñ, sedsi aliquid se haberet prætendere, in instanti eam commonstrare cum suis successoribus debebit, pœna vel pœnis xv, alias trium marcarum peccuniæ, nec eadem triplici pœna damnorum terrestrium solutionem nō subterfugieñ. Nec etiam ad euictorem seu ad euictores tam inscriptos quam non inscriptos dilationem sibi assumeñ. Non euadeñ prænominatā Sere: Dei gratia Reginam Poloniæ & eius successores, ratione præmissorum omnium & singulorum litteris dictisq; regalibus, terris, districtibus, præscriptionibus, terminibus, fataliis av taciturnitate quauis, euasionibus & condemnañ, nec legalibus impedimentis quibusuis, bello, abseñ Regis a Regno, interregno, colloquio, conuentionibus generalibus seu particularibus, [3v] legationibus intra & extra Regnum Poloniæ, etiam Reipub. causa, turbatione Reipub. quauis, seruitio militari, quauis expeditione bellica, peregrinatione, aura pestifera, inundatione aquarū, fractione pontium, detentionibus per hostes, litteris restium, insultu hostium, defectu aliquo inscriptionis præsentis, cittationum iuxta & ad eandem editarum mala insufficieñ inordinataq; eorū scriptione intempestiuaq; locoq: indebito positione & publicatione, iuramentis quoq; de ignorantiis ipsorum & processus iuridici

Appendix II.4 215

incompeteñ iudiciis seu locum teneñ officii, mala condemnatione in lucro & erroneo processu iuris recitatione, ministerialium eorumq́; autenticarum litterarum productione seu ipsorum ministerialium statuitione, procuratorumq́; mala obtentione, minorennitate successorum, ac ad annos eorum discretionis causæ & actionis prorogatione, statutis & constitutionibus Regni laudatis & laudañ. Tum nec consuetudinibus in iudicio & officio obseruari solitis. Et generaliter nullis aliis causis aut modis exquisitis & exquireñ iudicialiter siue extraiudicialiter fieri solitis, quæcunq; mens & ratio humana inuenire & excogitare possit contra prenominatam Sacram & Sere: Reginalem Mtātem & eius successores sese tueñ. Nec quicquam sibi in auxilium contra in scriptionem præsentem & illius omnia contenta assumendo. Nec specialitate quauis eidem generalitati derogañ. Immo quicquid obmissum esset, vt id generalitas in se concludat & complectatur. Nulla vt præmissum est præscriptione terrestri temporis diuturnitate abusuq́; inscriptionis in præmissis obstante, sub ammissione suæ & successorum totius causæ. Et hic idem coram eodem iudicio & actis præsentibus terrestribus Cracouieñ personaliter stans Gñosa Zophia filia olim Gñosi Nicolai Grodovvski, consors vero legittima præfati Gñosi Hieronymi Konarski, cum consensu præsentaneo eiusdem mariti sui, necnoñ Gñosorum Simonis & Andreæ Grodovvskich fratrum prūelium, hic idem penes eam personaliter stañ, & ad infrascripta omnia illi liberè consentieñ, recedeñ à terris & districtibus, iuribus iurisditionibusq́ue suis quibusuis propriis & competeñ & se cum bonis successoribusq́; suis iurisditioni præsenti terrestri Cracouieñ, quo ad actu hunc, incorporañ & subiicieñ, palam, libere, publicè & per expressum recognouit. Quia ipsa super inscriptionem suprascriptā donatoriam per prædictum Gñosum dominū Hieronymum Konarski maritum suum prædictæ Sacræ & Sere: Annæ Dei gratia Reginæ Poloniæ super inscriptionem præfatam donatoriam super bona totam & integram villa Szvvoszovvice cum curia ac prædio & sortes totas & integras in villa Mekarzovvice & Korytho fact, quo ad ius eius reformatorium & aduitalitium aliudq́; quoduis per eam in bonis præfatis inscriptione præsenti donat, onerāt & obligāt, à marito suo habotis & eidem suruieñ, pertinet & spectat, consensit & præsentibus consentit, ac randem inscriptionem donatoriam approbat, confirmat & ratificat, tenore præsentium mediante. Actum Cracouię in terminis terrestribus feria secunda post festum sanctorum Trium Regum proxima. Anno Dñi, Millesimo, Quingentesimo, Octuagesimo Quatro.

Comparens personaliter coram Iudicio & Actis præsentibus Cracouieñ Nobilis Ioannes Seceminski de Secemin, recedeñ à terris, districtibus, iuribus, iurisditionibusq́; suis quibusuis propriis & competeñ, & se ac suos successores cum bonis suis omnibus presenti terrestri Cracouieñ iurisditioni, quo ad actum hunc, in toto incorporeñ & subiicieñ, palam, liberè, publicè & per expressum recognouit. Quia Sere: Principi Dominæ Dñæ Annæ Reginæ Poloniæ &c. & Sere: successoribus suæ Reginalis Mtātis, de omni & integro iure suo, videlicet de inscriptione terrestri Wislicieñ eidē Ioanni Seceminski per Gñosum

Hieronymum Konarski bonorum Szvvoszovvice hæredem super summam sex millium florenorum peccuniæ communis monetæ & numeri Polonicalis fact & super bonis Szvvoszovvice cum prædio & necnon sortibus villarum Mekarzovvice & Korytho de facto obligat & assecurat, cum omnibusque eiusdem inscriptionis terrestris Wislicień obligatoriæ punctis, clausulis, tuitione, vadiis ac ligameń omnibus in ea descriptis. Tum & se summa præfata sex millium florenorum peccuniæ præfatæ, ac de tenua & possessione bonorum pradictorum eadem [4r] inscriptione obligatorum. Cum omni iure, dominio & proprietate, omnibus & singulis summæ prædictæ & bonorum præfatorum vtilitatibus, fructibus, prouentibus, redditibus & obuentionibus attinentiisq; & pertineń vniuersis, nullis penitus exceptis aut pro se & successoribus suis reseruatis, sed plenariè & in totum cessit & condescendit, ceditq, & condescendit præseń. Ac hoc idem omne ius suum inscriptionis summæ & bonorum prædictorum in personam Sere: suæ Mtãtis Regiæ & Sere: successorum ipsius transfert & incorporat præsentibus perpetuè, realemq; iam exnunc intromissionem & actualem pacificamq; possessionem idem Nobilis Ioannes Seceminski prædictæ Sere: Reginæ Poloniæ & Sere: suis successoribus in bona prædicta suprarecensita dat & admittit per ministerialem terrestrem, quemcunq; sibi eadem Reginalis Mtãs cum suis successoribus ad intromittendũ elegerit, ei & eis à iudicio præsenti iam ad id additum, per ipsam Sere: Regina Poloniæ & Seren: successores ipsius, bona prædicta Szvvoszovvice cum prædio necnon sortes villarum Mekarzovvice & Korytho præseń sibi cessa & condescensa cum eodem omni iure totoq; vti præfertur dominio & proprietate vtilitatibusq; vniuersis, nullis penitus exceptis, teneń, habeń, pacificeq; & quietè possideń, iuxta vim & formam latioremq; effectum inscriptionis prædictæ terrestris Wislicień originalis & capitalis, tum etiam præsentis condescensoriæ & transfusoriæ iuris. Nihilominus tamen prædictus recognoscens Ioannes Seceminski in bonis prædictis villarum Szvvoszovvice cum prædio, necnon sortium Mekarzovvice & Korytho, præsentibus condescensis, saluam sibi rũmationem sex septimanarum ad euehendes exportandasq; res suas reseruauit reseruatq; præsentibus, recognitione sua præseń mediante. Actum Cracouiæ in terminis terrestribus feria secunda post festum Trium Regum proxima. Anno Domini, Millesimo, Quingentesimo, Octuagesimo Quarto.

STEPHANUS DEI GRATIA REX POLONIÆ, Magnus Dux Lithuaniæ, Russiæ, Prussiæ, Mazouiæ, Samogitiæ, Liuoniæ, &c. Princeps Transyluaniæ. Significamus præsentibus litteris nostris quorum interest vniuersis & singulis. Quòd cùm intellexerimus eam esse mentem & voluntatem Serenissimæ Dominę Annę Dei gratia Reginæ Poloniæ, Magnæq; Ducissæ Lithuaniæ, &c. coniugis nostræ charissimæ, vt D.D. Poloniæ Regum antecessorum suorum, præsertim D. Sigismundi Primi parentis sui desideratissimi piissima imitata vestigia, ardentissimoq; cultus Diuini in primaria Arcis nostrę Cracouień Capella Regia promoueń studio desiderioq; incensa, constituerit prædium & villam

Appendix II.4 217

Szvvoszovvice necnon sortes totas & integras in villis Mekarzovvice & Korytho, in districtu Wislicień & Palatinatu Sendomirień sittas, à sui Sereni: propriis peccuniis à Gñoso Hieronymo Konarski emptam, & ei Capellæ Cracouień Regię propter augendos prouentus Sacerdotum illic Deo Opt. Max. sacrificantium, & in laudibus diuinis beatæque Mariæ virginis in cœlum assumptæ, assiduè perseuerantium, donare, resignare, & ordinationem quandam respectu auctionis prouentuum facere: istam singularem & eximiam eius Serenitatis in Deum Opt. Max. Matremq́; illius sanctissimam, pietatem & cultum gratissimo complexi animo, consentiendum duximus in hanc donationem, resignationem & ordinationem, quemadmodum authoritate nostra, qua tutor coniugalis ipsius Serenitatis sumus, consentimus, eaq́; per Mtātem eius facienda & ordinañ nos & successores nostros Reges Poloniæ semper intégrè obseruaturos esse pollicemur, ac nos obligamus præsentibus litteris nostris. Ita quidem vt possit Sereniss. Domina Anna Regina Poloniæ coniux nostra præfata charissima coram quibusuis actis Regni nostri autenticis hunc suam donationem recognoscere, & præfatum prædium & villam Szvvoszovvice cum sortibus in villis Mekarzovvice & Korytho, Præposito & Prebendariis præfatæ Capellæ Regiæ resignare. Per eos & pro tempore existeñ cum omni iure, dominio, proprietate, & redditibus, commodisq́; vniuersis, nullis prorsus exceptis, iure donationis ex præscripto ordinationis per eius Seren: facieñ, habeñ, teneñ possideñ, vtifrueñ [4v] perpetuis sequuturis temporibus in æuum. Iure tamen patronatus nostro Regio ad confereñ Præposituram & Prebendarios, duntaxat actu presbyteris cum obligatione nullum aliud beneficium præter hoc teneñ & resideñ, semper manente saluo. Quod ad notitiam Rñdi Domini Lociordinarii Cracouień deducimus, eumq́; requirimus, vt postquam præfata donatio & ordinatio suū fuerit sortita effectum, istud prædium & villam sortesque prædictas, cum dominio & iure prouentibusque omnibus, ex illis venieñ, iuri Spirituali incorporet, vniat & adiungat, cæteráque in talibus fieri solita conficiat pro officio suo. In cuius rei fidem præsentes subscriptas sigillo Regni nostri consignari instituimus. Datum Grodnæ, die vndecima mensis Februarii, Anno Domini, Millesimo, Quingentesimo, Octagesimo Quarto. Regni verò nostri anno Octauo.

    Stephanus Rex ſcāt   Sigillatum ad mandatum Sacra' Regiœ Mtātis per l̃ras

                                            Albertus Baranowski sczt.

SERENISSIMA DOMINA DOMINA ANNA Dei gratia Regina Poloniæ, Magna Dux Lithuaniæ, Russiæ, &c. Coram Iudicio & Actis præsentibus Cracouień recedeñ à terris, districtibus, iuribus, iurisditionibusque aliis quibusuis propriis & competeñ, & se ac successores suos Serenissimos cum bonis suis omnibus, præseñ terrestri Cracouień iurisditioni, quo ad effectum recognitionis infrascipæ, plenariè & in totum incorporañ & inuisceriñ, beniuolè & expressis verbis personaliter ipsa recognouit. Quia de omni & integro iure suo, videlicet de inscriptione terrestri Cracouień terminorum proximè preteritorum donatoria, per Gñosum Hieronymum Konarski de Korytho sibi Reginali Mtáti super bona sua hæreditaria, vczt totam & integram villam Szvvoszovvice cū prædio necnon sortes totas & integras in villis Mekarzovvice & Korytho in terra Sendomirień & districtu Wislicień iaceñ, modo & iure donatorio, acced eñ ad id personali consensu Gñosæ Zophiæ filiæ olim Gñosi Nicolai Grodovvski consortis ipsius Hieronymi Konarski legittimæ, amicorumq́; ipsius duorum de linea paterna proximorum, facta & recognita. Cum eodem omni iure ac titulo hæreditario omnibusq́; inscriptionis prædictæ donatoriæ punctis, clausulis, articulis, intromissione, tuitione, vadiis, ac ligamentis & conditionibus generaliter vniuersis. Necnon & de bonis supraspecificatis donatis, possessione hæreditaria, omniq́; iure, hæreditate ac dominio ipsorum, nihil pro se Serenissimisq́ue successoribus suæ Reginalis Mtátis in ibidem reseruañ seu excipień, sed plenariè & in totum, prout eadem bona supra expressa, vigore inscriptionis præfata donatoriæ, sua Reginalis Mtás renuit, habuit, & possidebat, tenereq́; & possidere deberet, generi per speciem & econuerso non derogañ, Honorabili Stanislao Zaiąc Præposito, & Præbendariis ac Clerico Capellæ in Basilica Cracouień nouæ fundationis olim Serenissimi Sigismundi Primi Regis Poloniæ, tituli Assumptionis beatissimæ virginis Mariæ, modernis pro tempore presenti existeñ & eorum successoribus, eadem munia & officia pietaris Christianæ, durante hac mundi machina, in eadem Capella perpetuo obituris, cessit & condescendit, ceditq́; & condescendit præsentibus perpetuò. Idq́ue eo animo, quod sua Reginalis Mtás, tanquam iam vnica superstes præclaræ à multis seculis Iageloniæ familiæ Serenissimorum Regum Poloniæ, cupiat & exoptet, cùm vbiq; locorum ad Dei cultum destinatorum, tum etiam præcipue in ea Capella (in qua piissimæ memoriæ diuorum Regum Polonię Sigismundi Primi patris, & Sigismundi Augusti fratris, Regia corpora condita iacent, tum quod suæ sæparata fuerit, ibidem reponetur & requiescet) laudem Diuinam, & fidem Christianam propagari, ac vt perpetua piaq́; sui memoria per laudem Dei in eodem Sacello exercenda elucescat. Omneq́ue [5r] & integrum ius suum præfatum inscriptionis prætactæ & bonorum donatorum in eadem descriptorum, in personas eorundem Præpositi, Præbendariorum ac Clerici Capellæ præfatæ modernorum, & pro tempore existentium, transfudit & incorporauit transfertq́; & incorporat presentibus perpetuo. Realemq́ue iam exnunc intromissionem cum actuali & pacifica possessione eadem Serenissima Reginalis Mtàs præfatis, Præposito, Præbendariis & Clerico modernis & pro tempore existeñ, in bona prædicta supra recensita, taliter sibi condescensa, dat & admittit per ministerialem terrestrem, quemcunq; sibi ad intromittendum elegerint, eis & eorum successoribus iam exnunc per iudicium præsens ad id additum, per ipsos, Præpositum, Præbendarios ac Clericum Capellæ præfatæ modernos & eorum successores eadem officia in eadem Capella, vt præmissum est, perpetuò obituros, bona prædicta Szvvoszovvice cum prædio necnon sortes villarum prædictarum Mekarzovvice & Korytho modo præmisso ipsis cessa & condescensa. Cum eodem omni iure totq́; vti præfertur dominio & proprietate vtilitatibusq́; vniuersis, nullis omnino exceptis, teneñ, habeñ, vtifrueñ, & pacificè ac quietè possideñ, iuxta vim & formam, latioremq; effectum & continentiam inscriptionis prædictæ terrestris Cracouieñ donatoriæ, & de eadem præsentis condescensoriæ & transfusoriæ iuris latius in se & suis tenoribus caneñ. Actum Cracouiæ in teminis terrestribus, feria secunda post Dñicam Reminiscere proxima. Anno Dñi, Millesimo, Quingentesimo, Octagesimo Quarto.

Ioan: Kmita N.T.C. ſſczt.

SERENISSIMA DOMINA DOMINA ANNA Dei gratia Regina Poloniæ, Magna dux Lithuaniæ, Russiæ, &c. Coram Iudicio & Actis præsentibus terrestribus Cracouieñ recedeñ à terris, districtibus, iuribus iurisditionibusque aliis quibusuis propriis & competeñ, & se ac successores suos Sereniss. cum bonis suis omnibus, præsenti terrestri Cracouieñ iurisditioni, quo ad effectum recognitionis infrascriptæ plenariè & in totum incorporañ & inuiscerañ, beniuolè & expressis verbis personaliter ipsa recognouit. Quia de omni & integro iure suo, videlicet de inscriptione sua terrestri Cracouieñ condescensoria & transfusoria suæ Serenissimæ Reginali Mtāti per Nobilem Ioannem Seceminski de Secemin, de inscriptione terrestri Wislicieñ, eidem Ioanni Seceminski per Gñosum Hieronymum Konarski bonorum Szvvoszovvice hæredem, super summam sec millium florenorum peccuniæ communis monetæ & numeri Polonicalis facṫ, & super bonis Szvvoszovvice cum prædio necnon sortibus villarum Mekarzovvice & Korytho, de facto obligāt & assecurāt, facta & condescensa. Cum omnibus inscriptionum prædictarum tam terrestris Cracouieñ condescensoriæ, terminorum proximè præteritorum, quàm etiam prædictæ originalis terrestris Wislicieñ obligatoriæ, punctis, clausulis, articlis, tuitionibus, vadiis, ac ligamentis omnibus ibidem descriptis. Nec non & de summa ipsa prænominata sex millium florenorum peccuniæ præfatæ, ac de tenuta & possessione obligatoria bonorum prædictorum, inscriptione prædicta terrestri Wislicieñ originali in eadē summa obligatorum. Cum omni iure, dominio & proprietate bonorum pręnominatorū, omnibusq; & singulis eorundem bonorum vtilitatibus, fructibus, prouentibus, redditibus & obuentionibus attinentiisq; & pertinentiis vniuersis, nullis prorsus exceptis, aut pro se & Serenissimis successoribus suis reseruatis, sed plenariè & integrè venerabili Stanislao Zaiąc Præposito & Præbendariis ac Clerico Capellæ in Basilica Cracouieñ nouæ fundationis olim Serenissimi Sigismundi Primi Regis Poloniæ, tituli Assumptionis beatissimæ virginis Mariæ, modernis & pro tempore præseñ existeñ & eorum successoribus eadem munia & officia pietatis Christianæ, durante hac mundi machina, in eadem Capella perpetuo obituris, cessis & condescendit præseñ perpetuò. Idq; eo animo, quòd sua Reginalis Mtās, tanquam iam vnica superstes præclaræ a multis seculis Iageloniæ familiæ Serenissimorum [5v] Regum Poloniæ, cupiat & exoptet, cùm vbiq; locorum ad Dei cultum destinatorum, tum etiam præcipuè in ea Capella (in qua piissimæ memoriæ diuorum Regum Poloniæ, Sigismundi Primi patris & Sigismundi Augusti fratris, Regia corpora cindita iacent, tum quòd suæ quoq; Serenissimæ reginalis Mtātis corpus, postquam ab eodem anima per Dei voluntatem seuincta & sæparata fuerit, ibidem reponetur & requiescet) Laudem Diuinam & fidem Christianam propagari, ac vt perpetua piaq̨; sui memoria per laudem Dei in eodem Sacello exercenda elucescat. Omneq̨; & integrū ius suum præfatum, inscriptionum summæ prætactæ, & bonorum in eadem summa obligatorum in personas eorundem venerabilium, Præpositi, Præbendariorum ac Clerici Capellæ præfatæ, modernorum & pro tempore existentium, transfudit & incorporauit, transfert & incorporat præseñ perpetuè. Realemq̨; iam exnunc intromissionem cum actuali & pacifica possessione, eadem Serenissima Reginalis Mtās præfatis, Præposito, Præbendariis & Clerico, modernis, nunc & pro tempore existentibus, in bona prædicta supra recensita dat & admittit, per ministerialem terrestrem, quemcunque sibi iidem, Præpositus Stanislaus Zaiąc, Præbendarii ac Clericus, nunc & pro tempore existētes ad intromittendum elegerint, eis & eorum posteris iam exnunc per iudicium pręsens ad id additum & deputatum, per ipsos, Præpositum, Præbendarios ac Clericum Capellæ præfatæ modernos, & eorum successores eadem munia & officia pietatis Christianæ, durante hac mundi machina, in eadem Capella perpetuò obituros, bona prædicta Szvvoszovvice cum prædio necnon sotrtes villarum prædictarum Mekarzovvice & Korytho modo præmisso ipsis cessa & condescensa. Cum eodem omni iure, totaq̨; vti præfertur dominio & proprietate vtilitatinsq̨; vniuersis, nullis omnino exceptis, teneñ, habeñ, vtifrueñ & pacificè ac quietè possideñ. Iuxta vim & formam latioremq́ue effectum & continentiam inscriptionum prædictarum, tam terrestris Wislicieñ obligatoriæ & de eadem condescensoriæ & transfusoriæ iuris latiùs in se & suis tenoribus caneñ. Actum Cracouiæ in teminis terrestribus, feria secunda post Dominicam Reminiscere proxima. Anno Domini, Millessimo, Quingentesimo, Octagesimo Quatro.

Ioan: Kmita N.T. Craco: sczt.

STEPHANUS DEI GRATIA REX POLONIÆ, Magnus Dux Lithuaniæ, Russiæ, Prussiæ, Mazouiæ, Samogitiæ, Liuoniæ, &c. Princep Transyluaniæ. Significamus præsentibus quibus interest vniuersis & singulis, præsentibus & futuris, harum notitiam habituris. Quòd cùm consideraremus zelum piæ deuotionis erga Deum incomprehensibilemq̨; eius Maiestatem Serenissimæ Principis Dñæ Annæ Dei gratia Reginæ Poloniæ, Magnæq̨; Ducissæ Lithuaniæ, &c. coniugis nostræ charissimæ, quæ cùm in aliis Regni nostri Ecclesiis, tum in Capella Regia Arcis nostræ Cracouieñ, more maiorum suorum Regum Poloniæ cultum Diuinorum augere & propagare animo desideratisiimo studet, hanc illius Serenit: propensam ad deuotionem mentem studiosissimo quoque complexi animo, voleñ & ipsi vnà cum Serenissima coniuge nostra præfata in fide prisca & relligione Catholica constantiam Regiam nostram testatam esse omnibus: vtq̨; in dicta Capella cultus Diuinus nocturnis & diurnis precibus augeatur, consentiendum esse nobis duximus, vti quidem consentimus præsentibus litteris nostris, vt ministria duorum Altarium, vnum videlicet tituli Sanctorum Fœlicis

& Aucti, alterum tituli Sanctæ Mariæ Ægiptiacæ, per Serenissimos antecessores nostros Poloniæ Reges fundata & erecta, Capellæ nostræ Regiæ in Arce Cracouień sittæ, per Lociordinarium vniantur, incorporentur & inuiscerentur, quæ Prępositus & Prębendarius eiusdem Capella senior, nunc & pro tempore existentes, cum suis fundis, censibus, decimis, iuxta illorum erectiones teneant, possideant sempiternis temporibus & in perpetuum. Iure tamen patronatus nostro Regio [6r] ad collationem Præpositurę & Præbeń in dicta Capella semper manente saluo. Cauemusq́; & pollicemut verbo nostro Regio pro nobis & Serenissimis successoribus nostris, quód neminem alium perpetuis temporibus ad Præpositarum & Præbeń præfatam dictæ Capellæ Regiæ in Arce Cracouień sittæ, ad inuestiendum Lociordinario præsentabimus & successores nostri præsentabunt, nisi actu presbyteros, & tales qui illic perpetuò resideń munia sua debita & officia ex fundatione competentia obeant, & qui vnico hoc sacerdotio sint contenti. In cuius rei fidem pręsentes subscriptas sigillo Regni nostri consignari iussimus. Dat.: Grodnæ die XI. Mensis Februarii. Anno M.D. LXXXIIII. Regni nostri octauo.

Stephanus Rex scāt.   Sigillatum ad mandatum Sacræ Regiæ Mtātis per litteras.

Albertus Baranowski ssczt.

AD LAUDEM DOMINI DEI, ET HONOREM beatissimæ virginis Mariæ in coelum assumptæ, perpetuæq́ue rei memoriam. Nos ANNA IAGELONIA Dei gratia Regina Poloniæ, Magna dux Lithuaniæ, Russiæ, Prussiæ, Mazouiæ, Samogitiæ, &c. Domina. Significamus p̄sentibus litteris nostris, omnibus & singulis præsentibus & futuris, harū notitiam habituris. Quoniam sanctus Deoq́; dilectus Rex Dauid, dum, ne cū impiis periret, Deum ardentissimè oraret, inter cætera pietatis suæ & amoris sui erga Deum ardentis argumenta, illud vt non postremum adducit: quòd decorem domus & locum habitationis eius dilexisset. Dilexi, inquiens, decorem domus tuæ, & locum habitationis gloriæ tuæ. Ne perdas cum impiis animam meam, & cum viris sanguinum vitam meam. Satis luculenter testatum nobis relinquens opera pietatis, & ornamenta domus sacræ, in qua gloria Dei habitat, Deo grata, accepta, hominibusq́; in discrimen positis auxilio esse, cùm Deus eiusmodi pietate nostra commoueatur, & prestò nobis memor eorum in periculis corporis & animæ adsit. Ideóque nos ANNA præfata, vltima prosapiæ Iageloniæ Regię Regina Poloniæ, & huius sancti Regis seruiq́; Dei Dauid, & maiorum nostrorum exemplum & pietatem imitantes, totum nostrum studium ad ornandam Ecclesiam Dei & habitationem gloriæ eius referimus. Eam enim pietatem ac relligionẽ maiores nostri ab Wladislao Iagelone orti, qui Euangelii lucem in familiam nostrā & totam Lithuaniam intulit, & idolorū impietate repudiatā, Christū Iesum recepit, receptumq́; subditis suis omnibus tanquam Apostolus genti suæ colendū tradidit, ob quam pietatem in sede Regni Poloniæ à Deo patre misericordiam positus, fœliciter & ipsa e regnauit, & posteritati suæ Regnum incolume & firmum reliquit, quod ad hanc vsq; diem illi successione continua & perpetua gubernarunt, multisq; & victoriis & cæteris ornamentis decorarunt, gloriamq; Dei, Regni sui authoris, magno studio complexi, multis & variis modis eam, & non modo integram conseruare, sed etiam omni ratione, & contentione propagare & illustrare semper contenderunt. Cuius corum pietatis clarissima in hoc Regno testimonia cùm reluceant, ac in omnium oculis posita versentur, non est quod plura dicamus. Nihil sanè quod gloriæ Dei inseruiret maiores nostri prætermissum reliquerunt: multa templa vel noua errexerunt, vel errecta exornarunt: multisq; opibus ac donis Ecclesiam in hoc Regno decorarunt, ac firmam reddiderunt: multa sacra, varios cantus, & symphonias in templis, quibus Deus iugiter laudatur, instituerunt. Atque vt ea laus Diuina ab eis instituta doctrinaque Euangelii magis illustretur, splendidiorq; in docendo Dei populo redderetur, Scholam vniuersalem, siue Academiam in hoc suo Regno Cracouie errexerunt. viros eruditos, & omnium scientiarum professores aduocarunt, & studium vniuersale constituerunt, quod seminarim Ecclesiæ & Regni adeò totius esse voluerunt, vt inde Euangelii doctrinæ Christi interpretes, populíque doctores ad omnes Ecclesias in suo Regno peterentur, & ad Rempub. consiliaque Regia viri [6v] vtilibus præceptis & institutis Philisophiæ instructi euocarentur. Videbant enim maiores nostri relligionem veram & puram maximè illustrari cognitione bonarum artium & litteratorum hominum industria: litteras bonas, & veræ Philosophiæ studia, lumen Ecclesiarum esse, qua luce Ecclesiam & Regnum suum priuari non passi sunt. Viderunt litteris ingenia ciuium perpolita faciliùs in officio contineri vtilitoresque & milites & Senatores rebus gerendis esse, eos qui in studio litterarum iuuentutem suam exercuissent, ac institutis præcetisque Philosophiæ & litterarum instructa pectora ad gubernacula Reipublicæ attulissent. Quam lucem Regni quòd antecessores eorum vel inferri Regno non curauerint, vel illatam extingui passi sunt, & Regnum sæpè varia in discrimina coniecerunt, & ipsi iglorii regnarunt, ignauia ignorantiæ litterarum alumna consumpti, melioribus gubernatoribus sedem Regni relinquerunt rectiùs constituendam atque amplificandam. Ad quam primus Proauus noster Princeps inclytus cùm vocatus esset luce Euangelii, quam tum primum hauserat, lucem litterarum adiungi voluit, Academiam erexit, virisque doctis compleuit: stipendiis, vt tum tempora erant, iustis & honestis eis propositis, vt Regnum suum non modo gloria armorum & rei militaris scientia, verumetiam litterarum studiis & eruditis viris florens & instructum posteritati suæ traderet, ac vtraque gloria Rempublicam florentem eis reliqueret, Regnum & foris virium robore & armorum tractandorum dexteritate, & domi viris in consiliis de Repub. capiendis, & litterarum studiis munitis instrueret. Quod consilium Proaui nostri, & vicini Principes admirati, & Auus noster Cazimirus, & filii eius Albertus & Alexander Patrui nostri, ac diuus Sigismundus Parens noster charissimus Principum clarissimus, postremoq; & Serenissimus Rex Sigismundus Augustus frater noster desideratissimus, amplexi, et Ecclesiam nunquã cultu suo augere, et litterarũ studio in hoc Regno propagere intermiserunt. Quorum nos ANNA Regina præfata, vltima in goc Regno Iagelonum stirps, & sancti Regis Dauid exemplum sequentes, studium omne nostrum, totamque curam ad cultum Dei, ac templa eius ornanda, a maioribus & parentibus nostris instituta & erecta, dirigimus, & maiorem partem fortunarum ornatusque nostri Regii ad eam rem seposuimus. Thesauros nostros in arcem cœli, vbi nec à furibus auferi, nec a tineis corrodi queunt, inferre consilio Saluatoris nostri decreuimus. Cuius propositi curæque nostræ exordium ab instauratione & propagatione sacrorum, à diuino patente nostro institutorum, & ea a fratre nostro prædicto auctorum, ducere voluimus. Sacerdotibus qui in Sacello nostro Regio, à parente nostro pro Regia magnificentia extructo ad sepulchra nostra, sacris assidue operantur diuinasque laudes cum deuotione canunt, stipendia & prouisiones augendo. Vt enim magis idonei digni & diligentes in obeundis Sacris in eodem Sacello nostro Regio efficiantur, habentes vnde pro sua conditione honeste viuant, emimus propria peccunia nostra villam hæreditariam terrestrem apud Nobilem Hieronymum Konarski, dictam Szvvoszovvice, cum prædio & sortibus Mekarzovvice & Korytho, in terra Sendomirień districtuque Wisliciensi iaceñ, quam cum omnibus ad eam pirtinentibus [sic] ad hoc idem Sacellum dotauimus, & cum consensa Serenissimi Domini coniugis nostri Præposito & Prebendariis, quos Rorantes vocant, donauimus euiternè, eamque illam eum cum omnibus ad eam pertineñ, nihil sibi & quibusuis successoribus suis reseruañ, Præposito & Præbendariis modernis & pro tempore existeñ eiusdem Sacelli officiose ad Acta terrestria Cracouień resignauimus. Insuper & duo Altaria antiquæ fundationis antecessorum nostrorum ad hoc idem Sacellum aliunde translata, alterum SS. Fœlicis & Aucti, alterum S. Mariæ Ægiptiacæ, vnum pro Præposito, alterum pro Præbendario iuxta receptionem & senium priori seu seniori, vt eidem Sacello nostro vniantur & incorporentur, apud Serenissimum coniugem nostrum, & Reuerendum Dñum Lociordinarium impetrauimus. Qua quidem auctione prouentuum & prouisionis nostræ interueniente, volentes vt Præpositus & Præbendarii ipsi eo digniores, & ad psallendum aptiores, continuoque eo vnico beneficio contenti residentes efficiantur, ordinationi præfatorum antecessorum nostrorum in eodem Sacello aliqua addenda esse existimauimus, prout quidem communicato prius cum Reuerendo Lociordinario consilio, addimus, ordinamus [7r] & statuimos, cum assensu & voluntate Serenissimi Domini coniugis nostri, in perpetuū ad hunc modum. Imprimis quia ex priori fundatione ius præsentandi Præpositum & Præbendarios est penes Serenissimum D. coniugem nostrum Regem Poloniæ & successores Mtātis eius similiter Reges Poloniæ, obnixè rogamus, & pro amore Domini nostri Iesu Christi, & sanctissimæ eius matris virginis Mariæ obtestamur, ne vnquam aulicum seu quempiam alium ad Præposituram ad hoc idem Sacellum præsentent, quam actu presbyterum, ex eodem collegio Præbendariorum, qui aptior digniorque videbitur, electum, sibi commendatum, cantum, figuratiuum psallere callentem. Qui quidem Præpositus cum vacatio alicuius Præbendarii occurrerit, non alium ad præsentandum Mtāti Regiæ commendabit, nisi priùs exactè probatum & idoneum, aptumque & valentem ad canenedum (prout mos in probando apud Vicarios eiusdem Ecclesiæ Cathedralis Cracouieñ est) repertum & iudicatum. Maiestas verò Regia taliter Probatum sibiqúe commendatum, & non alium, ad Præbendam vacantem Lociordinario ad instituendum præsentabir. Altaria vero prædicta Sacello vnita & incorporata, semper Præpositus & senior Præbendarius perpetuo possidebunt, oneraqúe ex priore fundatione debita adimplebunt, videlicet, Præpositus tituli SS. Fœlicis & Aucti, Præbendarius verò tituli S. Mariæ Ægiptiacæ. Item prædium & villam integram Szvvoszovvice cum omnib. ad eam spectañ solus Præpositus præsens, & pro tempore existens, semper tenebit, gubernabit, & possidebit quoad vixerit, ex eaqúe omnes fructus & commoda percipiet, ea conditione, vt quolibet anno præter alia quæuis onera sine aliqua defalcatione (exceptis tamen casibus fortuitis, veris & notoriis) quingentos florenos peccuniarum Polonicalium, quemlibet florenum triginta grossis computando, communitati Præbendariorum confratribus suis eiusdem Sacelli sine vlla procrastinatione pro quolibet festo Natiuitatis Domini simul integrè dare & numerare teneatur. Reliquum vero prouentuum & commodorum eiusdem villæ & prædii, pro se liberè tollet & percipiet, & hoc ratione onerum & curæ per cum in eadem villa sustuneñ. Ipsi verò Præbendarii seu corum collegium ex eisdem quingentis florenis per Præpositum datis & numeratis, quolibet anno inprimis ad carbanam seu cistam communem, pro fabrica eiusdem Sacelli ac domo Præbendariorum, quindecim marcas peccuniæ reponere & seruare tenebuntur, & hoc vltra illud quod ex priori ordinatione singulis annis reponi debet. Ad cistam verò communitatis claues, vnam penes Præpositum, aliam penes Præbendarium receptione seniorem, vel quem aptiorem ad id iudicauerint ac elegerint, habebunt, ita vt Præpositus sine Præbendariis, & Præbendarii sine Præposito, ex eadem cista nil vnquam capere & expendere possint. Item reponent annuatim pro cera ad hoc idem Sacellum marcas septem cum media. Item Clerico vltra prius stipendiam annuatim, pro quolibet festo Natiuitatis Domini, dabunt marcas peccuniæ decem. Item pro auctione prandii ad assaturam ad integrũ annum reponent marcas peccuniæ quinque, & ea omnia fient ex eisdem quingentis florenis, per Præpositum annuatim ex villa & prædio dandis. Residuum verò vltra præmissa quicquid superfuerit, Præbendarii numero nouem inter se partibus æqualibus diuident: partem vacantis quicunque acciderit, ad cistam, in necessitates Sacelli ac domus, semper reponendo. Ad bona verò & prædium Szvvoszovvice per nos Sacello donata ac dotata, duo Præbendarii capitulariter electi quolibet anno tempore congruo semel descendent eaqúe reuidebunt, & ad fratres rederent fideliter, vt si in aliquo excessum esse cognouerint, Prapositum officii omnes admoneant. Qui quidem Præbendarii non debent suscipi, nisi actu presbyteri, viri pii, exemplares, pacifici, modesti, sobrii, concinnam & sonaram vocem ad psallendum habeñ, qui ex arte fractum benè canere sciant & possint, alias non nisi benè probati, more Vicariorum suscipiantur, & Mtãti Regiæ ad præsentandum per Prapositum commendentur. Item isti iidem Præbendarii nostri præsentes, & corum successores, respectu eiusdem auctoris prouentuum per nos factæ, præter priora onera & ordinationes,

Appendix II.4

tenebuntur perpetuò ordine suo, quolibet die in eodem Sacello alternatim vnam lectam sacrificii Missæ, donec vixerimus, pro peccatis nostris, post mortem verò pro anima nostra, obire debebunt ac tenebuntur, in [7v] quo conscientias corum oneramus. Debentque esse secundum ordinationem Serenissimi D. fratris nostri vnà cum Clerico perpetui. At si Clericus pro tempore existens Præposito inobediens, negligens, excessiuusque fuerit, & admonitus non se emendauerit, potestas penes Præpositum erit eum alienandi, & loco illius meliorem ac diligentiorem instituendi. Item iidem Præbendarii cum Præposito moderni, & pro tempore existens, respectu eiusdem prouisionis nostræ, præter Missas beatiss. virginis Mariæ, quas in choro eiusdem Cathedralis Ecclesiæ fractu decantare soliti sunt, tenebuntur tres Missas, summas vocari solitas, cantu figuratiuo in eadem Ecclesia singulis annis perpetuò decantare. Primam die Natiuitatis Domini, Puer natus est nobis. Secundam die Paschæ. Tertiam ipso die Pentecostes. Cui sacro & aliis omnibus Sacelli officiis Præpositus præsens semper adesse. præesse, & in canendo Præbendarios iuuare tenebitur & erit obligatus, pro conscientia sua. Villam & prædium Szvvoszovvice si aliquando visitare & œconomiam reuidere, & aliquid aliud agere illic necesse fuerit, non diu ibi manebit: sed expeditis necessariis, Cracouiam ad sacra Sacelli curanda redibit: Tempore tamen mensis, vno mense abesse, & rem œconomicam in eadem villa & prædio curare poterit, officiis Sacelli ita ordinatis & instructis, nè interim aliqua negligentia, error & scandalum, oriatur. In reliquis vero omnibus & singulis ordinationes Serenissimorum Patris & fratris nostrorum ac item Lociordinarium satisfieri, easque saluas, integras, ac illæsas manere volumus. Quod ad notitiam Reuerendiss. in Christo Patris Dñi Petri Myszkovvski Episcopi Cracouień, & eius Ptis in Spiritualibus Vicarii seu Officialis generalis Cracouień, vel alterius cuiuspiam ad id potestatem habentis, præsentibus deducimus: ab eo postulañ & requireñ, vt eiusmodi dotationem, donationem, & ordinationem nostram superius specificatam, cum assensu & voluntate Sacræ Mtātis Regiæ Domini coniugis nostri obseruandiss. factam, suscipiat, villamque ipsam cum prędio & sortibus prouentibusque omnibus, iuri, libertati, & immunitati Ecclesiæ adscribat: tum & altaria duo, secundum præscriptum litterarum S. M. Regiæ, & ordinationem nostram eidem Sacello nostro, vnum pro Præposito, alterum pro Præbendario receptione seniore, vniat & incorporet: erectionemq́; nouam, in quantum necessaria fuerit, secundùm præscriptum & intentionem nostram faciat, cæteraque circa præmissa fieri necessaria, curari & exequi mandet pro officio debitoque suo pastorali. In quorum omnium & singulorum fidem ac testimonium hasce litteras manu nostra subscriptas sigillo nostrò appenso muniri iussimus. Dat. Cracouiæ die vigesima octaua Aprilis. Anno Domini, Millesimo, Quingentesimo, Octagesimo Quarto.

Anna Regina Poloniæ   Gaspar Sadlochius á Osiek, Schol̃: Warsouien, etc.
scát.   Sacræ Reginalis Mtātis Secretarius, ex mandato eiusdem
                              Reginalis Mtātis scripsit, et manu sua subscripsit. sczt.

Post quarum quidem litterarum præinsertarum, coram nobis exhibitarum, præsentationem, postulatum à nobis fuit nomine Sacræ Reginæ Mtātis præfatæ, vt ad effectum & executionem in eisdem litteris contentorum & expressorum procederemus. Nos verò modum & formam iuris, in talibus antiquitus obseruari solitam, seruare voleñ, litteras cittationis notræ in vim cridæ contra omnes interesse habere se ad præmissa putañ, ante omnia præmitteñ duximus, prout in Dei nomine præmisimus. In quorum legittimo termino. visis dictæ cittationis litteris debitè exequutis, nemine ex aduerso comparente neque contradicente, in contumaciam cittatorum, vltra horam solitam expectatorum non compareñ, ad litterarum suprasciptarum Sacræ Reginalis Mtātis exequutionem, consensuumq́ue Regiorum in audientia publica pro tribunali sedeñ, & causas audieñ, processimus, præinsertasq́ue litteras auctionis prouentuum Capellæ prænominatæ, per Sacram Mtātem præfatam modo præmisso fact, & dictorum duorum Altarium eidem Capellæ perpetuo vnionem & assciptionem in omnibus earum articulis, conditionibus, & clausulis, auctoritate nostra ordinaria approbauimus, [8r] ratificauimus & confirmauimus, approbamusq́ue, confirmamus & ratificamus per præsentes litteras nostras, villam Szvvoszovvice cum prædio integram, cum eiusdem villæ commodis & vtilitatibus quibusuis, ac duo Altaria præfata supramemoratæ Capellæ Regiæ, Præposito & Præbendariis in ea institutis, iuxta ordinationem infrascriptam perpetuo iure dotatam & donata, eorumq́ue vsui & proprietati hæreditariæ æuiternè appropriamus, ac ad priores dotes per Diuos Sigismundum Primum & Sigismundum Augustum Reges Poloniæ eidem Capellæ collatas, adiungimus & annectimus, applicamus, incorporamus, inuisceramus & immunitati Ecclesiasticæ asscribimus, per eosdem Præpositum Capellæ Regiæ & illius Præbendarios, iuxta infrascriptam ordinationem perpetuo iure habeñ, teneñ, vtifrueñ, diuideñ, & distribueñ, hoc videlicet modo: Inprimis igitur & ante omnia exnenc & in futuros perpetuos annos non debet per quemcunque & quomodocunque dari & institui alius quispiam Præpositus dictæ Capellæ regiæ, præter eum qui dignior & habilior interpresbyteros & Præbendarios, seu vt vocant Rorantos, censebitur fore, ex collegio eorum per eos ipsos Canonicè liberè electus, & Mtāti Regiæ, suæq́ue Mtātis successoribus Regibus Poloniæ pro tempore & in futurum existentibus, ad præsentandum Lociordinario declaratus, & qui sit actu præsbyter, eo ipso beneficio duntaxat contentus, continuè circa Capellam residens, nullis negociis alienis aut substituti onere implicatus. Cuius quidem Præpositi, dum eius legittima occurrerit vacatio, talis debet in perpetuum fieri electio. Mortuò Præposito, nunc & in futurum existente, absoluto funere demortui Præpositi, tandem Sacro solito cum inuicatione numinis Spiritis sancti, congregato fratrum Præbendarioru̅ Capellæ præfatæ integro capitulo, in loco secreto ad id & ad actum electionis huiusmodi constituto, in præsentia Notarii publici side digni hominis, pii, grauis, & in iure periti & discreti, seu Consistorii Cracouieñ Actorum Notarii. Antequam Præbendarii Capellæ præfatæ ad electionem noui Præpositi accedant, quilibet eorum singulatim & seorsim expressis verbis in manibus Notarii, tactis sacri

Appendix II.4

Euangelii scripturis, iuret, & iuramentum corporale præstare debebit. Quod videlicet ad electionem noui Præpositi accedit, illumque ex gremio confratrum suorum, qui sibi idoneus, & in psallendo ac musica magis peritior videbitur, non amore, fauore, factione, prece, vel pretio, aut aliqua spe recompensæ, sed pure & simpliciter pro conscientia sua eliget & nominabit, quem ibidem nominare tenebitur, & sic singilatim singuli, præmissis iuramentis, per vota secreta Præpositum nominare & eligere debebunt. Qui quidem Notaris, collectis & conscriptis eorum votis & nominationibus, in præsentia dictorum Prębendariorum ad hoc vocatorum, vota illorum collacionabit, & quem nominatum pluralitatem vocum habere considerauerit, & eorum collationem in præsentia dictorum Præbendariorum fecerit, talem qui pluralitate vocum habere considerauerit, & eorum collationem in præsentia dictorum Præbendariorum fecerit, talem qui pluraliter vocum suffultus fuerit, pro electo Præposito nominabit & declarabit. Et confecto huiusmodi electionis instrumento, electum pluralitatem vocum habeñ, ad Regia, Mtãtem pro præsentatione ad instituen Dño Lociordinario remittet. Mtãs autem Regia neminem alium præter huiusmodi electum & declaratum Lociordinario ad instituendum, iuxta Priuilegium super hoc per suam Mtẽm concessum, præsentabit. Quem quidem præsentatum Reuerendiss: Dñus Lociordinarius, seu illius in Spiritualibus Vicarius & Officialis generalis Cracouieñ pro tempore existens, seu aliquis alius ad id potestatem habens, instituet & inuestiet. Simili modo & Altaria duo præfata, per Sacram Mtãtem pro Præposito tituli sanctorum Fœlicis & Adaucti, & tituli sanctæ Mariæ Ægiptiacæ pro Præbendario seniore, in dictam Capellam receptione incorporata, eosdem binos occurrente vacatione, sine vlla quauis præsentatione Regia, de qua iam Mtãs sua regia suis Priuilegiorum litteris renunctiauit, instituet, & de eisdem ipsis prouidebit. Prædium & villam integram Szvvoszovvice præfatam solus Præpositus semper tenebit, administrabit, reget & gubernabit quoad vixerit, ex eaque omnes fructus & commoda percipiet, ea conditione, vt quolibet anno præter alia quæuis onera & sine aliqua defalcatione (exceptis tamen casibus fortuitis, veris & notoriis) quingentos florenos peccuniarum Polonicalium, quemlibet florenum triginta grossis Polonicalibus computañ, communitati Præbendariorum [8v] confratribus suis Capellæ præfatæ, sine vlla procrastinatione, pro festo Natiuitatis Dñi simul integre dare & numerare tenebitur. Reliquum vero commodorum & prouentuum eiusdem prędii & villæ Szvvoszovvice, liberè pro se tollet. Ipsi vero Præbendarii, seu illorũ collegium, ex eisdem quingentis florenis per Præpositum datis & numeratis, quolibet anno sine quauis retardatione ad carbonã seu cistam communitatis, pro fabrica eiusdem Capellæ & domo Præbendariorũ dictæ Capellæ, quindecim marcas peccuniæ Polonic. Item pro comparanda & emenda cęra ad Capellam pręfatam, marcas eptem cum media Polonicales. Clerico annuatim pro quolibet festo Ntãtis Dñi, pręter illius priorem prouisionem, marcas decem. Item pro auctione carnium, quas ssaturas vocãt, pro anno integro de eisdem quingentos florenis, quinq; marcas umerare tenebuntur, & ea omnia supra priorẽ prouisionẽ & dotationẽ annuatim ex dictis quingentis florenis perpetuo habebunt. Reliquum vero quod deductis præmissis pensionibus ex eisdem quingentis florenis residuum fuerit, Pręndarii nouem numero inter se partibus æqualibus diuident. partem vacantis, si eo tempore vacauerit, ad cistam communitatis, propter necessitatem futurã, imponere & seruare debent & tenebuntur semper. Qui quidem Præbendarii debent esse actu presbyteri, pii, exemplares, & pacifici ac sobrii viri, concinnam & sonorosam vocem habeñ, qui exactè fractū cantare & psallere sciant. alias prius & ante omnia examinati & in proba ad instar Vicariorum nostræ Cathedralis Ecclesiæ probati atq; idonei reperti, eligi & suscipi debebunt, & sic suscepti Sacræ Mtãti Regiæ per Præpositum ad præsetañ remittentur. Iidem Pręndarii ratione & respectu eiusmodi prouentuum auctionis, pręter priora onera & ordinationes, perpetuò quolibet die in eadem Capella alternatim vnam lectam sacrificii Missæ pro salute & peccatis Serenissimæ Reginæ Annæ quoad vixerit, post mortem vero illius pro anima, obire debebunt & tenebuntur, in quo conscientias eorum oneramus. Et debent esse præfati Præbendarii & Clerica[1] in dicta Capella perpetui. Ita tamen. quodsi & in quantū Clerica[2] negligens fuisset suo officio, Præpositoq́: non obediuisset, fuissetq́; excessiuus, exnunc quotienscunq; capitulariter admonitus, non fuerit correctus, potestas erit Præposito eum priuandi & alienandi, aliumq́; loco illius habendi & ordinañ. Item prædicti Præbendarii respectu præsentis auctionis prouentuum, præter Missas beatæ virginis Mariæ, quas decantare fractu sunt soliti in choro Ecclesiæ eiusdem, Missas loco Summæ tres: Vnam, quam vocant Puer natus, die natalis Dñi : Secundam ipso die Paschæ: Tertiam ipso die Pentecostes, fractu seu cantu figurato sonorã voce decantare perpetuò tenebuntur & erunt astricti. Ad villam præfatam Szvvoszovvice duo Præbendarii, à toto collegio electi, quolibet anno semel tempore competenti venire, & eiusdem villę prouentus, ac etiam si aliqua intercesserit damna reuidere, & confratribus referre debebunt. In aliis verò ordinationibus omnibus & singulis ac institutis, quę hic expressæ non sunt, erectiones ac fundationes ordinationesq́; dictæ Capellæ per Serenissimos Principes olim Sigismundum Primum & Sigismundum Augustum, Reges Poloniæ nostros, factas & constitutas, saluas & in suo robore conseruatas perpetuo esse volumus. Huic autem præsenti nouæ prouentuũ Capellæ præfatæ auctioni & Altarium suprātorum vnioni, dispositioni & ordinationi nostræ, auctoritatē nostram ordinariam pariter & decretum interponimus, eisq́; robur perpetuæ firmitatis valiturum decernimus, tenore præsentium mediante. In quorum omnium fidem & testimonium præmissorum præsentes litteras manu nostra & Notarii nostri infrapti subscripsimus, ac subscribi iussimus, sigigilliq́; [sic] nostri appensione communiri fecimus. Dãt Cracouiæ die Lunæ XI. Iunii. Anno Dñi, Millesimo, Quingentesimo, Octuagesimo Quarto. Præsentibus Rñdis, Venerabilib. ac Nobilib. Christophoro Podolski Kielczeñ Præposito. Christophoro Kárszynski Gnezneñ, Martino & Stanislao Skárszevvski Cracouieñ Canonicis, Stanislao Mánieckii sacratissimi Corporis Christi in Cazimiri Pręposito, Vicario in Spũalibus & Officiali gñali Cracouieñ, Nicolac

Appendix II.4

Romiszevvski, Adriano Wilczkovvski, Ioanne Sulovvski, Martino Strzemeszki. & aliis quam plurimis circa præmissa existentibus.

  petrus Miskovskj[3]
  eps̄ Crac ppt

  Et quia ego Petrus Nobilis Nicolai Goisjÿ clericus Dioceś Plocen, sacra aútate aplića publicus et prenominati Rḿi dńi Epí Crać curiæ' actorú Nórius, quia dict errectioni fundoḿ ordinationi aliisque omnibus et singulis premissis unacú prenominať testibus prńs interfui eaque sic fieri vidi et audiui Ideo prńtes lŕas fuńdonis cum appensione sigilli memorať Rmi dni Epí Crac manu mea subscripsi signoque meo solito quo in conficień instrútis. vtor. obsignaui et communiui in fidé et testimoniú premissoŕ rogatus et requisitus.

NOTES

[1] Changed to clericus.
[2] Ibid.
[3] This signature and the final text by Goiski was written by hand.

APPENDIX III: MEMBERSHIP OF THE RORANTISTS' COLLEGE (1543-1599)

Appendix III presents a chronological table of the Rorantists' membership from its inception in 1543 to the end of 1599. The information has been taken primarily from the Rorantists' account-book, the so-called *Elenchus* (Kk Inv. 56), supplemented by records of individual payments found in the royal accounts in Wagad and church records in Kku. The cut-off date of 1599 was determined not only by the general scope of the survey, but more significantly by the source material. Detailed accounts in the *Elenchus* cease in this year and subsequent yearly entries do not list members by name. The *Elenchus* has already been examined by Adolf Chybiński; his *Materiały* of 1910 presented an alphabetical list of prefects, prebendaries, and substitutes named therein. However, the graph here presents a more complete picture of the college membership, including those persons unnamed in the *Elenchus*, such as the prefects Krzysztof Borek and Benedykt of Stryków, as well as those referred to as 'a substitute', 'clerk', or 'singer'.

All dates of appointment or employment and departure or death accompany the respective member in brackets. Months are given in roman numerals (upper case). Employment is presented in the graph by a continuous line within two small vertical strokes; deaths are noted by a cross (†), resignations by an asterisk (*), and a promotion within the college is marked by an equals sign (=) before and after the move. Where precise dates are not given, the approximate time of employment and/or departure has been deduced from the salary received. Where the payments are too ambiguous, such as for the substitutes employed for less than a year at any one time, the name alone is given.

On the whole, the accounts were well kept, although there are some problems with the *Elenchus*. The manuscript does not contain accounts for the years 1566 and 1595-7. For these years, the table presents those members almost certainly employed with a broken line, whilst those whose employment is questionable are presented by a dotted line. Members are not always recorded in the same way in consecutive years. Whether a prebendary was presented by name only, surname only, birthplace only, or indeed a mixture of the three was of little significance at the time (as long as he was paid); it nevertheless presents some difficulties for the modern researcher. Inevitably, some deductions and assumptions have had to be made. At other times, names are illegible. These have been presented as closely as possible to the original.

Appendix III 231

	1543	1544	1545	1546	1547

Prefect | Mikołaj of Poznań (31 V 1543-28 XII 1556)

Prebendaries:
- Walentyn of Jastrząb (V 1543-27 VI 1547) †
- Szymon Radomski (V 1543-VI 1548)
- Walentyn of Mieszczyska (V 1543-12 VIII 1548)
  - *| Piotr of Samborz (VIII 1543-4 IV 1544)
  - *| Franciszek of Poznań (22 II 1544-8 VII 1545)
  - Andrzej Żmygród (13 V 1544-IV 1555)
  - Blasius of Przemąt (29 VII-30 XI 1544)
  - Jan Brzeźny (30 X 1544-14 IV 1547) †
  - Stanisław Radomski (30 XI 1544-1554)
  - Walentyn of Jasło (20 IX 1545-1546)
  - Jan of Wojnicz (14 XI 1546-XII 1549)
  - † Walentyn Żurowski (27 V-VI 1547)
  - Jan Busko (27 V 1547-7 IX 1549)

Clerk | Tomasz of Jadłownik (V 1543-1560)

Substitutes:
- Szymon Brzeżek
- Stanisław Łowicz

- Szymon Brzeżek
- Stanisław Łowicz
- Stanisław Curzelów
- Stanisław Bawoł
- Jan of Książe

Stanisław Łowicz

Stanisław Łowicz

Szymon Brzeżek
Stanisław Łowicz

Walentyn Brzozów
Jakub of Żarnowiec
(unnamed)

Jakub of Regnów
Walentyn Cieszkowice

Feliks de Strzelno

Jan of Działoszyce

	1548	1549	1550	1551
Prefect	Mikołaj of Poznań (31 V 1543-28 XII 1556)			
Prebendaries	*| Szymon Radomski (V 1543-VI 1548)			
	*| Walentyn of Mieszczyska (V 1543-12 VIII 1548)			
	Andrzej Żmygród (13 V 1544-IV 1555)			
	Stanisław Radomski (30 XI 1544-1554)			
	Jan of Woinicz (14 XI 1546-XII 1549)			
	Jan Busko (27 V 1547-7 IX 1549)			
	Andrzej Słomniki (4 III 1548-1597)			
	Sebastian of Książe (V 1548-1555/6)			
	Laurenciusz Warka (VI-IX 1548)			
Clerk	Tomasz of Jadłownik (V 1543-1560)			
Substitutes	Szymon Brzezek			
	Jan de Koszyczki			
	Feliks Mirmidoni			
	Marcin of Lelów			
	Baltazar			
	Jan Muka			
	Jakub of Proszowice			
	Józef Charziny			
	Mikołaj of Łęczyca			
	Jan Szalo			
	Bartłomiej Lipnica			
	Paweł of Bochnia			
	Jan Lipnica			
	WalentynCzieszkowice			
	Walentyn Stupia			
	Jakub Lwowko			
	Józef Krzecięcice			
	Stefan Brzozów			
	Andrzej of Lublin			

Appendix III

	1552	1553	1554	1555	1556	1557
Prefect	Mikołaj of Poznań (31 V 1543-28 XII 1555)				†	Krzysztof Borek (17 III 1556-2 II 1572)

Prebendaries:
- Andrzej Zmygród (13V 1544-IV 1555)
- Andrzej Słomniki (4 III 1548-1597) †
- Sebastian of Książe (V 1548-1555/6)
- Stanisław Grodziecz (IV 1552-VII 1555)
- Mikołaj Kochanowski (IV 1552-I 1555) *
- Feliks Skarzyński (V 1552-V 1559)
- Stanisław Zając (VI 1553-18 I 1601)
- Stanisław Kłomiczki (1555-VII 1557)
- Kasper Łańcut (VI 1555-4 III 1584)
- Augstinius (1557-1559)

Clerk: Tomasz of Jadłownik (V 1543-1560)

Substitutes:
- Walentyn Słupia
- Józef Krzecięcice
- Andrzej of Lublin
- Marek of Kołaczyce
- Stefan Rzeszów
- Stanisław Opatowiec
- Valentinus
- Walentyn of Skaryszów

	1558	1559	1560	1561	1562	1563
Prefect	Krzysztof Borek (17 III 1556-20 II 1572)					

Prebendaries:
- Anadrzej Słomniki (4 III 1548-1597)
- Sebastian of Książe (V 1548-1555/6)
- Feliks Skarzyński (V 1552-V 1559)
- Stanisław Zając (VI 1553-18 I 1601)
- Kasper Łańcut (VI 1555-4 III 1584)
- Augustinius (1558-VIII 1559)
  - Mikołaj of Odrzywioł (V 1558-1574)
  - Stephano (VI 1558-III 1563)
  - Matheo (VI 1558-VI 1559)
- Stanisław Bąkowski (VI 1560-XII 1578)
  - Stanisław Krakowita (VI 1561-XII 1570)
  - Jan Gliński (IV 1563-1565/6)

Clerk: Tomasz of Jadłownik (V 1543-1560)
 = Jacób Skwirmowita (I 1561-IX 1572)

Substitutes:
- (unnamed)
- (unnamed)

Jakób Skwirmowita =

Augustinus

(unnamed) ——— Stanisław Pokrzywnica

Appendix III 235

	1564	1565	1566	1567	1568	1569
Prefect	Krzysztof Borek (17 III 1556-20 II 1572)					
Prebendaries	Andrzej Słomniki (4 III 1548-1597)					
	Sebastian of Książe (V 1548-1565/6)					
	Stanisław Zając (VI 1553-18 I 1601)					
	Kasper Łańcut (VI 1555-4 III 1584)					
	Mikołaj of Odrzywiół (V 1558-1574)					
	Stanisław Bąkowski (VI 1560-XII 1578)					
	Stanisław Krakowita (VI 1561-XII 1570)					
	Jan Gliński (IV 1563-1565/6)					
	Erasmus (1564-1565/6)					
					= Jakub Skwirmowita (I 1561-IX 1572)	
					Jakub Głowny (I 1568-IV 1578)	
Clerk	Jakub Skwirmowita (I 1561-IX 1572)			= Jan of Piotrków (X 1567- IX 1571)		
Substitutes				Szymon		
				Michael		
				Jakub Kloński		
				Grula		
				Skiczki		
					Skiczki	
					Laurenciusz Zakroczym Laurenciusz Zakroczym	

	1570	1571	1572	1573	1574	1575
Prefect	Krzysztof Borek (17 III 1556-20 II 1572)	†			* Benedykt of Stryków (1574-5?) = S. Zając (23 III 1575-18 I 1601)

Prebendaries
Andrzej Słomniki (4 III 1548-1597)
Stanisław Zając (VI 1553-18 I 1601)
Kasper Łańcut (VI 1555-4 III 1584)
Mikołaj of Odrzywiół (V 1558-1574)
Stanisław Bąkowski (VI 1560-XII 1578)
  Stanisław Krakowita (VI 1561-XII 1570)
Jakub Skwirmowita (I 1561-IX 1572)
Jan Główny (I 1568- IV 1578)
  Jan Brzeski (VI 1570-IX 1574)
    Szymon Buczkowski (VII 1574- VI 1576)
      Tomasz Szadek (1575-1578)
      Skiczki (X 1575-1576)

Clerk
Jan of Piotrków (X 1567- IX 1571)   Michał   ------ Tomasz SMR [Szadek?] (IX 1572-II 1573)
                                                  Clerk

Substitutes   Laurenciusz Zakroczym Laurenciusz Zakroczym   Laurenciusz Zakroczym Laurenciusz Zakroczym

Appendix III

	1576	1577	1578	1579	1580	1581
Prefect	Stanisław Zając (23 III 1575-18 I 1601)					
Prebendaries	Andrzej Słomniki (4 III 1548-1597)					
	Kasper Łańcut (VI 1555-4 III 1584)					
	Stanisław Bąkowski (VI 1560-XII 1578)					
	Jan Główny (I 1568- IV 1578) †					
	Szymon Buczkowski VII 1574- VI 1576)					
	Tomasz Szadek (1575-1578)					
		Skiczki (X 1575-1576)				
		Tomasz Boruczki (XI 1576-I 1583)				
		Job of Wiślica (1577-IV 1601)				
				Wróblewski (VIII 1578-VI 1579)		
					Jakub Małuzyn (XI 1579-VI 1585)	
					= Kasper of Kleszów (X 1579-VI 1585)	
						Feliks (VIII 1581-IX 1582)
Clerk	Clerk					
Substitues	Laurenciusz Zakoczym					
		Drzewicza				
			substitute			
			Zygmunt			
			Cantori	Nicolao		
				Mateusz		
				Zygmunt	Zygmunt	
				Kaspar of Kleszów =		

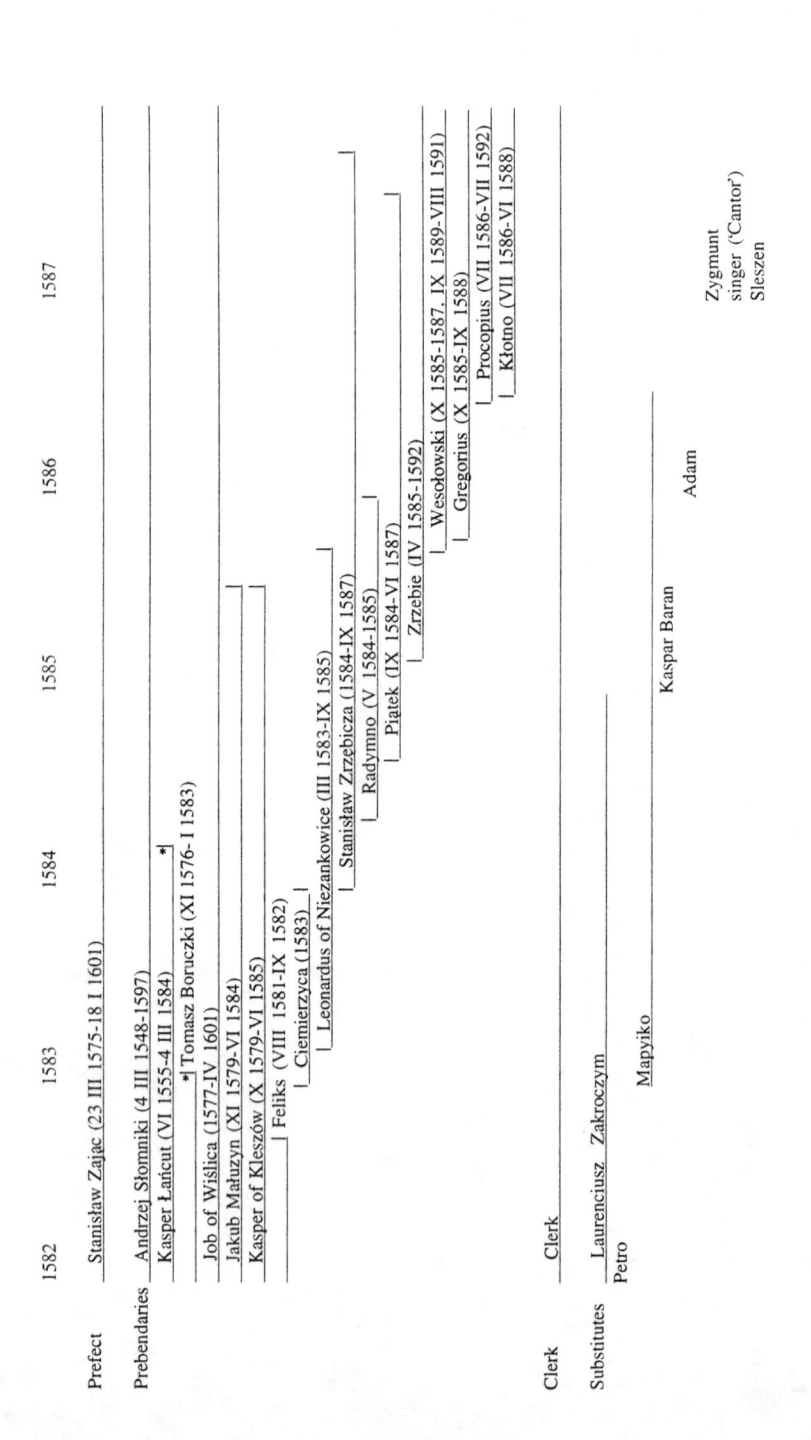

	1582	1583	1584	1585	1586	1587
Prefect	Stanisław Zając (23 III 1575-18 I 1601)					
Prebendaries	Andrzej Słomniki (4 III 1548-1597)					
	Kasper Łańcut (VI 1555-4 III 1584)					
			*| Tomasz Boruczki (XI 1576- I 1583)			
		Job of Wiślica (1577-IV 1601)				
		Jakub Małużyn (XI 1579-VI 1584)				
		Kasper of Kleszów (X 1579-VI 1585)				
			Feliks (VIII 1581-IX 1582)			
			Ciemierzyca (1583)			
			Leonardus of Niezankowice (III 1583-IX 1585)			
				Stanisław Zrzebicza (1584-IX 1587)		
				Radymno (V 1584-1585)		
				Piątek (IX 1584-VI 1587)		
				Zrzebie (IV 1585-1592)		
					Wesołowski (X 1585-1587, IX 1589-VIII 1591)	
					Gregorius (X 1585-IX 1588)	
					Procopius (VII 1586-VII 1592)	
					Kłotno (VII 1586-VI 1588)	
Clerk	Clerk					
Substitutes	Laurenciusz Zakroczym					
	Petro					
		Mapviko				
				Kaspar Baran		
					Adam	
						Zygmunt singer ('Cantor') Sleszen

Appendix III

	1588	1589	1590	1591	1592	1593
Prefect	Stanisław Zając (23 III 1575-18 I 1601)					
Prebendaries	Andrzej Słomniki (4 III 1548-1597)					
	Job of Wiślica (1577-IV 1601)					
	Zrzębie IV 1585-1592					
	Gregorius (X 1585-IX 1588)					
	Procopius (VII 1586-VII 1592)					
		Wesołowski (X 1585-1587, IX 1589-VIII 1591)				
	= Kłotno (VII 1586-VI 1588)					
	Tyczyn (XII 1588-1595/7)					
	Abraham (IX 1589- VI 1590)					
			Szymon (V 1591- 1592)	Szalony (1591)		
				Salomon	Sieciechowicze (1593-III 1597)	
				Franciscus of Wielopole (18 IV 1593-1599/1601)		
				Dobczyce (18 IV 1593-III 1597)		
				Christopherus (1 VI 1593-1595/7)		
Clerk	Clerk					
Substitutes	Lupa	Lupa	Lupa	Lupa		
	Feliks					
	Cantor					Radymno
	Stanisław Biecz					
	= Kłotno			Kłotno		
			Walentyn			
			Jakub			
				Maliczyn		
				Parzynczew		
				Czarnocin		
					Andrea Adolescentem	Andrea Adolescentem
					Blasio Adolescentem	Blasio Adolescentem

	1594	1595	1596	1597	1598	1599
Prefect	Stanisław Zając (23 III 1575-18 I 1601)					

Prebendaries:
- Andrzej Słomniki (4 III 1548-1597)
- Job of Wiślica (1577-IV 1601)
- Tyczyn (XII 1588-1595/7)
- Siecziechowicze (1593-III 1597)
- Franciscus of Wielopole (18 IV 1593-1599/1601)
- Dobczyce (18 IV 1593-III 1597)
- Christopherus (1 VI 1593-1595/7)
- Benedictus Pilcza (595/7-1616)
- Jan Mirmicus (1595/7-1622/3)
- Gregorius (1595/7- VII 1599)
- Jan Lwowko (1595/7- IX 1597)
    - Jan Pobiedziska (VI 1598-1616)
- Laurentius Tadiowski (1599-1611) =
    - Adam (1599-?)

Clerk: (Jan Krzepczów)

Substitutes:
- Andrea
- Blasius
- Stanisław
- Laurentius

Laurentius Tadiowski =
Jan Pobiedziska =
Adam =

APPENDIX IV: DOCUMENTS CONCERNING THE PREFECTS OF THE RORANTISTS' COLLEGE

IV.1: Mikołaj of Poznań.
Kk Inv. 56 (*Elenchus*), fols. IIv-IIIv.

Serenissimus Princeps et dóinus Dús Sigismúdus Rex Polonie ... iuxta sui propositi laudabilé institucioné mandavit. Huic ordini et rectoré laudibili dispositione sue Prepositum et rectoré pmú sacelli illius Venrabilé Doiñ Nicolaú de Poznania viccariú et Vicedecanú arcie Cracovień Anno 1543 Die 31 May institutus. [IIIr] ac per Reueredissimú in Chŕo prem et Dóim Dominū Samuelē Maczijeyowski Epm Ploceń Vicecācellariū regni ordinās curā et disposicionem totalem oñibus in rebus sibi cōmitteñ. . . [IIIv] Institucio Prepositi Venerabilis Dóinus Nicolaus de Poznania Viccarius et Vicedecanus Ecclesie Cathedrali Crać Preptus Capelle nove Fúdacionis Regie Maiét ac rector pmus Institutus est. Per Rńdissim̄ in Chró prém et dóim Dóim Petrú de Gamrat Archipsulé et Epm Cracouień legatú natú primatem Regni Anno dōī 1543 25 Junij.

Kku Episc. Crac. 20 (1543-44), fol. 211rv.

Die Sabato VVIII Junij
Decretum institucionis ad pposiúra in capella Regia
in ecclia cathedrali Cracouień nouiter errect'
Ad Prepositurá nouiter errecta' in capella Regia ecclie cathedralj Cracouien', Ad prñtacom sęrmi principis [211v] et dni dni Sigismunid dei gratia Regis Polonié Magni ducis Litwanié ect. eiusdem ppositure vnicj proví Venelem d Nicolaú a posnania Vicedecanú ecclié cathedralis Cracovień R̄mus dńs als Canriús Curié sue ꝑt R̄me per manus capituli suo impositoḿ Instituti et investivit curá administratoḿ spualiú et Spāliú rerú sibi eiusdem comisic recepto In prius ab eo obendientia, reverentia et nó alicu añ [?] a dicta pposiura bonis corporalj iuramto Irás de super necessario Dand̄ decrevit pụt h. Bartolomeo Siekiereczki plebano in Vilczina testibus, et Andrea hincza actis pñtis scriba.

IV.2: Krzysztof Borek
Kku Offic. Crac. 100 (1556), fol. 1154v (17 March, 1556)

Vdo. chrōfero Borek Sacelli Regii Novi in arce Crac̄ Preptus̄ et ad eccliam Parl̄em in Sandzissow pñtatus apud acta pńcia et. Ad comparenḍ coram dnś et ad poten' se ad eand eccliam in Sandissow institui et investici iura mentumque circa pmissa restari solitum in animam suam pstan ac lras desuper necerias obtineń ho. dmo Felicem Skarzinski eiusd saceli Prebendarium et Andream de Lubowycz Ecclie Cathedralis Cracc. vicariorum in suos constituit procures pntibus norys.

IV.3: Benedykt of Stryków
Kku Episc. Crac. 30 (1572-1577), fol. 207r.

Inst° ad Prepositoram Sacelli Regij in ecctia Cathedrali Crac Benedicti de Striikow. Anno quo supra [1574] Die Veneris, nona mensis Aprilis CRACOVIÆ

Ad præpositoram sacelli Erectionis novæ Divi Sigismundi Regis Poloniæ, in ecclesia Cathedralis Cracceń collationis Sacrae R. Mtis sitam, morte Venerlis Christopheri Borek, ultimi ilius et immediate possessoris vacań, ad presentationem SERmi principis et domini, domini Henrici, Dei gratia Regis polæ eius vnici et legitimi Patroni seu collatoris, Honorabilem Benedicti de Striików actupresbyteris Sacellanu defuncti Regis Sigismundi Augusti, Rmus dńs Episcopus seu manus suæ capiti eius impositionem. instituit [?] et investivit auctoritate ordria, Curam et administralioni spiritualium ac regimen temporaliu sibi in eodem præpositora comitteń et lras hmói instońis et investituræ dom Petro Chwalikowski, Alberto Pęgowski, Joanne Lagiewniky alys familiaribus Rmi domini testibus ad pmissa. Et me Martino ut supra.

R sig^{no}

IV.4: Stanisław Zając of Pabianice
Kku Offic. Crac. 107, p. 252 (Wednesday, 23 March 1575)

Institutio

Ad Prepositoram Sacelli noui Regii in Cathedrali eccla Cracouień Sit. per liberam resignationem honorabilis Benedicti de Strikow in Lukniczki plebani dicte ppture ultimi ac imediate posoris coram nobis facta et per nos ad missam vacań. hońlem Stanislaum Zaiączcz vicarium Cathedralę ecclesie Cracouień, ad pńtationem Serenissimi dni Henrici Dei grá Regis Polonie Magni Ducis Lithuanie etc. dicte prepture legitimi patroni In contumaciam omnium et Singulorum exo interesse pntantium lris cride citatorum et non comparentium seruatis særuandis instituit ac investivit et literas inuestiture desuper oportimus decreuit Pntibus quibus sup.

APPENDIX V: RORANTISTS' INVENTORIES CONTAINING LISTS OF BOOKS (SELECTIONS)

This appendix contains selected sections of four manuscript inventories of 1563, 1584, 1599, and 1834, which list the Rorantists' liturgical books and the music books. The first of these is taken from A. Bochnak, *Inwentarz katedry wawelskiej z roku 1563, (Źródła do dziejów Wawelu, x),* Kraków, 1979, pp. 1, 155, 159, 161-162; the other three have been taken from the original manuscripts. The material is arranged in tabular format. The first column provides the location in the source, the second gives the item number. The third column presents the item entry itself, reproduced as closely as possible to the original. The fourth gives a literal translation of the latter, although book titles are not translated. The fifth column provides further information on the item in question and possible identification. The numbering of the first three inventories is editorial and thus presented in square brackets, and the 1599 inventory has been further subdivided into the liturgical books and the music books. This has been done to facilitate their use in conjunction with the respective chapters of the book. The fourth inventory (of 1834) has an original numbering of items (by both numbers and letters), and this is given in the table. Editorial additions are presented in square brackets. Explanatory notes are provided as endnotes.

V.1: Kk Inv. 29 (1563), fol. 1r: *Anno Domini 1563 mense septembri Inventarium rerum, facultatum et suppellectillis sacrae ecclesiae cathedralis Cracoviensis* . . . . [112r:] Regium Sacellum novae fundationis . . .

Fol.	no.	Item	Translation	Identification
113v	[1]	Missale bonum pressurae Cracoviensis, reverendissimi olim Tomicii, cum clausuris et bullis alias puklie ex argento albo, in cuius medio arma Aquilae et in alia parte Pogonia ex argento, zonae vero regestri ex serico filato, cum gemmis.	A good printed Kraków Missal, of the late [Bishop] Tomicki, with clamps and studs or buldges of white silver, in the middle of which [there is] a shield of an Eagle and the Pogoń, [made from] silver, The rest [ie cover] sewn of cloth, with gems.	*Missale Secundum Ritum Insignis Ecclesie Cathedralis Cracoviensis Noviter Emendatum*, (P. Lichtenstein, Venice, 1532)
	[2]	Missale aliud novum impressum.	Another Missal, newly printed	
	[3]	Tertium missale scriptum in pargameno.	A third Missal, written on parchment	Kk 4
	[4, 5]	Alia quotidiana missalia duo.	Two other daily Missals	Possibly including the Fryderyk Missal recorded in *1599*
114v	[6]	Graduale bonum in pargameno notatum manu excellenti, cute obvolutum, bullis aereis ornatum.	A good Gradual noted on parchment [and] excellently written, covered with leather, ornamented with bulging studs	Kk 46
	[7]	Cantionale quattuor vocum in papyro notatum et pulchre concinatum pro officio Beatae Virginis solemniter decantando comparatum.	A four voice choirbook noted on paper and beautifully produced [and] prepared for the singing of solemn office of the Blessed Virgin Mary	Choirbook now lost.

Appendix V.2 245

V.2: Kk.Visit. 64 (1584), p. 12: *Apparatus Ecclesiasticus Capelle Sacræ Regiæ Mtis, nouae erectionis . . . die XXVI Aprilis . . . MCXXXiiij conscriptu Cracoviæ*

Page	no.	Item	Translation	Identification
13		Missalia	Missals	
	[1]	Missale impssu cū puklis et clausulis argenteis Thomicij.	A printed Tomicki Missal with studs and clamps	*Missale Secundum Ritum Insignis Ecclesie Cathedralis Cracoviensis Noviter Emendatum*, (P. Lichtenstein, Venice, 1532)
	[2]	Missale aliud Thomicij impressū.	A second printed Tomicki Missal	As above
	[3]	Missale quotidianū.	A daily Missal	Perhaps the Fryderyk Missal recorded in the 1599 inventory
	[4]	Missale pargameneum scriptū.	A Missal written on parchment	Probably Kk 4
		Item anno Doi Millsō Quingtō Septuago Sexto ante Festū Resurrectionis Crī, eadem Sacra Rgliś Mtas post felicem suū adventū Craćc eidem Sacello donavit in manus Stāo Zajączek dedit	[The following items were] given to Stanisław Zając, on the safe arrival of her royal highness the queen to Kraków prior to Easter 1584.	
	[5]	Inprimis Missale in pargameno pulcherrime illuminatū, et decem puklis argenteis clausurisque duabus decoratum.	A parchment Missal beautifully decorated with miniatures and ten silver studs and two [silver] clamps	The lost manuscript Missal donated by Anna Jagiellonka

V.3: Kk Inv. 67 (1599), p. 1: *Apparatus Ecclesiasticus Capellæ Sacre Regie Mtis Rorā dictæ, in Ecclia Cathedrali Crac . . . In revisioē visitatioīs Illustrisīsi Cardlis Radziwił . . . die xi Junij M.D.XC. nono conscriptus per Job*

Page no.	Item	Translation	Identification
23	Mszady	Missals	
[1]	Mszał Tomickẏ s puklami srebrnemi ktorich jest dziesieć clausuri srebrne. Sigismunus dedit[1]	A Tomicki Missal with silver studs of which there are ten [and] silver clamps. Given by Zygmunt [I Stary]	A copy of: *Missale Secundum Ritum Insignis Ecclesie Cathedralis Cracoviensis Noviter Emendatum*, (P. Lichtenstein, Venice, 1532)
[2]	Mszał drugi Tomicẏ stary (Sigismunus dedit)	A second Tomicki Missal, old (given by Zygmunt [I Stary])	Another copy of: *Missale Secundum Ritum Insignis Ecclesie Cathedralis Cracoviensis Noviter Emendatum*, (P. Lichtenstein, Venice, 1532)
[3]	Mszał Crac. Friderici (Sigismunus dedit)	A Kraków Missal of Frederyk (given by Zygmunt [I Stary])	*Missale secundum rubricam Cracoviensem* of Bishop Fryderyk Jagiellonczyk, which dates from 1494.[2]
[4]	Mszał Pargaminowy pissany. (Sigismunus dedit)	A written [i.e. manuscript] Missal [of] parchment (given by Zygmunt [I Stary])	Kk 4

Appendix V.3

[5]	Mszał kosztowny pargaminowy pissany s figurami, w bronattem axamicie: na ktorim puklow srebrnych poslocistich dziewiec, clausuri takze pozlociste Regina Anna dedit[3]	An expensive parchment Missal written with figures [miniatures], [covered] in brown velvet: on which [there are] nine gilded silver studs, [and] clamps likewise gilded Given by Queen Anna	
[6]	Mszał Rzymski 1595 Venetÿs excussū	A Roman Missal of 1595 printed in Venice	Most probably *Missale Romanum Pii V. Pont. Max. iussu editum* (Giuntas, Venice, 1595)
[7]	Mszał Rzymski drugi	A second Roman Missal	Probably a second copy of the *Missale Romanum Pii V. Pont. Max. iussu editum* (Giuntas, Venice, 1595)
31	Catalogus librorum Bibliotecæ Comunitatis Rorañ . . .	A catalogue of books of the library of the Rorantists' community . . .	
36	Libri aliquot at cantu pertineñ vulgo dicti partesy, nullus vsui.	Several books for singing, commonly called partbooks, no longer used.	An unknown quantity of books, possibly including Kk I.3.
37	[2] Cantionale in folio Officiorū Lutetiæ imp̄ssum Anno dñi 1557	A Choirbook in folio for the Office [Mass], printed in Paris in 1557	Probably a tract volume containing the choirbook format prints of Le Roy and Ballard, of which the first is dated from 1557.
	[3] Cancionale aliud simile huic Anno dñi 1558 impressum	Another similar Choirbook to this [the former] printed in 1558	Probably another tract volume containing the prints of A. Le Roy and R. Ballard, of which the first is dated from 1558.

[4]	Partes quor vocum æqualium, Introituum	Parts [partbooks] for four equal voices, [with mass] propers	Probably Kk I.4
[5]	Partes Quinque Vocum Officiorum.	Parts [partbooks] for five voices for the Office [Mass]	Probably Kk I.1
[6]	Partes Quinque Motetarum Orládi impreß Anno dñi	Five parts [partbooks] of motets by Orlando [di Lasso] printed in [no date]	A set of Orlando di Lasso's motets
[7]	Cancionale in folio motetarũ Josqn.	Choirbook in folio [containing] motets by Josquin	An unidentified choirbook of motets by Josquin des Prez

Notes

1 This note 'Sigismundus dedit' appears in the margin with a bracket encompassing the first four items.
2 See J. Ptaśnik, *Cracovia impressorum*, p. 37, footnote 1.
3 This note 'Regina Anna dedit' appears in the margin next to the item entry.

Appendix V.4

V.4: Kk Inv. 68 (1834), p. 1: Opisanie Kaplicy Królewskiej Zygmuntowskiej Rorantystów zwany (A description of Zygmunt's Royal chapel called the Rorantists' [chapel])

Page	no	Item entry	Translation	Identification/Kk call number
15		10 Regestr Ksiązek Bibliotyke Kaplicznę Składaiących	10. Register of books comprising the Chapel library	
	1	Mszałów przednieyszych większych z Regestrami 2	Prime Missals, large with registers 2	
	2	Detto mnieyszych 2	Ditto smaller 2	
	3	Detto Rekwialnych róznych 3	Ditto various requiem [items] 3	
	4	Kanonum Świętalnych w ramkach wżacanych za Szkłem	Canon of the Saints, in a gilded frame with glass	
	5	Detto Feryalnych ordynarnych 3	Ditto Ferial, ordinary 3	
	6	Missalia vetuss: Moguntina dla Dyecezyi krac Goczkim drukiem z Maluwanemi Wielkiemi Literami 2	Old Missals: Moguntina [?] for the Kraków dioces, in gothic print with large painted letters 2	
	7	Missalia Krakowskich, ieden w Wenecji drukowany 1532 roku 2	Kraków Missals, one printed in Venice in 1532 2	The last of these is *Missale Secundum Ritum Insignis Cathedralis Cracoviensis*, (P. Lichtenstein, Venice 1532)

8	Detto: w Krakowie z Kanonem Goczkim drukowanym w Krakowie 1607 1	Ditto with the canon in gothic [writing] printed in Kraków 1607 1	Probably: *Missae Propriae patronum et festorum Regni Poloniae*, (A. Petricovii, Kraków, 1607) Kk M. 129
9	Detto: in 4to ieden Krakowski, drugi Goczki 1510 1	Ditto: in 4° one [printed in?] Kraków, the other gothic 1510	The second of these is *Missale Itinerantium seu Misse Peculiares valde devote*, (W. Huber, Nuremberg, 1510) Kk M. 240
10	Detto: pro Defunctis dwa w Poznaniu ieden w Wenecyi drukowane	Ditto: for the dead, two printed in Poznań one in Venice	The last of these is *Missale in agenda defunctorum*, (Cireas, Venice, 1638) Kk M. 3
11	Breviarum Romanorum in fol: Cracoviae 1509 1	A Roman Breviary in folio: [printed] in Kraków 1509 1	Possibly: *Breviarum Cracoviensis* (J. Haller, Kraków 1509) Kk B. 70
12	Detto: in 4to Venetiis 1563 impressum 1	Ditto: in 4° printed in Venice 1	
13	Detto: in 8vo pomnieyszy -"- 1	Ditto in 8° smaller -"-	
14	Officia propria Sanctorum in 4to 2	Propers of the saints in 4° 2	

Appendix V.4 251

24	141	Libri due in quibus Vespe Missæ Vivor et defunctorum motetta etc cum falsis Bordonis, sectione gravium partiui - paribus 4 vocibus Auto. D: Greg: Zuchinie Brixiensi I.L: Mediol: 1611. 2 libr. Venet: 1613	Two books containing Vespe Missæ Vivor et defunctorum motetta etc cum falsis Bordonis, sectione gravium partium - paribus 4 vocibus Auto. D: Greg: Zuchinie Brixiensi, Book I Milan 1611, Book 2 Venice 1613.	Probably G. Zucchino: *Motectorum et missarum senis septenisque vocibus . . . liber secundum* (G. Vincenti, Venice, 1611) and *Missa quatuor vocibus decantanda cum non nullis psalmis integris, divisis falsis bordonibus, Magnificat / litanijs Beate Virginis . . .* (G. Vincenti, Venice, 1615)
	142	item Officium defunctorum 4 voć: Aut: F. Lud: Viadana Op. 11ᵐ Ven: 1609 inter duos libros medium Altus defect' Cantus deest 2	Office for the dead for four voices by L. F. Viadana op. 11, Venice 1609. In two books, Altus is incomplete, the Cantus is missing	L. Viadana: *Officium defunctorum . . . quatuor paribus vocibus decantandum . . . nunc denuo . . . opus undecim.* (G. Vincenti, Venice, 1619g)
		Libri defectuosi Missar' Mottetorum de Autorem Prenestini Gabr: de Pultis Passino, Joanelli - Merulla de Autor Galodae N Op: 6 1	Incomplete books masses [and] motets by Palestrina, Puliti Passino, Joanelli, Merulo Number of books 6	Various incomplete prints including masses and/or motets by G. P. da Palestrina, G. Puliti, S. Pasino, R. Joanelli and C. Merulo.
	143	Książki pisane Dzieta G: G: Gorczyńskiego Msze Hymny, Antyfony, Responsoria etc 6	Manuscript books with the works of G. G. Gorczycki Masses, hymns, Antiphons, responses etc. 6	Kk I.7
	144	Książki Roranczkie zamykaiace Msze, Introity, Graduały, Hymny etc 1	Rorantists' books comprising Masses Itroits, Graduals hymns etc 1	
	145	Detto Detto dawniejsze i w mniyeszym formacie, u iednych Alt brakuie 3	Ditto ditto older and of a smaller format, from one of them the Altus [part] is missing 3	The last of these is probably Kk I.3

146	Książki Anieliczkie w białey skórze zamyk. Msze Graduały Offertoria 1	Angelist's books in white leather comprising masses Graduals Offertories 1	
147	Detto: Roranczkie i Anielskie róznych Autoͬ defect 4	Ditto: Various incomplete Rorantists and Angelists' [books] 4	Possibly including Kk I.4 and Kk I.5
148	Msze, Hymny, Moteta, Introity, Graduały etc dawnieysze i nowsze róznych Autoruw, w osobnych Egzemplarzach lub Kopertach	Masses, Hymns, Motets, Introits, Graduals etc, old and new of various authors, in single copies or envelopes	
149	Mszał pargaminowy pisany Goczkim haraktterem z figurami maluwanemi przez K. Zygmunta I dany w Axamicie Niebieskim bez okucia 1	Parchment Missal written in gothic writing with painted figures [minatures] given by King Zygmunt I [bound] in blue velvet without any protective metal corners or studs	Kk 4
150	Listy N. Królewny Anny oryginalne w liczbie 20 przed ostatni wraz z kopią w iedney Ksiedze oprawne przy tym rozne szanowne monumenta oryginalne i w kopertach w Indexie na końcu teyże Książki wyszczególnione	Original letters of Queen Anna numbering 20 recently bound, together with copies, also various original acts in envelopes, listed in an index at the end of this book	
151	Elenchus oͥium perceptor̊ et expositor̊ ex oͥibus proventibus Sacelli Regii ab A° Erectionis 1543 ad a 1631 1	Elenchus omnium perceptorum et expositarum omnibus proventibus Sacelli Regii ab anno erectionis 1543 ad anno 1631 1	The Rorantists' account book, *Elenchus* (Kk Inv. 56)

152	Aparatus Eclesiasticus cum Inventarys Capellae Sue Regiae	Aparatus Eclesiasticus with inventories of the Royal Chapel	Kk Inv. 67: *Apparatus Ecclesiasticus* . . . (See Appendix V.2)
25 a	choralis Officina divina/: Missae et Antiphona etc:/ Juxta erectionem Sensmi Sigismundi I Regis Pol cura et industria Adm Rndi Nicholai de Posnania primi Capellae Rorant' Praepositi A° 1543 Ksiega na pargaminie gockim charakterem z wyzlacanemi i malow: literami pisana w mosiądz na rogach i w szrodku okuta 4	Chant Divine Office (Masses and Antiphons) According to the foundation of Zygmunt I King of Poland and the work of the Reverend Mikołaj of Poznań, the first chapel prefect, 1543 A parchment book with gothic characters with gilded and painted letters with metal corner and centre pieces 4	The Rorantists' Gradual, Kk 46
b	Figural: Thome Ludovici à Victoria Abulensis Himni totius anni, qui quatuor cunnantę vocibus una cu' Psalmis pro praecipuis Fest: qui 8 modulant vocibus Fol: magno Romae 1581 1	Figured [music]: Tomas Ludovico a Victoria Himni totius anni, qui quatuor cunnantę vocibus una cu' Psalmis pro praecipuis Fest: qui 8 modulant vocibus Large folio, Romae 1581 1	T. da Victoria: *Hymni totius anni quatuor vocibus*. . . (V. Dorico, Rome, 1581a) Kk II. 52
c	Marci Scacelin Romani Sereniss: ac potentiss: Vladislai IV pol: et Suecie Regis etc: Capellae Musicae Moderatoris Missar' 4 vocibus Lib: I^m Romae 1633 1	Marco Scacchi Sereniss: ac potentiss: Vladislai IV pol: et Suecie Regis etc: Capellae Musicae Moderatoris Missarum 4 vocibus Lib: I^m Romae 1633 1	M. Scacchi: *Missarum quatuor vocibus liber primus* (G. B. Robletti, Rome, 1633)

d	Missarum in benedictione Nuptiar' 6 vocum Authore Stephano Lando S.D.N. Urbano VIII diceta Romae 1628 1	S. Lando: *Missa in benedictione nuptiarum sex vocum* (G. Robletti, Rome, 1628)
	Missarum in benedictione Nuptiarum 6 vocum Authore Stephano Lando S.D.N. Urbano VIII diceta Romae 1628 1	
e	Missae variorum praestantiss' Author/: Sermisi, Cadeac, Herrissant Goudimel Mailland, Certon:/ Lutetiae 1558 4	Various choirbook prints of masses produced by A. Le Roy and R. Ballard.
	Masses by various excellent authors (Sermisi, Cadeac, Herrisant, Goudimel Mailland, Certon) Lutetia [Paris] 1558 4	
f	Liber 1 Missarum Caroli Luython Sacrae Cies: Martis Organistae et Componistae 7.6.5. et 3 vocum Pragae 1609 1	C. Luython: *Liber I missarum . . .* (N. Straus, Prague, 1609) Kk II. 50
	Liber 1 Missarum Caroli Luython Sacrae Cies: Martis Organistae et Componistae 7.6.5. et 3 vocum Pragae 1609 1	
g	Missarum Joan. Petri Aloysi Brenestini Basilcae S.Petri Almae Urbis Capellae Magistri 4.5.6.voc. Liber 2 dus Romae 1600 1	G. P. da Palestrina: *Missarum liber secundus . . . quaternis quinquis ac senis vocibus.* (N. Mutti, Rome, 1600c)
	Missarum Joan. Petri Aloysi Prenestini Basilcae S.Petri Almae Urbis Capellae Magistri 4.5.6.voc. Liber 2 dus Romae 1600 1	
h	Detto d° d° Missarum Liber 5us Romae 1590 1	G. P. da Palestrina: *Missarum Liber Quintus Quatuor, Quinque ac Sex vocibus . . .* F. Coattino, Rome, 1590a) Kk G. 441
	Ditto ditto Missarum Liber 5us Romae 1590 1	
i	Missae 5 quinis vocibus a diversis et aetatis nostrae praestantis musicis (Praenestini, Lasso etc:/ compositae stud: et op. Frid Lindeneri Norimbergae 1590 in 4to 4	*Missae quinque, quinis vocibus . . . studio & opera Friderici Lindeneri.* (C. Gerlach, Nuremberg,1590[1])
	Missae 5 quinis vocibus a diversis et aetatis nostrae praestantis musicis (Praenestini, Lasso etc) compositae studio et opera Frid Lindeneri Norimbergae 1590 in 4to 4	

Appendix V.4

k	Ibidem Missarʹ selectissimarʹ Flores ex Praestantiss: Authoritȷ̃ 4.5.6.et plurium vocum op: M.Pottier Cath Ecclae D. Mariae Phonasci Antverpiae 1599	Missarum selectissimarumFlores ex Praestantissmis Authoribus 4.5.6.et plurium vocum opus M.Pottier Cathedrali Ecclae D. Mariae Phonasci Antverpiae 1599	*Selectissimarum missarum flores . . . Opera D. Mathiae Pottier . . .* (P. Phalèse, Antwerp, 1599[1]) Kk R. 412
l	Idem Harmoniae Miscelle Cantionũ Sacrarʹ ab exquisetʹ Auct/: Praenestini, Missaini, Asulae, Viadanae Lasso/ 5 et 6 vocum stud: Leonardi Luchneri Athesini 1	Harmoniae Miscellae Cantionum Sacrarum ab exquisitissimis Auctore (Praenestini, Missaini, Asulae, Viadanae Lasso) 5 et 6 vocum studio Leonardi Luchneri Athesini	*Harmoniae miscellae cantionum sacrarum . . . studio Leonardo Lechneri . . .* (Gerlach, Nuremberg, 1583[2]) Kk R. 412
l	Continuatio ejusdem 5.6.7.8. et pluriũ vocũ de Festʹ vocũ praecipius Ani stud: Frid: Linderin Norimbergae 1588 1	Continuatio 5.6.7.8. et plurium vocũ de Festʹ praecipius Ani stud: Frid: Linderin Norimbergae 1588	*Continuatio cantionum sacrarum quatuor, quinque, sex, septem, octo et plurimum vocum . . . studio & opera Friderici Lindneri . . .* (K. Gerlach, Nuremberg, 1588[2]) Kk R. 412
m	Corollariũ cantionum sacraẽ ejusdem Collectioris Norimbergiae 1590 1	Corollarium cantionum sacrae Collectioris Norinbergiae 1590 1	*Corollarium cantionum sacrarum quinque, sex, septem, octo et plurimum vocum studio & opera Friderici Lindneri* (C. Gerlach, Nuremberg, 1590[5]) Kk R. 412
n	Item Selectissimae cantiones quas vulgo Motetas vocant 6 et pluribus vocibus compositae 2 partes per ExeII Musicũ Orlandũ Lassum Norimbergae 1587 in 4to Libri 6 6	Selectissimae cantiones quas vulgo Motetas vocant 6 et pluribus vocibus compositae 2 partes per ExeII Musicũ Orlandum Lassum Norimbergae 1587 in 4to Libri 6 6	O. di Lasso: *Selectissimae cantiones . . . sex et pluribus vocibus compositae.* (C. Gerlach, Nuremberg, 1587e) and *Alter pars selectissimae cantiones . . . quinque et quatuor vocibus compositarum.* (C. Gerlach, Nuremberg, 1587f) Kk R. 412

26	o	Primus liber modulorum quinis vocibus Authõ Orlando Lassaiio Lutetae Parisioĩ Nu libri 4 Superior - Tenor ctratener Bass Altus deẽ 1571 4	Primus liber modulorum quinis vocibus Authõ Orlando Lassaiio Lutetae Parisiorum 1571. Number of books 4: Superius, Tenor Contratenor, Bassus, the Altus is missing	O. di Lasso: *Primus liber modulorum quinis vocibus* . . . (A. Le Roy & J. Ballard, Paris, 1571c)
	p	Missar̃ 5 vocum ad Normã Concilli Proviɳ Mediol: sub Carolo Boromeo Card. habiti Authore Orpheo Vecchino Mediolan Presb: quibus accessit Missa Jac.. Antoni Piccioli Liber 1us Mediolani 1588 1	Missarum 5 vocum ad Normam Concilli Proviɳ Mediol: sub Carolo Boromeo Card. habiti Authore Orpheo Vecchino Mediolan Presb: quibus accessit Missa Jac.. Antoni Piccioli Liber 1us Mediolani 1588	O. Vecchi: *Missarum quinque vocum . . . liber primus.* (F. and S. Tini, Milan, 1588)
	q	Missae brvi a quatro voci piene di Guisepe Ant Litoani Maistro di Cap: nella Basil: di S. Stepɦ in Bologna op 11^m con Violne Bologna 1720 1	Missae brevi a quatro voci piene di Guisepe Ant Litoani Maistro di Cap: nella Basil: di S. Stepɦ in Bologna op 11^m con Violne Bologna 1720 1	
	r	Missa a 4 voci le tre prime dal Palestina et la Quarta della Bataglia di Gio Fran: Anerio 5ta di Pietro Heredia 6ta per idef: del medesimo - con il Basso continuo per l'Org in Roma 1646 Cant et Org des̃ 1	Missa a 4 voci le tre prime dal Palestina et la Quarta della Bataglia di Gio Fran: Anerio 5ta di Pietro Heredia 6ta per idef: del medesimo - con il Basso continuo per l'Org in Roma 1646. Cantus and Organ missing 1	*Misse a quattro voci* . . . *prime dal Palestina* . . . *& la Quarta della* . . . *Gio Francesco Anerio* (L. Grignani, Rome, 1646^1) Kk II.2
	s	Musica 4 vocum quae materna lingua Moteta vocant ab opt: et variis Auth elaborata, paribus voc: decantanda Venetiis 1549 1	Musica 4 vocum quae materna lingua Moteta vocant ab opt: et variis Auth elaborata, paribus voc: decantanda Venetiis 1549 1	*Musica quatuor vocum quae materna lingua Moteta vocantur . . . paribus vocibus decantanda.* . . (A. Gardane, Venice,1549^9)

Appendix V.4

t	Gomberti Excell et inventione in hac arte facile principis, Chori Carole V Imperatoris magistri, Musia 4 Voc./: vulgo Motetta:/ Lyris Majoribus ac Tibiis imparibus aĉomodata q̃ Lib 1ᵘˢ Vene 1541 1	Gomberti Exceĩl et inventione in hac arte facile principis, Chori Carole V Imperatoris magistri, Musia 4 Voc. (vulgo Motetta) Lyris Majoribus ac Tibiis imparibus accomodata, Liber Primus, Venice 1541	N. Gombert: *Musica Quatuor vocum . . . liber primus* (A. Gardane, Venice, 1541e) Kk II.14
u	Missae ac Litaniae B.M.V. Flamini Nuceti parmen: Octonis vocibus concinendae Venetiis 1602. Cantus 1 Chori deest 1	Missae ac Litaniae B.M.V. Flamini Nuceti parmen: Octonis vocibus concinendae Venetiis 1602. Cantus of choir I missing 1	F. Nocetti: *Missae ac litaniæ beatæ Mariæ Virginis Octonis vocibus conciendae* (A. Gardane, Venice, 1602). Kk II.18
v	Ibidem Missarum Quatuor Florii Zacharii Ord. Min: con: quinque et octo vocibus concinandum Lib. 1ᵐ ut supra 1	Missarum Quatuor Florii Zacharii Ord. Min: con: quinque et octo vocibus concinandum Lib. 1ᵐ as above 1	
w	Responsoria Feriae V. VI. et Sabbati Hebdomadae Sᵉ pro quatuor Musica arte contexta a Rndo D. pandufo Zallamella Raveñate quibus addit Motectum ad Deũ Sacrlũ Altaris Beata Virg et SSᵐ Ven: 1590 1	Responsoria Feriae V. VI. et Sabbati Hebdomadae Sᵉ pro quatuor Musica arte contexta a Rndo D. pandufo Zallamella Raveñate quibus addit Motectum ad Deũ Sacrlũ Altaris Beata Virg et SSᵐ Ven: 1590 1	Lost print by P. Zallamella.
x	Ibidem Vespertini Concentus 4 concinendi vocibus Authore Gabriele pingirolo Laudensi Venetiis 1589 1	Vespertini Concentus 4 concinendi vocibus Authore Gabriele pingirolo Laudensi Venetiis 1589	G. Pingirolo: *Versprtini concentus quatuor concinendi vocibus* (A. Gardane, Venice, 1589)

y	Ibidem Missarum cum 4 vocibus Aut^re Hieronymo Bello Argentenii Liber primus Venetiis 1585/: una de Requiem:/ 1	Missarum cum 4 vocibus Autore Hieronymo Bello Argentenii Liber primus Venetiis 1585/ (una de Requiem) 1	Lost print by H. Bello.
z	Ibidem Missae sex Hipoliti Sabini Anxianensis quae vulgo pari voci dicunt Quatuor vocum Venetiis 1591 1	Missae sex Hippoliti Sabini Anxianensis quae vulgo pari voci dicunt Quatuor vocum Venetiis 1591 1	An unknown edition of I. Sabino: *Misse sex . . . qua vulgo apri voce dicuntur* (A. Gardane, Venice,1575)
zz	Ibidem Tibiertii Massaini Cremensis Concentus 5 voc: 1ª deest in universos Psalmos à Cath Ro: Eclee in Vesperis Omnius Fest' per totum Annú frequentatos cum Cantico B.M.V. venet 1588 1	Tibiertii Massaini Cremensis Concentus 5 voc: 1ª deest in universos Psalmos à Cath Ro: Eclee in Vesperis Omnius Fest' per totum Annú frequentatos cum Cantico B.M.V. venet 1588	T. Massaini: *Concentus quinque vocum in universos psalmos. . .* (A. Gardane, Venice, 1588)
zzz	Ibidem Missa cum Introitu/: Gaudeamus oés in Dnó :/ ac tribus Motetii 12 vocibus canenda 3^bus choris distincta R. d. F. Thomá Gratiano a Bagnacavalle Ord: m: e: Chorus primus Venetiis 1587 1	Missa cum Introitu/: Gaudeamus oés in Dnó :/ ac tribus Motetii 12 vocibus canenda 3^bus choris distincta R. d. F. Thomá Gratiano a Bagnacavalle Ord: m: e: Chorus primus Venetiis 1587	T. Graziani: *Missa cum Introitu, ac tribus motectis duodecim vocibus canenda, tribus choris distincta* (A. Gardane, Venice, 1587a)

APPENDIX VI: THE CALENDAR OF THE RORANTISTS' MISSAL, Kk 4

All of the abbreviations and contractions are left unchanged. Items entered in red in the original are presented here in bold type.

Januarius

		Vigilia	
1	Circumcisio domi		**Solenne**
2	Octava scti Stphani		iii l'
3	Octava scti iohannis evangeliste		iii l'
4	Octava sctorú innocentum		iii l'
5		Vigilia	
6	**Epiphania domi**		solenne
7			
8			
9			
10	Pauli primi hermite		cmeo
11			
12			
13	Octä epiphanie		iii l'
	hilary epi		c⁰
14	Felicis in pincis		iii l'
15			
16	Marcelli ppe + mris		iii l'
17	Anthony abbatis		iii l'
18	Prisce virgis + mr.is		iii l
19	Mary + Marthe + abacu. mrm		iii l'
20	Fabiani + sebastiani mrm		
21	**Agnetis vgis + mr.is**		duplex
22	Vincenti mris		iii l'
23	Emerenciane virgis + mris		iii l'
24	Thimothei apli		iii l'
25	Cõversio s. pauli		duplex
26	Pollicarpi mris		iii l'
27	Johanis crisostomi		iii l'
28	Octava agnetis		iii l'
29			
30	Aldegundis vgis		iii l'
31	Ignacy epi + mris		iii l'

Februarius

1	Brigide virgis	cmeo
2	**Purificaco s. marie virgis**	solène
3	Blasy epi	iii l'
4		

5	Agathe virginis		
6	**Dorothee virgis + m̃ris**		dux
7			
8			
9	Apollonie virgĩs + m̃ris		dux
10	Scolastice virgĩs + m̃ris		iii l'
11			
12	Eulalie virgĩs + m̃ris		iii l'
13			
14	Valentini m̃ris		dux
15			
16	Juliane virgĩs		iii l'
17			
18			
19			
20			
21			
22	Cathedra petri		iii l'
23		Vigilia	
24	**Mathie apl̃i**		dux
25			
26			
27			
28			

Marcius

1	Albini confess		
2			
3			
4	Translatõ s. venceslai		dux
5			
6	Perpetue + felicitatis		ix l'
7	Thome de aquino		dux
8			
9	Ciruli + metudy		ix l'
10			
11	Quadraginta militũ		dux
12	**Gregory pp̃e**		dux
13			
14	Longini militis		
15			
16			
17	Gertrudis virgĩs		cmeo
18	Joseph nutricy dñi		ix l'
19			

Appendix VI

```
20                                              ix  l'
21  Benedicti abbatis
22
23
24
25  Annūciaco s. ma̍ie + icarnacō dni   Soleñe
26
27  Castuli m̃ris
28
29
30
31
```

Aprilis
```
 1
 2  Marie egiptiacæ                     dux
 3
 4  Ambrosy ep̃i                        dux
 5  Vincency cfesś                      ix  l'
 6
 7
 8
 9
10
11
12
13
14  Tiburcy + valeriani mr̃m            ix  l'
15
16
17
18
19
20
21
22
23  Adalberti ep̃i + m̃ris              dux
24  Georgy mris.                        dux
25  Marci euägeliste                    dux
26
27  Cleti p̃pe + mris                   cmeo
28  Uitalis m̃ris                       cmeo
29  Petri noui m̃ris                    cmeo
30  Octä adalberti                      iii  I
```

Mayus
```
 1  Philippi + iacobi aplōr.            dux
```

2	Sigismundi regis	iii l'
3	**Invencio scte crucis**	dux
4	Floriani m̃ris	ix l'
5	Gothardi ep̃i	cmeo
6	Joānis ante portā latinam	dux
7		
8	**Stanislai epi**	dux
9		
10	Gordiani + epimachi m̃rm	cmeo
11		
12	Nereï + achilei m̃rm	cmeo
13	Seruacy ep̃i	cmeo
14		
15	Zophie regine. Octa. s. Stanislai	iii l
16		
17		
18		
19	Potenciane virgĩs	cmeo
20	Bernhardini cfess	dux
21	helene regine	dux
22		
23		
24		
25	Urbani p̃pe	ix l'
26		
27		
28	Germani ep̃i	cmeo
29		
30		
31	Petronelle virgĩs	cmeo

Junius

1	Nicomedis m̃ris	cmeo
2	Marcelli + petri m̃rm	iii l
3		
4	Erasmi ep̃i m̃ris	dux
5	Bonifacy ep̃i + socōr.	iii l'
6	Vincency ep̃i	cmeo
7		
8	Medardi m̃ris	cmeo
9	Primi + feliciani	iii l'
10		
11	Barnabi ap̃li	dux
12	Basilidis + socōr.	iii l'
13	Anthony cfess.	iii l'
14		
15	Uiti + modesti + crescencie mrm	dux

Appendix VI

16			
17			
18	Marci + marcelliani m̄rm.		iii l'
19	Geruasy et prothasy m̄rm		iii l'
20			
21	Albani m̄ris		iii l'
22	Decem miliū mrm		ix l'
23		Vigilia	
24	Johañis baptiste nativitas		dux
25			
26	Joañis et Pauli		iii l'
27			
28	Leonis pape **cmeo**	Vigilia	
29	**Petri et pauli aplōr.**		dux
30	Cōmemoratō s. pauli		ix l'

Julius
1	Octā iohānis baptiste		iii l'
2	**Uisitaco scte marie**		Solēne
3			
4	Procopy cfess.		cmeo
5			
6	Octā petri et pauli		ix l'
7	Villibaldi ep̄i		cmeo
8	Kyliani m̄ris		cmeo
9	Octā visitacōnis marie		ix l'
10	Septem frm̄		iii l'
11	Tn̄slacō s. bn̄diciti		iii l'
12	Naboris + felicis m̄rm		iii l'
13	**Margarethe virgīs + m̄ris**		dux
14	Henricis regis		
15	**divisio aplōrum**		dux
16			
17	Allexy cfessoris		iii l'
18	Arnolphi ep̄i		iii l'
19	Arseny cfessoris		iii l'
20			
21	Praxedis virgis		iii l'
22	**Marie magdalene**		dux
23	Apollinaris m̄ris		iii l'
24	Cristine virgis	Vigilia	cmeo
25	**Jacobi apli**		dux
26	Anne m̄ris marie		dux
27	Cristoferi m̄ris		dux
28	Panthaleonis m̄ris		iii l'
29	Marthe hospite dn̄i		dux
30	Abdon + sennen m̄rm		iii l'

Augustus
31	Germani ēpi	iii l'

Augustus
1	Petri ad vincula	dux
2	Stephani p̄pe	iii l'
3	Inuentio s. stephani	iii l'
4	Dn̄ici cfess	iii l'
5		
6	Transfiguraćo dn̄i	dux
7	Donati epi.	iii l'
8	Ciriaci + sočor.	iii l'
9	Romani m̄ris	iii l'
10	**Laurency m̄ris**	dux
11	Tiburcy m̄ris	iii l'
12	Clare virgīs	iii l'
13	Ipoliti + socōr. eius	iii l'
14	Euseby cfess.	iii l'
15	**Assumptio btē marie vgīs**	Solēñe
16		
17	Octa laurency	cmeo
18	Agapiti mris	cmeo
19	Magni mris	cmeo
20	Bernhardi abbatis	ix l'
	Stephi reg. huga^e	c.
21	Thimothei + simphoriani	cmeo
22	Octä assūptōis marie	ix l'
23		
24	**Bartholomei apli**	dux
25	Tn̄slaco s heduigis	ix l'
26	Lodouici regis	
27	Ruffi mris	iii l'
28	Augustini ēpi	dux
29	Decollaćo s. iohan̄is	dux
30	felicis + adaucti	iii l'
31		

September
1	Egidy abbatis	
2		
3		
4	Magni + socōrum	iii l'
5		
6		
7	Adriani m̄ris	iii l'
8	**Nativitatis marie**	solēne
9	Gorgony + socōr.	
10		

Appendix VI

11	Prothi + iacinc m̃rm	cmeo	
12			
13			
14	**Exaltacō sctē crucis**	dux	
15	Octā natiuitatis marie	ix	l'
16	Eufemie virgis	iii	l'
17	Lamperti epi	iii	l'
18			
19	January + socōr. eius	iii	l'
20		Vigilia	
21	**Mathei apli + evāgeliste**	dux	
22	Mauricy + socōr eius	dux	
23	Tecle virgis	iii	l'
24			
25	Iustine virgis	iii	l'
26	Cosime + damiani m̄rm	iii	l'
27	**Trīslacō s. Stanislai**	dux	
28	**Venceslai m̃ris**	dux	
29	**Michaelis archangeli**	dux	
30	hyeronimi cfess.	dux	

October
1	Remigy germani vedasti epor.	iii	l'
2			
3			
4	Francisci cfessoris	dux	
5			
6	Fidis virgis	iii	l'
7			
8	Sergy + bachi n̄rm	iii	l'
9	Dionisy rustici elenthery m̄rm	iii	l'
10	Gereonis + socōrū	iii	l'
11			
12			
13			
14	Calixti ppe	dux	
15	**Hedvigis electe**	iii	l'
16	Galli cfessoris		
17			
18	**Luce evāgeliste**	dux	
19	Ianuary epi.	iii	l'
20	Translaco s. adalberti	dux	
21	Vndecī. milia virginū	dux	
22	Cordule + severi cfess	iii	l'
23	Severini epi.	iii	l'
24			
25	Crispini + crispiani	iii	l'

26			
27		Vigilia	
28	**Simonis + iude**		duplex
29	Narcisci eṗi		iii l'
30	Amandi cfess		iii l'
31	Quintini m̃ris	Vigilia	

November

1	**Omnium sctorum**		Solēne
2	Cōmemoraco aṁarum		ix l'
3	Eustachy m̃ris + socōr. eius		ix l'
4	Uictoriani pont. + m̃ris		iii l'
5			
6	Leonardicfess		dux
7	Villibrordi epi		iii l'
8	Quatuor coronator		iii l'
9	Theodori m̃ris		iii l'
10	Ludimille electe		iii l'
11	**Martini eṗi**		dux
12	Guniperti eṗi		cmeo
13	Brucy eṗi.		ix l'
14			
15			
16	Othimari abbatis		cmeo
17			
18	Octava s. martini		iii l'
19	Elizabeth electe		dux
20			
21	**Presentaco marie**		dux
22	Cecilie virgĩs		ix l'
23	Clementis ṗpe		dux
24	Crisogoni m̃ris		iii l'
25	**Katherine virgis m̃ris**		dux
26			
27	Lini ṗpe		iii l'
28			
29		Vigilia	
30	**Andree apli**		dux

December

1			
2			
3			
4	**Barbare virgĩs + m̃ris**		dux
5			
6	**Nicolai eṗi**		
7	Octã s. andree		

Appendix VI

8	Conceptio btē marie virgĩs		Solēne
9			
10			
11			
12			
13	Lucie virgĩs mris		ix l'
14			
15			
16			
17	Lazari epĩ		ix l'
18			
19			
20		Vigilia	
21	Thome apĩĩ		dux
22			
23			
24		Vigilia	
25	Nativitatis dñi		Solēne
26	Stephani protomĩris		dux
27	Johañis apĩĩ + evāgeliste		dux
28	Sctōr. innocentū		dux
29	Thome epĩ canthuriēn		iii l'
30			
31	Siluestri pp̄e		iii l'

APPENDIX VII: EXTRACT FROM BISHOP JERZY RADZIWIŁŁ'S DECREE OF 1597 (Kk 239, pp. 26-9) MANDATING THE USE OF THE ROMAN MISSAL

[p. 26] GEORGIUS miseratione divina, tituli sancti Sixti, S. R. E. presbyter Cardinalis, Radziwil nuncupatus, perpetuus administrator Episcopatus Cracouień . . . ad visitañ Comunitatem Vicariọr eiusdem Ecclesiæ transtulimus, atque Anno Dńi 1597 a die tercia Ianuary . . .
[p. 27]   DE DIVINIS Officys.
Horæ Canonicæ diurnæ, & nocturnæ, et Breuiario Romano, decantari debent, nil addendo, minueń, vel immutan, exceptis festis Regnii proprÿs, quæ licet aliqua habeát propria, secundum rubricas tamen, Breviary Romani ordinań sút. Similiter officium Beatæ Mariæ Virginis, officium defunctọr, Psalmi graduales, & Pœnitentiales cum Litanÿs, temporibus suis, secundum formam Breuiarÿ Romani fiant.
. . . Missa tamen de die, quam Votiua quæcunque atque etiam pro defunctis, ex Missali Romano celebretur qua id Pius V[1] virtute Sanctæ obedientiæ præcipit & conciliú Tridentinú Ses. 7. c. 13. anathema pronunciat, Ecćlæ Catholicæ ritus contemneń, aut pro libitu ońitteń, aut in nouos alios mutań.
Verba in Missæ officio, addita, vel interiecta ommittantur vt in Kyrie eleysó, Gloria in excelsis
A sequentys inter natos & verbum Dei, quas in Ecclesia nŕa fundatas esse vidimus, Vicarios liberamus: cum eæ, in Ecćlia Romana. non canantur, in cuius fide, confessione, & obedientia, dicti fundatores, mortui sunt, sed vt Vicary legatæ, pro ÿs, bona conscientia percipiat, ÿs diebis, Missæ intersint Conuentuali, & pro anima fundatọr, De profundis cum Versu, & Collecta per defuncto orent.
[p. 28] Concianes, quæ fiunt diebus Dńcis, festivis, & tempore Quadragesimæ, ab omnibus Vicarÿs superpiliciatis, in Choro audiantur, sub poena vnius grosi, per diuisiores [p. 29] e distributionibus detrahenda In choro nullus colloquÿs, ious, aut clamoribus, ofensionis alÿs præbat; sed omnes, reuerenter, distinctè, deuoteque psallant. Ses. 24. c. 12. sub poena simili.
. . . Datum Cracouiæ die Vigesima Mensis Ianuarÿ. Anno Domini. Millesimo Quingentesimo Nonagesimo Septimo.

NOTES

[1] The note 'Pius V' is written not in the main text but added in the margin.

APPENDIX VIII: CATALOGUE OF THE RORANTISTS' GRADUAL

This appendix contains a catalogue of the Rorantists' Gradual, Kk 46. It is presented in tabular format, by item, together with concordances in local manuscripts. The first four columns catalogue the Rorantists' Gradual, providing the item number (editorial), location in the manuscript, the textual incipit, and the title (with subsequently added marginalia in brackets). The next columns record the concordances in the three volumes of the Olbracht Gradual Kk 42-44 (1501-6), and the last column gives concordances in two other manuscripts, a Gradual from Kraków (fifteenth century), Kk 45, and a Cancionale from Kraków (1498), Kk 58. All textual incipits are standardized, but the titles are presented exactly as given in the source. Original entries are presented in normal type-face; italic type-face denotes later additions.

The missing folio of the Rorantists' Gradual (between fols. 46 and 47) has been indicated in the catalogue by a dash in square brackets, and the 'Alleluia. Angelus ad virginem' which began here, has been included as item 43.

VIII: Kk 46: Catalogue of chant with concordances in local manuscript.

No	Rorantists' Gradual (Kk 46) Fol.	Text incipit	Title (Marginalia)	Olbracht Gradual vol. I Temporale (Kk 44) Fol. Title	Olbracht Gradual vol. II Sanctorale (Kk 43) Fol. Title	Olbracht Gradual vol. III Marian (Kk 42) Fol. Title	Other sources (selection) Source. Fol. Title
1	2r-2v	Kyrie virginitatis		1r: Fons bonitatis	1v-2r: (fons bonitatis)	2v-3r: Kyrie virginitatis	
2	2v-4r	Kyrie. Gloria	Aliud in duplicibus festis cum sequentia et in terra (Feria Quinta, Solenne Gloria)		3r-4v: De patronis	14v-16r: Item de patronis Canite	
3	4r-6r	Kyrie. Gloria	Aliud per octauas (per octauas)	6r: Angelicū siue per octauas	6v-7v: Per octouas	13v: Per octavas	
4	6r-8r	Kyrie. Gloria	Paschale	4r: Paschale	4v-6v: Istud cant' festuibus tpr paschali	12r-13v: Paschale	
5	8r-10v	Kyrie. Gloria	Sabbatuis diebus (Sabbatho de B.V.M.)		18r-21r: De domina sabbativis diebus	4v-7r	
6	10v-12v	Kyrie. Gloria	Item aliud (Feria Quarta)		14v-16r: De electa	7r-9r: Item aliud	
7	12v-13r	Kyrie	Item aliud (Feria secunda)		23v: De beata virgine in adventum	9rv: De domina in adventum	
8	13r	Kyrie	Aliud (Feria Tertia)		23v: Item aliud de beata virgine in adventum	11rv	

Appendix VIII

9	13v-15r	Kyrie. Gloria	Item aliud (Diebus Dominicis Gloria feria 2da feria 3tia Idem)		11v Kyrie: Aliud in adventum; 9v-11 Gloria: De domina in adventum
10	15r-17r	Kyrie. Gloria	Aliud cum et 1 fra ferialibus diebus (Feria Sexta)		
11	17r-18v	Et in terra	(Feria 4)		
12	19r-19r	Sanctus. Agnus Dei	Solenne	13rv: Solenne	13r: De virginibus
13	20r-21r	Sanctus. Agnus Dei	Aliud solẽne Angelic̃ (Paschale)	14r-15r: Angelicum	17v-18r
14	21r-22r	Sanctus. Agnus Dei	Aliud solẽne		26v-27v 27v-28v: Angelicum 18v-19v: Angelicum
15	22r-23r	Sanctus. Agnus Dei	Aliud pulchrũ (Feria tertia)		28v-30r: Aliud solenne 19v-20v: Aliud
16	23r-24r	Sanctus. Agnus Dei	Aliud sabbativale (De BVM)		48r-49r: Aliud quando placet 31r-32r
17	24r-25r	Sanctus. Agnus Dei	Aliud de eodẽ (Feria secunda)		51r-52r: Item aliud 34v-36v
18	25r-26r	Sanctus. Agnus Dei	Aliud (Dominicis diebus)		25r-26r: aliud 34r-35r: De beata virgine 23v-24v
19	26r	Sanctus. Agnus Dei	Aliud (Feria Sexta)		31r-32r: Item aliud
20	26v-27v	Sanctus. Agnus Dei	Aliud Quando Placet		38r-39r: Aliud quando placet 22v-23v: aliud
21	28r-29r	Sanctus. Agnus Dei	Aliud (Feria Quarta)		46v-47r: Item aliud 33r-34r

22	29r-30r	Sanctus. Agnus Dei	Aliud decorū		47r-48r: Item aliud	32r-33r: Item aliud
23	30r-31r	Sanctus. Agnus Dei	Aliud naydobne		49r-50r: Item aliud	35v (Sanctus)
24	31r-32r	Sanctus. Agnus Dei	Ungarić (Per octavas)	16r-17r: Ungaricum	39r-40r: Aliud ad placidum	28v-29v: Item aliud
25	32v-33r	Sanctus. Agnus Dei	Aliud Iocundum Roskoschne		41r-42r: Aliud de b. virgine	26r-27v: aliud
26	33v-34v	Sanctus. Agnus Dei	Aliud per octavas (Per octavas tritum)	15r-16r: Per octavas	37r-38r: Quando placet per octavas	21v-22v: aliud
27	34v-35v	Sanctus. Agnus Dei	Aliud Ferys Qūtis (Feria Quinta)	19r: De corpore Christi		
28	35v-36v	Sanctus. Agnus Dei	Aliud pulchrum			
29	36v-38r	Sanctus. Agnus Dei	Decorumaliud		50r-51r: Item aliud	37v-38v
30	38r-39r	Sanctus. Agnus Dei	Aliud nobile et regale			
31	39r-40r	Sanctus. Agnus Dei	De Angelis		30r-31r: De apostolis	
32	40r	Kyrie	De Apostolis		7r: De apostolis	
33	42r	Kyrie	De martyribus		9rv: De Martiribus	
34	40v	Gloria (incipit only)	Aliud et in terra vide a latera dextro instantia post vigilium		9v	
35	40v-41r	Kyrie	De confessoribus		11r: De confessoribus	
36	41rv	Gloria	A.M.D.G.B.e G.M. AD 1658 M.M.P.R. Subsubscripsit 10 feb (Feria Quinta)			

Appendix VIII

				35v-36r: Feria quarta in quatuor temporibus	83v-84r: In annunciacone beate virginis marie	39v-40r
		Rorate celi desuper	Officium Misse Introit			
37	42rv	Tollite portas	graduale	36r	84r:graduale	40rv
38	42v-43r	Prophete sancti				41r
39	43r	Alleluia. Prophete sancti				
40	43v-44v	Alleluia. Ave benedicta Maria	Aliud			41v-42v: Aliud
41	45r-46v	Alleluia. Ab arce siderea gabriel	Aliud			42v-44r
42	46v [-]	Alleluia. O Maria rubens rosa (incomplete)	Aliud			44r-45r: Aliud
43	[-]47r-48r	Alleluia. Angelus ad virginem (incomplete)				45r-46v
44	48rv	Alleluia. Prophete sancti praedicaverunt	Item aliud			46v-47r
45	48v-50v	Alleluia. Salve rosa paradisi	Aliud			47r-49r
46	50v-51r	Alleluia. Angelus ad virginem Christi	Aliud			49rv
47	51rv	Alleluia. Ave plena gracia				79rv

48	51v-52r	Alleluia. Ave virgo maria	Aliud		
49	52rv	Alleluia. Spiritus sanctus	Aliud		
50	52v-53r	Alleluia. O Maria ancilla	Aliud		
51	53rv	Alleluia. Angelus ad virginem Christi	Aliud		
52	53v-54r	Alleluia. Angelus ad virginem subintransit	Aliud		
53	54rv	Alleluia. Post partem inviolata	*Aliud*		
54	55r	Alleluia. Haec dies	Sabato in conductum pasche primum de Beata Virgine Maria	235v: Sabbato	73rv: Sabbato in conductum pasche. Primum all. de beata virgine
55	55r-56r	Alleluia. Pascha nostrum. Epulemur	Dominicis diebus post pascha	223: Paschale	89rv: de sanctis tempore paschali primo	135rv: Si die dominico contigerit
56	56r	Alleluia. In die resurrectionis	Ferialibus diebus post pascha	231v-232r: Feria quinta	90v: Istud alla canitoi di feriali usque ad vigilia ascensionis	73v: Post conductum Pasche
57	56rv	Alleluia. Ascendit deus	In die asscēsionis domini et per octavas	249rv: In die sancto	107rv: De ascensione Domini Officium	74rv: In die ascensionis et per totam octavam	79v-80r	90rv	Kk 45. fol. 2r.

Appendix VIII

58	56v-57r	Alleluia. Veni sancte Spiritus	Seques alleluia pro scūdo cantendur	75v-76r
59	57rv	Alleluia. Emitte Spiritum Tuum	Aliud de eodem	75rv: Spiritus Domini
60	57v-58v	Ave Maria gratia plena	Tractatus de Beata Virgini Maria a septuagisima ad palmarum (Tractus de BVM)	68v-70r: Tractus
61	59rv	Gaude Maria virgo	Alter tractus	90r-91v: Tractus
62	60r-61r	Laus Tibi Christe	Tractus	67r-68v: De beata virgine a septuagesima usque ad palmarum Tractus
63	61v-63v	Mittit ad virginum	Prosa de annuncione	143r-145r
64	63v-65v	Rex celi et terre	Alia de eodem	145r-147r: Item alia de eodem
65	65v-68r	Mittittur archangelus fidelis	Alia de eodem	147r-149v: Alia de eodem
66	68r-70v	Ab arce siderea	Alia de eodem tempore paschali	149v-152r: Alia de eodem
67	70v-74r	Aurea Virga	Prosa sequens infra octavas assumptionis V. M.	185r-188v: Item alia
68	74v-77r	Verbem dei dicens	Alia quando placet	209r-213r: Joannis añ portam latinam [text: Verbum dei deo natum]

69	77v-79r	Nunctiemus nunctium iocundum	Tempore nativitatis domini		152r-153v: A Nativitate domini usque ad purificatio [text: Letabundus exultet]
70	79v-80r	Virgini Marie ave intonent	Prosa de anunciacione tempore a pascha		156r-157r: Item alia (de tempore pasce) [text: Virgini marie laudes]
71	80v-81v	Venit caeli nunctius	Prosa tempore Penthecosten		157v-158: Infra octavam p̄teco [Text: Veni virgo virginem]
72	82r-83r	Nunctiavit archangelus	Alia quando placet		181r-182v: [text: Verbum bonum et suave]
73	83rv	Ave Maria Gratia plena	offertorium	86v: Offertorium	50r-51r: Offertorium
74	83v-84r	Ecce virgo Concipiet	Communio	87rv: Communio	51r: Communio
75	84r-86r	Patrem omnipotentem		38r: (Feria quarta in quatuor temporibus)	
76	86r-88r	Patrem omnipotentem	Aliud Pulchrum quando placet		
77	88r-90r	Patrem omnipotentem	Dominica	27r-28v	
78	90v-92v	Uterum virgineus thronus			213v-214r

Kk 45, fol.1r-2r.

Appendix VIII

79	93rv	Alleluia. Angelus intulit		
80	93v-95v	Patrem omnipotentem		
81	95v	Alleluia. Ave Maria gratia plena		
82	96r	Alleluia. Virga Jesse		
83	96v	Alleluia. Ave Maria	Graduale Omnia in Albis et per Annum	
84a	97r-99r	Circumdederunt me genitus		Kk 58, p. 339-45: Incipiunt Vigilie et Invitatori^m
84b	99v-101v	In loco pasche	In secundo nocturno	Kk 58, p. 345-50: In secundo nocturno antiphō
84c	101v-4r	Non derelinquas me	In tercio nocturno	Kk 58, p. 350-55: In tercio nocturno antiphō
85	104v-5v	Exultabant domino	Adlaudes	Kk 58, p. 356-7.
86	105v	Assumpta est Maria	Offertorium de Assumptione BVM	
87	105v	Optimam partem	Comunio	
88	106r-7r	Et in terra		

89	107r-8v	Ave salvatoris mater	Prosa de Beata ac Intermerata semper Virgine Maria	182v-4r: Item alia [Text: O Beata beatorum]
90	109rv	Patrem omnipotentem	Tempore Paschali	
91	110r	Et in terra	De Nativitate Domini	
92	110rv	Patrem omnipotentem		
93	110v-11r	*Gaudeamus omnes*	Introitus de Assumptione BVM	
94	111v	*Propter veritatem*	Graduale	
95	112r	*Audi Filia*		
96	112r	*Alleluia. Assumpta est Maria*	*Verte retro 6 folia* Offertirium	
	112v-19v	[Printed insert:]		
97	120v	Media vita	Officium Defunctorum	
98	120v	Sanguine proprio	1599 tempore pestis Ferys sextis per anno pro elevatione Cantandu	

APPENDIX IX: CATALOGUES OF THE RORANTISTS' PARTBOOKS

This appendix contains a catalogue of the four manuscript partbooks belonging to the Rorantists discussed in this survey, Kk I.3, Kk I.1, Kk I.4, and Kk I.5. The catalogues are presented in tabular format, with respective columns giving the item number, location in the partbooks, title of composition, incipit, name of composer, scribes, concordances, and finally other comments. All the catalogues have been compiled from the manuscripts themselves, although a significant portion of the information duplicates that published in *Musicalia Vetera* (fascicli 3, 1, 4 respectively, with fascicle 4 covering Kk I.4 and Kk I.5). Each composition has been given a separate number. Groups of pieces which form a clear unit, such as the sections of a mass ordinary or a mass cycle of propers, are given one number collectively and each individual section distinguished by an additional letter. Kk I.3 and Kk I.4 have a new numbering system, different from that found in *Musicalia Vetera*, due to problems and inconsistencies with it. The *Musicalia Vetera* numbering has nevertheless been given in brackets, and all cross-references to later manuscripts not discussed in this study but included in the published catalogues (Kk I.2, Kk I.7) also use the *Musicalia Vetera* numbering. Due to the limited amount of space, prints are referred to only by their *RISM* numbering. They are all discussed in full within the body of the book.

    Original text underlay, titles, and other annotations are presented in normal type-face; subsequent additions are given in italics. Second texts, original, or later additions are only acknowledged where they appear in all the partbooks of a given set. Spellings of the textual incipits have been standardized. This has been necessary due to the inconsistencies of the texts between the partbooks themselves as well as abbreviations which appear in some or all of the books. A slightly different approach has been taken for the titles and annotations. Here, the most complete example is given in its original form, regardless of which partbook it comes from. Where different annotations are found in the books, all the relevant information is provided. Editorial additions and expansions have been placed in square brackets. The compositions are presumed to be for four voices unless otherwise stated.

    Information on the scribes, based principally on the *Elenchus* (Kk Inv. 56), has also been included in the catalogues. The identified scribes are represented by their initials; single letters refer to scribes whose writing also appears in the *Elenchus*, but who are not identified (i.e. signatures or entries are not autographed). Scribes not found in the *Elenchus* are shown by a question mark '?'. A small number of compositions were copied into the partbooks by two or more scribes; the table presents all those responsible, with their initials separated by a slash (/). Additional scribes presented in italic type-face refer to subsequently added text, titles, or annotation, and are accompanied by the respective annotations in other columns of the catalogue. A table of scribes referred to in the catalogues, including relevant information is given below.

Rorantist scribes

a) Known scribes (autograph) in chronological order

Name, College membership (initials)	Entries in Inv. 56	Entries in music ms
Mikołaj of Poznań,1543-56 (MP)	1543-56	Kk I.3
Walentyn of Jastrząb, 1543-7 (WJ)	1543-7	Kk I.3
Andrzej Słomniki, 1548-97 (AS)	1550-6	Kk I.1
Krzysztof Borek, 1556-73 (KB)	1556-72	Kk I.1
Stanisław Zając of Pabianice, 1550-1601 (SZ)	1575-94	Kk I.4
Job of Wiślica, 1577-1601 (JW)	1578-1601	Kk I.1, 4, 5.
Jan Mirmicus, 1595/7-1622/3 (JM)	1597-1621	Kk I.3, 1, 4, 5.
Jan Borimus, 1602-23 (JB)		Kk I.4
Mikołaj Pieszkowicz, 1672-94 (MPi)	[Kk Inv. 64]	Kk I.4
Jan Porębski, 1686-1730 (JP)	[Kk Inv. 64]	Kk I.4

b) Anonymous scribes in chronological order

Scribe (Abbreviation)	Entries in Inv. 56	Entries in music ms
Scribe A (A)	1543-50	Kk I.3
Scribe B (B)	1543-8	Kk I.3
Scribe C (C)	1547-54	-
Scribe D (D)	1549	-
Scribe E (E)	1551-3	Kk I.1
Scribe F (F)	1551-3	-

Appendix IX.1

IX.1: Kk I.3: Catalogue of compositions

Item no. (*MV no.*)	Discantus	Location: Tenor	Bassus	Title	Incipit	Composer	Scribe	Concordances	Comments
1a (1)	1rv	1rv	1rv		Et cum spiritu tuo. Amen		A		
1b (1)					Gloria tibi Domine		A		
1c (1)				ad Prefacionem	Amen. Et cum spiritum tuo		A		
1d (1)				Mediocris	Habemus ad Dominum		A		
1e (1)					Dignum et iustum est		A		
1f (2)				In festo solemi	Habemus ad Dominum		A		
1g (2)					Dignum et iustum est		A		
1h (2)					Sed libera nos a malo		A		
1i (2)				ad benedictionem	Deo gratias		A		
2 (3)	2rv	2r	2rv		Veni Sancte Spiritus		A		
3 (4)	-	2v-4v	-		Patrem omnipotentem		1		Tenor only

4a (5a)	9r-10v	8r-9r	6r-7r	Officium de Assumcione BMV	Gaudeamus omnes in Domino	B
4b (5b)	10v-12r	9r-10r	7v-8v		Propter veritatem	B
4c (5c)	12rv	10r-11r	9rv		Alleluia. Assumpta est Maria	B
4d (5d)	13r-14v	11r-12r	9r-11v		Congaudent angelorum chori	B
4e (5e)	14v-15v	12v-13r	11v-12v		Diffusa est gratia	B
4f (5f)	–	13rv			Sanctus. Benedictus	B Tenor only
4g (5g)	–	13v-14r			Agnus Dei	B Tenor only
4h (5h)	16rv	14rv	12v-13r		Dilexisti iustitiam	B/II
5a (6a)	16v-17v	15r-16r	13r-14v	Introitus Primi Officij de Anunctiacione B. M. Virginis	Rorate caeli	B/II
5b (6b)	17r-19r	16v	15rv	Kirie Primi Officij	Kyrie eleison	B/II
5c (6c)	18rv	15v	14rv		Gloria Patri	B/II
5d (6d)	19r-20v	16r-17v	15v-17v	Graduale Primi Officij	Tollite portas	B/II
5e (6e)	20v-21v	17v-18r	18r-19r	Alleluya Primi Officij	Alleluia. Prophetae sancti praedicaverunt	B/II
5f (6f)	21r-23v	18r-19r	19r-20v	Prosa Primi Officij	Mittit ad virginem	B/II
5g (6g)	23v-25r	19r-20r	20v-22r	Offertorium Primi Officij	Ave Maria gratia plena	B/II

Appendix IX.1

5h (6h)	25r-26r	20rv	22r-23r	Sanctus Primi Officij	Sanctus. Benedictus	B/II
5i (6i)	26r-27r	20v-21r	23v-24r	Agnus Primi Officij	Agnus Dei	B/II
5k (6k)	27rv	21r	24rv	Comunio Primi Officij	Ecce virgo concipiet	B/II
5l (6l)	27r-28r	21r	24v-25r		Deo gratias	B/II
6a (7a)	28v-29r	21v-22r	25v-26v	Officium Secundu̅ Introitus secundi Officij	Rorate caeli	II
6b (7b)	29r-30r	22rv	26v-27r	Kirie secundi Officii	Kyrie eleison	B/II
6c (7c)	30r-32r	22v-24r	27r-29r	Et in terra secundi Officij	Et in terra	B/II
6d (7d)	32v-33r	24r-25r	29r-31r	Graduale secundi Officij	Tollite portas	II
6e (7e)	33r-34r	25rv	31r-32r	Alleluya secundi Officij	Alleluia. Prophetae sancti praedicaverunt	II
6f (7f)	34r-36r	25v-26v	32r-33v	Prosa secundi Officij	Mittit ad virginem	II
6g (7g)	36r-37r	27rv	34r-35r	Offertoriu[m] Secundi Officij	Ave Maria gratia plena	II
6h (7h)	37r-38r	27v-28r	35rv	Sanctus S[ecun]di Officij	Sanctus. Benedictus	B/II
6i (7i)	38rv	28r	36r	Agnus S[ecun]di Officij	Agnus Dei	B/II
6k (7k)	38v-39r	28v	36v-37r	Com[m]unio Secundi Officii	Ecce virgo concipiet	II

7a (8)	39v-48r	29r-35r	Kirie virginitatis solenne	Kyrie virginitatis/ Kyrie fons bonitatis	B/II	Second text (fons bonitatis) by II
7b (8)			Et in terra solenne	Et in terra		
7c (8)				Patrem omnipotentem		
7d (8)				Sanctus. Benedictus		
7e (8)				Agnus Dei		
8a (9)	48r-51v	35r-37r	Kyrie per Octavas	Kyrie	B/II/ WJ (title)	
8b (9)				Et in terra		
9a (10)	51v-57v	37r-39v	Sabbativis	Kyrie	B/II, WJ (title)	Kk I.32 Kk I.32 has part of Kyrie only
9b (10)				Et in terra		
10a (11)	58r-61v	39v-42r		Kyrie virginitatis	B	
10b (12)				Et in terra		
11 (12)	61v-65r	42v-45r	Ungaricu[m]	Patrem omnipotentem	B/WJ (title)	
12a (13)	65r-67r	45r-46v		Sanctus. Benedictus	B	
12b (13)				Agnus Dei		
13a (14)	67r-69r	46v-47v	Angelicum	Sanctus. Benedictus	B/WJ (title)	
13b (14)				Agnus Dei		
14a (15)	69r-71r	47v-49r	Sabbatis	Sanctus. Benedictus	B	Kk I.32
14b (15)				Agnus Dei		Kk I.32

Appendix IX.1

15a (16)	71v-72v	49v-51r	De electa	Sanctus. Benedictus	B/JM
15b (16)				Agnus Dei	B/?
16 (17)	73v-76r	51v-53v	Tractus ad Officium in Sabbatho	Ave Maria gratia plena	B
17 (18)	76r-79r	53v-55v	Tractus	Laus tibi Christe	B
18 (19)	79r-82v	56v-59v	Alter Tractus	Ave Maria gratia plena	B/MP	Tenor fol. 57 & Bassus fol. 76 by MP
19a (20)	83v-86v	62r-64v	Kyrie Paschale	Kyrie	B/WJ (title)
19b (20)				Et in terra	
20 (21)	86v-87v	64v-65v		Alleluia. Angelus intulit (Alleluia. Surrexit pastor bonus)	B/JW	Second text by JW incomplete in Discantus and Bassus
21 (22)	8r-89v	65v-66v		Alleluia. Angelus intulit	B	Kk I.4 item 28	Text incomplete in Discantus and Bassus
22 (23)	89v-90v	66v-67r		Alleluia. In die resurrectionis	B
23 (24)	90v-91v	67v-68r		Alleluia. In die resurrectionis	B
24 (25)	91v-94r	68r-70r		Ab arce siderea descendens	B
25 (26)	94v-95r	70r-71r	Prosa pro festis Resurrectionis Domini	Virgini Mariae ave intonent	B/?

26 (27)	95v-96r	71rv	Pro festis Pentecosten	Alleluia. Ascendit Deus in iubilatione/ Emitte Spiritum tuum	B/?
27 (28)	96v-97v	71v-72v	Prosa pro Festis Pentecosten	Alleluia. Veni Sancte Spiritus/ Ave virgo Maria	III
28 (29)	97v-99v	72v-73v		Venit caeli nunctius	III
29 (30)	99r-100r	73v-74v	Tractus pro Festis Pentecosten	Alleluia. Veni Sancte Spiritus (Alleluia. Ave virgo Maria)	III/?
30 (31)	100r-101r	74v-75r	Alia pro festis Pentecoste	Alleluia. Ave plena gratia (Alleluia. Ave Maria gratia plena)	III/?
31 (32)	101r-102r	75v-76r		Nunctiavit archangelus Mariae	III
32 (33)	102r-105r	76v-78v		Nunctiemus nunctium iocundum fratres	B
33 (34)	105r-107v	78v-80v		Nunctiemus nunctium iocundum fratres	B
34a (35)	108r-112r	81r-84r		Kyrie virginitatis/ Kyrie fons bonitatis	B
34b (35)				Et in terra	B
35 (36)	112r-115v	84v-87r	Furmańskie	Patrem Ominipotentem	B/JM

Appendix IX.1

36 (37)	115v-116r	87rv	111v-112v		Alleluia. Pascha nostrum	B
37 (38)	116rv	87v-88r	112v		Alleluia. Haec dies quam fecit Dominus	B
38a (39)	116v-118v	88r-89r	113r-114v	Per octavas	Sanctus. Benedictus	B/JM
38b (39)					Agnus Dei	B
39 (40)	118v-119v	89v	114v-115r	Feria quinta	Kyrie eleison	B/JM
40 (41)	119v-121v	90r-91r	115v-117r		Venit caeli nunctius	B
41a (42)	122v-124r	92r-93r	118r-120r		Rorate caeli	B
41b (43)	124r-125r	93r-94r	120rv		Kyrie eleison	
41c (44)	125v-127r	94r-96r	120v-122v		Tollite portas	B
41d (45)	127v-128r	96rv	122v-123v		Alleluia. Prophetae sancti praedicaverunt	B
41e (46)	128r-131r	97r-99v	123v-126v		Mittit ad virginem	B
41f (47)	131v-133r	99v-100v	127r-128r		Ave Maria gratia plena	B
41g (48)	133r-135r	100v-102r	128r-130r		Sanctus. Benedictus	B
41h (49)	135v-136v	102r-103r	130r-131v		Agnus Dei	B
41i (50)	137rv	103rv	131v-132v		Ecce virgo concipiet	B
42a (51)	138r-140v	103v-105r	132v-135r	Quintis ferijs	Sanctus. Benedictus	A/WJ (title)
42b (51)					Agnus Dei	

43a (52)	140v-146v	105v-107v	135v-140v		Sanctus. Benedictus	IV
43b (52)					Agnus Dei	
44a (53)	147r-151r	108r-111v	141r-145r	Sabato de B. M. V.	Kyrie	JM
44b (53)					Et in terra	
45 (54)	151r-152v	111v-112	145r-146r		Alleluia. O Maria ancilla	JM
46 (55)	152r-153v	112v-114v	146r-147v	Prosa	Ave salvatoris mater	JM/ JW (title)
47 (56)	-	114r	-	Quinta vox	Magnificat	JM	Tenor only
48 (57)	153v-155v	114v-116r	147v-149v	Prosa pro Ferijs Quartis	Rex Caeli et terra	JM
49 (58)	155v-157v	116r-119v	*149v-151r*	Prosa (pro Feria Tertia)	Mittitur archangelus	JM/ JW (title)
50 (59)	157v-159v	119v-121v-	151v-153r	*Alia*	Uterus virgineus	JM/?
51 (60)	159v-162v	121v-123v	153v-155v	Aliud per octavas	Sanctus. Benedictus	JM
					Agnus Dei	
52a (61a)	162v-163v	123v-124r	-	Officium pro Feria Quinta	Kyrie eleison	V
52b (61b)	163v-165v	124v-125v	(155v)-157v		Et in terra	

Appendix IX.2

IX.2: Kk I.1: Catalogue of compositions

Item no.	Cantus	Location: Altus	Tenor	Bassus	Title	Incipit	Composer	Scribe	Concor-dances	Comments
1	1r	[missing]	1r	1r	Fons bonitatis/Solenne	Deo gratias		?JM		Altus has missing page
2a	2r-11v	1r-12r	2r-12r	12r-12r	Alma redemptoris mater	Kyrie eleison	V. Ruffo	E	1542^3	
2b						Et in terra				
2c						Patrem omnipotentem				
2d						Sanctus				
2e						Agnus Dei				
3a	12r-21r	12v-20v	12v-21v	12v-20v		Kyrie eleison	[Anon]	E	1542^3	
3b						Et in terra				
3c						Patrem omnipotentem				
3d						Sanctus				
3e						Agnus Dei				
4a	21v-30v	21r-31r	22r-31r	20v-30r	Quam pulchra es	Kyrie eleison	Jachet of Mantua	E	1542^3	Altus, fol. 189r has C & A part for the 'pleni sunt'and 'Benedictus' sections (SZ)
4b						Et in terra				
4c						Patrem omnipotentem				

4d				Sanctus		
4e				Agnus Dei		
5a	30v-41r	31v-42v	31r-42r	30v-40r	Gaude virgo M[ate]r Chri[sti]	[Anon]	E	1542³	Altus, fol. 190rv has C & A part for the 'pleni sunt' and 'Benedictus' sections (SZ)
5b				Kyrie eleison		
5c				Et in terra		
5d				Patrem omnipotentem		
5d				Sanctus		
5e				Agnus Dei		
6a	41v-52v	43r-52r	42r-51r	40v-50v	Ave Maria gratia	C. Morales	E	1542³
6b				Kyrie eleison		
6c				Et in terra		
6c				Patrem omnipotentem		
6d				Sanctus		
6e				Agnus Dei		
7a	52v-59r	52v-59v	51v-58r	51r-58r	Missa Mater Matris		KB		adaptation of a mass attributed to Josquin de Prez
7b				Kyrie eleison		
7b				Et in terra		
7c				Patrem omnipotentem		
7d				Sanctus		
7e				Agnus Dei		

Appendix IX.2

8	59v-60v	60r-61r	59v-60v	58r-59r	Ad aequales 5 vocum Mart. Paligony	Rorate caeli	M. Paligon	JM	Kk 1.360	Kk I.360 is a five part copy
9	60v-61r	61rv	60v-61r	59rv	Valentinus Gawara ad aequales vocum	Per merita Sancti Adalberti	W. Gawara	JM	Kk 1.360	Kk I.360 is a five part copy
10	61v	61v-62r	61r-v	59v-60r		Quoniam rex noster		JM	Kk 1.360	Kk I.360 is a five part copy
11	62r-64v	63r-65v	62r-63r	61r-63r		Patrem omnipotentem		AS		
12a	65r-68v 69r-75r	66r-72v	64r-70v	64r-70r	5 vocum Borek	Kyrie eleison	K. Borek	JW/?		Cantus has two copies: the first by JW is the later copy
12b						Et in terra				
12c						Patrem omnipotentem				
12d						Sanctus				
13a	75r-81v	73r-78v	71r-76r	70v-76r	Te Deum laudamus C.B./MR1573	Kyrie eleison	K. Borek	?	Kk I.5 item 14	Kk I.5 is a later copy of Cantus by JW
13b						Et in terra				
13c						Patrem omnipotentem				
13d						Sanctus				
13e						Agnus Dei				
14a	82r-90r	79r-86v	76v-83r	76v-85v	Auctore Petro Certon	Kyrie eleison	P. Certon: Missa ad imitationem moduli 'Le temps qui court'	JW	1558c	
14b						Et in terra				
14c						Patrem omnipotentem				
14d						Sanctus				

14e				Agnus Dei	JB	
15	-	-	87v-88r	Assumpta est Maria	?	
16	97v	93v	88v (89)	Offertorium Assumptionis		
			92v	Communio de Assumpt[ione] BMV		
17	98r-101v	94v-96v	93v-95r	Gaudeamus omnes	E	Kk I.161
18	101v-103r	96v-97v	95v-96v	Audi filia *Propter veritatem*	E/*MPi*	
19	103r-104r	98r-99r	96v-97v	Alleluia. Ave stillans melle alvearium *Assumpta est Maria*	E/*MPi*	
20	104r-105v	99r-101r	97v-99r	Ave verbi Dei parens	E	
21	106rv	101r-102r	99v-100r	Communio Diffusa est gratia	E	
22	107r-108v	102r-103v	100r-(100v)	Graduale de Ass[umptione] BMV Propter veritatem	E	Bassus incomplete (end missing)
23	109r-110r	104r-105r	(missing)	*Pro Graduali* Alleluia. Assumpta est Maria	E/*MPi*	
24	110r-112r	105r-107r	(101r)-102r	Congaudent angelorum	E	Bassus incomplete (lacking opening)
25	112v-113r	107v-108r	102r-103r	Com[mu]nio Dilexisti iustitiam	E	
26	113r-114r	108r-109r	103r-104r	Off[ertoriu]m Diffusa est gratia	E	
27	114v-115v	109v-110v	104r-105r	Alleluia. Nativitas gloriosae	E	

Appendix IX.2

28	115v-117r	110v-112r	100r-101r	Prosa	Stirpe Maria	E
29	117v-118r	112v-113r	101v-102r	105v-107r	Sanguine proprio	JM	Kk Kk I.360 is a five 1.360 part copy
30	119v-120v	114v-116r	102v-103r	107rv	Ad equales 5 vocum	Egredimini et videte Ave Maria	E/MPi
31	121r-122v	116r-117v	103r-104r	108r-109r		Qualis est dilecta	E
32	112v-123r	117v-118v	104r-v	109v-110v	Pro tempore Paschali	Alleluia. Veni regina nostra	E/?
33	123v-126r	118v-121v	104v-106v	111rv		Festum Mariae celebramus	E
34	126v-127r	121v-122r	107r	111v-114v		Gloriosa dicta	E
35	127r-129r	122v-124r	107v-108v	114v-115r		Hortus conclusus	AS
36	129v-131r	124v-126r	109v-110r	115r-117r	Introitus pro festo Purificationis BMV	Suscepimus Deus	E/JM
37	131r-135r	126r-128r	110v-111r	117v-119v		Suscepimus Deus	E
38	133r-134r	128r-129r	111v	119r-120v		Alleluia. Post partum virgo Senex puerum	E/JM
39	134r-136v	129r-131v	112r-113r	121rv		Laetabundus exultet	E
40	136v-139v	131v-134v	113r-114r	121v-124r	Tractus de BMV	Audi filia	E	Kk I.4, item 35
41	139v-140r	134v-135r	114r-115r	124r-126v		Responsum accepit	E
42	140r	-	115r	127rv		Deo gratias	JM

#							
43	140v-141r	135v-136r	128rv		Terribilis est locus iste		JM
44	141v-142r	136v-137r	129rv		Alleluia. Vox exultationis		?
45	142rv	137r-138r	116v-117v	Prosa	Haec domus aulae caelestis		?
46	143rv	138rv	117v-118r	Communio	Domus mea		?
47	144-145r	139r-140r	118v-119r		Protexisti me Deus		?
48a	145v-152r	140v-147r	119v-126v	Officium Dies est laetitiae Tomae Szadek 1578/ Thoma Szadek eiusdem Capelae Pb	Kyrie eleison	T. Szadek	?
48b					Et in terra		
48c					Patrem omnipotentem		
48d					Sanctus		
49a	152v-160r	148r-156r	127v-136r	Officium in melodiam motetae Pisneme Thomas a Szadek Vic. Castriensis fecit/ 1580	Kyrie eleison	T. Szadek	JW
49b					Et in terra		
49c					Patrem omnipotentem		
49d					Sanctus		
49e					Agnus Dei		
50	160v-161r	156r-157r	136r-v	Quinque vocum	Salve Sancta parens		JM/? Kk I.6 item 1
51	161r-162v	157v-158v	136v-138r	Grad[uale]	Benedicta et venerabilis		JM Kk I.6 item 2

294

Appendix IX.2 295

52	162v-163v	159r-160v	138r-v	148v-150r	Quatuor	Salve Sancta parens	JM
53	164r	160v-161r	139r	150rv	Communio	Beata viscera	JM
54	164v-165v	161v-162r	139v-140r	150v-151r	Sebastiani Felstin De Conceptione Visitatione Nativitate	Alleluia. Felix es sacra	Sebastian of Felsztyn	JW/?
55a	166r-173v	162v-170r	141r-146r	152r-159v	[Missa] Dominicale/I.B.	Kyrie eleison		IB/?/? Several scribes were responsible for this entry, all unknown. The I.B. appearing in the Altus at the beginning may refer to Jan Borimus, as being the scribe or even the composer.
55b						Et in terra		
55c						Patrem omnipotentem		
55d						Sanctus		
55e						Agnus Dei		
56a	173v-176r	170r-173r	146v-148v	159v-162r	Feria Tertia	Kyrie eleison		?/MPi
56b						Sanctus		
56c						Agnus Dei		
57	177rv	174r	149r	162v-163r		[Textless]		
58	182v-183r	185v	164v	180v	Quatuor vocum	Et cum spiritu tuo. Amen		JM
						Gloria tibi Domine		
					Praefatio	Et cum spiritu tuo		
						Habemus ad Domino		
						Dignum et iustum est		

No.					Section	Text		Note
59	183v	186v	165v	181v	Co[mmun]io	Sed libera nos a malo / Deo gratias. Amen / Vos qui secuti	?	
60	184rv	187rv	166r	182rv	Quinque vocum / Praefatio	Amen. Et cum spiritu tuo / Gloria tibi Domine / Amen. Et cum spiritu tuo / Habemus ad domino / Dignum et iustum est / Sed libera nos a malo	?	
61	185rv	188rv	-	183rv	Quatuor vocum / Prafatio	Amen. Et cum spiritu tuo / Gloria tibi domine / Amen. Et cum spiritu tuo / Habemus ad domino / Dignum et iustum est / Sed libera nos a malo / Deo gratias	JM	Tenor book ends fol 166v.

Appendix IX.3

IX.3: Kk I.4: Catalogue of compositions

Item no. (MV no.)	Location Discantus	Tenor	Title	Incipit	Composer	Scribe	Concordances	Comments
1 (1)	1r-2v	1r-2v		Ave Maria gratia plena		SZ		
2 (2)	2v-(3v)	2v-5r		Nunctiemus nunctium iocundum fratres		SZ		Incomplete(end missing)
3 (3)	(missing)	5r-5v		Ab arce siderea descendens		SZ		
4 (4)	(missing)	6v	Paschale	[textless]		JW		title written by JW
5 (5)	(missing)	7rv		Resurrexi et adhuc tecum sum		SZ		
6 (6)	(missing)	7v		Sicut erat in principio		JW		
7a (7)	4r-6r	8r-9v	Paschale	Kyrie		SZ/?		
7b (7)				Et in terra		SZ		
8 (8)	6r-7r	9v-10r		Alleluia. Pascha nostrum immolatum est		SZ		
9 (9)	7rv	10v	Prosa pro Paschale	Virgini Mariae laudes	Sebastian of Felsztyn	SZ/MPi	Kk I. 2 item 14, Kk I.7 item 5, Kk I. 335	In Kk I.335 attributed to S. of Felsztyn
10 (10)	7v-9v	11r-12v	Lubelskie	Patrem omnipotentem		SZ/?		
11 (11)	10r	13r		Alleluia. In die resurrectionis		SZ		

12a (12)	10v-14v	13v-17r	Prima classis cum et in terra solenne	Kyrie eleison	SZ/MPi
12b (12)				Et in terra	
12c (12)				Sanctus	
12d (12)				Agnus Dei	
12e (12)				Deo gratias	
13a (13)	15r-21r	17r-14r	Quinque vocum Fabricii	Kyrie eleison	SZ/MPi Copy of Bassus part in Kk I. 110. This mass is perhaps by Wacław of Szamotuły.
13b (13)				Et in terra	
13c (13)				Patrem omnipotentem	
13d (13)				Sanctus	
13e (13)				Agnus Dei	
14 (14)	21v	24v	De Spiritu Sancto Quolibet Anno Graduale à Dnica Pentecosten ad Trinitatem canitur	Alleluia. Ave virgo Maria	SZ/MPi
15 (15)	22rv	25rv	Prosa ad praecendens Graduale	Venit caeli nunctius	SZ/MPi
16 (16)	23rv	26rv	Introitus de Spiritu Sancto in Electione Novi Praepositi Coro Rorate	Spiritus Domini replevit	SZ/MPi
16a (16)				Confirma hoc Deus Exurgat Deus	SZ/MPi Original text is the Off. for Pentecost, the added text is the Intr. verse

Appendix IX.3

17 (17)	23v-24r	26v-27r	Graduale de Spiritu Sancto pro electione praepositi	Alleluia. Veni Sancte Spiritus	SZ/MPi	
18 (18)	24r-25r	27r-28r	Et Prosa sequens	Veni Sancte Spiritus	SZ/MPi	
19 (19)	25rv	28rv	Communio	Factus est repente de caelo sonus	SZ	
20 (20)	26rv	29rv		Alleluia. Margarita quae decreta	SZ	
21 (21)	26v-27v	29v-30v		Margaritam pretiosam	SZ	
22 (21)	28rv	31rv		Sacerdotes Dei benedicite Dominum	SZ	
23 (23)	28v-29v	31v-32v		Beatus vir	SZ	
24 (24)	30rv	33r		Alleluia. Prophetae sancti praedicaverunt	SZ	
25 (25)	30v-31v	33v-34r		Nunctiemus nunctium iocundum fratres	SZ	
26 (26)	32rv	35rv		Alleluia. O Maria ancilla Trinitatis	SZ	
27 (27)	32v-33r	35v-36r		Nunctiavit archangelus Mariae	SZ	
28 (28)	33v-34r	36v-37r		Alleluia. Angelus intulit	SZ	Kk 1.3 item 21
29 (29)	34v	37v		Alleluia. Qui creavit omnia	SZ	Tenor book has 'Bassus'.

30 (31)	36rv	Graduale	Haec dies quam fecit Dominus		JM	
31 (32)	37rv	Communio	Pascha nostrum immolatus		JM	
32 (30)	35rv	Annuntiationis BMV Introitus Thomae Schadek Poenitentiarii Eccle. Cathedr. et vicarii artiu lib. Bac.	Vultum tuum	Tomasz Szadek	JM	
33 (33)	37v-38v	Graduale Annuntiationis BMV	Diffusa est gratia		JM	
34 (34)	39r		Gloria Patri et Filio		JW	
35 (35)	39v-40v	Tractus in Festo Annuntiationis BMV	Audi filia		JW/JM	JW (title) JM (text)
36 (36)	40v-41r	Sebastiani Felstyn All[eluj]a. ad Rorate	Alleluia. Ave Maria gratia plena	Sebastian of Felsztyn	JW/JM	JW (title) JM (text)
37 (37)	41v-42r		Rorate caeli		JM	
38 (38)	42rv		Kyrie eleison		JM	
39a (39)	42v-44r	Aliud de Beata	Kyrie		JM/MPi	
39b (39)	44r-46r		Et in terra			
40a (40)	46r-48v	Paschale	Kyrie		JW/JM	JW (title) JM (text)
40b (40)			Et in terra			
41 (41)	48v-49r		Alleluia. Ave Maria		JM	

Appendix IX.3

42 (42)	48rv	49r-50r		Alleluia. Virga Jesse floruit	JM
43 (43)	48v-50v		Lubelskie	Patrem omnipotentem	JM
44 (44)	51rv		Offertorium	Ave Maria gratia plena	JM
45a (45)	51v-53r		Angelicum *Pro paschale*	Sanctus. Benedictus	JM/*MPi*
45b (45)				Agnus Dei	
46 (46)	53r		Communio	Ecce virgo concipiet	JM
47 (47)	53v-54r		Aliud Rorate V.G.	Rorate caeli	[?W. Gawara]
48a (48)	54v-56r	55rv		Kyrie	JM
48b (48)		56r-57v		Et in terra	
49 (49)	56v-57r	57v-58r	*Post Tollite à Dica Trinit. et Purificatione BVM durante Alla ad Septuages.*	Alleluia. Ave Maria gratia plena	JM/*MPi*
50 (50)	57r-58v	58r-59v	Prosa	Mittit ad virginem	JW/JM	JW (title) JM (text)
51 (54)	59r-60v	65r-66r	Tractus de BMV á D. Septuagesimae ad Pascha	Gaude Maria Virgo	JM/ *P/P*	Discantus has date 1606 at end
52a (55)	61r-65r	66v-69v	Feriis Quartis	Kyrie eleison	JM
52b (55)				Et in terra	
52c (55)				Sanctus	
52d (55)				Agnus Dei	

53a (52)	65v-69r	Feriis Sextis *Ferialibus*	Kyrie eleison		JM/*MPi*
53b (52)	60r-62v		Et in terra		
53c (52)			Sanctus		
53d (52)			Agnus Dei		
54 (53)	69rv		Sanguine proprio		JB/*MPi*
	62v, 71v-72r				Original incomplete version in T is by JB, and complete version in D and T by *MPi*
55 (56)	69v-71v	Joannis Petri Biandri Romani a 4 / tempore paschali	Alleluia. Ave Maria gratia plena	J. Petrus Biandra	JM/*MPi*
56 (57)	70v-71r		Alleluia. Virga Jesse floruit		?/*MPi*
57 (58)	71v-72r	Feriis Quartis in Ferialibus Excepto tempore paschalis	Media vita		JB/*MPi*
58a (59)	72v-78v	Ave Sanctissima	Kyrie eleison		?/*MPi*
58b (59)			Et in terra		
58c (59)			Patrem omnipotentem		
58d (59)			Sanctus		
58e (59)			Agnus Dei		
59 (60)	78v-79r, 72v		Sancte Sebastiane magna est fides tua		JB/*MPi*
60 (61)	79v-80r, 70r		O adoranda Trinitas		?/*MPi*

Appendix IX.3

61 (62)	80rv	De Sancto Michaele Antiphona	Princeps gloriosissime Michael	?/MPi	
62 (63)	80v-81r		Sub tuum praesidium	?/MPi	D: original is incomplete and finished by MPi
63 (64)	81rv		Quoniam Rex noster	MPi	
64 (65)	81v-82r		Jesus Nazarenus rex Judaeorum	MPi	
65 (66)	82rv		Per merita Sancti Adalberti	MPi	
66 (51)	82v		Domine Rex Deus Abraham	MPi	
67 (67)	83v-84r		Grates nunc omnes reddamus	MPi	
68 (68)	83rv		Regina caeli laetare	MPi	
69 (69)	84r		Da pacem Domine	MPi	
70 (70)	84rv	De Sancto Stanisalo	Vir inclite Stanislae	MPi	
71 (71)	85rv	De Sancto Martino	Deus noster, cuius gratia beatus Martinus	MPi	
72 (72)	85v		Da pacem Domine	MPi	
73 (73)	86rv		Sub tuum praesidium	?	
74 (74)	87rv		Sub tuum praesidium	?	

IX.4: Kk I.5: Catalogue of compositions

Item no.	Location: Discantus	Title	Incipit	Composer	Scribe	Concordances	Comments
1	1r-4v	Niepolomiciis Anno Dni 1585 in Maio	Kyrie eleison		?		Probably not produced by Rorantists
1b			Et in terra				
1c			Patrem omnipotentem				
1d			Sanctus				
1e			Agnus Dei				
2a	4v		Et cum spiritu tuo. Amen		?		Probably not produced by Rorantists
2b			Gloria tibi domine				
2c			Et cum spiritu tuo				
2d			Habemus ad Dominum				
2e			Dignus et iustum est				
2f			Sed libera nos a malo				
3	5rv		Agnus Dei		JM		
4	5v-6r	Communio	Ecce virgo concipiet		JM		
5a	7r		Et cum spirits tuo		?		

Appendix IX.4

5b		Gloria tibi Domine			
5c		Et cum spiritu tuo			
5d		Habemus ad Dominum			
5e		Dignum et iustum est			
5f		Deo gratias			
6	7rv	Veni Creator Spiritus		?	
7	8rv	Rorate caeli		JW	
8	8v	Kyrie		JW	
9	9rv	Tollite portas	Graduale	JW	
10	10r	Alleluia. Prophetae sancti praedicaverunt		JW	
11	10v	Ave Maria gratia plena		JW	
12	11r	Ecce virgo concipiet	Communio	JW	
13a	13r-17v	Kyrie eleison	Antoii Scandelii	A. Scandello	?	Probably not produced by the Rorantists
13b		Et in terra			
13c		Patrem omnipotentem			
13d		Sanctus			
13e		Agnus Dei			

14	18r-21v	Te Deum laudamus C. B.	Kyrie eleison	K. Borek	JW	Kk I.1 item 13
14b			Et in terra			
14c			Patrem omnipotentem			
14d			Sanctus			
14e			Agnus Dei			
15a	21v-24v		Kyrie eleison		JW	
15b			Et in terra			
15c			Patrem omnipotentem			
15d			Sanctus			
15e			Agnus Dei			
16a	25r-28r	Auctore Jo: Peio Praenestino. Papae Marcelli	Kyrie eleison	G. P. da Palestrina	JW	1590	Copy of four part vesion of Palestrina's Papae Marcelli mass in *Missarum cum quatuor vocibus. Liber primus* (J. Vincenti. Venice. 1590)
16b			Et in terra			
16c			Patrem omnipotentem			
16d			Sanctus			
16e			Agnus Dei			
17a	29r-33v	Officium Sancta Maria C. Clabon	Kyrie eleison	K. Klabon	JW	
17b			Et in terra			
17c			Patrem omnipotentem			

Appendix IX.4

17d			Sanctus		
17e			Agnus Dei		
18a	34r-37v	Octavi Toni offm quor	Kyrie eleison	[G. M. Asola]	JM	1581[a], Kk I.6. item 18	Probably copied from 1581[a]. Kk I.6 is a later copy.
18b			Et in terra		
18c			Patrem omnipotentem		
18			Sanctus		
18e			Agnus Dei		
19a	39r-44r	Missa supra Intravit Jesus / Caspar Baviera	Kyrie eleison	K. Baviera	JM
19b			Et in terra		
19c			Patrem omnipotentem		
19d			Sanctus		
19e			Agnus Dei		
20	44r		Veni Creator Spiritus		JM
21a	45r-49r	[Missa]	Kyrie eleison		JM
21b			Et in terra		
21c			Patrem omnipotentem		
21d			Sanctus		
21e			Agnus Dei		

APPENDIX X: REGISTER OF COURTIERS AND SERVANTS EMPLOYED AT THE COURT OF ZYGMUNT II AUGUST (RK 110) (SELECTION)

This appendix presents a transcription of the terms of employment of the singers and instrumentalists employed at the court of Zygmunt II August, as found in the register of courtiers and servants, 1543-72 (RK 110). The transcription is diplomatic, and an attempt has been made to recreate the layout of the original manuscript. It adopts the most recent and most comprehensive page numbering found on the bottom right-hand corner of each page (recto).

As the manuscript was a practical guide for the treasury, it was constantly updated. New members were entered on arrival, often under the terms of employment of a given group. Some deaths and departures were recorded; elsewhere, the name was simply crossed out. In this transcription, I have presented all entries referring to terms of employment, and all names of individuals in normal type. Additions and annotations made to these at a later stage are denoted by italic type. Deletions of individual words or phrases in the original are placed in brackets in the transcription.

The peculiar order of the instrumentalists deserves comment. The manuscript seems to have been initially divided up into sections of the court, with space left after each group to allow for later additions. However, only a few pages were left free following the terms of the wind-players and before those of the trumpeters. Within a few years these pages themselves were taken up by soloists given similar terms to the wind-players. Thus with the employment of the 'Musici Fistulatores' in 1550, the scribe decided to enter their terms on the page immediately preceding those of the wind players (fol. 936v). He did the same for the 'Musici Itali' in 1556 (fol. 936r), and again for the new terms of the original wind-players in 1560 (fol. 930r).

Appendix X: RK 110

875r   Wijrschbkowskj Joańes p̓ptus sacel:
Cui cóstitutú est salariú denuo in Olitha ex
Thezauro Ḿtis sue, donec meliori beneficio
prouisus erit, a die 2 februarij Anni 1544 sinǵlis
annis nuŕi et monete Polo: fl sexaginta
Et pro vesté undulata in anno fl decé

Pro Componista
Id' dnús Wijrschbkowskj pro Wladislao
Componista, vel alteri in locú illius qué servaré
debet. penes se, habebit pro annuo salario nuŕi et
monete Polonićlis flor vigintj
Et panni Purpuriaí vlnas 8 vel recione Illius fl 6

Pro pueris
Seruabit id' dńus Wijrschbkowskj 4 pueros ad
canend' aptos, Quos cóponista, et iṕe docebunt
canere. ac expésis seruabit, providebitque
reformatione vestiú. quorúcunque ac interalis
nouis Tú focaria pro ablucione, & ad paranda
cibaria hababitque ex Thezauro M. R. in
provisione eaŕ reŕ in Anno nuŕi et monete Polo:
fl 24

875v   Pannú vero
Pannú vero et pellicea pro vestita istoŕ pueroŕ
dabit M. R. de grá et arbitrio suo sinǵlis annis,
ac pro Jopulis et caligis
Faciet suḿa singlís qŕtalibus eid. dáda róne illius
ac Cóponiste et Pueroŕ focarieque salaria fl 26
Rońe vero expensaŕ coquiné et celarÿ pro se.
componista et pueris, habebit singulis septimáis
a dispensatore Mtiś R. fl 2 gr 15
sed eid' de diarys dempti gr 20 Quia Componista
hźt seorú asignata diaria. Habet itaque singulis
septimanis loco diariorú suṕscriptorú fl 1/25
Idem ex stabulo M R hźt singlís diebus Auene
Cor 1.
Iam est provisus per Mtém Regiá Beneficiis
ideo hoc sallario carebit

902r

Sacellani M. R.
Habuit quilibet eorum de Tesauro R. M. senioris
pro anno salario. Nunc vero habent de Tesauro
Mtiś Regiæ Junioris per florenos vigint'
Fać pro quolibet quartuali floŕ 5
Preterea habet quilibet eorum pro veste panni
purpuriani per vlnas 8.

Et clerice additi floŕ 8 in anno, ita qui equale cum
ceteris salarium habet et ultra panni purpuriani
vlń 8 habet pro diploide armisini vlń 7

Adolescentes vero cantores habent pannum equale
cum ceteris et pro stipendio anno per floŕ 12 vcżt
Klimek et Jurek.
Facit pro quartuali cuilibet floŕ 3

Preterea dantur eisdem loco diariorium coquinæ
et cellarÿ a dispensatore Regio in loco singuliś
septimanis per floŕ 1. In itinere vero dantur
eisdem diaria et coquina et celario.

903r

Nomina sacrifficorum.

Sebastianus Strzeschkowskj

Mathias Raszek *Mortuus*

Joannes Jasscz *dimissus in opaszzon*

mortuus Simon Lieliow *apud mtem RJém*

Joannes a Gamratis *mortuus post festum pasche*

Andreas calans *subduxit se a servicÿs M R*

Martinus clerica *mortuus Cracć*

Jacobus piąnthek susceptus vilnae die 15 decebr.   *apdM*
anno dominj 1544   *RJém*

Appendix X 311

	Daniel Masouita susceptus Vilnae die 3 aprîll Anno domjni 1545 *Mortuus Vilne*	*apud Mtem Ŗlém*
	Franciscus de Posnania Susceptus Cracowie die 2 Jully Anno dominj 1545	*dimissus*
	Mattĥ clerica Pośn susceptus ex servicio M. R. senioris post mortem Mtiś sue, die 24 Junij A⁰ 1548, qui antea nullú salariú habuit, nisi ad provisioné Iniebat, sed et eidé Mtás Regia Senior. Pietrkowie cócessit, quos et núc habebit, ad provisioné usque annuatim fl 20	*Mortuus*
	Stanislaus de Ssamothulli. Quamuis ańea Iniebat M. R. I quia trennio abbens erat a Curia, ideo denuo die 19 Jully A⁰ 1548 est insertus in Rgtrú	*dimissus*
903v	*dimissus*	Ambrosius de Beldrzichow Susceptus in seruitiú M R die 8 aprillis Anno domini 1549
		Benedictus a Strikow susceptus in servitiú M. R. die 2 februarii Anó 1551
	Mortuus	Klimek
	dimissus	Andreas de Opoczno die 23 Maii 1551 Crac susceptú
	mortuus	Bartholomeus Wiszogrod susceptus Petric. 16 Aṗll 1552
	dimissus ad Mrasam[?]	Stanislaus Zagorski susceptus Margenburgi die 5 Jvnii 1552 *Cracc*
		Martinus a Droiczin Susceptus 24 Aprilis ad relatione Dḿ Dowoino
	dimissus	Adam de Belzicze Saccellanus Susceptus Cracc. die 22 Augusti 1553
		Adam Smiglod sacéll suscepti A M R^li seniori Petrus Adol. 16 maÿ 1556 Vilné

vide aĩs   Schimek susceptus Warschauiae iñt Musicos M
R die 29 Octobŕ 1558 ad rolḿ D. Georgii Clerice
M R *Eidem ex grá M R additi Die 14 Juny 1566
Fl 10 Armisini vln 7*

            Thomas Sandecz susceptus die 24 Aprilis 1569
Cracć

Dimissus   Martinus Compositor Cantus susceptus *vil:* 1 May 1560

Dimissus   Albertus Francusz Musicus suscept' 1 Junij 1560 vil.

mortuus   Theodolski Translatus ex pueris cantoŕ inter
Warschauia adolescentes 1 Aug 1562 habebit pro dyary ąlibzt
e 1564   sept' fl 1/-/

                    Nomina adolescétú cantorú

            Jurek *Apud mtém Rlém*

            Klimek

            Albertus Odolinski susceptus Vilnae A^o 1551
Die 27 Decembris habebit oḿem provisionis
sicut alys capellani

            Stephanus Lesser stiirus adolescens. susceptus ab
eo tempore quo vienna abenit in seruitiú M R die
19 Junii Anno doḿi 1552   *Expeditus a Curia*

            Is omém prouisione habebit vt saccellani M R

Appendix X

> Georgius clerica quaᵛis habuit sing
> septm' fl 1 sed ei M ℞ meliorauit
> aliú floŕ polonicú die 29 Octobŕ 1554

Vcź
        Tres pueri Cantorú
Suscepti Torunniæ die 8 Iunii 1552 habebunt
pro Diariis a dispensatore Regio singulis sepť
quilibet grosos 20 poť.
Item singulis quattuor sepť habebunt ad calceas
per gr 4 et pro Ablutrice gr sex simul tres et a
reparatione vestium etiá simul 3 gr 8
Vestitum pro libitu M R
        Hi commissi sunt Georgio clerica

904v

        Venceslaus cóponista
Susceptus in servicium Mtiś R. die 6 Maii Anno
domini 1547 pro componista, Cui ᵽ constitutum
est sallarium annuum pol. fl 30 facit pro quilibet
quartuali flor 7/15
Vestitum annuum, et diaria septimanatio habet

mort.   vt ceteri sacellani
Eidem Mtaś. ℞. Piotrć die prima Maÿ 1552 de
grá addidit sallarii Annvi fl 20
        faciet pro quolibź qrť pol. flo. 12 $^1/_2$
Eidem M ℞ Anúatim concessit dari Adamascú
pro diploide

        Nicolaus Kochanowski Sacallanus
Idem a Mté Reginali acceptus, anno 1558 Habet
prouisionem vt reliqui sacellani Sacræ M. ℞

        Stanislaus Petronius Sacellanus
Susceptus in servitium M. R 17 Maÿ 1561
Piotrć Habebit prouisionem similem reliquis

        Martinus Syeradz Sacellanus
susceptus die 13 Martÿ 1563 Piotrć Habebit
provuisionem similem reliquis

Martinus Raczulski sacellanus
Susceptus in seruitiú M R die 21 January 1570
Habebit sing. sept. fl 1/- Panni Lund: vĩ 9 sing
annú. salariú ut reliqui sacellani.

905r

Georgius Clerica Mtiś Regiæ

Habet sing qrt' fl 6 poloni Et vestitu' omné vt
Sacellani Mtiś R.
Eo tamé M R attento quod pueros cantores M R
exercet in arté Musices concessit ei sing Ańis
vltra prius Sallariú Polon fl 10 incipień a die 9
Aug 1554
It loco Armesini ańis sing. Adamasci vl 6
Nouú salariúilli M R constituit folio sequét

Pueris Cantoribus
Posthanowienie iako schathei maią bicz dawane
Pacholiethom Spiewakom Masczi vedlie wolei
a roskazanya k. Je⁰. M.

Lethne
Svkna Lunskie⁰ Sukienki Axamit' Bramowane
Kabath kithaiczani podniem plothno
vbraniezamschowe
Birethek Axamithni poden Plothno

Zimne
Sukna czeskie⁰ albo Morawskie⁰ Ciermaczki
podschite futhrem

905v

Zupicze svkna Lunskie⁰ albo Barchanove
podschite Vbranie Sukna thegosch czo zupicze
czapki Podschite
   Item na Sok czali kazdemv Plothna na
koschul 3
   Item na rok Skorzenki

Appendix X 315

> Pueris Cantoribus Sex
> Die 6 January 1565 Petrcouiæ eisdem Mtás Regia
> constituit hanc inferius specificatam soluendi
> methodum, In primis ratione coquinæ et celarÿ
> singulis septimanis in quamĺbt personam gr 24 poto.
> Facit vna septimana fl 4/24/-
>
> Pro vestitu annis singulis omnibus in simul hæc oĩa
> dari debebuntur cum reliqua familia curiæ Sacrae M:
> R panno providebitur
> Panni Lundineń vlnæ 34
> Telle ɉvidusÿs et sub toraces ut peciæ 2
> Veluti sub beretha et ad fenbrias v́l 15
> Telle nigræ vlnae 3
> Alutæ pelles 15
> Panni Carasia dicti vlnae 18
> Pro thoracibus et eǫɼ attinentÿs annis singulis fl 12/-
> Pro vestibus subductis pro peliceis ocreis incluso
> sartore et pellione cuíbt annis singulis fl 12/-

906r   *Mortuus*   Georgius Jassziuczÿcz Clerica Mt̃is R
       Crac̀   Die 6 Januarÿ 1565 Petrc. Sacra Mt̃is Regia constituit
illi nouum stipendium et habebit annis singulis ɉ gr
30 fl 70/- fac̃ pro qŕt fl 17 $^{1}/_{2}$
Ratione coquine et celary singulis septimanis fl 3/-
Pro vestitu annis singulis   fl 20/-
Ad officiú clericaturæ qui sibi cerca solutionem
vestimentorum solventur habebit annis singulis fl 10/-
Die 29 Marty 1567 Mtás R rońe stipendÿ quod in
Thesauro Lithwanico habuit ad prius salarium addidit
singulis septimanis ɉ gr 30   fl 2/-
Habebit itaque singulis septimanis per gr 30   fl 5/-
Eidem M. R die 4 Nobŕ 1569 Knyszini meliorauit et
ad prius salariú addidit fl 50. Et habebit quolzt anno
fl 120 fac̀ pro qŕt fl 30.

906v   Joannes Baston flander
            compositor cantus
Susceptus in seruitiú M. R. die 8 Marcii 1552 Habebit
singulis mensibus Auf Hungaf 12
Et in puerum Bernhardum Raizaber pro diariis septimanat
gr 15
            dimissus

907r   Mvsicis et alÿs Cantoribvs
            Christoff Klabon
Die 6 Januarÿ 1565 Petrć. translatus ex pueris
Cantoribus ad numerum fistulatorum.   Habebit ex
Thesauro S M R̂ Annui stipendij cum omnibus
attenentÿs per gr 30 fl 56/- facit pro quartali fl 14/-/-
Item rons coquine et cellarÿ tam in loco quam in itinere
singulis septimanis fl 1/-

            Stepha: Reder *Translatus ad*
                Fistulatores maiores
Die 6 January 1565 Petrć assignatus ad numerum
fistulatorum et habebit roñe coquinæ et cellarÿ ex
thesauro S M R̂ singulis septimanis tam in loco quam in
itinere gr 24 pol.
Item pro omni vestitu annis singulis per gr 30 habebit fl
15/-
Stipendium ex pensionibus a domino Georgio Clerica

            Simon Trubiczki
Die 6 January 1565 Petrć ex pueris cantorib: assignatus
inť fistulatores et habebit roñe coquinæ et cellarÿ sing:
septi gr 24.
Item roñe vestitius annis singulis fl 15/-
Stipendium ex pensionibus a dnó Georgio Clerica

            Bartho:Kecher
Die 6 January 1565 Petrć ex pueris cantoribus assignatus
int iuuenes musicos et h̃bebit roñe coquæ̃ et cellarÿ
septimanatí gr 24
Pro omni vestitu annis singulis p gr. 30 fl 15/-
Stipendiú ex pensionibus a dñō Georgio Clerica

Appendix X

907v
Thomas Sądecz
Die 6 Januarÿ 1565 Petrć Mtas R de nouo constituit illi
rone coquinæ et cellarÿ singulis septimanis fl 1/-
Pro vestitu annis singulis p gr 30   fl 10/-
Stipendiú datur ille nullum, ob id quia bńficÿs bonorum
spiritualium puesus est.

Schimek
Die 6 Januarÿ 1565 Petrć sacrae M R de nouo constituit
illi róne coquinæ et celarÿ singulis sept' fl 1/-
Pro vestitu annis singulis p gr 30   fl 10/-
Stipendium datur illi nullú, ob id quia bńficys bńorum
spualium prouesus ē

Bartho: Zingier
Die 6 January 1565 Petrć Sacra M: R constituit illi de
nouo rone coquine celarÿ singulis septimanis fl 1/-
Pro omni vestitu annis singulis fl 10/-
Stipendium v̄l ex bnficiys bnōr spualium vel ex
pensionibus eorundem

Leonard: Jankowski
Die 6 Januarÿ 1565 Petrć sacra mtas R constituit illi
rone coquinæ cellarÿ singulis sept' fl 1
Pro vestitu annis singulis fl 10
Stipendiú v́l ex bńficÿs bnōŕ spualium v́l ex ea eorúdé
pensionibus
*Item die 4 Sept 1570 Mtaś Regia ex grá sua illi per
panno anno dedit qźlźt anno fl 10/-*

908r   *mortuus*
Laurentius Pabianus
Die 18 Decembŕ 1564 Petrć ińt musicos adolescentes
Habebit roñé coquinae et celarÿ singulis septimanis fl 1/-
Pro vestitu annis singulis   fl 10/-
Stipendiú ex pensionis bonoŕ spualium a dnó Georg.
Clerica

Mart' Warteczki
Susceptus inter adolescentes Cantores die 10 Februarij
1565 Petrcoviæ Habebit rone sept. a dispensatore p gr
24/-
Rone panni annui   fl 15/-/-
Stipendiú ex pensionibus bonoŕ spualium a dnō Georgio
Clerica

Profugit

Jan Skiczki
Susceptus die 17 Aprilis 1568. Habebit sing sept' rone celarÿ et coquinae fl 1/- Salariu ex pensionibus. Pro panno annis sing fl 10/-/-

Thomas Szadek
Susceptus Crac die 25 Junÿ 1569 p Georg: Clericá in seruitiú M R
Habebit Rone coquinæ et celarÿ sing. sept. gr 24
Item Rone Panni annui fl 10/-
Stipendiu uel ex bńficys bonoŕ spum uel ex eoŕd' pensionibus

Jacobus Bronowski.
Susceptus in seruitiú M R p d. Georgi: Clericá Crac die 13 Aug 1569. Habebit rone coqná et celarÿ sing sept' fl 1/- Róne Panni annui p fl 10/-
Stipend^m ex pensionibus bonoŕ spum.

908v

Joannes Ramulth
Susceptus die 27 Aug Crac 1569 Habebit rone coqnae et celarÿ sing sept' fl 1/- Rone panni annui fl 10/-
Stipendiú ex pensionibus bonoŕ spualiú.

Stanislaus Rohatin.
Susceptus inter Sacellanos M R die 27 Aug 1569
Habebit sing sept' fl 1/- It. Ratione Panni Lund': vl 9 vt ceteŕ Sacellanis.

Nicolaus Klaus
Susceptus die 8 Januarÿ 1569 Crac. Habebit sing sept' fl 1/-
It. Rone panni annui quolźt anno fl 15/-
Stipendiú annis sing fl 40/-

929r

Bebenniczi

Niemiecz Thudesko *Dimissus a Curia 1570 Warszawia*.
Pieniaiecz
motuus NiemieczTudesko *Denuo susceptus 9 Sept 1570 Warszawia*

Appendix X

Suscepti die 20 Febrÿ Vilnæ 1560.
Habebit quilźt illoŕ in anno ex Thesauro Saċ
Mtiś Ŗ fl. 12 faċ‚p quart' fl. 3
Panni Ludineń v̄l 6.

Macziek Ianowicz.
Susceptus Vilnae die 30 Aug 1563.
Habebit omné prouisioné ut sup

Omnibus his Mtis Ŗ die 4 Febŕ 1567 ad prius
salarium annis singulis addidit ‚p g. 30 fl. 8.
Habebit itaque quilzt eoŕ singulis annis fl. 20
fać pro quartuali fl. 5/-

930r

Fistulatores Germani

Claus   Thomas *Mortuus*
Hanus   Iachim
Mortuus Rheder

Istis M R ex gratia singulari Die 7 Maii 1560
constituit nouum salarium. Habebit itaque
quilibet eorum annis singulis ex Thesauro M. R.
cum omnibus panno. Auena et aliis rebus illis
ex Thesauro dari soluis per fl 56 fać pro qŕti fl
14/- A Dispensatore sing sept' fl 2/-

Carolus uero quia nullam ex zuppis habet
prouisionem ideo hic habebit ex thesauro M.R.
pro anno sal: fl 96 fać pro qŕti fl 24 A
dispensatore sing sept' fl 2/-

Et illud obseruandum est quod postéque aliquis
illorum seru'ire propter ingrauescentem aetatem
non poterit ab hec tépore non amplius ex
Thesauro M.R. quicquid speret. Sed tantum in
hac Zuppe prouisione se continere usque ad
finem uitae debet. Quod si uero alienbi eis
discedere una M. Ŗ. uiserit Tunc M. R. ex gratia
sua singulari dare tenetur ad fistulas et alia
musicæ instruméta vectorem cum curru vno
equis 2.

Claus die 14 Iunii 1559 meliorati ex grá M. R.
fl 50/-

Iachim Keppel

Habuit oém prouisionem, vt hi fistulatores
superiores sac M: R. sed quia pensionem quæ illi
ex Zuppis dabatur certo contractu M: R. cessit,
Habet itaque singulis septimanis fl 2/- rone
coquinæ et celarỹ. It pro stipendio annuo annis
singulis fl 56/-

Laurentius Margonski

Susceptus Warschawie die 13 Februarỹ 1564.
Habet omnem prouisionem prout Carolus.

Christopherus Klabon

Eid' M. R. die 4 Februarỹ 1567 ordinauit et
constituit salarium simile reliquis fistulatoribus
qui nullam in Zuppis puisionem hńt.

930v *Dimissus* Joannes Kappa Italus Fistulat.
Susceptus in seruitiú M. R. Vilnæ die 1 Januarỹ
Anno 1561. Habebit a M. R. annis sing cum
omnibus attinentỹs per gr 30 flor 96. fać pro qŕt
fl 24/-
It' Roe coquinæ et cellarỹ sing sept' Pól. fl 2/-

Schimek Muzik

Die 5 Augusti 1568 Knischini assignatus et
ordinatus ińt fistulatores maiores. Habebit itaque
singulis septimanis fl 2/- Annui salarỹ singulis
annis fl 96/-

Stephanus Rheder

Die 5 Augusti Anno 1570. Idem translatus ad
Fistulatores maiores Sue Mtás Regia vna cum fl
15/- quos pro panno habuit ad prius salariá
addidit. Tumque Fistulatoribus ad æquavit p gr
30 fl 56/- fac pro qrt' 24/- Item singulis sept' fl
2/- It' hoc die 1 Apŕ 1570

936r   Mvsici Itali   *Dimissi*

Suscepti in seruiciú M R̃ et inscripti iussuv M
sue A die 10 Nobr̃ 1556 qva egressi ex
Anthwerbia Ab eoque tempore illis salariú cedet

Gwido Hoberean flander

Paulus Baninch Anthwerbień   *mortuus vil: die*
                                       29 Januarÿ 1560

Arnoldus Veracter flander   *Sufocatus in aquis*
                                       die 4 Junij 1560

Philiphus Mansart flander

Cuilibet eoŕ M.R^a assignauit pro Annuo
Sallario talleros centú quinqvaginta

Item tempore itiner. M.R̃^{e}. expeń victus A M
Sua habebunt. Et Currú liberí

936v   Musici Fistulatoē

A R̃n^{do} Do Epo' Crac. Suscepti in seruitiú M
Regiæ Crac' die 29 Novembŕ Anno dói 1550
Quibus est per M. Regiam constitutú sallariú.
Vestitus et omnes provisio vt fistulatoribus aliis
Pro diariis coquinæ et cellarii singulis septiś A
dispensatore Regio habebunt per   fl 1

Stephanus

Dziano

Theodoricus

Hugo

Anthonius

Franciscus Italus Lyricen Susceptus Crac̀ die 28
July 1553 oém prouisionem habebit ut supra
scṕti. Eid' M. Rᵃ. meliorauit ad Annú salariú die
13 Sept' 1556 Ad vln 8 svecamerąr fl.

Dziano Musico suprasepto Die 2 Decembris
1553 In Knischin additi sunt per M. R. pro
diarys coquinæ et Cellary vltra floŕ 1 qui illi sept
dabatʳ gr pól 10

Expeditus Pawlik puer qui Apud Dziano est M R mandauit
dare pro diarys sing̀ sept' gr 20 Pol
incipień a die 2 Decembris 1553 In kniszin
Hvic M R om̀ prouisioné concessit vt aliis die
16 Nobŕ 1555 ad vluá decem svecameraɽ

937r   Fistulatores Salariati

Habebant ex Thezauro Seɽ ᵐⁱ Regis antiqui
annuá infrascriptá prouisionem quam ex
Thezauro M.R. Iunioris iam habent, viczt quílbt
eoŕ moneté et nuŕi Polo: per flor. quadraginta.
Facit pro vno quoque quartuali per flor 10.

Preterea cuíblt ɛoŕ in anno dantur pro vestibus,

Panni Lundineń.	ꝑ vlnas 8
Panni Stameti pro caligis	ꝑ vln 1 ¹/₂ 2
Panni Czwikouień	ꝑ vlnas 8
Panni futtertuchu	ꝑ vlnas 1 ¹/₄
Barchani vlmeri	ꝑ vlnas 5
Futter barchani	ꝑ vlnas 5
Armesini	ꝑ vlnas 7

Huc vsque vero dabátur in quattuor eorum vnum
Lundineń Alteŕ Czwikouień stamen panni.
Reliquis vero per vlnas 8 utriusque panni, aut per
¹/₂ Stamen. hoc in eoŕ Stat arbitrio, si
staminibus an vlnis accipient,

Appendix X

937v

Habuerút etiá ex Thezauro Ser ᵐⁱ Regis antiqui pro diarÿs coquiné et celarÿ singulis septimanis per gr. 12, Mtas vero [937v:] Regia Junior illis Grodne a 15 Septembŕ per gr 8, et iteŕ Vilné 21 Octobŕ Anno 1543 per gr 10 addidit, Eá ob causá quod debent he se submiserút omnes Claus excepto, semper cum tubicinatoribus ad mensam Regiá tubis caneré, vltra officia sua fistulatoria,

Itaque habent iam pro diarÿs prefatis singulis sept' per floŕ 1 a dispenstoré Regio.

Et ex stabulo M.R. habent singuli diebus singliś Auene Coŕ 1.

Item Duo pueri discipuli Klaus ratione diarior. Coquine et Cellarÿ habét singlís septimanis a dispensatore Regio p gr 30   fl 1

Iis M Rᵃ peccunia auená soluere constituit singulu' coret. per groś 2 ¹/₂ fac pro qrt' singulo fl 7/17 ¹/₂

Idque a die 1 Januarÿ 1558 Eis ex Thesauro vna cum sallario soluetur

938r

	Fistulatoŕ nomina	
Claus	vczt pueros discipulos	Pieniązek
		Gomolka

Jurek

Hanus Rheder Cuj Crać. datj. ad r͞om servicÿ de mádato Regio fl 60 Ita per singliś qŕtalibus p trienniú p fl 5 defalcari debet a die 20 Junij 1[545]

Hanus tenorista

Thomas

Joachim Kepel. Susceptus Crac' die 15 decembr'
Anno 1549 Cui constitutú sallariú et omnis
prouisio. vt ceteris fistulatoribus M. Regiæ

Carolus fist' a d de Gorka susceptus ad M R̄ª 9
May 1556 om' vt alii ex the⁰ puisioné habebit.

Nicolao Gomolka puero sup̄to Mtás Regia
constituit Crac' die 22 Aprilis 1550. Sallarii
anvi per gr 30 florenos (duodece) *Viginti qvinque
fac' pro Quar.* fl 6/7 $^1/_2$
Vestitú oém vt Fistulatoribus.
Pro expensis septimátim per gr 20
Huic M. R. constituit habé om' prouisioné
quemadmod. alii fistulatores habét Vilne die 20
Januarii Anno 1555

938v

Dominicus Italus de Verrona Arfista
Vilne Anno domini 1545 Die 20 Decembris.
Susceptus in seruiciú Mtis Regie. Cui M sua
Salarium et vestitum ac Diaria equalia sicut
fistulatores habent constituit.
*Expeditus a Curia M.R. die
26 Aprīll a⁰ 1550. Crac'*

939r

Sobek Organista
Huic a principio ex Thezauro Ser^{mi} Regis Iunior.
et núc pro annuo salario soluunt ei flor' 12, fac'
singlís quar̄tlibus flor' 3
Eidem Mtás Regia die 15 februarÿ vilne Anno
1545 adscribere mandauit pro annuo salario
singlis qr̄tualibus et iam pro preterito soluere
flor' 2
Eidem Pańi Purpuriani vl̄ 8
Eidem M R die 25 Juny 1560 addidi annis sing'
ad prius sallarÿú p gr 30 fl 20
Habebit iam annis sing. fl 40 fac. p qú fl 10
Item Amesini pro thorace vl 7.

939v

Valentinus Bakfark
Hungarus Ciitaredus
Anno domini 1549 die 12 Jvnii Cracouiæ
Susceptus in seruituum Mtiś Regiæ.
Habebit prouisionem omnem sicut Fistulatores
M. Regiæ.
Vilnæ Die 13 Aug. A⁰ 1554. Mtaś R ei
concessit semper liberú habere hospiciú
It. vectoré cú equis 2 quá M R aliensi profiscetur
It. vltra Sallariú et ońi prouisioné eius prioré
Mtá Regia ei concessit ańis sing Polonić fl 50
Incipień a die 30 Aug 1554
Die 8 Maÿ 1558 eidem M.R. Vilnæ addidit flor
60 fać cum priori flor centú quinquaginta et pro
q̄ri 37$^1/_2$
Die 6 Maij 1564. Assignati p M.R. pro panno et
toto illius vestitu p gr 30   fl 25/-/-

940r

Tubicinatores salariati

Czÿemÿorka.
Id' habet ex Zuppis censum vitalem, ex Thezauro
illi ńil datur preterque ex grá in exitu Ser^e M. R.
dantur illi aliquot floreni
Tantum datur ille pannus Lundineń, sicut cæteris
tubicinatoribus vlnas 6
Dant' et eid' pro diarÿs coquine et celarÿ singulis
septimatiis a dispensatore Regio gr 20
        Melioracio eidem
Die 28 Julÿ 1546 vilnæ M: R. ex eo ꝗ iuuenes
in tubis et timpanis docere dźt constituit pro
annuo solario fl 20. ft' sińgliś qrtualibus fl 5.
Preterea racione diariorum illi addidit gr 10 itaque
singulis septimanis habebit fl 1.
*Habent pterea ex stabulo M R singlís diebus
Aueni p Cor. 1$^1/_2$ omnes infra sequen'.
Iis M.R. pecuniæ Auenam soluere constituit
sing Coreth per gross 2$^1/_2$ fac pro qrti fl
3/23/13$^1/_2$*
Idque a die 1 January 1558 eis thesauro una cú
sallario soluetur.

941r

Præterea M. R. die 21 octobŕ 1563 singulatim omnibus addidit sinǵ sept' gr 10 Habebit itaque quilibzt eoŕ ut Cziemior. fl 1/-

Ÿenczi
Tubicinator

Eid' ex Thezauro R. M. Senioris soluebátur pro annuo salario, Quod et núc ex Thezauro M. Regie Iunioris soluunt' floŕ 20 Facit ad quaŕtle anni floŕ 5
Preterea pro pelliceo floŕ 5
Panni Lundinen vlnas 6
Dantur etiam eid' pro diarÿs coquine & celarÿ singulis septimanis a dispensatore Regio gr 20
Mortuus Vilne 5 Marcij Anno 1545 solutus in toto ad manus Georgÿ fris̃ eius iuxta Regestrum̃ expositorú

941v *mortuus die 4 April' Vilnæ 1557*

Jrzÿk
Tubicinator

Eidem ex Thezauro M R senioris soluebantur pro annuo salario Qui & núc ex Thezauro M. R. Junioris soluuntur florem 20 Facit ad quaŕtle anni floŕ 5
Preterea pro pelliceo floŕ 5
Panni Lundineń vlnas 6
Dantur etiam eid' pro diarÿs coquine' & celarÿ sinǵlis septimanis a dispensatoré Regio gr 20

942r

Joachim Spangel
Tubicinator

Susceptus Vilne die 28 Marcÿ in seruiciú Mtiś Regie Anno 1545. Cui Mtás sua concessit pro Annuo salario ex thezauro Polo: fl 20 Facit ad quartuale anni   floŕ 5
Preterea pro pelliceo   fl 5
Panni Lundineń   vlnas 6
Dantur eciam eidem pro diarÿs coquine et celarÿ singulis septimanis a dispensatore Regio gr 20
Expeditus

Appendix X

942v

  Thomek Cracowczyk
  Tubicinator
Susceptus Vilne die 25 Aprilis Anno 1545 Cui
constitutú é pro annuo salario ex thesauro Pol̄
fl. 20
Facit ad quartuale anni fl. 5
Preterea pro pelliceo   fl 5
Panni Lundinen vl̄   6
Dantur eciam eidem pro diarÿs coquine et celarÿ
singulis septimanis a dispésatore Regio gr 20

943r

  Stanislaus Doyzwon
Susceptus Vilne die 19 July Anno 1546 Cui
constitutum est pro Anno salario ex Thesauro
Pol̄ fl 20
facit ad quartuale anni fl 5
Preterea pro pelliceo   fl 5
Panni Lvndineń vl̄   6
Dantur eciam eidem pro Diarÿs Coquine et
Celarÿ singulis septimanis a Dispensatore Regio
gr 20   *Mortuus Piotrc. die 18* A^o *1548*

943v

  Hanzel Ibrol
  tubicinator
Susceptus in seruicium M R ab ea diæ qua
dimissionem actepit a seruicio Dom̄i episcopi
wratislawień vczt a die 10 decembris anno domini
1546 Qvi servicium et omnem provisionem aliis
tvbicinatoribus Regijs eqvalem habebit
Die
Cui Mtaś Regia die 25 Juny Cracoviæ denuo
sallarium et oém prouisionem constituit sić
fistulatoribus Mtiś suæ Anno 1549

Joannes Rogoschka puer susceptus in serviciú
Mtiś R. et datus Hansel supto ad discendú Tubis
cané. Cvi tantú rńe expensarú constituti singvlis
septís in manus Hansel dań gr 6 a die 17
Februarii A^o 1550
Eidem Pańi Mistinén vlń 7

944r

Stephanus Vilneń
Tubicinator
Susceptus in serviciú M R. die 18 Octobŕ A⁰ domini
M⁰ D⁰ XLvii, Vilne.
Qui seruiciú et oem͂ prouisioné cú aliis
Tubicinatoribus Regis equalem habebit

*Mortuus
Vilne
Anno
1555*

944v

Joannes Koributh
Ssurmcz *de Kasei*
Susceptus in servitiú M R Vilnæ pro servitoé M R.
die 6 Jullii Anno domí 1548 Cracouiæe. Qui pro
Mortuus   timpana turcica debet seruare laicellum perfectum.
Habebit pro salario annuo ex Thesauro pól fl 20
Facit ad quartuale anni   fl 5
Preterea pro peliceo   fl 5
Panni lundineń   vln 6
Dantur ecciá eidem pro diariis coquine et celĩ
singulis septimanis a dispensatore Regio gr 20

945r

Jenik Czech Tubicinator
Qui ex seruitio M. R. Senioris susceptus est in
servitiú Mtiś suæ die 24 Junii Anno dom͂i 1548
Cui ex Thesauro Mtiś R. senioris soluebátur
annuatim qui et nunc ex Thesauro Mtís Regiæ
habebit fl 20
Facit pro quilibet quartuali   floŕ 5
Preterea pro pelliceo   floŕ 5
Panni Lundineń   vln 6
Roé diariorum coquine et cellarii singulis septimáis
per groś 20

945v   *mortuus
Cracc'*

Pavlus Lancz Tubicinator
Susceptus in seruitiú Mtiś Regie ex Seruitio Mtiś
Regiæ senioris die 24 Junii Anno domini 1548 Cui ex
Thesauro Mtiś Regiæ senioris soluebantur annuatim
Qui et núc ex Thesauro M. R. habebit fl 20
Facit pro quartuali quolźt   floŕ 5
Preterea pro pelliceo   fl 5
Panni lundinensis   vln͂ 6
Róe diariorú coquine et cellarii singulis sept' ꝑ gr 20

Appendix X

946r

Georgius Chromi tubicinator
Qui ex seruitio M. R. senioris susceptus é in seruitiú Mt' sue die 24 Junii Anno domini 1548 Cui ex Thesauro Mtiś R senioris soluebantur annuati qui et nuć ex Thesauro M. R. habebit flor 20
Facit pro quolibet quartuali   fl 5
Preterea pro pelliceo   fl 5
Panni lundinensis   vlń 6
Róe diarioru coquine et cellarii singliś sepf per gr 20

Anno domii 1549 die 11 Januarÿ
Mortuus in Nowemiasto

946v

Raczlawski
Stanislaus   Timpanista
Susceptus in seruitiú M. R. die 24 Junii A⁰ dói 1548 post mortem M. R. senioris ex seruicio M. sue.
Habebit pro anno salario fl 12 Fać pro quartuali fl 3
Diaria septimanatim a D. Dispensatore M. R. per gros 20
Cui constitueń Per M. R. die 10 februarii a⁰ 1549 Sallariú et omnis provisio, Aliis Tubicinatoribus similis etc.

Mathias Liubelczik
Albertus Zeliazowski
Joan: Goniwiecha
Suscepti Liubleni die 16 Apŕ 1564 Habebunt omnem prouisionem ut reliq̨ Tubicinatores

947r

Stanislaus Tubicinator *Krassowski*
Quamvis ańea pro discipulo, et de gratia M. Regiæ serviebit. Cui tamen Mtas R. sallarium annuum et omńe prouisionem sicut aliis tubicinatoribus Piotrcouiæ die 11 Novembris Anni 1548 constituit *Mortuus Vilnae die 5 Octobŕ*

Mortuus Vilnae die (10 Febr) 5 Octobris 1554

Sczessni Molda Tubicinator
Susceptus Vilnæ ad Cedulá D Tharlo Mgři
Curiæ die 19 Decembris 1554 Qui om̃
prouisioné vt ceteri Tubic' M R habebit

947v

Joachim Kepel fistulator.
Susceptus in servitium M. Regiae Crać die 18
Decembŕ Anno domini 1549, Cui cóstitutú
salarium et omnis prouisio Vt ceteris Fistulatoŕ
M R. Inter fistulatores est inscriptus

Nicolaus Sokol Tubicinator
Susceptus Vilnæ Ad cedulá Dm̃ Tharlo Mgři
Curiæ die 6 Januarÿ 1555 Cui om̃ prouisioné vt
ceteri Tubic' habebit.

948r

Paulus Juszko Tubicinator
Susceptus in serviciú Sacræ M.Regiæ Crać die
27 Aprilis Anno dñi 1550, Cui Mtás sua
Sallariú et omné provisioné, aliis Tubiccinis
constitvit simile.

Mathias Garn Susceptus Vilne die 23 Sept'
1563. Habebit omné prouisioné vt cæteri
Tubicinat' M R.

Andreas Kolakowski. Susceptus die 23 Augusti
1567 Grodnæ Habebit omnem prouisionem
prout cæteri tubicinatores Sać Mtiś R

Blasius Kosczielski Susceptus in seruitiú Sać
M: R die 19 Junÿ 1568 Grodnæ Habebit omnem
prouisionem vt reliqui tubicinatores Mtĩs R

Antonius Neuman Susceptus in seruitiú M: *Dimissus a*
R. die 3 July 1568 Grodnæ Habebit omnem *Curia 22 Aprilis*
prouisioné vt reliqui tubicinatores Mtĩs R *1570 Warscha*

Appendix X   331

948v   Marthinus Organista
           Susceptus Pietric' Die 18 Aprillis in seruitore Mtís
           Regiæ Anno domi 1552.
           Quamuis Cracc' manere debet tamé qńdocumque per
           M. R. vocatus fuerit debet venire in expeń et vectore
           Regio. quam vero ex necessitate M. R. illum in
           Curia habere voluerit obligatus erit manere Ita tú ͜p
           M R eum prouidebit victu et amictu [?] Interim tú
           tantum mó habebit rońe sallarii Anni per gr 30 fl 20
           fac' ad quart fl 5

949r   *Mortuus*   Stanislaus et Andreas   *Duscha*
       Cracc'   Timpaniste M. Regiæ   *factus tubicinator*
       1559
              Quibus constitutum sallarium annuú per Mteḿ
              Regiam Crać die 12 Maii Anni domí 1549 cuilżt per
              flor 12   Fac pro quartuali per fl 3
              Panni lundineń per   vlń 6
              Eisdem róe diariorum coquine et ceĺl cuilżt
              septimanatim per gr 15
              Anno 1551 die 10 Februarii Crać eisdé M Regia de
              grá sva constitvit sicut Tvbiccinatoribus similem
              oeḿ prouisioné et sallarium.

                              Nicolaus Sokol.
              Susceptus die 7 Julÿ 1569 Crac' Habebit omnem
              prouisioné vt cæteri Tubicinatores M Ʀ.

                         Antonius Klabon Tubicinator
              Susceptus in seruiciú Mtĩs Regiæ Liublini die 25
              Junÿ 1569 Habebit omné ͜puisioné similem reliquis.

949v   Jacob Brinik
              Susceptus Vilnæ die 9 Martys 1557

            ͜pfuit   Mart. Tarnowczik
              Susceptus Vilnæ die 3 Apŕ 1558.

                             Sczessni Skoczek
              Susceptus die 15 Aug. 1561 Vilnæ Habebit omné
              prouisioné ut caeteri Tubic'.

APPENDIX XI: PENSIONS (PRIVILEGIA) GRANTED TO MUSICIANS AT ZYGMUNT II AUGUST'S COURT

This appendix contains the privileges granted by Zygmunt August to some of his instrumentalists. These were copied into a book of privileges, now preserved in the Ossoliński library in Wrocław (WRo MS 180 II). These consisted of pensions, usually given for life, and were paid directly from the keeper of the royal salt-mines. Some of the musicians' terms as found in the register RK 110 have a note to this effect, and on occasion, the salary given from the treasury was appropriately reduced. For this reason, they should be seen as an important supplement to the register.

The transcriptions here are selective, and contain only the relevant information for the wind players, Dziano Bali, Marcin of Jędrzejów, Hansel Ibrol and Krzysztof Klabon. The text is reproduced exactly, with all abbreviations and contractions. Foliation is given in square brackets.

XI.1: The Wind Players

[46v] Sigismundus Augustus Dei Gratia Rex Polonia . . . significamus præsentibus literis quorum interest universis. Quod cum honestis Georgius vilhelmi Tibicen noster ab annos compluribus fideliter et diligenter nobis serviat æqum putauimus vt nostram suosque gratiam experiatur. Quamobrem ipsi pensione annuam Quadraginta flor. dandum et concedendam in Zuppis nostris constituendam et demonstrań duximus [47r] . . . Datum Cracouiae in vigilia sancti Mathei Apostoli Anno Domini Millesimo Quingentesimo Quinquagesimo Tertio
Sigismundi Augustus Rex
Reliqui quattuor Tibicines similia privilegia habent videlicet
Johannes Vilhelmus
Ioannes Ryder
Nicolaum Brugner
Thomas Georg

XI.2: Dziano Bali

[59v] Sigismundus Augustus . . . significmus pńtibus lŕis quorum interest Vniuersis. quod nos fidelium servitorum nobilis Joannis Bali Musici nostri begnigná habentes ratione tum ad nónulloru consiliariof ńrorum intcessienibus pro eo ad nos facta addicti . . . Ipsi stipendium annum centum florenof ŕóné salarii quod a nobis assignatú habet dandú cóstituend' et assignand' ex zuppis nŕis Crać. duximus damusque constituimus et assigmamus pńtibus litteris ad vitę eius extrema. . . . Dat Vilne ipse die Sancti Andree apostoli 1554, Regni vero nŕi Ańo vigesimo quarto.
Sigismundus Augustus Rex

XI.3: Marcin of Jędrzejów

[65v] Sigismundus Augustus Dei Gra Rex Poloniæ Generoso Hieronimo Buzinski Zuppario nostro Craccˊ. fideli dicto graciarum Regia Generose fidelis delicte non noscit. f. tua quia ingenius Joseph Magister et Concinnator instrumentof musicof insigne alequod opus Wielicię conficere debuerat, Cu' vero hu'eusque hand' parvo peracta tempore perfectu' non sit coniicimus negligentia eius alÿs laboribus intentu fieri Quamobrem cu' inactura' temporis maiorem pocevinæ habemus, comissius hoc negotiu' honesto Martino Andropolitano musico nostro vt apud dictu' Jozephu' in conficiendo hoc opere et ordinandis ad ea necessariis diligens admouitor errator et inspector fiet, ibidemque in Zuppa Wielicien cohabitet, Quem f tua habitatione comode prouidebit eu'que una duos servitores pueru' et Agazonem equos duos in eu' usu' ex Zuppis nostris

alat volumus Mandavimusque et tuc vt pro necessarias huic artifici operisque nostro conficiendo vid Martino per florenos Centu extradat, quibus Pictores Cęlatores et alios artefices conducas illisque necessaria admistret et salaria pacta solvat, De qua peccunia quaprimum ratione fecerit alios Centenos in eund vsu illi et tua huic nostro Mandas insequendo iteru numerabit ac sit deinceps faciat vt ceptu instrumentu tanto [66r] Cómodius et eicius absolvatur Ceteru ememus [?] ab eod Martino Instrumenta duo simphoniale & Regale, in vsu Musicæ nostre pro florenis Centu numeri et monete polonicę Cvius solutionem apud f. tuam ac demonstravimus Mandamus itaque vt eu f tua de his et alijs supra scriptis contentet qua solutionem et expensas ipsas nos in rationibus f tuae suscepturi sumus pro gra et debita officij sui a leter non faciat. Datu Wolboriæ Die 21 Junij Anno dni M⁰ D⁰ V⁰ Regni vero nri Anno XXVI

Sigismundus Augustus Rex

[66v]   Martino Organisto
Sigismundus Augustus . . . Honestum Martinum Andreopolitanus Musicus noster habuerat hueusque de manibus Generosi Josti Ludovici Decii Zupparii Illcussien Carbarii Wielicien rationé salarij ańui pro quolźt festo Pascharu monete et numeri poloni florenos viginti cui nunc iteru de gra nra additimus florenos viginti et solutionem istius salarii anni quadragin: fczt florenoŕ ad F [?] sua transferimus ex proventibus Zupparu pro quolźt festo Paschę solvendo, Mandamus . . . Datum Piotrcowiæ Dię vigessima prima Junii Anno Millesimo Qvingentesimo Quinquagesimo qvinto Regni vero nostri vigesimo Sexto.

Sigismundus Augusti Rex

[87v-88r]   Martino Organistæ
Sigismundus Augustus Quod quemadmod' Honestum Martino Andreopolitanus Musicus nro prioribus lŕis nŕis pro salario ańuo Quadraginta florenos peccvniaru : Item alijs lŕis nŕis ipsius persona seruitoribus duobus expensas victus desegnauimus, quarum rońe ex prouentibus Zupparu nostraru Cracouien septimanatim tres floreni ei soluébantur : Nos eá sumam peccuniam in vnu cóinugenda, atque annua pensionem, tam pro salario, quam pro expensis victus ipsius, servitoŕ duoŕ Agazonis pueri et equoru duoru Ducentos Florenos peccvniaru Monete et numeri Polonicaŕ in Zuppis nris Crac ex demonstań ut assignań ... singulis quadratibus anni sczt per quinquaginta florenos solvendos. Quod si vero in negotÿs nŕis ipsi ad nos venire aut abire ac res certos secú adducere et reducere iusserimus, tam viatico ipsius, qua pro vectore conducendo, ex thesauro ńro eidem dicens summa peccuniaŕ numerabitur, Astrictusque et obligatu erit ipse Martinus Musicus eius salarii et expensaru victus noie servitus nris adesse vbecúque locorú in Regno et domińys nŕis fieremus, vel quocúque alio loco propter seruitia nŕa ab eunda, cu ageri iussimus. Datu Varsschowiæ Die Sexta Mensis Octobris Anno Domi Millesimo Qingentesimo Qinquagesimo Sexto; Regni vero nŕi Anno Vigesimo Septimo.   S. A.

Appendix XI

[158v] Privilegium Martini Andreopolitani
Musici Regii

Sigismundus Augustus Dei gra Rex Poloniæ . . . Quia nos cu' consiliarys nostris habentes perspectam in nos fide ac integri talem et nobis seruindi studio Nblis Martini Andreopolitani quotidiani Musici nri quo nob a multis ańis non minus fidler quam diligent' præstitit ac etiam num præstare intermittit ipi itaque stipendiu' seu annuam pensionem ducentaru' Marcarum peccuniae numeri et monetae Regni in thesauro Regni vel in proventibus ad Thesuaru' nostru' ex Zuppis Cracc' pertineń tam pro salario quá pro expeń victualibus vite ipius ducanto demonstra' ac assignań esse duximus vte quid' assignatus . . . pro tempore futuris . . . noticiam deduceń mandamus vt memorati Martino Musico et servitori ńro quottidiano summa' ducentam Marcar' nomine stipendij sive pensiois annuæ sigulis anni qŕtalibus ad vitæ suæ extrema ipa per quinquagita marcas . . . Dat Varssouia d' 29 Mensis May Anno domî Millesimo quingentesimo septuagesimo primo. Regni Vero nŕi Anno Quadragesimo scdo.

Sigismundus Rex.

XI.4: Hansel Ibrol

[105v] Sigismundus Augustus Quia nos habentes ratione obsequioń honesti Johanne Iberhan Tibicen nostri áplicimus [?] annis nobis exibtoru' illi stipendiu' annu' Quadraginta florenos in singulis triginta gros. Regni nri computando. in Zuppis nŕis Vieliceń assignan duximus prout præsentibus assignamus quotamus pro festo Pentecostes ad vitæ suæ extrema tpa percipień . . . Die xvij May [1559] Regni nŕi trigesimo . . .

XI.5: Krzysztof Klabon

[160r] Christophori Klawon als Pisczek

Sigismundus Augustus . . . fidelium servitorum honesti Christophori klawon servitor' nostre qua nobis ea' a multis ańis præstat præstaveque . . . Eid' pensioń annua' in Zuppis nŕis Wieliceń qua olim klaus Brukner musicus nosrti habebat et percepiebat, danda' et assignatus esse duximus prout damus et assignamus pńtibus lŕis nŕis ad extma vsque vitæ ipiús tépore per eudé Chŕophoru' Klawon . . . pension eis annua' pro quolibet quartali per decé flor . . . Dat Varszauiæ d' 24 mensis februarij A° 1572 Regni vero nŕi Ano xliii

Sigismundu' Augustu' Rex

APPENDIX XII: MEMBERSHIP OF ZYGMUNT II AUGUSTS' MUSICAL ESTABLISHMENT

This appendix presents the composition of the musical establishment at the court of Zygmunt August between 1543 and 1574. The information is presented in three tables, dividing the establishment primarily by function. The first table comprises the royal chapel (including the organists), the second includes the trumpeters and drummers, and the third encompasses the wind players, the 'Musici Fistulatores' and the 'Musici Itali', the soloists and the organists. The duplication of the organists is intentional since their activities included both chapel and chamber duties.

The tables presented here are the result of research on the source material itself, preserved in State Archives in Warsaw (Wagad) and Wrocław (Wro). Whilst there is some duplication of information presented in E. Głuszcz-Zwolińska *Muzyka nadworna* (which also contains tables compressed onto three A3 pages), the tables here are much clearer to read, and present a more realistic picture of the respective groups of the musical establishment.

Within these tables, each individual is named, with the dates of service in brackets (months given in upper case Roman numerals), and the duration of employment shown by a continuous line within two small vertical strokes. Where a person's employment is uncertain, the respective line is dotted. As with the Rorantists' table, Poles are given their Polish form of names, with the birthplace, the city, town or village where appropriate, the latter is recorded in its modern version. Foreigners and those whose nationality is uncertain, are presented by their name as found in RK 110. The preciseness of the dates of membership reflects the information given in the sources. Almost all of the members have a date of employment, many also have a date of death or departure (marked by a † and * respectively). Where no such information is available, approximate dates are deduced from the actual payments made. Promotions and moves by members are denoted by an equals sign (=). In the majority of cases, such movement was restricted within a given group, and the status of the given person can be observed on the same table. The one exception is the movement of the boys of the chapel to the wind players in 1565.

Appendix XII.1

XII.1: The royal chapel (membership)

	1544	1545	1546	1547	1548	1549
Prefect		—— Jan Wierzbkowski (2 II 1544 - 10 XI 1549)———————————	*			
Boys (no.)	4	4	4	6	6	?
Composer	|. . . .	Władysław 1544		|—— Wacław of Szamotuły (6 V 1547-23 V 1555)—————————		

Chaplains:
- |—— Maciej Raszek (1544-V 1551)———————————|
- |—— Jan Jaszcz (1544-III 1557)—————————————————|
- |—— Szymon of Lelów (1544-VIII 1553)———————————|
- |—— Jan of Gamrat (1544-3 VI 1549)—————————|
- |—— Marcin of Iża cl. (1544-10 II 1557)————————————| †|
- |. . . . | Calans (1544)
-       |—— Jakub of Piątek (15 XII 1544-III 1564)——————————————|
-         |—— Daniel Mazowita (3 IV 1545-IV 1552)——————|
-           |—— Franciszek of Poznań (2 VII 1545-V 1555)—————————|
-             |—— Sebastian Strzeszkowski (VIII 1545-IX 1561)———————————————|
-                       = Jurek Jasiwczyc cl (1544-30 VI 1572)
-                         |— Maciej of Poznań cl (25 VI 1548-V 1555)
-                           |— S. of Szamotuły (19 VIII 1548-IX 1561)
-                     Ambrozy of Bełdrzychów (8 IV 1549-2 X 1559) =

Young Singers:
- |—— Jurek Jasivcicz (1544-30 VI 1572)———————————|
- |—— Klemens of Sandomierz (1544-1 XII 1559)——————|

Organist:
- |—— Sobek (1544-V 1565)—————————————|

Music at the Royal Court and Chapel in Poland c. 1543-1600

	1550	1551	1552	1553	1554	1555
Master				= Jurek Jasivcicz cl (1544-30 VI 1572)		
Boys (no.)	-	-	-	3 3 8 5	5	5
Composers	Wacław of Szamotuły (6 V 1547-23 V 1555)					
Chaplains	Maciej Raszek (1544-V 1551) †				Johannes Baston (8 III 1552-6 IX 1553)	
	Jan Jaszcz (1544-III 1557)					
	Szymon of Lelów (1544-VIII 1553)		*			
	Marcin of Iłża cl. (1544-10 II 1557)					
	Jakub of Piątek (15 XII 1544-III 1564)					
	Daniel Mazowita (3 IV 1545-IV 1552) †					
	Franciszek of Poznań (2 VII 1545-V 1555)					*|
	Sebastian Strzeszkowski (VIII 1545-IX 1561)					
	Jurek Jasivcicz cl (1544-30 VI 1572)	=				
	Maciej of Poznań cl (25 VI 1548-V 1555)					
	Stanisław of Szamotuły (19 VIII 1548-1561)					
	Ambroży of Bełdrzychów (8 IV 1549-2 X 1559)					†|
		Benedykt of Stryków (2 II 1551-1574)				
		= Klemens of Sandomierz (1544-1 XII 1559)				
		Andrzej of Opoczno (23 V 1551-V 1559)				
			Bartłomiej of Wyszogród (16 IV 1552-15 I 1560)			
			Stanisław Zagorski (5 VI 1552-7 XI 1558)			
				Marcin of Drohiczyn (24 IV 1553-V 1555)		
					Adam of Bełżyce (22 VIII 1553-1559)	
				Wojciech Odoliński (27 XII 1551-V 1561)		
				Stephanus Lesser (19 VI 1552-III 1554)		
			= Klemens of Sandomierz (1544-1 XII 1559)			
Young Singers	Sobek (1544-V 1565)					
		Joannes Bali (25 X 1550-V 1574)				
			Marcin of Jędrzejów (18 IV 1552-XII 1573)			
Organists		Pawlik b. (X 1550-6 XI 1561)				(= organist)

Appendix XII.1

	1556	1557	1558	1559	1560	1561
Master	Jurek Jasivcicz cl (1544-30 VI 1572)					
Boys (no.)	5	6	5	8	5	5
Composer						Marcin of Lwów (1 V 1560-XI 1661)
Chaplains	Jan Jaszcz (1544-III 1557) *					
		†| Marcin of Iłża cl. (1544-10 II 1557)				
	Jakub of Piątek (15 XII 1544-III 1564)					
	Sebastian Strzeszkowski (V 1545-IX 1561)					
	Stanisław of Szamotuły (19 VIII 1548-1561)					
	Ambroży of Bełdzychów (8 IV 1549-2 X 1559)					
	Benedykt of Stryków (2 II 1551-1574)					
	Andrzej of Opoczno (23 V 1551-V 1559) *					
	Stanisław Zagorski (5 VI 1552-7 XI 1558)					
	Klemens of Sandomierz (1544-1 XII 1559)					
	Bartłomiej of Wyszogród (16 IV 1552-15 I 1560) †					
	Adam of Bełżyce (22 VIII 1553-1559) †					
	= Wojciech Odoliński cl. (27 XII 1551-V 1561) *					
	Adam of Żmigród (16 V 1556-II 1573)					
				Marcin Leszczyński (III 1558-IX 15678)		
				Mikołaj Kochanowski (29 IV 1558-V 1574)		
				Albert Francuz (1 VI 1560-9 IX 1561)		
Young Singers		Piotr of Bodzentyn (16 V 1556-V 1574)				
				Szymek (29 X 1558-1568)		
				Tomek of Sącz (24 IV 1559-V 1574)		
Organists	Sobek (1544-V 1565)					
	Joannes Bali (25 X 1550-V 1574)					
	Marcin of Jędrzejów (18 IV 1552-XII 1573)					
	Pawlik (X 1550-6 XI 1561)					

	1562	1563	1564	1565	1566	1567
Master	Jurek Jasivcicz cl (1544-30 VI 1572)					
Boys (no.)	4	4	6	6	6	6
Composer						
Chaplains	Jakub of Piątek (15 XII 1544-III 1564) *⏐					
	Benedykt of Stryków (2 II 1551-1574)					
	Adam of Żmigród (16 V 1556-II 1573)					
	Marcin Leszczyński (III 1558-IX 1567)					
	Mikołaj Kochanowski (29 IV 1558-V 1574)					
	⏐ Marcin Brzykowski of Sieradz (13 III 1563-V 1574)					
	= Piotr of Bodzentyn (16 V 1556-V 1574) ⏐					
	Stanisław Petronius (17 V 1567-II 1573) ⏐					
Young Singers	Piotr of Bodzentyn (16 V 1556-V 1574) =					
	Szymek (29 X 1558-1568)					
	Tomek of Sącz (24 IV 1559-V 1574)					
	⏐ Teodolski (1 VIII 1562-III 1564) †⏐					
	†⏐ Laurentius of Pabianice (18 XI 1564-III 1566)					
	⏐ Bartłomiej Zinger (6 I 1565-V 1574)					
	⏐ Leonard Jankowski (6 I 1565-V 1574)					
	⏐ Marcin Wartecki (10 II 1565-VIII 1568)					
Organists	Sobek (1544-V 1565)					
	Joannes Bali (25 X 1550-V 1574)					
	Marcin of Jędrzejów (18 IV 1552-XII 1573)					

Appendix XII.1

	1568	1569	1570	1571	1572	1573	1574
Master	Jurek Jasivcicz cl (1544-30 VI 1572)					†	
Boys (no.)	6/8	[6/8]	9	9	9	-	

Composer

Chaplains:
- Benedykt of Stryków (2 II 1551-1574)
- Adam of Żmigród (16 V 1556-II 1573)
- Mikołaj Kochanowski (29 IV 1558-V 1574)
- Stanisław Petronius (17 V 1561-II 1573)
- Marcin Brzykowski of Sieradz (13 III 1563-V 1574) †
- Piotr of Bodzentyn (16 V 1556-V 1574)
- Stanisław Rohatyn (27 VIII 1569-V 1574)
- Marcin Raczulski (21 I 1570-V 1574)
- Szymon Buczkowski (1571)
- Jerzy Kałowski of Łowicz (V 1571-V 1574)
- Paweł Rostkowski (IX 1572-V 1574)
- Leonard Jankowski cl. (6 I 1565-V 1574) =

Young Singers:
- Szymek (29 X 1558-1568) (to wind players)
- Tomek of Sącz (24 IV 1559-V 1574)
- Bartłomiej Zinger (6 I 1565-V 1574)
- Leonard Jankowski (6 I 1565-V 1574)
- Marcin Wartecki (10 II 1565-VIII 1568)
- Jan Skiczki (17 IV 1568-V 1574)
- Mikołaj Klaus (8 I 1569-IV 1572)
- Tomasz Szadek (25 VI 1569-V 1574)
- Jakub Bronowski (13 VIII 1569-V 1574)
- Jan Ramult (27 VIII 1569-V 1574)
- Marcin Przeworsko (4 VIII 1571- 5 I 1572)

Organists:
- Joannes Bali (25 X 1550-V 1574)
- Marcin of Jędrzejów (18 IV 1552-XII 1573)

XII.2: Trumpeters and drummers (membership)

	1543	1544	1545	1546	1547	1548	1549

Trumpeters
- Maciej Ciemiorka (19 VIII 1543-V 1574)
- Jenczy (19 VIII 1543-5 III 1545) †
- Irzyk (19 VIII 1543-4 IV 1557)
- Joachim Spangel (28 III-22 XI 1545)
- Tomek Krakowczyk (25 IV 1545-3 II 1573)
- Stanisław Doidzwon (19 VII 1546-V 1548)
- Hansel Ibrol (10 XII 1546-V 1565)
- Stefan Ząbek (18 X 1547-1554)
- Jenik Czech (24 VI 1548-4 I 1562)
- Paweł Lancz (24 VI 1548-IX 1553)
- Gegorius Chromi (24 VI 1548-11 I 1549) †
- Stanisław Racławski (24 VI 1548-V 1574) =
- Stanisław Krasowski (1 1545-5 X 1554) =

Apprentice Trumpeters
- Stanisław Krasowski (1 1545-5 X 1554)
- Ragoszka b. (1548-1549)

Drummers
- Stanisław Kot ap.(1 1545-V 1559)
- Andrzej Dusza ap. (V 1545-1572)
- Stanisław Racławski (24 VI 1548-V 1574) = drummer
- Johannes Korybut (6 VII 1548-7 IV 1554) = drummer

Appendix XII.2

	1550	1551	1552	1553	1554	1555

Trumpeters
- Maciej Ciemiorka (19 VIII 1543-V 1574)
- Irzyk (19 VIII 1543-4 IV 1557)
- Tomek Krakowczyk (25 IV 1545-3 II 1573)
- Hansel Ibrol (10 XII 1546-V 1565)
- Stefan Ząbek (18 X 1547-1554) †
- Korybut (6 VII 1548-7 IV 1554)
- Jenik Czech (24 VII 1548-4 I 1562)
- Paweł Lancz (24 VII 1548-IX 1553) †
- Stanisław Racławski (24 VI 1548-V 1574)
- Stanisław Krasowski (I 1545-5 X 1554)
- Paweł Josko (27 IV 1550-9 IX 1572)
- Szczęsny Molda (19 XII 1554-15 IX 1571)

Drummers
- Stanisław Kot (1 1545-V 1559)
- Andrzej Dusza (V 1545-1572)
- Johannes Korybut (6 VII 1548-7 IV 1554) †

Music at the Royal Court and Chapel in Poland c. 1543-1600

	1556	1557	1558	1559	1560	1561

Trumpeters
- Maciej Ciemiorka (19 VIII 1543-V 1574)
- Irzyk (19 VIII 1543-4 IV 1557) †
- Tomek Krakowczyk (25 IV 1545-3 II 1573)
- Hansel Ibrol (10 XII 1546-V 1565)
- Jenik Czech (24 VII 1548-4 I 1562)
- Stanisław Racławski (24 VI 1548-V 1574)
- Paweł Josko (27 IV 1550-9 IX 1572)
- Szczęsny Molda (19 XII 1554-15 IX 1571)
  - Paweł Brinnik (9 III 1557-11 XII 1560)
    - Marcin Tarnowczyk (3 III 1558-V 1565)
      - Jurek Pawłowski (V-XII 1558)
    - = Andrzej Dusza (V 1545-V 1574)
  - Szczęsny Skoczek (15 VIII 1561-8 I 1574)

Drummers
- Stanisław Kot (1 1545-V 1559)
- Andrzej Dusza (V 1545-1572)
  - = boy (IV 1558-)
    - = Stefan Pieniajecz ap. (20 II 1560-31 XI 1573)
    - Maciej Tudesko ap. (20 II 1560-31 XII 1571)

Appendix XII.2

	1562	1563	1564	1565	1566	1567

Trumpeters
- Maciej Ciemiorka (19 VIII 1543-V 1574)
- Tomek Krakowczyk (25 IV 1545-3 II 1573)
- Hansel Ibrol (10 XII 1546-V 1565)
- Jenik Czech (24 VII 1548-4 I 1562)
- Stanisław Racławski (24 VI 1548-V 1574)
- Paweł Josko (27 IV 1550-9 IX 1572)
- Szczesny Molda (19 XII 1554-15 IX 1571)
- Marcin Tarnowczyk (3 III 1558-V 1565)
- Andrzej Dusza (V 1545-V 1574)
- Szczesny Skoczek (15 VIII 1561-8 I 1574)
- Maciej Garn (23 IX 1563-14 IX 1572)
- Maciej Lubelczyk (16 IV 1564-1 XII 1572)
- Wojciech Żelazowski (16 IV 1564-18 XI 1572)
- Jan Goniwiecha (16 IV 1564-22 April 1570)
- Andrzej Kołakowski (23 VIII 1567-V 1574)

Drummers
- Stefan Pieniajecz ap. (20 II 1560-31 XI 1573) = drummer
- Maciej Tudesko ap. (20 II 1560-31 XII 1571) = drummer
- Maciej Janowicz (30 VIII 1565-V 1574)

	1568	1569	1570	1571	1572	1573	1574

Trumpeters
- Maciej Ciemiorka (19 VIII 1543-V 1574)
- Tomek Krakowczyk (25 IV 1545-3 II 1573)
- Stanisław Racławski (24 VI 1548-V 1574)
- Paweł Josko (27 IV 1550-9 IX 1572)
- Szczęsny Molda (19 XII 1554-15 IX 1571)
- Andrzej Dusza (V 1545-1574)
- Szczesny Skoczek (15 VIII 1561-8 I 1574)
- Maciej Garn (23 IX 1563-14 XI 1572)
- Maciej Lubelczyk (27 IV 1564-1 XII 1572)
- Wojciech Żelazowski (27 IV 1564-18 X 1572)
- Jan Goniwiecha (27 IV 1564-2 IV 1570)
- Andrzej Kołakowski (23 VIII 1567-V 1574)
- Błażej Kościelski (19 VI 1568-V 1574)
- Antoni Neuman (3 VII 1568-22 IV 1570)
- Antoni Klabon (25 VI 1569-V 1574)
- Mikołaj Sokoł (2 VII 1569-V 1574)
- Jan Słowik (V 1571-1 VIII 1572)

Drummers
- = Stefan Pieniajecz (20 II 1560-31 XI 1573)
- = Maciej Tudesko (20 II 1560-31 XII 1571)
- Maciej Janowicz (30 VIII 1565-1574)

XII.3: Wind players, 'Musici Fistulatores', 'Musici Itali', soloists and organists.

	1543	1544	1545	1546	1547	1548	1549
Wind players		Claus Brugner (VIII 1543-2 X 1571)					
		Jurek Wilhelm (VIII 1543-V 1559)					
		Hanus Rheder (VIII 1543-5 II 1563)					
		Hanus Wilhelm (VIII 1543-V 1574)					
		Thomas Georg (VIII 1543-8 V 1563)					
		? Silvestro (1543-1544)					
				Mikołaj Gomółka b. (I 1545-19 VIII 1563)			
				Andrzej Pieniążek b. (I 1545-X 1549)			
							Joachim Kepel (18 XII 1549-21 IX 1572)
Soloists					Dominicus de Verona harpist (20 XII 1545-26 IV 1550)		
							Bálint Bakfark lutenist (12 VI 1549-V 1565)
Organists			Sobek (1544-V 1565)				

348   Music at the Royal Court and Chapel in Poland c. 1543-1600

	1550	1551	1552	1553	1554	1555

Wind players
- Claus Brugner (VIII 1543-2 X 1571)
- Jurek Wilhelm (VIII 1543-V 1559)
- Hanus Rheder (VIII 1543-5 II 1563)
- Hanus Wilhelm (VIII 1543-V 1574)
- Thomas Georg (VIII 1543-8 V 1563)
- Joachim Kepel (18 XII 1549-21 IX 1572)
- = Mikołaj Gomółka adol. (I 1545-19 VIII 1563)   = wind player

Musici Fistulatores
- Stephanus (29 XI 1550-VIII 1552)
- Theodoricus (29 XI 1550-VIII 1552)
- Antonius Ruffo (29 XI 1550-VIII 1553)
- Hugo (29 XI 1550-III 1554)

Soloists
- Dominicus de Verona harpist (20 XII 1545-26 IV 1550)
- Balint Bakfark lutenist (12 VI 1549-V 1565)
- Franciscus Lyricen violinist (28 VII 1553-XI 1562)

Organists
- Sobek (1544-V 1565)
- Joannes Bali (29 XI 1550-V 1574)
- Marcin of Jędrzejów (18 IV 1552-XII 1573)
- Pawlik b. (XI 1550-6 XI 1561)   (= organist)

Appendix XII.3

	1556	1557	1558	1559	1560	1561

Wind players
- Claus Brugner (VIII 1543-2 X 1571)
- Jurek Wilhelm (VIII 1543-V 1559)
- Hanus Rheder (VIII 1543-5 II 1563)
- Hanus Wilhelm (VIII 1543-V 1574)
- Thomas Georg (VIII 1543-8 V 1563)
- Joachim Kepel (18 XII 1549-21 IX 1572)
- Mikołaj Gomółka (1 1545-19 VIII 1563) =
- Carolus (9 V 1556-V 1574)
- Joannes Kappa (1 I 1561-6 II 1562)

Musici Itali
- Guido Hoberean (10 XI 1556-7 VIII 1561)
- Arnoldus Veracter (10 XI 1556-4 VII 1560) †
- Philipus Mansart (10 XI 1556-7 VIII 1561) †
- Paulus Baninch (10 XI 1556-29 I 1560) †

Soloists
- Balint Bakfark lutenist (12 VI 1549-V 1565)
- Franciscus Lyricen violinist (28 VII 1553-XI 1562)
- = Mikołaj Gomółka (1 1545-19 VIII 1563)

Organists
- Sobek (1544-V 1565)
- Joannes Bali (29 XI 1550-V 1574)
- Marcin of Jędrzejów (18 IV 1552-XII 1573)
- Pawlik (XI 1550-6 XI 1561)

Music at the Royal Court and Chapel in Poland c. 1543-1600

	1562	1563	1564	1565	1566	1567
Wind players	Claus Brugner (VIII 1543-2 X 1571)					
	† Hanus Rheder (VIII 1543-5 II 1563)					
	Hanus Wilhelm (VIII 1543-V 1574)					
	Thomas Georg (VIII 1543-8 V 1563) †					
	Joachim Kepel (18 XII 1549-21 IX 1572)					
	Carolus (9 V 1556-V 1574)					
	Joannes Kappa (1 I 1561-6 II 1562)					
			Laurentius Margoński (13 II 1564-V 1574)			
				= Krzysztof Klabon adol. (6 I 1565-V 1574) = wind player		
				= Stefan Reder adol. (6 I 1565-V 1574)		
				= Szymon Trubicki adol. (6 I 1565-30 X 1572)		
				= Bartłomiej Kicher adol. (6 I 1565-V 1574)		
Soloists	Balint Bakfark lutenist (12 VI 1549-V 1565)					
		Franciscus Lyricen violinist (28 VII 1553-VIII 1562)				
	Mikołaj Gomółka (I 1545-19 VIII 1563) *					
Organists	Sobek (1544-V 1565)					
	Joannes Bali (29 XI 1550-V 1574)					
	Marcin of Jędrzejów (18 IV 1552-XII 1573)					

Appendix XII.3

	1568	1569	1570	1571	1572	1573	1574
Wind players	Claus Brugner (VIII 1543-2 X 1571) †						
	Hanus Wilhelm (VIII 1543-V 1574)						
	Joachim Kepel (18 XII 1549-21 IX 1572) †						
	Carolus (9 V 1556-V 1574)						
	Laurentius Margoński (13 II 1564-V 1574)						
	Krzysztof Klabon (1 I 1565-V 1574)						
	Stefan Reder adol. (6 I 1565-V 1574) = wind player						
	Szymon Trubicki adol. (6 I 1565-30 X 1572) = wind player †						
	Bartłomiej Kicher adol. (1 I 1565-V 1574) = wind player						
	[= Szymek (5 VIII 1568-V 1574)						
				Stephan Bauman (3 II 1572-V 1574)			
Soloists			David König (18 VI 1569-15 XII 1571) †				
Organists	Joannes Bali (29 XI 1550-V 1574)						
	Marcin of Jędrzejów (18 IV 1552-XII 1573)						

APPENDIX XIII: THE INVENTORY OF
JUREK JASIVCICZ (1572)

This appendix presents the inventory of Jurek Jasivcicz, made on his death in 1572. It includes the opening explanatory paragraph, all the partbooks and choirbooks, the lute tablature, the two instruments, the writing utensils, and finally the concluding statement regarding the transfer of the music books to the palace on Wawel Hill. Also provided within the text are the location markings. The information is presented in a tabular form: the first column provides the page location in the manuscript and the item numbers (editorial). The second presents the original text with all abbreviations and contractions, and the third has a literal translation of the latter, though titles of prints are not translated. The fourth column includes identification or other information. Prints listed here are given in their *RISM* version, and only the first edition (or earliest in the given format) is provided. All editorial additions are given in square brackets.

XIII: The inventory of Jurek Jasivcicz, 1572 (Kpa, K 446, pp. 26-37)

Item	Original entry	Translation	Identification
[p. 26]	Feria sexta post festũ sctæ Margarethæ Anno Domini 1572 Postulantibus Genroso Doṅó Thoma Postekalský viceproctore Castri Crać. veluti executore Testamẽti Nobilis olim Georgÿ Jazwýcz S. M. R. Clericæ Ac noié Gṅosi Dōi Ludovici Decÿ Magni Gṅalis Cracć Procuratoris, Necnon Nobili Joanne Szelmiczký aĩs Vaÿsz, et Famato Joanne Miernik Consule kasimireń eiusd Testamti exequitoribus, res infranotatae a morte pfati Georgÿ Jazvýcz relictae, In pṅtia Famatoɫ Andreae Naczovicz, et Bartholomei Bieglowsky scabinorú, ex offitio ad id misf-p. 26 - Jsorum in pṅtia quoque Honesti Adolescétis Georgý ex sorore Nepotis, eiusḍ D: Georgý Jazwýcz sũt officiosæ in domo eiusḍ Georgý Jazwýcz hæreditaria cóscriptae	The sixth day after St. Margaret's feast [19 July,] the year of our Lord 1572. On the request of the Noble Thomas Postekalski, Vice-procurator of the castle of Kraków, the venerable executor of the will of George Jazwicz [ie Jasivcicz], His Royal Highness' clerk, And the noble Ludovicus Decius, Procurator of all Kraków, also the noble Jan Szelmiczki, called Waisz, and the famous Jan Miernik, Consul of Kazimierz, the things noted below, left on the death of the said George Jazwicz, were obligingly written in the presence of the famous Andrzej Naczowicz and Bartłomiej Bieglowski, sent as the designated municipal officers, and also in the presence of respectable youth George, [son] of the sister of the deceased George Jazwicz, in the home of the same George Jazwicz.	

[p. 27]	Naprzod visbie na Gorze ku vliczi	Firstly, in the chamber on the first floor off the street
	It. Rastra 2 do Liniovania	2 rulers for drawing lines
	It. Instruméta do gładzenia papierv 2	2 instruments for smoothing paper
	It. Piorka miedziane do Notovania 3 a mosiądzove 4	copper nibs 3 and brass [nibs] 4 for notating
	It. ołowu trocha, czo na księgi kładą	A little lead which is used for books
	W kownaczie theý Iszbý	In that chamber of the house
[p. 29]	W skrzini iedneý tham ze wteý komnaczie	In one chest in that chamber
[1]	Ité Partessow vÿazanich iednakich in folio 5	5 tied partbooks in folio
[2]	It. Partessow czervonich 3	3 red partbooks
[3]	It. Partessow zoltich durkovaných zbrzegamý posloczisthemý sescz	Six printed partbooks, yellow with golden borders
[4]	It. Partessow w bialeý skorcze durkovanich 5	5 printed partbooks in white leather

Appendix XIII 355

[5]	It. Drugich partessow wbialey skorcze 6	6 other partbooks [printed?] in white leather
[6]	It. Madrigał Doico Phinoth 5	Madrigal[s] by Dominique Phinoth [à] 5. Probably D. Phinot: *Premier livre contenant trent et sept chansons*. (G. & M. Beringen, Lyons, 1548b) or *Second livre contenant vingt et six chansons*. (G. & M. Beringen, Lyons, 1548c)
[7]	It. Muteti Cipriani Parteskow 4	Motets by Cipriano 4 partbooks. C. de Rore: *Motetta D. Cipriani de Rore et aliorum auctorum quatuor vocum parium* ... (G. Scotto, Venice, 1563[4])
[8]	It. Madrigał Cipriano 5	Madrigal by Cipriano 5. One of C. de Rore's five books of madrigals for five voices, 1542 - 1566.
[9]	It. Drugi Madrigałi Cipriano 4	Another [book of] madrigals by Cipriano [à] 4. Possibly C. de Rore: *Il primo libro de madrigali a quatro voci*. (G. Buglhat & A. Hucher, Ferrara, 1550) or *Di Cipriano de Rore il secondo libro de madregali a quatro voci* ... (A. Gardane, Venice, 1557[24])
[10]	It. Madrigał Janequin	Madrigal by Janequin. Possibly C. Janequin: *Second livre des inventions musicales*. ... (A. Chemin, Paris 1555b) or *Verger de musique contenant partie des plus excellents labeurs de M. G. Janequin à 4 & 5 parties ... premiere livre.* (A. Chemin, Paris 1555a)
[11]	It. Clementis Janequin 4	Clement Janequin [à] 4. A four part composition (or book of four part compositions) by C. Janequin.

[12]	It. Magnificat tonorů 8	Magnificat tonorum 8	Possibly: *Postremum Vespertini Officii . . . Magnificat tonorum* (G. Rhau, Wittenberg, 1544[4])
[13]	It. Muteti Joańis Pÿenner 5	Motets by Johannes Pionner [à] 5	One of three books of motets by Johannes Pionner, 1548, 1561 and 1564, of which only the first survives: *Cantiones quinque vocibus . . . liber primus* (A. Gardane, Venice, 1548) (incomplete).
[14]	It. Lamentacieÿ Parthesÿ 2	Lamentations 2 partbooks	
[15]	It. Parthesÿ Dihangero 3	3 partbooks of Ihan Gero	Jehan de Gero: *Quaranta madrigali a tre voci.* (A. Gardane, Venice, 1553) or *Il secondo libro di madrigali a tre voci.* (A. Gardane, Venice, 1556)
[16]	It. Parthessow ad pares voces 4	4 partbooks for equal voices	
[17]	It. Parthessÿ Constancÿ porte voces 5	Constanzo Porta partbooks [for] voices	A book of madrigals or motets by Constanzo Porta.
[18]	It. Plami Cipriani Jakkieth voces 4	Cipriano [and] Jachet psalmi [for] voices	Cipriano de Rore and Jachet of Mantua: *Di Cipriano et di Jachet i salmi a quattro voci a uno choro . . .* (C. da Correggio, Venice, 1570[2])
[19]	It. Muteti Adriani Vilath voces 4	Adrian Willaert motets [for] 4 voices	One of Adrian Willaert's *Musica quatuor vocum . . . liber primus . . .* (G. Scotto, Venice, 1539a) or *Motetti . . . libro secondo a quattro voci.* (B. & O. Scotto, Venice, 1539b).

Appendix XIII

[20]	It. Psalmi Phinoth voces 4	Phinoth Psalms [for] 4 voices	D. Phinot: *Il primo libro di salmi a quatro voci* . . . (A. Gardane, Venice, 1555a)
[21]	It. Muteti Jakieth 5	Jachet motets [à] 5	Jachet de Mantua: *Motecta quinque vocum* . . . *liber primus* (G. Scotto, Venice, 1539), or *Primo libro di motetti* . . . *a cinque voci* (A. Gardane, Venice, 1540)
[22]	It. Muteti drugie Adriani Jakieth 5	Other motets by Adrian Jachet [à] 5	Probably Jachet de Mantua: *Motetti* . . . *a cinque voci, libro secondo* . . . (G. Scotto, Venice, 1565)
[23]	It. Parthessÿ Lupachini 4	Lupacchino 4 partbooks	B. Lupacchino: *Madrigali a quattro voci*. (G. Scotto, Venice, 1543), or *Il segondo libro di madrigali* . . . *a quatro voci*. (A. Gardane, Venice, 1546)
[24]	It. Parthessÿ Axamithnem Brunathem oblieczone in mod' cordis 4	4 partbooks covered with brown velvet in modum cordis	
[25]	It. Partessÿ pissane stare wpargaminie vocum 6	Old manuscript partbooks in parchment for 6 voices	
[26]	It. Parthessÿ wloskie pissane wpargaminie bialem 4	4 Italian manuscript partbooks in white parchment	
[27]	It. Psalmi Adriani voces 4	Adrian Psalms for 4 voices	A. Willaert: *I sacri e santi salmi* . . . *a quatro voci*. (A. Gardane, Venice, 1555)
[28]	It. Parthessÿ wbrunathneÿm papierze 5	5 partbooks in brown paper	

[p. 30]

[29]	It. Parthessẏ pissane ad voces equales 4	4 manuscript partbooks for equal voices	
[30]	It. Rapturki ku spievanẏu pospolithe	Songs for common singing	
	Tham ze wdrugieij skrzinẏ	In another chest there	
[31]	Parthessẏ wczervoneẏ skorze chedogo opravione Adriani villa 7	7 partbooks sumptuously bound in red leather [music by] Adrian Willaert	A. Willaert: *Musica nova* . . . (A. Gardane, Venice, 1559a)
[32]	It. Parthessẏ ploczienne slothem vissivane 4	4 partbooks sewn with gold [thread]	
[33]	It. Parthessow czarnẏch wstegamẏ 5	5 black partbooks with ties	
[34]	It. Parthessow czarnẏch zczervonemẏ wstegamy 6	6 black partbooks with red bands	
[35]	It. Parthessow czervonich zorlem 6	6 red partbooks with an eagle	
[36]	It. Parthessow czervonich brzegẏ opravione zlotem 4	4 red partbooks with golden borders	
[37]	It. Parthessẏ wmodreẏ skorze zbrzegi pozloczistemij 6	6 partbooks in dark blue leather with golden edges	

Appendix XIII

[38]	It. Parthessÿ w czarneÿ skorze zbrzegamij dzikiemij 5	5 partbooks in black leather with rough edges	
[39]	It. Parthessow Missarũ Doĩcaliũ w deboweÿ skorze wstegami czervonemi 4	4 partbooks with sunday masses in wooden boards with red bands	Possibly one of three *Missarum dominicalium* (Attaingnant, Paris, 1534) mentioned in A. Schmid's book on Petrucci of 1845.
[40]	It. Psalmi czarne 4	4 black [partbooks with] psalms	
[41]	It. Parthessÿ biale zbrzegamij zoltemij przesz wstag officialne 4	4 white partbooks with golden borders with ties, containing masses	
[42]	It. Parthessÿ w czervonem pargaminie z brzegamij zlotemÿ piecz	Five partbooks in red parchment with golden borders	
[43]	It. Parthessÿ wbialeÿ skorze zorlem, zbialemÿ wsthegamÿ 4	4 partbooks in white leather with an eagle with white ties	
[44]	It. Parthessÿ czarne mutetne z brzegamy zielionemi 4	4 black partbooks with green borders containing motets	
[45]	It. Parthessÿ czarne pissane zzoltemÿ wstegamÿ 5	5 black manuscript partbooks with yellow ties	
[46]	It. Parthessÿ czarne pissane krom wstag 5	5 manuscript partbook, black without ties	

[47]	It. Parthessý czarne Niemieczkie mnyeisse krom wstąg 4	4 smaller German partbooks, black without ties
[48]	It. Parthessý Debiane pissane zbrzegamý zoltemý 5	5 brown manuscript partbooks with yellow borders
[49] [p. 31]	Item Parthessý czarne pissane małe zzoltho cziemnemý Brzegami 4	4 small manuscript partbooks, black with dark borders
[50]	It. Parthessý Niemieczkie czarne zczervonamý wstęgamý 3	3 German partbooks, black with red ties
[51]	It. Villaneský w papierze zaviazane 3	Villanellas [à] 3 tied up in paper
[52]	It. Parthessow pissanich na malý Jezik 5	5 manuscript partbooks on a small tongue
[53]	It. Parthessý, na vielký Jezik wzieloneý skorze 4	4 partbooks in green leather on a large tongue
[54]	It. Parthessý wbialem Pargaminie zczervonemý wstęgamý 4	4 partbooks in white parchment with red ties
[55]	It. Parthessý pissane nadlugý Jezyk stare 5	5 old manuscript partbooks on a long tongue

[56]	It. Parthessỳ Madrigał wpapierze kłyonem 4	4 partbooks of madrigals stuck in paper	
[57]	It. Parthessỳ durkovane maluskie mutectae czarne zbrzegami słothemỳ 4	4 small printed partbooks containing motets, black with golden borders	
[58]	It. Parthessỳ wpargaminie białem vnỳch brzegỳ posloczisthe 4	4 partbooks in white parchment with goldenborders	
[59]	It. Psalmi wloskie maluskie 4	Italian psalms, small, 4 [partbooks]	
[60]	It. Villaneczkỳ wkłyonem Papierze 4	Villanellas stuck in paper, 4 [partbooks]	
[61]	It. officia moralis w papierze kłyonem 4	Masses [à] 4 [by] Morales stuck in paper	One of *Excellentissimi musici Moralis hispani, Gomberti, ac Jacheti cum quatuor vocibus missae . . . liber primus.* (G. Scotto, venice, 1540[4]), *Missae cum quatuor vocibus paribus decantandae, Moralis hispani, ac aliorum authorum . . .* (G. Scotto, Venice, 1542[3]), or *Christophori Moralis hyspalensis missarum quinque cum quatuor vocibus secundus liber.* (A. Gardane, Venice, 1544[5])
[62]	It. Muteti maluskie zbrzegamỳ zlothemỳ krom clausor 5	5 small partbooks with golden borders without a clasp	
[63]	It. Muteti stare surge propera 4	Old motets [à] 4 with 'surge propera'	

[64]	It. Muteti Helisei wklyonem papierze5	Motets by Heliseo [à] 5 stuck with paper	H. Ghibelli: *Motectorum . . . cum quinque vocibus liber primus*. (G. Scotto, Venice, 1548), or *Motetta super plano cantu cum quinque vocibus . . .* (Venice, 1546)
[65]	It. Labathagilia wklyonem papierze 4	Labathagilia [à] 4 stuck in paper	Probably C. Janequin: *La bataglie, La louette, Le critz de Paris, Le chant des oyseaux, Le rossignol, libro primo*. (A. Gardane, Venice, 1545)
[66]	It. Parthessy wkompathorze wsithe Pissane media vita 6	6 manuscript partbooks sewn in a folder [with] 'Media vita'	A six part motet 'Media vita' by N. Gombert can be found in *Sextus tomus Evangeliorum, . . . de Poenitentia*. (J. Montanus & U. Neuber, Nuremberg, 1556⁹).
[67]	It. Parthessy, wsithe wkompathurze plesth 6	6 partbooks sewn in a folder	
[68]	It. Psalmodię niesporne wsithe wpargamin 4	Vesper psalms [à] 4 sewn in parchment	Possibly: *Vesperarum precum officia psalmi feriarum et dominicalium dierum tocius anni . . . quatuor vocibus ab optimis & celeberrimis musicis compositi . . .* (G. Rhau, Wittenberg, 1540⁵)
[69]	It. Parthessy czarne sbrzegamy pozloczistemy krom wstag 4	4 black partbooks with golden borders without ties	
[70]	It. offitia na durkovanych linjach notovane w kompathurze 4	Masses [à] 4 written on printed staves in a folder	
[71]	It. officia notovane wkompathurze wsithe 5	Masses [à] 5 written, sewn in a folder	

Appendix XIII

[72]	It. Muteti na drukovanich liniach pissane 6	Motets [a] 6 written on printed staves
[p. 32]		
[73]	It. Parthessỹ, muttaetne notovane na Jezỹk 5	5 manuscript partbooks with motets on a tongue
[74]	It. Parthessỹ stare in qřto Madrigali pissane 4	4 old partbooks in quarto [containing] madrigals
[75]	It. Polskie piesnỹ pissane, na Jezỹk malỹ 4	Polish songs [a] 4 written, on a small tongue
[76]	It. Parthessỹ zbrunathnemỹ brzegamỹ 2	2 partbooks with brown borders
[77]	It. Parthessỹ notovane wczervonem Pargaminie zzakladaniem 3	3 manuscript partbooks covered with red parchment
[78]	It. Parthessỹ vỹazane notovane stare 2	2 old manuscript partbooks tied up
[79]	It. Tabulatura stara do Luthnỹeỹ na Jezỹk 1	1 old tablature for the lute on a tongue
[80]	It. Partesz na Jezỹk durkovani wstegamỹ zzielonemi 1	1 printed partbook with green ties

[81]	It. Partes mutetni, durkovani na Jezýk przesz wstąg	Printed motets on a tongue without ties	
[82]	It. Muteti dum deambulareth male wsithe notovane 4	Written motets [à] 4 [with] 'dum deambulareth', small	
[83]	It. Villaneczký wloskie durkovane wsithe na Jezýk 3	Printed Italian Villanellas a 3 sewn on a tongue	
[84]	It. Villaneczký durkovane wklyone wkompathurze 4	Printed Villanellas [à] 4 stuck in a folder	
[85]	It. Muteti durkovane w sexterniech na Jezýk 6	Motets [à] 6, printed in sexterns and on a tongue	
[86]	It. Parthessý Greczkie muteti	Parts with Greek motets	Possibly ΠΡΟΤΕΛΕΙΟΣΕΥΧΗ qua chorus musicus bene precatur optimo sponso ornamentis ingenij . . . (J. von Berg & U. Neuber, Nuremberg, 1550[21])
[87]	It. Parthessý na Jezýk durkovane fugi 1	1 partbook with printed fugi, on a tongue	
[88]	It. fasciculi male rozmaithego spievania 5	5 small fascicles with various songs	
[89]	It. Sexterni durkovane Labatalia 4	4 printed sexterns with 'Labatalia'	
[90]	It. fascicul výethssý wnyem exclamacie 1	1 fascicle with some exclamations	

Appendix XIII 365

[p. 34]	W ysbie na Dolie ... w sienij	In the room downstairs ... in the hallway	
[p. 35]	Wskrzincze wozoweẏ	In a travelling chest	
[91]	Cancional wczervoneẏ skorze Missarú 10 ieden	One choirbook in red leather Missarum 10	Probably R. Rodio: *Missarum decem liber primus ... cum quatuor, quinque et sex vocibus*. (V. Dorico, Rome, 1562)
[92]	Passiones 4 na pargaminie opus 1	Passiones 4 written on parchment, opus 1	
[93]	It. Psalteriú figuralr̄ notovane 1	One written psalter figuraliter	
[94]	It. Liber selectarú Cancionú opus vielkie 1	One large choirbook, Liber Selectarum Cancionum	*Liber selectarum cantionum quas vulgo Mutetas appellant sex quinque et quatuor vocum*. (Grim & Wyrsung, Augsburg, 1520[4])
[95]	It. Cancional w skorze czarneẏ na przodkv wnẏch fecit potenciá	A choirbook in black leather with 'fecit potenciam' at the front	
[96]	It. Liber 15 Missarú electarú per excellétissimos Musicos compositarú	Liber 15 Missarum electarum per excellentissimos musicos compositae	*Liber quindecim missarum electarum quae per excellentissimos musicos compositae fuerunt* (A. Antico, Rome, 1516[1])
[97]	It. Liber cú 4 vocibus ad imitatióem Cantilenæ Misericordiæ	Liber cum 4 vocibus ad imitationem Cantilenae Misericordiae	Clemens non Papa: *Missa cum quatuor vocibus, ad imitationem cantilenae, Misericorde, condita ...* (P. Phalèse, Louvain, 1556)

[98]	It. Cantionale 6 Missarů suavissimæ modulacionibus referte partem 4 parté 5 vocum Jacobo de kierl	A Choirbook 6 Missarum suavissimae modulationibus referte partim 4 partim 5 vocum Jacobo de Kerle	J. de Kerle: *Sex misse suavissimis modulationibus referte partim quatuor partim quinque vocibus concinendae... liber primus.* (A. Gardane, Venice, 1562b)
[99]	It. Præstantissimorů divinæ Musicæ Autorů, missæ decé 4 et 5 et 6 vocú	One [volume,] Praestantissimorum divinae Musicae Autorum misse decem 4 et 5 et 6 vocum	*Praestantissimorum divinae musices auctorum missae decem, quatuor, quinque & sex vocum...* (P. Phalèse & J. Bellère, Louvain, 1570[1])
[p. 36]			
[100]	It. Liber 10 missarů wczervonych desczkach 1	One liber 10 missarum in red boards	*Liber decem missarum a praeclaris musicis...* (J. Moderne, Lyons, 1532[8])
[101]	It. Gradual Craccovien͂	Graduale Cracoviensis	
[102]	It. Passye 1	Passions 1	
[103]	It. Cancional polsky	a Polish choirbook/Cancional	
[104]	It. Te deú laudamus na vielkie moḍ na pargaminie 5 et 6 vocú 1	Te Deum laudamus for 5 and 6 voices written in the grand style on parchment	This manuscript was donated to Zygmunt August by J. Wirker in 1563.
[105]	Musica Glareani	Glareani's Musica	H. Glareanus: *Musica epitome sive compendium ex Glareani Dodecachordon* (H. Petri, Basle, 1557)
[106]	It. Parthessy wczervoney skorze zerbamy Je° K M Thesaurus partes 6	Partbooks in red leather with the royal highness' emblem, Thesaurus 6 parts.	*Thesauri musici tomus tertius continens cantiones sacras ... Sex vocum...* (J. Montanus & U. Neuber, Nuremberg,1564[3])

Appendix XIII

[107]	It. Parthessỷ wczervoneỷ skorze, iedna Missa wných Gott jsth man vocú 5	Partbooks in red leather with the mass gott ist man for 5 voices	
[108]	It. Parthessỷ wzolteỷ skorze, Labathaỷ vocum quinque	Partbooks in yellow leather with 'labathaỷ' for 5 voices	Probably C. Janequin: *Premiere livre des inventions musicales . . . contenant La guerre, Bataille de Metz, Jalouzie, le tout à cinq parties* . . . (N. du Chemin, Paris, 1555a)
[109]	It. Parthessỷ wdebneỷ skorze, orzel na ných offitia Vaczlavove 6	6 partbooks in brown leather with an eagle [on them] containing masses by Wacław	Six part masses by Wacław of Szamotuły, probably in manuscript, which have not survived.
[110]	It. Parthessỷ wczervonei skorze o regé cæli 4	4 partbooks in red leather with 'O regem caeli'	*Primus liber cum quatuor vocibus. Motteti del fiore* (J. Moderne, Lyons, 1532[10])
[111]	It. exclamacie i Lamentacie vaczlavove Zerbem kroliewskỷem vocú 4	Exclamations and Lamentations by Wacław, with the king's emblem, for 4 voices	Wacław of Szamotuły's Lamentations and Passion responses, either in manuscript or print: *Quatuor parium vocum Lamentationes* . . . (Ł. Andrysowic, Kraków, 1553). Only the Discantus and Tenor books survive.
[112]	It. Parthessỷ wskorze białeỷ sex Misse Gomberthi vocú 5	Partbooks in white leather containing six masses by Gombert	Sex missae cumquimque vocibus quarum tres sunt excellentissimi musici Jacheti, reliquae vero celeberrimi Gomberti . . . (G. Scotto, Venice, 1542[2]) (ATB and 5:*Missarum sex Gomberti et Jacheti*)
[113]	Item exclamacie drugie Vaczlavove w skorze białeỷ vocum 5	Second Exclamations for 5 voices by Wacław in white leather	5 part settings by Wacław of Szamotuły probably in manuscript, lost.

[114]	It. Parthessÿ wkompathurze Doici notovane vocum 5	Written partbooks in a folder for 5 voices by Do[min]ici	Perhaps music by D. Phinot
[115]	It. Parthessÿ wkompathurze Magnificat Orlandi ad octos Thonos vocú 6	Partbooks in a folder with Magnificat ad octo tonos for 6 voices by Orlando	O. di Lasso: *Magnificat octo tonorum, sex, quinque, et quatuor vocum* . . . (T. Gerlach, Nuremberg, 1567b)
[116]	It. offitia wpargaminie wsithe Vaczlavove 4	Masses [à] 4 by Wacław, sewn in Parchment	4 part masses by Wacław of Szamoty, probably in manuscript, lost.
[117]	It. Parthessÿ Orlandi lasso Madrigalÿ vocum 5	Partbooks of madrigals by Orlando di Lasso for 5 voices	One of four books of madrigals by Orlando di Lasso for five voices (1555-1567).
[118]	It. Parthessÿ D: Paulo Magri do Bologna vocum 5	5 partbooks d. Paulo Magri da Bologna	The earliest extant print by Paolo Magris is his first book of motets of 1581. It is possible that this item refers to a book of madrigals which has not survived, or perhaps a manuscript containing his music.
[119]	It. Parthessÿ Madrigali D: Jacobo Corfini vocú 5	Partbooks with madrigals for 5 voices by Jacopo Corfini	J. Corfini: *Il primo libro di madrigali a cinque voci* . . . (A. Gardane, Venice, 1565) or *Il secondo libro de madrigali a cinque voci*. (A. Gardane, Venice, 1568)
[120]	It. Parthessÿ Francisci Londariti vocú 5	Partbooks for 5 voices by Francesco Londariti	F. Londariti: *Modulationum quinque vocum . . . liber primus*. (A. Gardane, Venice, 1566)
[121]	It. Psalmi Adriani Jacheti vocú 8	Psalms by Adrian [and] Jachet [for] 8 voices	*Di Adriano et di Jachet. I salmi appertinenti alli vesperi per tutte le feste dell'anno* . . . (A. Gardane, Venice, 1550¹)

Appendix XIII

[122]	It. Misse vincentio ruffo vocú 5	Masses for 5 voices by Vincenzo Ruffo	V. Ruffo: *Messe . . . a cinque voci.* (A. Gardane, Venice, 1557)
[123]	It. Misse 4 Jakieth de Manthva vocú 5	4 masses by Jachet of Mantua for 5 voices	Jachet de Mantua: *Il primo libro de le messe a cinque voci . . .* (G. Scotto, Venice, 1554a), *Messe del fiore a cinque voci libro primo* (G.Scotto, Venice, 1561a) or *Messe del fiore a cinque voci, libro secondo* (G.Scotto, Venice, 1561b)
[124]	It. Tricinia wpargaminie	Tricinia [bound] in parchment	Possibly: *Tricinia. . . .* (G. Rhau, Wittemberg, 1542[8]), or *Tricinia sacra . . .* (T. Gerlach, Nuremberg, 1567[2])
[125]	It. Villaneski Neapolitanskie male vocú 3	Small Neapolitan Villanellas for 3 voices	Possibly: *Canzone villanesche alla napolitana . . . Libro primo* (G. da Colonia, Napoli, 1537[5])
[126]	It. drugie villanesky orládi vocum 3	Other villanellas by Orlandi for 3 voices	O. di Lasso: *Villanelle d'Orlando di Lassus e d'alti eccellenti musici libro secondo.* (V. Dorico, Rome, 1555[30])
[127] [p. 37]	It. Trzeczie villanesky cansoni vocú 3	A third set of villanellas canzonas for 3 voices	Possibly: *Secondo libro delle muse a tre voci. Canzon villanesche alla napolitana . . .* (A. Barré, Rome, 1557[20])
[128]	It. Msza iedna na Heinal w papierze i wsitha vocum 5	One morrow mass in paper and sewn 5 voices	
[129]	It. Polskie piesnij parthessý 3	3 partbooks of Polish songs	

[130]	It. Parthessỳ w ných egredienté vocú 4	Partbooks with 'Egredientem' for 4 voices	
[131]	It. Msza Vaczlavova vocú 8	Mass for 8 voices by Wacław	This 8 part mass, probably in Manuscript is not extant.
[132]	It. Msza Antonỳ Scandelin vocú 8	Mass for 8 voices by Antonio Scandello	Scandello is not known to have writen an 8 part mass, it may be his lost 6 part mass of 1558, or a lost manuscript.
[133]	It. Fascicul rosmaithich Authrow Missarum	Fascicle with masses by various authors	
[134]	It. Villanewskỳ wrozmaithých skorkach 5	Villanellas in various leather [bindings] 5 [partbooks]	
[135]	It. Fascicul ieden Villaneskow 4	One fascicle with villanellas 4 [parts ?]	
[136]	It. Cancional Misse Surgens Jesus 1	One choirbook with the mass 'Surgens Jesu'	P. Colin: *Missa cum quinque vocibus, ad imitationem moduli Surgens Jesus, condita.* (N. du Chemin, Paris, 1556)
	Item Arpha 1	1 harp	
	Item Cithara Gusmanowa	A cittern by Gusman (?)	
	Thi wsistkỳ partessỳ wýsseỳ opissane wsietho na zamek. do Jego Mcźi Pana Vielkiego Rzancze do drugich Instrumétow K. J. M.	All of these partbooks described above were taken to the castle of the great ruler, and deposited with the other instruments of His Royal Majesty.	

APPENDIX XIV: MUSIC FROM THE RORANTISTS' REPERTORY: TRANSCRIPTIONS

This appendix contains transcriptions of music from the Rorantists' partbooks. All these compositions are presented anonymously in the sources, and it has not been possible to identify any of the composers, though the last composition may be by Wacław of Szamotuły. Nevertheless, they represent a small cross-section of music available to the college, including the original falsobordone style and items of particular interest. Modern clefs have been used and note-values have been halved. The text underlay has been standardized, with editorial additions placed in square brackets. Missing parts have been left blank. Editorial accidentals have been placed above the notes. Barring and bar numbers are also editorial.

Critical Commentary

XIV.1 Anon., Sanctus 'Sabbatis'. Sources: Kk I.3: Discantus, Tenor, and Bassus; Kk I.32: Altus.
Comments: Altus part is called Tenor II in Kk I.32. This seventeenth century copy does not have the second 'Hosanna' section. Some textual repetitions found in this source have been removed and the pre-Tridentine trope 'Marie filius', absent from the manuscript, has been re-introduced here. This later copy also contains some accidentals, which were most probably not in the original; these have been printed small before the note.
b. 25/Altus/Kk I.32 has crotchet c, quavers b♭ and a, dotted crotchet b♭, quaver b♭.

XIV.2. Anon., 'Missa Gaude Virgo Mater Christi', Credo (extract). Sources: *Missae cum quatuor vocibus paribus* (Scotto, Venice, 1543[2]) and Kk I.1
Comments: The 'Missa Gaude Virgo Mater' found in Kk I.1 was copied from *Missae cum quatuor vocibus paribus* (Scotto, Venice, 1543[2]), with several additions, presumably the work of the Rorantists' themselves. These additions are presented here in small notes.

XIV.3. Anon., 'Diffusa est gratia'. Source: Kk I.1
Comments: b. 19-20/Bassus/rests are presented as brevis followed by semibrevis.

XIV.4 Anon. (Wacław of Szamotuły?), 'Fabricii' [mass], Gloria. Sources: Kk I.4: Discantus and Tenor; Kk I.110: Bassus.
Comments: b. 35/Discantus/1st note is a brevis; bb. 36-40 - Discantus and Tenor have text 'Jesu Altissimus', Bassus has repeat sign for 'Jesu Christe'; b.39/Discantus/ d, e, f, d are crotchets.

XIV.1 Anon., Sanctus 'Sabbatis'. Kk I.3, item 14

Appendix XIV.1

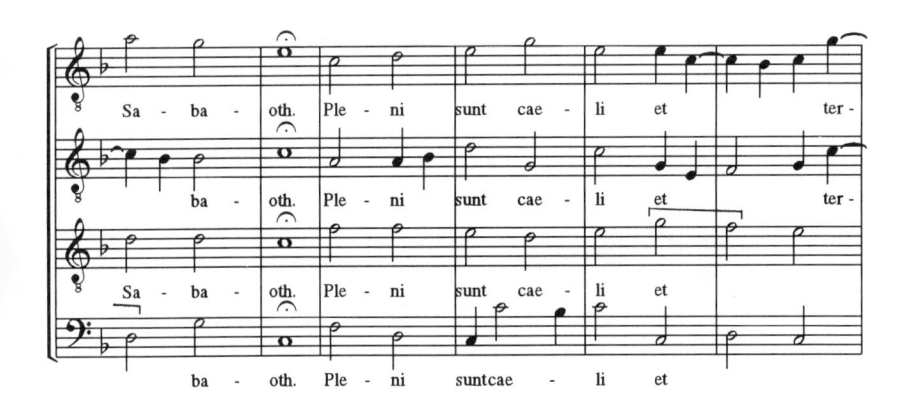

a.
a.
a.
a.
Ho - san - na in ex -
Ho - san - na in ex -
Ho - san - na in
Ho - san - na in ex -
ex - cel -

cel - sis. Be - ne - dic - tus
cel - sis. Be - ne - dic - tus
sis. Be - ne - dic - tus
cel - sis. Be - ne dic - tus
Ma - ri - ae fi - li - us qui ve - nit in no -
Ma - ri - ae fi - li - us qui ve - nit in
Ma - ri - ae fi - li - us qui ve - nit in
Ma - ri - ae fi - li - us qui ve- nit in
mi - ne Do -
no - mi - ne Do -
no - mi - ne Do -
no - mi - ne Do -

mi - ni. Ho - sa - [na in ex -
mi - ni.
mi - ni. Ho - san - na in ex - cel -
mi - ni. Ho - san - [na in ex - cel -

cel - sis
sis.
sis.]

XIV.2 Anon., 'Missa Gaude Virgo Mater Christi', Credo (extract). *Missae cum quatuor vocibus* . . . and Kk I.1, item 5c

[pas - sus et se - pul - tus est] pas - sus et se -
sus et se - pul - tus est pas - sus et se - pul -
pas - sus et se - pul - tus est [pa -
pul - tus est.
tus est [et se - pul - tus est.
ad dex - te -
sus et se pul - tus est. Et
Et re - su - re - xit [ter - ti - a di - e] ter -
Et re - su - re - xit ter - ti a di -
ram Pa - tris. se - det ad
re - sur - re - xit ter - ti - a di - e

ti - a di - e et
e se - cun - dum scri - ptu - ras. Et a - scen - dit in
dex - te - ram Pa - tris. Et re - sur - re -
se - cun - dum scri - ptu - ras. Et a - scen- dit in
a - scen - dit in cae - lum [et a - scen - dit in cae -
cae - lum [et a - scen - dit in cae - lum,]
xit ter - ti - a di - e secun - dum scri - ptu - ras
cae - lum [et a - scen - dit in cae -
lum,] se - det ad
se - det ad dex - te - ram Pa tris.
Et a - scen - dit in cae - lum [et
lum,] se - det ad dex - te - ram Pa - tris.

dex - te - ram Pa - tris.
[se - det ad dex - te - ram Pa - tris]
se - det ad dex - te - ram Pa - tris.
se - det ad dex - te - ram Pa - tris.

XIV.3. Anon., 'Diffusa est gratia'. Kk I.1, item 26

is tu - is] in la - bi -
in la - bi - is tu - is [in la - bi - lis tu -
bi - is tu - is
la - bi is tu - is] in la - bi - is tu -
is tu - is, pro- pter - e - a
is] pro- pter - e - a be -
pro - pter - e -
is pro - pter - e - a
be - ne - di - xit be - ne - di -
ne - di - xit te De - us
a be - ne - di -
be - ne - di - xit be - ne - di - xit te

Appendix XIV.3

cu - li in se - cu - lum [se -
lum se - cu - li [et in se - cu - lum] [se
cu - lum se -
cu - li in se - cu - lum se - cu - li in se -
cu - li] [in se - cu - lum se -
cu - li] et in se - cu - lum et in se - cu -
cu - li
cu - lum se - cu - li [se - cu - li] et in se -
cu - li] in se - cu - lum se - cu - li.
lum se - cu - li in se - cu - lum se - cu - li.
cu - lum se - cu - li in se - cu lum se - cu - li.

XIV.4 Anon. (Wacław of Szamotuły?), 'Fabricii' [mass], Gloria. Kk I.4, item 13

ca- mus te. Gra - ti - as a - gi - mus ti - bi prop-
mus te. Prop-
mus te. Gra - ti - as a - gi - mus ti - bi
ter ma- gnam glo - ri - am tu - am. Do - mi - ne De - us rex cae -
ter ma- gnam glo - ri - am tu - am. Do - mi - ne De - us rex cae -
Do - mi - nus De - us rex cae -
le - stis De - us Pa- ter om - ni - po - tens. Do- mi- ne
le - stis De - us Pa- ter om - ni - po - tens.
le - stis De- us Pa - ter om - ni - po - tens.

Appendix XIV.4

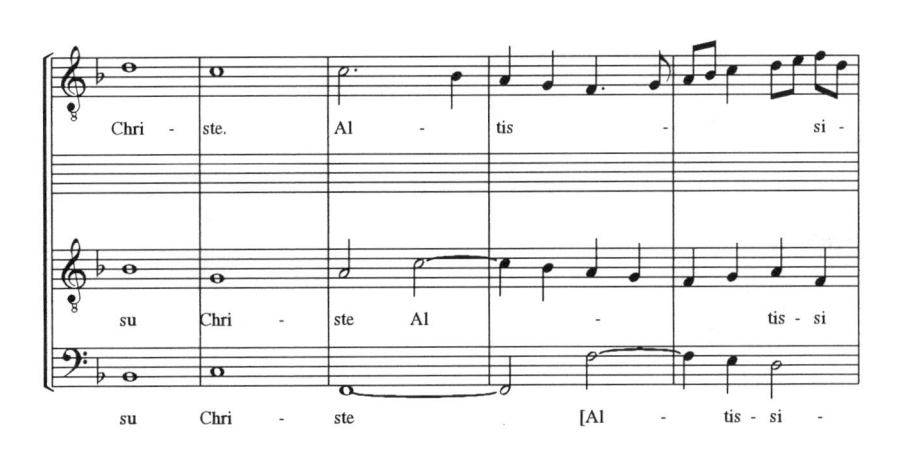

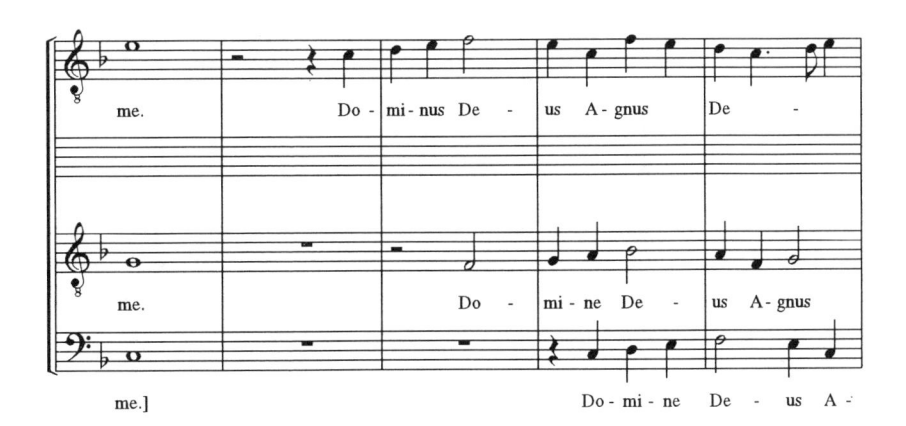

i Fi - li - us Pa - tris. Qui tol - lis pec - ca -
De - i Fi - li - us Pa - tris. Qui tol - lis pec -
gnus De - i Fi - li - us Pa - tris Qui Tol - lis pec - ca - ta
ta mun - di mi - se -
ca - ta mun - di mi - se - re - re no -
Mun - di mi - se - re -
re - re nobis bis. Qui tol - lis Su -
bis. Qui tol - lis pec - ca - ta mun - di
re no - bis. Qui tol - lis pec - ca - ta mun - di

Appendix XIV.4

ctus, tu so - lus Do mi - nus, tu so - lus al - tis - si -
Tu so - lus Do - mi - nus, tu so - lus al - tis - si -
lus san - ctus tu so - lus al tis - si -
mus Je - su Chri - ste.
mus Je - su Chri - ste.
mus Je - su Chri - ste. Cum san - cto
Cum san - cto spi - ri-tu [spi - ri] - tu in glo - ri -
Cum san - cto spi - ri - tu in glo - ri - a De - i Pa - tris De
spi - ri-tus cum san - cto - spi - ri - tu in glo - ri - a De - i Pa -

Appendix XIV.4

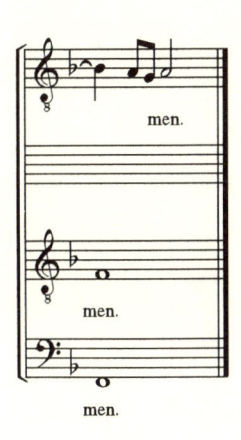

BIBLIOGRAPHY

EDITIONS OF POLISH MUSIC

Chomiński, J., and Lissa, Z. (eds.), *Music of the Polish Renaissance* (Kraków, 1955).

Chybiński, A. (ed., 1928-52); H. Feicht (ed., 1953-62); H. Feicht, and Z. Szweykowski (eds., 1963-67); Z. Szweykowski, (ed., 1967-   ), *Wydawnictwo Dawnej Muzyki Polskiej* (Kraków, 1928-).

Feicht, H. (ed.), *Antiquitates musicae in Polonia*, 15 vols. (Graz, 1963-8).

Feicht, H. (ed.), *Muzyka staropolska* (Kraków, 1966).

Gołos, J., *The Organ Tablature of the Warsaw Musical Society* (Antiquitates musices in Polonia, 15; Graz, 1968).

Nowak-Dłużewski, J. (ed.), *Kolędy polskie* (Warsaw, 1966).

Siedlecki, J. (ed.), *Cantionale ecclesiasticum ad usum Poloniae juxta decreta synodorum praesertim synodii petricoviensis* (Kraków, 1885).

Surzyński, J. (ed.), *Monumenta musices sacrae in Polonia*, 4 vols. (Poznań, 1885-96).

Szweykowski, Z. (ed.), *Muzyka w dawnym Krakowie* (Kraków, 1964).

PUBLISHED CATALOGUES

A. POLISH

Polkowski, I., *Katalog rękopisów kapitulnych Katedry Krakowskiej* (Archiwum do dziejów literatury i oświaty w Polsce, iii; Kraków, 1884).

Szweykowski, Z. (ed.), *Musicalia Vetera: Thematic Catalogue of Early Musical Manuscripts in Poland* (Kraków, 1969-   ). Volume I of this series (in six fascicli) is devoted to *Collections of Music Copied for Use at Wawel.*

Wisłocki, W., *Katalog rękopisów Biblioteki Uniwersytetu Jagiellońskiego* (Kraków, 1877).

B. OTHERS

Bohn, E., *Die musikalischen Handschriften des XVI. und XVII. Jahrhunderts in der Stadtbibliothek zu Breslau* (Breslau, 1890).

Davidsson, Å., *Catalogue critique et descriptif des imprimés de musique des XVIe et XVIIe siècles conservés a la Bibliothèque de l'Université Royale d'Upsala, T. II: Musique profane. Musique dramatique. Musique instrumentale. Additions au t. I* (Uppsala, 1951).

------ *Catalogue critique et descriptif des imprimés de musique des XVIe et XVIIe siècles conservés a la Bibliothèque de l'Université Royale d'Upsala, T. III: Recueils de musique religieuse et profane* (Uppsala, 1951).

------ *Catalogue critique et descriptif des imprimés de musique des XVIe et XVIIe siècles conservés dans les Bibliothèques Suédoises (excepté Bibliothèque de l'Université Royale d'Upsala)* (Uppsala, 1952).

Eitner, R., *Biographisch bibliographisches Quellen-Lexikon der Musiker und Musikgelehrten der christlichen Zeitrechnung bis zur Mitte des neunzehnten Jahrhunderts*, 10 vols. (Leipzig, 1900-4).

Gaspari, G., *Catalogo della Biblioteca del Liceo Musicale di Bologna*, 2 vols. (Bologna, 1890-2).

Hamm, C., and Kellman, H. (eds. vol. i); H. Kellman (ed. vols. ii-v), *Census-Catalogue of Manuscript Sources of Polyphonic Music 1400-1500*, 5 vols. (Renaissance Manuscript Studies, 1; Neuhausen-Stuttgart, 1979-88).

Mitjana, R., *Catalogue des imprimés de musique des XVIe et XVIIe siècles. Bibliothèque de l'Université Royale d'Upsala, T. I: Musique religieuse* (Uppsala, 1911).

Répertoire International des Sources Musicales. Series A: Einzeldrucke vor 1800, 11 vols. (Kassel, 1971-86).

BOOKS AND ARTICLES

Baliński, M., *Historya miasta Wilna* (Wilno, 1837).

Bierzanówna, J., and Małecki, J., *Kraków w wiekach XVI-XVIII*, ed. J. Bierzanówna, J. Małecki, and J. Mitkowski, (Dzieje Krakowa, 2; Kraków, 1984).

Biskup, M. (ed.), *Historia dyplomacji polskiej*, i: *Połowa X wieku - 1572* (Warsaw, 1982).

Bochnak, A., *Inwentarz katedry wawelskiej z roku 1563* (Źródła do dziejów Wawelu, 10; Kraków, 1979).

------ 'Mecenat Zygmunta Starego w zakresie rzemiosła artystycznego', in J. Szablowski (ed.), *Studia do dziejów Wawelu* ii (Kraków, 1961), pp. 131-301.

Briquet, C.M., *Les Filigranes: Dictionnaire historique des marques du papier de leur apparition vers 1282 jusqu'en 1600* (facsimile edition of the Paris 1907 print, ed. A. Stevenson, Amsterdam, 1968).

Busch, H.J., *Giovanni Francesco Anerio, and Francesco Soriano: Two Settings of Palestrina's Missa Papae Marcelli* (Recent Researches in the Music of the Baroque Era, 16; Madison, 1973).

Carter, T., 'Music-selling in Late Sixteenth-Century Florence: The Bookshop of Piero di Giuliano Morosi', *Music & Letters*, 70 (1989), no. 4, pp. 483-504.

Chomiński, J. (ed.), *Słownik muzyków polskich*, 2 vols. (Kraków, 1964-7).

Chybiński, A., 'Bekwarek. Lutnia i polityka', *Przegląd Muzyczny* (1918), no. 6, pp. 1-3.

------ 'Do biografii Sebastjana z Felsztyna', *Kwartalnik Muzyczny* (1932), nos. 14-15, pp. 594-8.

------ 'Jan Fabrycy z Żywca (XVII wiek)', *Kwartalnik Muzyczny* (1932), no. 16, pp. 665-70.

------ 'Krakowskie inwentarze muzyczne z XVI wieku', *Kwartalnik Muzyczny* (1912), no. 3, pp. 253-8.

------ Materyały do dziejów król. kapeli rorantystów na Wawelu, i: 1540-1624 (Kraków, 1910).

------ 'Mikołaj z Chrzanowa', Przegląd Muzyczny (1925), no. 20, pp. 1-6, and no. 21, pp. 1-5.

------ 'Miscellanea polonico-italica', Przegląd Muzyczny (1910), no. 7, pp. 4-5.

------ 'Nowe materjały do dziejów królewskiej kapeli rorantystów w kaplicy Zygmuntowskiej na Wawelu', Księga pamiątkowa ku czci Oswalda Balzera (Lwów, 1925), pp. 133-51.

------ 'O kulcie Palestriny w dawnym Krakowie', Przegląd Muzyczny (1925), no. 23, pp. 2-5, and no. 24, pp. 1-6.

------ Słownik muzyków dawnej Polski do roku 1800 (Kraków, 1948).

------ Stosunek muzyki polskiej do zachodniej w XV i XVI wieku (Kraków, 1909).

------ 'Stosunki muzyczne Polski z Francją w XVI stuleciu', Przegląd Muzyczny (1928), no. 3, pp. 1-6, and no. 4, pp. 1-8.

------ 'Walentyn Gawara-Gutek', Przegląd Muzyczny (1927), no. 11, pp. 1-3.

------ 'Zbiory muzyczne na Wawelu', Przegląd Muzyczny (1910), no. 1, pp. 1-4, and no. 2, pp. 4-7.

------ 'Ze studiów nad polską muzyką wielogłosową w XVI stuleciu', Przegląd Muzyczny: parts of this article were printed throughout 1910 issues.

------ 'Ze studiów nad stosunkiem muzyki polskiej do niemieckiej od XVI do XVIII wieku', Przegląd Muzyczny (1910), no. 16, pp. 1-6.

------ 'Z dziejów muzyki w Krakowie: 1500-1600', Przegląd Muzyczny (1912), no. 9, pp. 3-5.

Cramer, E., 'Związki z muzyką hiszpańską w Lamentacjach Wacława z Szamotuł', Muzyka, 24 (1979), no. 3, pp. 35-43.

Czapliński, W., and Ładogórski, T. (eds.), The Historical Atlas of Poland (Wrocław, 1986).

Bibliography

Davies, N., *God's Playground: A History of Poland*, i: *The Origins to 1795* (Oxford, 1981).

Dunning, A., 'Baston', *New Grove Dictionary of Music and Musicians*, ed. S. Sadie (London, 1980), ii, p. 282.

Federhofer, H., *Musikpflege und Musiker am Grazer Habsburgerhof der Erzherzöge Karl und Ferdinand von Innenösterreich (1564-1619)* (Mainz, 1967).

Fenlon, I., *Music and Patronage in Sixteenth-Century Mantua*, 2 vols. (Cambridge, 1980-2).

Gąsiorowski, A., 'Itineraria dwu ostanich Jagiellonów', *Studia Historyczne*, 16, (1973), no. 2, pp. 249-75.

Gierowski, J., *Historia Polski, ii: 1505-1764* (Warsaw, 1986).

Gloger, E., *Encyklopedia staropolska*, 2nd edn. (Warsaw, 1972).

Głuszcz-Zwolińska, E., Introduction to *Collections of Music Copied for Use at Wawel.* Vol. I, fasc. 1 of *Musicalia Vetera*, ed. Z. Szweykowski (Kraków, 1969).

------ Introduction to *Collections of Music Copied for Use at Wawel.* Vol. I, fasc. 6 of *Musicalia Vetera*, ed. Z. Szweykowski (Kraków, 1983).

------ 'Missa Mater Matris z repertuaru rorantystów wawelskich', *Muzyka*, 15 (1970), no. 3, pp. 73-7.

------ *Muzyka nadworna ostatnich Jagiellonów* (Kraków, 1988).

------ see also Zwolińska, E.

Gołębiowski, E., *Zygmunt August: żywot ostatniego z Jagiellonów*, 2nd rev. edn. (Warsaw, 1968).

Gołos, J., 'Zaginiona tabulatura organowa Warszawskiego Towarzystwa Muzycznego (ca. 1580)', *Kwartalnik Muzyczny* (1960), no. 3, pp. 70-9.

Gombosi, O., *Der Lautenist Valentin Bakfark, Leben und Werke, 1507-1576*, ed. Z. Flavy (Musicologia Hungarica, Neue Folge, Veröffentlichungen des Bartók Archivs in Budapest, 1; Budapest, 1967 (repr. of Budapest, 1935 edn.).

Grabowski, A., *Kraków i jego okolice* (Warszawa, 1981; repr. of 5th edn., Kraków, 1866).

------ *Starożytności historyczne; czyli, Pisma i pamiętniki do dziejów dawnej Polski* (Kraków, 1840).

Jachimecki, Z., *Muzyka polska w epoce Piastów i Jagiellonów* (Warszawa, 1927).

------ *Muzyka polska w rozwoju historycznym od czasów najdawniejszych do doby obecnej* (Kraków, 1934).

------ *Wpływy włoskie w muzyce polskiej*, i: *1540-1640* (Kraków, 1911).

Jaroszewski, T. (ed.), *Renesans. Sztuka i ideologia* (Warszawa, 1976).

Kalinowski, L., 'Treści artystyczne i ideowe kaplicy Zygmuntowskiej', in J. Szablowski (ed.), *Studia do dziejów Wawelu*, ii (Kraków, 1961), pp. 1-129.

Kawecka-Gryczowa, A., *Biblioteka ostatniego Jagiellona: pomnik polskiej kultury renesansowej* (Wrocław, 1988).

Kitkauskas, N., *Vilniaus pilys, statyba ir architektūra* (Vilnius, 1989).

Kłobukowska, J., 'Msze francuskie w repertuarze kapeli roranckiej' *Muzyka*, 16 (1971), no. 3, pp. 85-6.

Koczirz, A., Introdution to Bakfark's compositions in Denkmäler der Tonkunst in Österreich, 37 (Jg. 18/2) (1911).

Kolankowski, L., *Zygmunt August, Wielki Książę Litwy do roku 1548* (Lwów, 1913).

Komornicki, S., 'Kaplica Zygmuntowska w katedrze na Wawelu', *Rocznik Krakowski* (1932), no. 23, pp. 47-120.

Konopczyński, W. (ed.), *Polski słownik biograficzny* (Kraków, 1935-1979).

Bibliography

Kurczewski, J., *Kościół Zamkowy czyli Katedra Wileńska w jej dziejowym, liturgicznym, architektonicznym i ekonomicznym rozwoju* (Wilno, 1908).

Kurpiński, K., 'Wiadomości o kompozytorach polskich, a szczególnie o muzyce dawnej i teraźniejszej w Krakowie', *Tygodnik Polski* (1819), no. 36, pp. 236-41.

Lesure, F., and Thibault, G., *Bibliographie des éditions d'Adrian Le Roy et Robert Ballard (1551-1598)* (Paris, 1955).

Leszczyńska-Skrętowa, Z., *Księga dochodów beneficjów diecezji krakowskiej z roku 1529 (tzw. Liber Retaxationum)* (Materiały Komisji Nauk Historycznych, 13; Wrocław, 1968).

Łobaczewska, S., 'O utworach Sebastjana z Felsztyna (XVI wiek)', *Kwartalnik Muzyczny* (1929), no. 3, pp. 227-44, and no. 4, pp. 347-65.

Marciniak, R., Muszyński, M., and Wiesiołowski, J. (eds.), *Katalog rękopisów staropolskich Biblioteki Kórnickiej*, ii (Kraków, 1985).

Morawski, K., *Czasy zygmuntowskie na tle prądów Odrodzenia*, 2nd edn. (Warsaw, 1965).

Nugent, G., Introduction to *Jachet of Mantua, Opera omnia*, (CMM 54/4; Neuhausen-Stuttgart, 1982).

Perz, M., *Mikołaj Gomółka. Monografia*, 2nd rev. edn. (Kraków, 1981).

------ 'Rękopiśmienne partesy olkuskie', *Muzyka*, 14 (1969), no. 2, pp. 18-44.

------ 'Szesnastowieczne księgi wielogłosowe z Olkusza i Sandomierza', *Muzyka*, 13 (1968), no. 4, pp. 11-27.

------ 'Ze studiów w bibliotekach i archiwach włoskich' *Muzyka*, 15 (1970), no. 2, pp. 53-64.

------ and Zwolińska, E., 'Do dziejów kapeli rorantystów w XVI stuleciu oraz biografii Krzysztofa Borka', *Muzyka*, 18 (1973), no. 2, pp. 34-47.

Piccard G., *Wasserzeichen Die Kronen*, I (Stuttgart, 1961).

------*Wasserzeichen Werkzeug & Waffen*, IX.1 (Stuttgart, 1980).

------ *Wasserzeichen Lilie*, XIII (Stuttgart, 1983).

------ *Wasserzeichen Verschiedene Vierfüssler*, XV.3 (Stuttgart, 1987).

Pikulik, J., 'Analiza źródłoznawcza MS 46 z Biblioteki Kapitulnej na Wawelu', in J. Pikulik (ed.), *Muzyka religijna w Polsce: materiały i studia*, ii (Warsaw, 1978), pp. 59-138.

------ 'Rorantyści wawelscy oraz ich graduał', *Tradycje muzyczne katedry krakowskiej* (Kraków, 1985), pp. 20-6.

------ 'Sekwencje polskie' (Musica medii aevi, 4; Kraków, 1973), pp. 7-125.

Pociecha, W., *Królowa Bona*, 4 vols. (Poznań, 1949 and 1958).

Poliński, A., *Dzieje muzyki polskiej w zarysie* (Lwów, 1907).

Popławski, F. (ed., vols. i-iv); M.R. Mayenowa (ed., vols. v-), *Słownik polszczyzny XVI wieku* (Wrocław, 1966-).

Prus, J., 'Król Zygmunt August i jego zasługi dla polskiej kultury', *Studia Historyczne*, 17 (1974), no. 4, pp. 533-65.

Przeździecki, A., *Jagiellonki polskie w XVI wieku*, 5 vols. (Kraków, 1868-78).

Przybyszewski, B. (ed.), *Wypisy źródłowe do dziejów Wawelu 1530-1533* (Źródła do dziejów Wawelu, 11/1-4; Kraków, 1984-7).

Przywecka-Samecka, M., *Drukarstwo muzyczne w Europie do końca XVIII wieku* (Wrocław, 1987).

------ *Drukarstwo muzyczne w Polsce do końca XVIII wieku* (Kraków, 1969).

Ptaśnik, J. (ed.), *Cracovia impressorum XV et XVI ss.* (Monumenta Poloniae Typographica, 1; Warsaw, 1979; repr. of Lwów, 1922 edn.).

Rożek, M., *The Royal Cathedral on Wawel Hill* (Warszawa, 1981).

Schmid, A., *Ottaviano dei Petrucci da Fossombrone* (Vienna, 1845).

Simmons, J.S.G. (ed.), *Tromonin's Watermark Album*, ed. E.J. Labarre (Monumenta Chartae Papyriceae Historiam Illustrata, 11; Hilversum, 1965).

Siniarska-Czaplicka, J., *Filigrany papierni położonych na obszarze Rzeczypospolitej Polskiej od początku XVI do połowy XVIII wieku*, ed. A. Gryczowa, W. Korotaj, and H. Kapełuś (Książka w dawnej kulturze polskiej, 15; Wrocław, 1969).

Sowiński, A., *Słownik muzyków polskich dawnych i nowoczesnych* (Warsaw, 1982; repr. of Paris, 1874 edn.).

Sternfeld, F. (ed.), *Music from the Middle Ages to the Renaissance* (A History of Western Music, 1; London, 1973).

Suchodolski, B., *Dzieje kultury polskiej*, 2nd rev. edn. (Warsaw, 1986).

Surowiak, Z., Introduction to *Collections of Music Copied for Use at Wawel*. Vol. I, fasc. 4 of *Musicalia Vetera*, ed. Z. Szweykowski (Kraków, 1974).

------ see also Surowiak-Chandra, Z.

Surowiak-Chandra, Z., 'Fabricius', *Encyklopedia muzyczna PWM, Część Biograficzna*, ed. E. Dziębowska, iii (Kraków, 1987), p. 55.

------ Introduction to *Collections of Music Copied for Use at Wawel*. Vol. I, fasc. 3 of *Musicalia Vetera*, ed. Z. Szweykowski (Kraków, 1976).

Surzyński, J., 'Muzyka figuralna w kościołach polskich od XV do XVII wieku', *Rocznik Towarzystwa Przyjaciół Nauk Poznańskiego*, 16 (1889).

Szweykowska, A., 'Początki krakowskiej kapeli katedralnej', *Muzyka*, 4 (1959), no. 2, pp. 12-21.

------ 'Przeobrażenia w kapeli królewskiej na przełomie XVI i XVII wieku', *Muzyka*, 13 (1968), no. 2, pp. 3-21.

Szweykowski, Z., Editor's Note to *Collections of Music Copied for Use at Wawel*. Vol. I, fasc. 1 of *Musicalia Vetera*, ed. Z. Szweykowski (Kraków, 1969).

------ 'Kilka uwag o twórczości mszalnej Giovanni Francesco Aneria związanej z Polską', *Muzyka*, 17 (1972), no. 4, pp. 53-64.

------ 'Rozkwit wielogłosowości w XVI wieku', in Z. Szweykowski (ed.), *Z dziejów polskiej kultury muzycznej*, i: *Kultura staropolska* (Kraków, 1958).

------ and Szweykowska, A., 'Wacław z Szamotuł - renesansowy muzyk i poeta. Szkic biograficzny', *Muzyka*, 9 (1964), no. 1, pp. 3-28.

Ulewicz, T., *Wśród impresorów krakowskich doby renesansu* (Kraków, 1977).

Wiliński, S., 'O renesansie wawelskim', in T. Jaroszewski (ed.), *Renesans* (Warsaw, 1976), pp. 213-26.

Wójcik-Góralska, D., *Niedoceniona królowa* (Warszawa, 1987).

Zwolińska, E., 'Borek', *Encyklopedia muzyczna PWM, Część Biograficzna*, ed. E. Dziębowska, i (Kraków, 1979), pp. 364-5.

------ 'Musica figurata w Jagiellońskim mauzoleum. Kilka uwag o polifonii rorantystów wawelskich w XVI wieku', in *Tradycje muzyczne katedry krakowskiej* (Kraków, 1985), pp. 27-37.

------ 'Muzycy włoscy na dworze królewskim Jagiellonów', *Pagine*, 2 (1972), Warszawa, pp. 71-7.

------ 'Studie über die Musik am Hofe der letzten Jagiellonen', in C.H. Mahling (ed.), *Florilegium musicologicum: Helmut Federhofer zum 75. Geburtstag* (Tutzing, 1988), pp. 501-15.

------ see also Głuszcz-Zwolińska, E.

INDEX

Adam, chaplain, 132
Adam of Bełżyce, 136, 154
Albert 'Francuz', 137, 155, 178
Albrecht V, Duke of Munich, 167
Aleksander Jagiellończyk, King of Poland, 4, 5, 6, 7
'Alleluia. In die resurrectionis', 75
Ambroży of Bełdrzychów, 136, 153
Andreas de Silva, 164
Andrysowic, Łukasz, 148
Andrzej of Opoczno, 153, 155
Annunciation of the BVM, feast of the, 30
  Mass Propers of the, 103-6, 113
Antonio, chaplain, 136
Antwerp, 146
Asola, Giovanni Matteo, 'Octavi toni', Mass, 115
Assumption of the BVM, feast of the, 30,
  Mass Propers of the, 82-3
'Ave Maria', 55, 69

Bakfark, Bálint, 148, 171, 178
Bali, Joannes, 146-7, 150
Ballard, Robert, 63, 64-5, 79, 115-6
Baninch, Paulus, 147
Barbara Radziwiłł, *see* Radziwiłł, Barbara
Barbara Zapolya, Queen of Poland, 6
Bartłomiej of Wyszogród, 134
Baston, Johannes, 134, 135, 136, 150, 171
Batory, Stefan, *see* Stefan Batory
Bayer, Melchior, 21
Benedykt of Stryków, 36, 42, 134

Berrecci, Bartolomeo, 8, 20, 38
Biegłowski, Bartłomiej, 163
Biskupice, 34
Bochnia, salt-mines of, 25, 143, 145
Bodzeniec, Piotr, 140
Bohemia, 7
Bolesław III Krzywousty, King of Poland, 3
Bolesław Chrobry, King of Poland, 3
Bona Sforza, *see* Sforza, Bona
Boner, Seweryn, 21
Boniface IX, pope, 17
Borek, Krzysztof, 31-2, 36, 42, 79, 85-93, 111, 115, 117
  mass, 89-91, 113-4
  'Te Deum laudamus' mass, 89-93, 113
Borimus, Jan, 102
Brandenburg, Albert, Duke, 148
Branicki, Sebastian, Bishop of Poznań, 22
Bronowski, Jakub, 140, 156
Brugner, Claus, 144, 145
Brześć, 67
Brzykowski, Marcin, 137
Buczkowski, Szymon, 36
Buda, 5, 6, 8

Cadéac, Pierre, 63
'Caeli enarrant', 72-3
Cancionale, 118
Cannonic hours, 18
Carolus, wind-player, 145
Cathedral on Wawel Hill, Kraków, 3, 6, 15-20, 30, 94, 113, 117, 182

Cathedral on Wawel Hill (cont'd)
   High Mass at the main altar, 30, 104, 116
   St. Christopher's altar, 18, 37
   staff, 16-20, 131
   vicars, 40
Certon, Pierre, 63-4, 79, 99, 115, 117
Chantries, 16-7
   Assumption of the BVM, 23, 24, 25, 26
   St Mary of Egypt, 23, 34, 48
   Sts Felix and Adauct, 23, 34, 48
Chapels
   Assumption of the BVM, 16, 20
   Assumption of the BVM, Sts Sigismund and Barbara, 8, 20-21
   Holy Cross, 17, 18
   Holy Trinity, 18
   Nativity of the BVM, 17
   rotunda of the BVM, 23
   Sts Peter and Paul, 18
   Sts Felix and Adauct, 23
Charles IX Valois, King of France, 10
Chocianowice, 30
Chodkiewicz, Hieronim, 173
Chotelski, Wojciech, 36, 43
Christmas, 34, 103, 113, 125
Chromi, Georgius, 142, 158
Chybiński, Adolf, 63, 64-5, 68, 76-7, 94, 100, 108-9, 111
Ciemiorka, Maciej, 14-2, 143, 144, 157
Cipriano de Rore, 167, 168, 169
Clemens non Papa, 176
Conception of the BVM, feast of the, 30,
   Mass Propers of the, 82-3, 85, 98
Corfini, Jacopo, 167, 169
Crecquillon, Thomas, 176

'Pis ne me peuly venir', 95-8, 123
Cytaredis, *see* Wind-players, Musici Itali
Czech, Jenik, 142, 158
Czerwona Niwa, 24
Czołowski, Aleksander, 76-7

Danikowski, Sebastian, 140
Danzig, *see* Gdańsk
Decius, Ludwik, 163
'Diffusa est gratia', 84
Długosz, Jan, 5
Doidzwon, Stanisław, 142, 157
Dominicus de Verona, 148
Drummers, 143, 151
Dusza, Andrzej, 142, 143, 157, 158
Dzierzkowski, Mikołaj, Archbishop of Gniezno, 29

Easter, 34, 103-4, 106, 113, 116, 125
'Egredimini et videte', 84, 122
Elenchus, Rorantists' accout-book, 25, 28, 31
Elizabeth of Austria, Queen of Poland, 5, 18, 38
d'Este, Ippolito, Cardinal, 19

'Fabricii' mass, 108-111, 117, 174, 179
Fabricius, Jan, 108-9
Falsobordone, 71-4, 76, 84, 113, 116
Fistulatores, *see* Wind-players
Florence, 20
Franciscus 'Italus' of Florence, 8, 38
Franciscus Italus 'Lyricen', 148
Franciszek of Poznań, 29, 132, 153, 155
Frankfurt, 169, 171

Gamrat, Piotr, Bishop of Kraków, 22, 23, 27, 41
Gardane, Antonio, 164

Index

Gatka, 30
'Gaude Maria Virgo', 108
'Gaude Virgo Mater Dei', Mass, 82
Gdańsk, 5, 151, 171
Georg, Thomas, 144, 145
Gerlach, Catherine, 65
Ghibelli, Heliseo, 167, 168
Głogów, 5
Głuszcz-Zwolińska, Elżbieta, see Zwolińska, Elżbieta
Gniezno, Congress of, 15
Gombert, Nicholas, 166, 176
Gomółka, Mikołaj, 145, 147, 149
  Melodiae na psałterz polski, 149, 159
Goniwiecha, Jan, 143
Górna Wieś, 24
Górnicki, Łukasz, 129, 148, 170
Gosławski Cancionale, see Sources, Kk 58
Grodno, 143
Grunwald, 4

Habsburgs, 7
  Catherine, Queen of Poland, 10, 134-5, 136, 148, 151, 173
  Elizabeth, Queen of Poland, 9, 132, 136, 137
  Ferdinand, Holy Roman Emperor, 7, 9
  Maximilian, Holy Roman Emperor, 7
Henry Valois, King of Poland, 10, 32, 140
Hérissant, Jean, 63
Hoberean, Guido, 147
Hohenzollern, Albrecht von, 6, 171
Holy Cross, College of, 18, 19, 20, 26, 27, 39
Holy Trinity, College of, 18, 19, 20, 27, 131, 154, 155
Hozjusz, Stanisław, Bishop of Warmia, 129, 167

Hugo, wind-player, 147-8
Hungary, 7, 20

Ibrol, Hanzel, 143
Instruments, 158, 159, 160, 163
'Intravit Jesu', Mass, 115
Irzyk, trumpeter, 141, 142
Italy, 11

Jachet of Mantua, 81, 99, 165, 166, 167, 168, 173, 176
Jacobus de Kerle, 167, 168
Jadwiga, Queen of Poland, 4, 17
Jagiellończyk, Fryderyk, Bishop of Kraków, 48, 58
Jagiellonka, Anna, Queen of Poland, 10, 11, 32-6, 44, 45-6, 103
Jakub of Piątek, 132, 133, 153
Jan of Gamrat, 132, 153
Jan Olbracht, see Olbracht, Jan
Janequin, Clément, 165, 166, 169
Jankowski, Leonard, 139, 156
Janowicz, Maciej, 143
Janusz III Piast, Prince of Mazowsze, 7
Jasivcicz, Jurek, 125, 132, 133, 135, 136, 137-8, 139, 140, 143, 153, 155, 156, 157, 161-2
  inventory of 1572, 162-73
Jaszcz, Jan, 132
Jean de Gero, 167, 169
Jenczy, trumpeter, 141
Job of Wiślica, 46, 51, 56, 62, 64, 79-80, 98, 102, 113-4, 121, 124,
Jogaila, see Władysław II Jagiełło
Johannes of Vienna, 138, 156
Josko, Paweł, 142
Josquin des Prez, 65, 93, 99, 166
  'Missa Mater Patris', 85-9
Józef, organ builder, 149

Kąski, 24
Kazimierz, 3, 162, 177
Kazimierz III Wielki, King of Poland, 3-4, 16, 20, 23, 26
Kazimierz IV Jagiellończyk, King of Poland, 4, 5, 18
Keppel, Joachim, 145
Kesner, Zacheus, 170
Kettler, Gottard von, 9
Kicher, Bartłomiej, 139, 145-6
Klabon, Krzysztof, 114, 126, 139, 140, 146
  'Officium Sancta Maria', mass, 114
Klaus, Nicolaus, 140, 157
Klemens of Sandomierz, 132, 134
Knyszyn, 10, 135, 140, 162
Kochanowski, Jan, 129, 148, 149
Kochanowski, Mikołaj, 137
König, David, 149
Königsberg, 6
Kołakowski, Andrzej, 143
Korybut, Johannes, 143
Kościelski, Błażej, 143
Koszucki, Stanisław, 170
Kot, Stanisław, 142, 143
Kraków, 3, 5, 133, 140, 141, 144, 153, 157, 161, 162, 169, 170, 172, 173, 181
  booksellers, 170, 172
  cathedral, see Cathedral on Wawel Hill
  Wawell Hill, 8, 11, 28, 93, 140, 172
  university, 3
Krakowczyk, Tomek, 141, 142
Krasowski, Stanisław, 142
Kromer, Marcin, 129
'Kyrie Sabbativis', 69, 70, 71-2
'Kyrie Virginitatis', 55, 69, 70, 72

'Laetabundus exultet' 84
Lancz, Paweł, 142, 158

Lasłowice, 30
Lasso, Orlando di, 64-5, 167, 168, 169, 170, 176
Laurenciusz of Pabianice, 139
Leo X, pope, 39
Leopolita, Krzysztof, 136
Le Roy, Adrian, 63, 64-5, 79, 115-6
Lesser, Stephanus, 135, 137, 178
Leszczyński, Marcin, 137
Lithuania, Grand Duchy of, 4, 6, 7, 11, 151, 157
Livonia, 9, 11, 136, 142
Łobzów, 34
Londariti, Francesco, 167, 168
Louis Jagiellończyk, King of Hungary, 7
Louis of Anjou, King of Poland, 4, 17
Lubelczyk, Maciej, 143
Lublin, 136
  Union of, 9, 140, 151
Luppacino, Bernardo, 167
Luther, Martin, 8
Lwów, 39
Lyons, 171

Maciej of Poznań, 133
Maciejowski, Bernard, Bishop of Kraków, 34
Maciejowski, Samuel, Bishop of Kraków, 146
Maillard, Jean, 63
Mansart, Philipus, 147
Mansionarii, 17, 19, 20, 26, 39
Marcin of Drohiczyn, 135
Marcin of Iłża, 132
Marcin of Jędrzejów, 135, 150
Marcin of Lwów, 138, 155
Margoński, Laurentius, 145
Maria of Castile, 7
Mathias, clerk, 132
Matins, 17, 18, 19, 26, 54, 56, 57

Index

Mazowita, Daniel, 132, 133, 134, 153
Mazowsze, 6-7, 11
Miernik, Jan, 163
Mieszko I, King of Poland, 3
Mikołaj of Poznań, 23, 27-8, 29, 31, 41, 42, 50-1, 54, 67
Mińsk, 140
Mirmicus, Jan, 51, 56, 69, 70, 80, 98, 102, 113, 114-5, 121
Miskiewicz, Maciej, 56
Missale Cracoviensis (1532), 48-9, 53, 69, 82-3, 121
Missals, 46-7, 48
Moldavia, 22, 39
Morales, Cristóbal de, 80-1, 99, 164, 167, 168
Mouton, Jean, 93
Muscovites, 7, 9, 11, 136
Myszkowski, Piotr, Bishop of Kraków, 33

Naczowicz, Andrzej, 163
Nativity of the BVM, feast of the, 30, Mass Propers of the, 82-3, 98
Neubaur, Johannes, 138, 156, 170
Niepołomice, 41
Nigra, 34
Nihil Novi, 5

Obrecht, Jacob, 93
Odoliński, Wojciech, 134, 137-8, 155
Olbracht Gradual, *see* Sources, Kk 42-44
Olbracht, Jan, King of Poland, 4, 5, 7, 38
Opaliński, Piotr, 8
Opawa, 5
Orgas, Annibale, 102
Orsza, 7
Orzechowski, Stanisław, 135, 175

Pabianice, 30
Palestrina, Giovanni Pierluigi da, 114, 167
'Papae Marcelli' mass, 114, 117
Parczew, 136
Paris, 171
Parliament, 5, 8, 134, 136, 140, 142, 171
Paulo de Magri, 167
Paulus, chaplain, 132
Pawlik, organist, 149
Pękalski, Józef, 71
Pentecost, 34, 103, 106, 113, 116
Perz, Mirosław, 79
Pesenti, Alexander, 19
Petronius, chaplain, 156
Petrucci, Ottaviano dei, 85
Phinot, Dominique, 166, 168-9, 170
Pieniajecz, Stefan, 143, 158
Pieniążek, Andrzej, 144-5
Pieszkowicz, Mikołaj, 102
Pikulik, Jerzy, 50
Pinczestein, Georgio, 21
Pińczów, 174
Pionner, Johannes, 167, 168
Piotr of Bodzentyn, 137
Piotr of Samborz, 29
Piotrków, 30, 41, 134, 136, 142, 157, 172
Polish-Lithuanian union, *see* Lublin, Union of
Polkowski, Ignacy, 76
Porta, Costanzo, 164, 167, 168
Postekalski, Tomasz, 163
Poznachowice, 24
Poznań, 67, 173
Prussia, 5, 6, 9, 11, 148
Przeworsko, 157
Psaltarists, 17-18, 19, 20, 27, 41
Purification of the BVM, feast of the, 30, 82-3

Racławski, Stanisław, 142, 158
Radlica, Jan, 17
Radomski, Andrzej, 22
Radomski, Szymon, 68
Radziwiłł, Barbara, Queen of Poland, 10, 28, 133-4, 142, 144, 153
   Mikołaj, 10, 137, 174
   Jerzy, Bishop of Kraków, 46, 47, 62, 66
Ragoszka, Johannes, 144
Raizaber, Bernard, 134
Ramult, Jan, 140
Raszek, Maciej, 132, 153
Reder, Stefan, 139, 145
Reformation, 5, 6, 8
Rener, Adam, 168
Requiem mass, 17, 18, 19, 27
Rheder, Hanus, 144, 146
Robatyn, Stanisław, 140
Rodio, Rocco, 168, 170
Roman Missals, 47-8
Rome, 171
Rorantists, 19, 21-36, 181-2
   clerk, 24, 27, 30, 34
   finances, 24-5, 29, 34
   Gradual, see Sources, Kk 46
   liturgical duties, 26-7, 30, 34-5, 99
   Missal, see Sources, Kk 4
   prebendaries, 23-4, 29, 33, 43
   prefect, 23, 24, 26-7, 33, 34, 43
   senior prebendary, 34
   size and organization, 23-4, 33, 181
   substitutes, 29, 41
'Rorate caeli desuper', 13, 104
Rorate mass, see Votive mass of the Annunciation of the BVM
Rostok, Paweł, 156
Royal Chapel, 129-40, 150, 182
   boys, 130, 133, 135, 139, 140, 150, 151, 161
   cantores, 139, 140, 150, 152
   chaplains, 130, 131-2, 134, 135, 136, 139, 140, 150
   clerk, 130, 131-2, 133
   composer, 130, 131, 138, 150, 174
   duties, 168
   organists, 130-1, 147, 150
   prefect, 130
   singers, 130, 137, 150
Royal Prussia, 4, 5, 151
Rudnik, 162
Ruffo, Antonio, 147
Ruffo, Vincenzo, 81, 99, 167, 168
Rzgów, 30

Scandello, Antonio, 113, 168
Sebastian of Felsztyn, 99, 123, 124
   'Alleluia. Felix es sacra', 99, 124
   'Alleluia. Ave Maria', 107
   'Virgini Mariae laudes', 107
Sebastian of Książe, 78
Sejm, see Parliament,
Senate, 4
Sermisy, Claudin de, 63
Sforza, Bona, Queen of Poland, 6, 7, 8, 29, 31, 32, 85, 89, 137
   Gian Galeazzo, Duke of Milan, 6
Silesia, 4, 6, 12, 141, 144, 157
Silvestro, wind-player, 144
Silvius, Andreas, 8
Skiczki, Jan, 140
Sliezak, Jurek, 158 see also Chromi, Georgius
Słomniki, 24, 124
Sobek, organist, 132, 135, 149
Sokół, Mikołaj, 143
Sources,
   Kj 1267, 83, 122
   Kk I.1, 64, 66, 76-100, 106, 111, 113, 115, 116-7
   Kk I.3, 65, 66-76, 83, 106, 111, 116

Index

Kk I.4, 64, 66, 100-11, 116-7, 174, 179
Kk I.5, 65, 66, 112-5, 116-7
Kk I.7, 108
Kk I.32, 71
Kk 4, 48-9
Kk 42, 54-5, 59, 83
Kk 43, 54-5, 59, 83
Kk 44, 54-6, 59, 83
Kk 46, 48, 50-7, 71
Kk 58, 56
Kk dyp. 1172, 29
Kk dyp. 1184, 23
Kk dyp. 1190, 33
Kk Inv. 29, 45, 61
Kk Inv. 67, 46, 62-3
Kk Inv. 68, 48, 63, 64
Kk Visit. 64, 45
Kpa K 466, 162-3
Wagad, RK 110, 129
Spangel, Joachim, 142, 157
Stanisław of Szamotuły, 133, 155
Stefan Batory, King of Poland, 11, 33, 44, 113, 114, 140, 151
Stefanus, wind-player, 147, 171
String players, 147-9
Strzeszkowski, Sebastian, 132, 155
Styria, 135
Surowiak-Chandra, Zofia, 100
Surzyński, Józef, 63-4, 76, 115
Szadek, Tomasz, 36, 80, 93-8, 111, 117, 122, 140, 156
  'Officium Dies est laetitiae', Mass, 94-5
  'Officium in melodiam motetae Pisneme', Mass, 95-8
  'Vultum tuum', 107
Szarfenberg, Maciej, 170
Szczepanowice, 24
Szelmiczki, Jan, 163
Szweykowski, Zygmunt, 91
Szymek 'Muzyk', 137, 139, 146, 156

Szymon of Lelów, 132, 153, 154, 155
Szyszkowski, Marcin, Bishop of Kraków, 117

Tarło, Stanisław, 170-1
Teodolski, singer, 137
Teutnic Order, 4, 6, 7
Thenaud, Jan, 170
Theodoricus, wind-player, 147, 171
'Tolilite portas', 55
Tomek of Sącz, 137, 139, 156
Tomicki, Piotr, Bishop of Kraków, 21, 22, 46, 48, 58
Toruń, 135
  Treaty of, 6
Trent, Council of, 9, 129, 167
Tridentine Rite, 66, 103, 113
  Propers of, 98-9, 103-6, 108
Trubicki, Szymon, 139, 146
Trumpeters, 141-4, 151
  apprentices, 142
Trzecieski, Andrzej, (father), 169
Trzecieski, Andrzej, (son), 169
Tudesco, Maciej, 143
Tykocin, 140, 170

'Veni caeli nuntius', 73
Venice, 171
Veracter, Arnoldus, 147
Vienna, Congress of, 7
Vilnius, 10, 11, 19, 22, 28, 65, 75, 101, 131, 133, 136-7, 138, 141, 142, 143, 144, 148, 151, 153, 154, 161-2, 169, 170, 172, 173, 174
Visitation of the BVM, feast of the, 30,
  Mass Propers of the, 82-3, 98
Votive masses,
  Annunciation of the BVM, 26, 40, 53, 57, 69, 70, 72, 76, 103-6, 116

Votive masses (cont'd)
Assumption of the BVM, 17, 18, 27, 56, 69, 70, 72
Corpus Christi, 18
Holy Cross, 19
Holy Trinity, 18

Wacław of Szamotuły, 94, 111, 132, 134, 135, 137-8, 150, 153, 161, 167-8, 170, 173-6
'Ego sum pastor bonus', 175
'In te Domine speravi', 109, 175
works, 174-5
Walentyn of Brzozów, 94
Walentyn of Jastrząb, 50-1, 67
Walentyn of Mieścisko, 68
Warsaw, 10, 36, 41, 136, 140, 162, 172, 182
Warszawa, see Warsaw
Wartecki, Marcin, 139
Wawel Hill, see Kraków, Wawel Hill
Wielowieś, 41
Wierzbkowski, Jan, 19, 131, 133, 135, 153, 154, 161
Wilhelm, Hanus, 144, 145
Wilhelm, Jurek, 144, 145
Willaert, Adrian, 165, 166, 167, 168, 169, 170, 173
Wilno, see Vilnius
Wind-players, 139, 144-7, 151
    Fistulatores Germani, 144-6, 151
    Musici Fistulatores, 146-7, 151, 171
    Musici Itali, 146, 147, 151, 171
Wircker, Johannes, 138, 155, 165, 169, 170
Wisła, 5
Wiślica, 36
Wiszkitki, 22, 24
Wittemberg, 171
Władysław I Łokietek, King of Poland, 3, 15
Władysław II Jagiełło, King of Poland, 417, 37
Władysław III Warneńczyk, King of Poland, 4
Władysław, composer, 131
Władysław Jagiellończyk, King of Hungary, 4, 5, 7, 8, 12

Ząbek, Stefan, 142
Zagorski, Stanisław, 134, 136
Zając, Stanisław, 32, 336, 43, 44, 56, 101-2, 106, 108, 121
Zapolya, John, 148
Zawisza of Kurozwęki, Bishop of Kraków, 17
Zborowski, Piotr, 8
Zebrzydowski, Andrzej, Bishop of Kraków, 29, 30
Żelazowski, Wojciech, 143
Zinger, Bartłomiej, 139
Żmygród, Andrzej, 78-9, 137, 156
Zofia, Queen of Poland, 18
Zwolińska, Elżbieta, 79, 85
Zygmunt I Stary, King of Poland, 5-8, 11, 12, 17, 19, 20, 21-23, 28, 29, 32, 36, 38, 46, 48-9, 133, 141, 142, 144, 153
    chapel of, see Assumption of the BVM, St Sigismund and St Barbara
    royal chapel, see Rorantists
Zygmunt II August, King of Poland, 6, 7, 8-10, 11, 23, 28-31, 32, 75, 81, 93, 104, 113, 114, 129, 132, 133-4, 135, 136-7, 139-40, 141, 142, 144, 147, 148, 150, 154, 161-2, 169, 171, 173
    chapel, see Royal Chapel
    musical establishment, 129-60, 181
Zygmunt III Vasa, King of Poland, 11, 33, 34, 44, 114, 182